THE IMPERIAL IRISH

McGILL-QUEEN'S STUDIES IN THE HISTORY OF RELIGION

Volumes in this series have been supported by the Jackman Foundation of Toronto.

SERIES ONE G.A. RAWLYK, EDITOR

1 Small Differences
Irish Catholics and Irish Protestants, 1815–1922
An International Perspective
Donald Harman Akenson

2 Two Worlds
The Protestant Culture of Nineteenth-Century Ontario
William Westfall

3 An Evangelical Mind
Nathanael Burwash and the Methodist Tradition in Canada, 1839–1918
Marguerite Van Die

4 The Dévotes
Women and Church in Seventeenth-Century France
Elizabeth Rapley

5 The Evangelical Century
College and Creed in English Canada from the Great Revival to the Great Depression
Michael Gauvreau

6 The German Peasants' War and Anabaptist Community of Goods
James M. Stayer

7 A World Mission
Canadian Protestantism and the Quest for a New International Order, 1918–1939
Robert Wright

8 Serving the Present Age
Revivalism, Progressivism, and the Methodist Tradition in Canada
Phyllis D. Airhart

9 A Sensitive Independence
Canadian Methodist Women Missionaries in Canada and the Orient, 1881–1925
Rosemary R. Gagan

10 God's Peoples
Covenant and Land in South Africa, Israel, and Ulster
Donald Harman Akenson

11 Creed and Culture
The Place of English-Speaking Catholics in Canadian Society, 1750–1930
Edited by Terrence Murphy and Gerald Stortz

12 Piety and Nationalism
Lay Voluntary Associations and the Creation of an Irish-Catholic Community in Toronto, 1850–1895
Brian P. Clarke

13 Amazing Grace
Studies in Evangelicalism in Australia, Britain, Canada, and the United States
Edited by George Rawlyk and Mark A. Noll

14 Children of Peace
W. John McIntyre

15 A Solitary Pillar
Montreal's Anglican Church and the Quiet Revolution
Joan Marshall

16 Padres in No Man's Land
Canadian Chaplains and the Great War
Duff Crerar

17 Christian Ethics and Political Economy in North America
A Critical Analysis
P. Travis Kroeker

18 Pilgrims in Lotus Land
Conservative Protestantism in British Columbia, 1917–1981
Robert K. Burkinshaw

19 Through Sunshine and Shadow
The Woman's Christian Temperance Union, Evangelicalism, and Reform in Ontario, 1874–1930
Sharon Cook

20 Church, College, and Clergy
A History of Theological Education at Knox College, Toronto, 1844–1994
Brian J. Fraser

21 The Lord's Dominion
The History of Canadian Methodism
Neil Semple

22 A Full-Orbed Christianity
The Protestant Churches and Social Welfare in Canada, 1900–1940
Nancy Christie and Michael Gauvreau

23 Evangelism and Apostasy
The Evolution and Impact of Evangelicals in Modern Mexico
Kurt Bowen

24 The Chignecto Covenanters
A Regional History of Reformed Presbyterianism in New Brunswick and Nova Scotia, 1827– 1905
Eldon Hay

25 Methodists and Women's Education in Ontario, 1836–1925
Johanne Selles

26 Puritanism and Historical Controversy
William Lamont

SERIES TWO IN MEMORY OF GEORGE RAWLYK
DONALD HARMAN AKENSON, EDITOR

1 Marguerite Bourgeoys and Montreal, 1640–1665
Patricia Simpson

2 Aspects of the Canadian Evangelical Experience
Edited by G.A. Rawlyk

3 Infinity, Faith, and Time
Christian Humanism and Renaissance Literature
John Spencer Hill

4 The Contribution of Presbyterianism to the Maritime Provinces of Canada
Edited by Charles H.H. Scobie and G.A. Rawlyk

5 Labour, Love, and Prayer
Female Piety in Ulster Religious Literature, 1850–1914
Andrea Ebel Brozyna

6 The Waning of the Green
Catholics, the Irish, and Identity in Toronto, 1887–1922
Mark G. McGowan

7 Religion and Nationality in Western Ukraine
The Greek Catholic Church and the Ruthenian National Movement in Galicia, 1867–1900
John-Paul Himka

8 Good Citizens
British Missionaries and Imperial States, 1870–1918
James G. Greenlee and Charles M. Johnston

9 The Theology of the Oral Torah
Revealing the Justice of God
Jacob Neusner

10 Gentle Eminence
A Life of Cardinal Flahiff
P. Wallace Platt

11 Culture, Religion, and Demographic Behaviour
Catholics and Lutherans in Alsace, 1750–1870
Kevin McQuillan

12 Between Damnation and Starvation
Priests and Merchants in Newfoundland Politics, 1745–1855
John P. Greene

13 Martin Luther, German Saviour
German Evangelical Theological Factions and the Interpretation of Luther, 1917–1933
James M. Stayer

14 Modernity and the Dilemma of North American Anglican Identities, 1880–1950
William H. Katerberg

15 The Methodist Church on the Prairies, 1896–1914
George Emery

16 Christian Attitudes towards the State of Israel
Paul Charles Merkley

17 A Social History of the Cloister
Daily Life in the Teaching Monasteries of the Old Regime
Elizabeth Rapley

18 Households of Faith
Family, Gender, and Community in Canada, 1760–1969
Edited by Nancy Christie

19 Blood Ground
Colonialism, Missions, and the Contest for Christianity in the Cape Colony and Britain, 1799–1853
Elizabeth Elbourne

20 A History of Canadian Catholics
Gallicanism, Romanism, and Canadianism
Terence J. Fay

21 The View from Rome
Archbishop Stagni's 1915 Reports on the Ontario Bilingual Schools Question
Edited and translated by John Zucchi

22 The Founding Moment
Church, Society, and the Construction of Trinity College
William Westfall

23 The Holocaust, Israel, and Canadian Protestant Churches
Haim Genizi

24 Governing Charities
Church and State in Toronto's Catholic Archdiocese, 1850–1950
Paula Maurutto

25 Anglicans and the Atlantic World
High Churchmen, Evangelicals, and the Quebec Connection
Richard W. Vaudry

26 Evangelicals and the Continental Divide
The Conservative Protestant Subculture in Canada and the United States
Sam Reimer

27 Christians in a Secular World
The Canadian Experience
Kurt Bowen

28 Anatomy of a Seance
A History of Spirit Communication in Central Canada
Stan McMullin

29 With Skilful Hand
The Story of King David
David T. Barnard

30 Faithful Intellect
Samuel S. Nelles and Victoria University
Neil Semple

31 W. Stanford Reid
An Evangelical Calvinist in the Academy
Donald MacLeod

32 A Long Eclipse
The Liberal Protestant Establishment and the Canadian University, 1920–1970
Catherine Gidney

33 Forkhill Protestants and Forkhill Catholics, 1787–1858
Kyla Madden

34 For Canada's Sake
Public Religion, Centennial Celebrations, and the Re-making of Canada in the 1960s
Gary R. Miedema

35 Revival in the City
The Impact of American Evangelists in Canada, 1884–1914
Eric R. Crouse

36 The Lord for the Body
Religion, Medicine, and Protestant Faith Healing in Canada, 1880–1930
James Opp

37 Six Hundred Years of Reform
Bishops and the French Church, 1190–1789
J. Michael Hayden and Malcolm R. Greenshields

38 The Missionary Oblate Sisters
Vision and Mission
Rosa Bruno-Jofré

39 Religion, Family, and Community in Victorian Canada
The Colbys of Carrollcroft
Marguerite Van Die

40 Michael Power
The Struggle to Build the Catholic Church on the Canadian Frontier
Mark G. McGowan

41 The Catholic Origins of Quebec's Quiet Revolution, 1931–1970
Michael Gauvreau

42 Marguerite Bourgeoys and the Congregation of Notre Dame, 1665–1700
Patricia Simpson

43 To Heal a Fractured World
The Ethics of Responsibility
Jonathan Sacks

44 Revivalists
Marketing the Gospel in English Canada, 1884–1957
Kevin Kee

45 The Churches and Social Order in Nineteenth- and Twentieth-Century Canada
Edited by Michael Gauvreau and Ollivier Hubert

46 Political Ecumenism
Catholics, Jews, and Protestants in De Gaulle's Free France, 1940–1945
Geoffrey Adams

47 From Quaker to Upper Canadian
Faith and Community among Yonge Street Friends, 1801–1850
Robynne Rogers Healey

48 The Congrégation de Notre-Dame, Superiors, and the Paradox of Power, 1693–1796
Colleen Gray

49 Canadian Pentecostalism
Transition and Transformation
Edited by Michael Wilkinson

50 A War with a Silver Lining
Canadian Protestant Churches and the South African War, 1899–1902
Gordon L. Heath

51 In the Aftermath of Catastrophe
Founding Judaism, 70 to 640
Jacob Neusner

52 Imagining Holiness
Classic Hasidic Tales in Modern Times
Justin Jaron Lewis

53 Shouting, Embracing, and Dancing with Ecstasy
The Growth of Methodism in Newfoundland, 1774–1874
Calvin Hollett

54 Into Deep Waters
Evangelical Spirituality and Maritime Calvinist Baptist Ministers, 1790–1855
Daniel C. Goodwin

55 Vanguard of the New Age
The Toronto Theosophical Society, 1891–1945
Gillian McCann

56 A Commerce of Taste
Church Architecture in Canada, 1867–1914
Barry Magrill

57 The Big Picture
The Antigonish Movement of Eastern Nova Scotia
Santo Dodaro and Leonard Pluta

58 My Heart's Best Wishes for You
A Biography of Archbishop John Walsh
John P. Comiskey

59 The Covenanters in Canada
Reformed Presbyterianism from 1820 to 2012
Eldon Hay

60 The Guardianship of Best Interests
Institutional Care for the Children of the Poor in Halifax, 1850–1960
Renée N. Lafferty

61 In Defence of the Faith
Joaquim Marques de Araújo, a Brazilian Comissário in the Age of Inquisitional Decline
James E. Wadsworth

62 Contesting the Moral High Ground
Popular Moralists in Mid-Twentieth-Century Britain
Paul T. Phillips

63 The Catholicisms of Coutances
Varieties of Religion in Early Modern France, 1350–1789
J. Michael Hayden

64 After Evangelicalism
The Sixties and the United Church of Canada
Kevin N. Flatt

65 The Return of Ancestral Gods
Modern Ukrainian Paganism as an Alternative Vision for a Nation
Mariya Lesiv

66 Transatlantic Methodists
British Wesleyanism and the Formation of an Evangelical Culture in Nineteenth-Century Ontario and Quebec
Todd Webb

67 A Church with the Soul of a Nation
Making and Remaking the United Church of Canada
Phyllis D. Airhart

68 Fighting over God
A Legal and Political History of Religious Freedom in Canada
Janet Epp Buckingham

69 From India to Israel
Identity, Immigration, and the Struggle for Religious Equality
Joseph Hodes

70 Becoming Holy in Early Canada
Timothy Pearson

71 The Cistercian Arts
From the 12th to the 21st Century
Edited by Terryl N. Kinder and Roberto Cassanelli

72 The Canny Scot
Archbishop James Morrison of Antigonish
Peter Ludlow

73 Religion and Greater Ireland
Christianity and Irish Global Networks, 1750–1950
Edited by Colin Barr and Hilary M. Carey

74 The Invisible Irish
Finding Protestants in the Nineteenth-Century Migrations to America
Rankin Sherling

75 Beating against the Wind
Popular Opposition to Bishop Feild and Tractarianism in Newfoundland and Labrador, 1844–1876
Calvin Hollett

76 The Body or the Soul?
Religion and Culture in a Quebec Parish, 1736–1901
Frank A. Abbott

77 Saving Germany
North American Protestants and Christian Mission to West Germany, 1945–1974
James C. Enns

78 The Imperial Irish
Canada's Irish Catholics Fight the Great War, 1914–1918
Mark G. McGowan

The Imperial Irish

Canada's Irish Catholics Fight the Great War, 1914–1918

MARK G. McGOWAN

McGill-Queen's University Press
Montreal & Kingston • London • Chicago

ISBN 978-0-7735-5069-8 (cloth)
ISBN 978-0-7735-5078-0 (ePDF)
ISBN 978-0-7735-5079-7 (ePUB)

Legal deposit second quarter 2017
Bibliothèque nationale du Québec

Printed in Canada on acid-free paper that is 100% ancient forest free (100% post-consumer recycled), processed chlorine free.

This book has been published with the help of a grant from the Canadian Federation for the Humanities and Social Sciences, through the Awards to Scholarly Publications Program, using funds provided by the Social Sciences and Humanities Research Council of Canada.

McGill-Queen's University Press acknowledges the support of the Canada Council for the Arts for our publishing program. We also acknowledge the financial support of the Government of Canada through the Canada Book Fund for our publishing activities.

Library and Archives Canada Cataloguing in Publication

McGowan, Mark, 1959–, author
The imperial Irish : Canada's Irish Catholics fight the Great War, 1914–1918 / Mark G. McGowan.

(McGill-Queen's studies in the history of religion. Series two ; 78)
Includes bibliographical references and index.
Issued in print and electronic formats.
ISBN 978-0-7735-5069-8 (cloth). – ISBN 978-0-7735-5078-0 (ePDF). – ISBN 978-0-7735-5079-7 (ePUB)

1. World War, 1914–1918 – Religious aspects – Catholic Church. 2. World War, 1914–1918 – Canada. 3. Catholic Church – Canada – History – 20th century. 4. Irish – Canada – History – 20th century. 5. Catholics – Canada – History – 20th century. I. Title. II. Series: McGill-Queen's studies in the history of religion. Series two ; 78

RD622.M44 2017 940.3088'282 C2017-900881-1
C2017-900882-X

This book was typeset by True to Type in 10.5/13 Sabon

In memory of

Hugh Francis de Sales McNally, MD, Royal Navy
Lance Corporal William McGowan, 15th Battalion, CEF
George M. McGowan, Royal Flying Corps

and in the hope that

Róisín Elizabeth Lea
is spared the witness to war
experienced by her ancestors

Contents

Tables xiii

Acknowledgments xv

Illustrations xxi

Introduction: The Complicated Worlds of Canada's Irish Catholics 3

1 The Long Road to War 21

2 "Let All Come to the Battle": Catholics Embrace the Imperial War 71

3 Ned Murray's War: Canada's Irish Catholics and the Call to Serve 105

4 Irreligion, Immorality, and Blasphemy: Faith at the Front 163

5 Between Resistance and Rebellion 201

6 Winning the War, Saving the Peace 249

Conclusion: The Principles and Outcomes of War 287

Notes 301

Index 375

Tables

1.1 Migration from the United Kingdom to British North America, 1843–48 30
1.2 Irish migration to North America from all United Kingdom ports, 1846–56 31
1.3 Distribution of Irish Catholic sample among Canadian recruits in the Boer War 63
1.4 Irish Catholic recruits to the Boer War, by place of birth 65
1.5 Irish Catholic Canadian recruits to the Boer War, by occupation 66
3.1 Voluntary recruitment in the Canadian Expeditionary Force, by religion, to 1 June 1917 108
3.2 The 208th Toronto Irish Battalion, by religion and previous service 121
3.3 Designated Irish units, recruitment and social characteristics 124
3.4 25th Battalion, Canadian Expeditionary Force, Halifax recruits by religion, birthplace, and military service 128
3.5 40th Battalion, Canadian Expeditionary Force, Halifax Recruits by religion and place of birth 130
3.6 40th Battalion, Canadian Expeditionary Force, by religion and militia regiment 132
3.7 25th Battalion, Canadian Expeditionary Force, Halifax recruits by religion and occupation 135
3.8 40th Battalion, Canadian Expeditionary Force, Halifax Recruits by religion and occupation 136
3.9 Recruitment and social characteristics of Irish Catholics in regional battalions 140

3.10 Irish Catholics on parish honour rolls 144
3.11 Irish Catholic Canadian nurses: recruitment and social characteristics, 1914–18 148
3.12 Characteristics of Ottawa Valley recruits, by religious group 155
3.13 Characteristics of Ottawa Valley recruits, by religious group: percentages 157
3.14 Occupational classifications of Ottawa Valley recruits, by religious group 158
3.15 Occupational classifications of Ottawa Valley recruits, by religious group: percentages 159
4.1 Venereal disease (VD) among Catholic soldiers, 1914–18: Irish Catholics predominant 194
4.2 Venereal disease (VD) among Catholic soldiers, 1914–18: French Catholics predominant 195
4.3 Venereal disease (VD) among Catholic soldiers, 1914–18: mixed ethnicities 196

Acknowledgments

This book may be a classic case of "Librus Interruptus." The idea for this project hatched nearly thirty years ago at a Remembrance Day ceremony at the cenotaph in front of Toronto's Old City Hall. I had come to believe, during my doctoral research, that there needed to be a study of the war that incorporated Catholics of Irish birth or descent from across Canada, because examining the Toronto experience alone would offer one particular and perhaps skewed view of Irish Catholic Canadians. But my progress with this idea was constantly interrupted by other projects and books, teaching, moving from university to university, and much more pressing family matters.

Sometimes even in the flow of completing the project, I was beset by the challenges and hazards built into this topic. Let one story suffice: I was in Dublin researching the papers of "home ruler" John Redmond when, one morning before the National Library opened, I decided to visit the Irish National War Memorial Gardens designed by Sir Edwin Lutyens at Islandbridge. I hired a cab on the north side of the Liffey and, as is often the case in Dublin, the driver was an animated conversationalist. When I asked to go to the war memorial he promptly told me that his father had fought for the British Army in World War II, and that his grandfather had fought in the British Expeditionary Force during the "first war." We continued talking about the wars, Ireland's role in them, and his own interest in military history. When I suggested he must know the memorial gardens well, he confessed he had never been there, and then had great difficulty finding the north entrance. He had been born and raised in Dublin and had lived there his entire life.

The perspective of my affable driver appeared to typify how, until recently, the Great War has survived weakly in Irish public memory and how the service of tens of thousands of Irish in the British Army has been understated and made subordinate to the Easter Rising and the road to Irish independence. I suspected that an alternative narrative of Irish men and women who believed, even for a time, in the cause of Empire would be difficult for me to write, and for many readers even more difficult to believe. In the end, however, my research has suggested otherwise, defying the conventional wisdom that the Irish were simply not interested in fighting Britain's imperial wars. As I discovered, in Canada, Ireland, and in much of the rest of the Empire, this presupposition was wrong.

I'm relieved that the project is now between two covers, and for this I owe much to many people who assisted me over nearly three decades. I wish to thank many archivists in public and religious archives across Canada, in particular those at the archives of the Archdiocese of St John's, the Archdiocese of Halifax, the Diocese of Charlottetown, the Archdiocese of Quebec, the Archdiocese of Montreal, the Archdiocese of Ottawa, the Diocese of Alexandria-Cornwall, the Diocese of Pembroke, the Diocese of Peterborough, the Archdiocese of Kingston, the Diocese of Hamilton, Debra Majer at the Diocese of London, the Diocese of Thunder Bay, the Archdiocese of Winnipeg, the Archdiocese of St Boniface, Margaret Sanche at the Diocese of Saskatoon, the Diocese of Calgary, the Archdiocese of Edmonton, the Diocese of Whitehorse, and the Archdiocese of Vancouver. In particular, I must acknowledge Marc Lerman, who for thirty years directed the Archives of the Roman Catholic Archdiocese of Toronto. He not only offered kind, generous, and expert assistance in mining the wealth of the archives in his care, but was also a wise and judicious fellow traveller in unlocking the challenging historical questions engaging the Catholic Church in Canada. Many public archivists also provided invaluable assistance. Tim Wright opened the wealth of the National Personnel Records Centre to me; without his assistance, I would never have established my initial database of over two thousand soldiers and nurses. Glenn Wright, now retired from Library and Archives Canada, offered me advice, opened doors, and read the entire draft manuscript, giving helpful comments. Any errors that remain are entirely of my commission. I would also like to thank librarians and archivists at the Commonwealth War Graves Commission, the Archives of Alberta, the Archives of Ontario, the Pontiac County Archives, the City of Toronto Archives, the Kelly Library at the University of St Michael's College, the General Archives of the Basilian Fathers, the Nova Scotia Archives, the Jesuit Archives Upper Canada Province, the Bruce County Museum and Archives (Southampton, Ontario), the St Paul's College Library (Winnipeg), the Concordia University Archives, the Archives of St Francis Xavier University (particularly Kathleen MacKenzie), the Morisset Library of the University of Ottawa, the Archives of Newfoundland and Labrador, the Secret Vatican Archives (and particularly Dr Matteo Sanfilippo and Professor Luca Codignola in Rome), the National Library of Ireland, and the Archives of the Archdiocese of Dublin (especially Noelle Dowling).

Over the years I have benefited from excellent research assistants, all of whom were diligent and good humoured. Ronalda McCarl, one of the finest genealogical researchers in Canada, pulled materials for me out of French-Canadian and small-town Ontario newspapers; Dr Michael Wilcox, my former graduate student, worked with me on Orange Order newspapers and Nova Scotia materials; former undergraduate student and friend, John O'Brien, also assisted me with newspaper work and opened up his grandfather's diary to me. I am deeply grateful to the O'Brien family and particularly the late Jim "Reg" O'Brien for allowing me to use William O'Brien's personal papers. Similarly, I offer my sincerest thanks to Madame Mariette Morin-Gonthier and her family, who gave me permission to research the papers of the Rt Hon. Charles J. Doherty. I also would like to thank my graduate students Laura Smith and Julia Rady Shaw for their excellent research assistance. My late grandfather, Albert G. Giesler, spent many car rides with me in the initial phases of the research as I explored and as he explained the war memorials in Grey and Bruce Counties. Finally, I am indebted to the Social Science and Humanities Research Council for a variety of grants that assisted with this research, including in 2013–14 a substantial Community Partnership Grant to research, with a large team of colleagues, the history of the Irish Catholic community in Halifax.

Over the years many colleagues offered their ideas, suggestions, research leads, and constructive criticisms. I am deeply grateful that my esteemed colleague, the late Professor Craig Brown, introduced me to personnel records at the National Personnel Records Centre, at a time when none were digitized. He said that I might sample about a dozen or so. In the end, I guess I went a little wild. In addition to periodic constructive questions, David Wilson offered me helpful advice on Irish nationalism and Irish history; the Hon. Sean Conway guided me through the thickets of Ottawa Valley Irish history;

Michael Vance, Peter Ludlow, and Terry Murphy were very helpful as I explored the Maritimes, particularly Nova Scotia. Simon Jolivet was insightful in his unpacking of Irish–French Canadian relations in Montreal. Brian Clarke, Stuart Macdonald, David Marshall, Gordon Heath, and my former PhD student Thomas Hamilton were sound advisors on the interface between religion and war. Jeff Kildea and Richard Reid gave me invaluable advice on comparing the Canadian and Australian war experiences. Many years ago, Dr Evan Patrick and Dr David Patrick offered me their medical insights as we reviewed the health records of many of the men in the database. Susan Martin generously shared her family history with me and informed my understanding of some expatriate Irish making their way back from Canada to fight in the Great War. I am very grateful to my colleague Sheila Eaton, web designer and photographer at St Michael's College, who helped me prepare and enhance the quality of the photographs in the volume. This is the second book for which Sheila has given me her time and talent most graciously.

As always, I have deeply appreciated working with McGill-Queen's University Press, particularly Philip Cercone and Kyla Madden, who never seemed to lose faith in this project. I would also like to thank copy editor Anne Marie Todkill, whose perspicacious eye and skilful edits helped me transform the manuscript into a much more pleasing read. Any gaffes, typos, and awkward prose are entirely of my creation.

This long journey could not have been completed without the support of many friends and family members. In recent years, Alan Keefer kept me moving in the final stages of the project by insisting on monthly updates on the writing. Fellow rugby enthusiasts (Seamus Beattie, Donnie Pettit, Dave Thompson, Mike Stones, Mike Clayton, Greg "Abby" Abbott, and George Burford) gave me confidence that this book "might" be interesting and cured me of any pretensions. John McManus and Dan Cormier gave me the gift of music to keep life in balance. My children – Erin, Patrick, Brendan, Kathleen, and Johnnie – endured many ventures to cemeteries and war memorials, although I suspect they learned something of the great conflict that had engulfed their family and the world in 1914. My gratitude to them is immeasurable. My wife Eileen has been with me long before this book was an idea. She has been a constant support, a wonderful companion, and an expert navigator, as we sailed our "heartships," à la Neil Young, through many harbours and adventures. Her love and patience keeps me afloat.

This book is dedicated to three veterans: Eileen's great uncle, Ship's Surgeon Hugh Francis de Sales McNally, who died 2 June 1916, on the HMS *Hampshire* (before enlisting he had been a captain in the Irish Volunteers in West Belfast); Lance Corporal William McGowan, who, as an expatriate Glaswegian of Irish Catholic descent, enlisted in 15th Battalion CEF and was one of the few originals in this storied unit to survive the war; and his brother and my grandfather, George M. McGowan, RFC, who served as a reconnaissance pilot and flew daily missions, without weapons, over the Western Front. I was not fully struck by their service and sacrifice until my own visits to St Julien, Passchendaele, Vimy, and Beaumont Hamel, while in the course of writing the final chapters. This book is for them, that we may not forget, even though this painful history can be a burden on our emotions and memories. Finally, this book is also dedicated to my granddaughter, Róisín Elizabeth Lea. I hope she will never see such human torment and tragedy as the Great War in her lifetime.

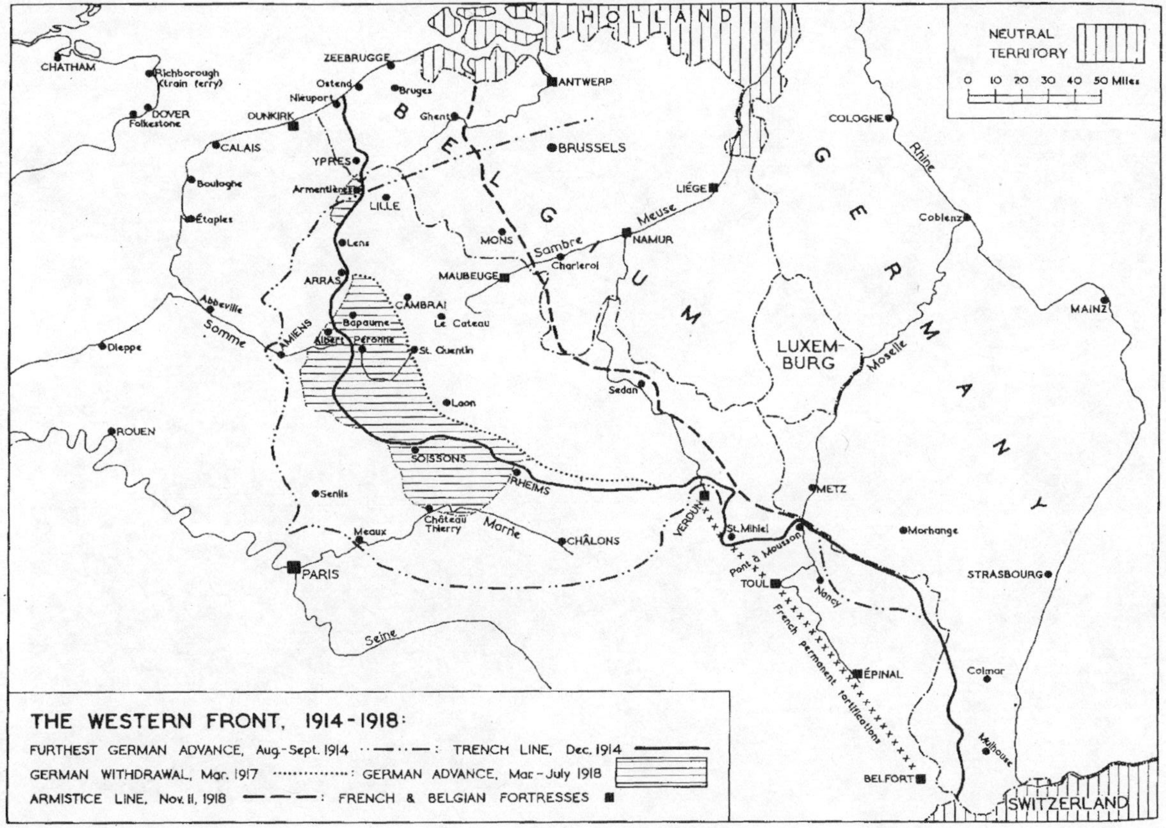

Map of the Western Front, 1914–18

Rev. Major John J. O'Gorman (author's collection)

Bishop Michael F. Fallon and chaplains in France, 1919 (author's collection)

Lt. William O'Brien, CFA, Veterans Parade, Canadian National Exhibition, c. 1936 (courtesy O'Brien family)

Monsignor Alfred E. Burke, editor of the *Catholic Register* (1908–15) and CEF chaplain (ARCAT)

Archbishop Neil McNeil of Toronto (1912–34) (ARCAT)

Captain Robert Manion, CAMC and MP (Port Arthur) (author's collection)

Nursing Matron-in-Chief, Major Margaret C. Macdonald, CAMC (author's collection)

Sir Charles Fitzpatrick, solicitor general (1896–1902), minister of Justice (1902–1906), and chief justice of Canada (1906–1918) (courtesy Catholic Missions in Canada)

Canadian infantry in training at Mount St Patrick, Renfrew County, Ontario, pose with parishioners at St Patrick's Parish, c. 1916 (author's collection)

Major General Sir David Watson and Hon. Charles J. Doherty, France, 1919
(LAC, PA-004207)

THE IMPERIAL IRISH

INTRODUCTION

The Complicated Worlds of Canada's Irish Catholics

The partisan crowd in Toronto erupted in cheers and thunderous applause as Charles Fitzpatrick paused in the middle of his speech on Britain's troubles in South Africa. "Wheresoever the British subject goes," continued the federal solicitor general, "he carries with him all that is right, the might and power of the British Empire."[1] For those in the crowd on that November day in 1899 who doubted the allegiance of Irish Catholics, here before them stood an Irish Catholic MP from Quebec making both a passionate defence of Britain's military campaign in South Africa and a declaration that those who enjoy the rights and privileges of the Empire had better do their duty and defend it. Across town, however, the *Catholic Register*, one of Ontario's prominent Catholic newspapers, was preparing to counter Fitzpatrick's rhetoric. Appalled by the minister's mixing of jingoism with religion, and suspicious of the conspiratorial hand of British and Canadian imperialists, the *Register* had been expressing concern about what it felt was a needless war against the Boers. Irish expatriate Patrick F. Cronin, the *Register*'s editor, was openly critical of Canada's hawkish imperialists and took aim at Sam Hughes – former newspaper editor, member of Parliament, and future minister of the Department of Militia and Defence – as "the cheapest talker in Canada. He insists upon taking command himself and of course he knows that except from the idiot asylums of the land, he could never get a corporal's guard to follow him across a potato patch."[2]

In reality, neither the Irish-born Cronin of Toronto nor the Canadian-born Fitzpatrick of Quebec City could claim to speak for all of Canada's Irish Catholics on the issue of Canadian participation in the

Second Boer War in South Africa, or on many other issues, political or otherwise. To place Canada's Irish Catholics, or any ethnic group in Canada, into a neat pigeonhole of identity does them a great disservice. The Irish, as all peoples, wore a variety of hats according to circumstance and adhered to overlapping identity narratives with varying degrees of intensity during the different phases of their migration and settlement in Canada. Cecil Houston and William "Seamus" Smyth were correct when they pointed out in their seminal study of Irish migration to Canada that one would be hard pressed to identify a single entity known as the Irish Canadian.[3] Religious differences notwithstanding, Irish communities evolved in varied ways across British North America, and each was affected by, among other factors, their place of origin in Ireland, motivation for leaving, time of settlement, region of settlement in Canada, and reception by the host community. Upon migration, the Irish themselves tended to be more attached to their home county – Cork, Limerick, or Kerry, for example – than to any abstract notion of Ireland.[4] In St John's, Newfoundland, Irish Catholics from Wexford and Waterford certainly placed more stock in their respective counties and their political differences than in their shared Irishness, as they beat each other senseless in the turf wars within the port city.[5] Although Irish Catholics in Toronto, across several generations, shared the same faith as their Irish Catholic brothers and sisters in Montreal, Halifax, Saint John, or the Ottawa Valley, other factors also shaped the distinctive ways in which they responded to their neighbours, made their own professions of self-identification, and expressed emotional or political ties to their homeland.

In 1971 John Moir probed what he called the "problem of a double minority," by which some Irish Catholics in Canada found themselves identified in some regions of the country as a religious minority in their linguistic group, or a linguistic minority within their faith group.[6] In such places as Montreal, St Boniface, and Ottawa, when Irish Catholics faced such a situation, it was frequently the Irish badge of identity that they clasped so dearly as the feature that made them distinct in their double minority status. In these social spaces, the Irish Catholics' proximity to the "others" – anglophone Protestants and francophone Catholics – may have prompted an overheated Irish nationalism because it was the distinguishing feature that separated them from these two majorities. Not so in other places in Canada. In any event, the Great War marked a time when these communities would be brought more closely together by the Catholic Church and its leaders and by the flowering of the English-language Catholic press.

In the past thirty years or so, the historiography of the Irish in Canada has demonstrated just how complicated writing the history of this people can be. In 1984, Donald Harman Akenson dispelled misconceptions about the Irish Catholics and Protestants in Canada, thereby clearly distinguishing the experience of the Irish in Canada from that of their American counterparts. Akenson's three major revisions to Irish Canadian historiography have been the source of heated academic discussion to this day. These are, first, that Irish Catholics and Irish Protestants in Canada were essentially rural people who did not cluster in the cities; second, that Irish Protestants outnumbered Irish Catholic migrants before 1845, by nearly two to one, although the clustering of each group might vary from province to province; and, third, that the Great Famine (1845–51) was not central to the Irish migration experience to Canada. Before Akenson's work – and certainly this is still a persistent view – the Irish Catholic Canadian experience was read by some historians, as well as by journalists, teachers, and broadcasters through the lens of the Famine migration, particularly "Black '47."[7] Akenson, as well as historical geographers Cecil Houston and William Smyth, begged to differ. In a later work, Akenson extended his revisionism by claiming that there were essentially "small differences" between Protestant and Catholic Irish. For their part, while challenging some of the details of Akenson's work, Houston and Smyth uncovered the regional differences between Irish communities and the importance of pre-Famine Irish migrations. Bruce Elliott's ground-breaking study of Irish Protestant migration to Upper Canada affirmed the importance of purposeful migration chains between Ireland and Canada and the agency of the Irish themselves in making the decision to migrate. American images of Irish "exile," "alienation," and "uprootedness" have been significantly challenged by scholars examining the Canadian–Irish migration nexus on its own terms.

Certainly, there has been a post-revisionist backlash in which scholars have tried to restore greater relevance to the Famine, to accent the prominence of Irish nationalism, and to restore a narrative of sectarian conflict predominating over denominational containment and peaceful coexistence. One scholar has suggested that a strong affinity existed between Irish nationalists and French-Canadian nationalists in Montreal during the early years of the twentieth century.[8] At times, the characterization of the Irish has verged on the excessively romantic. Take, for instance, those who might argue the Irish in Canada have been "exceptional" or "heroic," citing Irish notables such as Thomas D'Arcy McGee, whose idea of a new nationality set an early precedent for Canadian pluralism, tolerance, and national autonomy.[9] Others have argued the Irish Catholic eye never lost sight of Ireland and that priority was given to issues of home rule and independence above most other things.[10] The problem remains, however, that if we assign paramount importance to Irish nationalism among the Canadian Irish, particularly by the late 19th century, or regard the Famine as a source of transgenerational resentment of anything English, it is difficult indeed to visualize an Irish Catholic Canadian, clad in khaki, sporting the crested royal insignia, crouched on the South African veldt, pointing his rifle at the head of a Boer commando, and doing so voluntarily. Even more startling might be an image of this same soldier surviving the Boer expeditions and, if age and condition permitted, volunteering fifteen years later to fight for the King against the Kaiser.

The idea of exile made popular by the American historian, Kerby Miller, has cast a long shadow over Irish historiography on both sides of the border. Miller argues that Irish Catholics, for reasons of their communal behaviour, particular theology, and other-worldliness, regarded themselves as involuntary immigrants and therefore exiles from Ireland.[11] Part of this collective ethos, in Miller's view, was a penchant for blaming England for their situation and a feeling of alienation from their homes in a hostile new world. Donald Akenson has argued persuasively against this notion of the Irish Catholic as victim in the process of migration and settlement. He situates the Irish Catholic experience in Canada on a much wider canvas and argues that, with respect to numbers, the Famine migration was merely an aberration and was actually built upon a migration process that was decades old, largely Protestant in faith, and voluntary. Finally, if Houston and Smyth are correct about the Irish in Canada being a community of communities – and the qualitative and quantitative data suggest this was the case in the nineteenth century – one suspects that the Canadian experience lies somewhere between the positions staked out by Akenson and Miller.

The Irish Catholics of Canada fit no cookie-cutter definition. There is no denying that, even across generations, in the Catholic media, in politics, in social interactions, and in literature, persistent themes, images, and rhetoric affirmed their nostalgic, religious, and cultural ties to Ireland. Although there are elements of the exile motif in Canadian Irish publications as late as 1899 – in fact, the Copp Clark readers published for Ontario Catholic schools that year still included the "Exile of Erin" as its only overtly Irish piece – there was much more to Irish Catholic Canadian life than pining for the motherland.[12] Similarly, while many things brought Irish Catholics and their Protestant neighbours together in politics, on the shop floor, in public celebrations, and (in some provinces) in schools, the persistence of anti-Catholic sentiment in the public press, in civic cultures, in social mores, and from the pulpit is not easily dismissed. Although, as the careers of J.J. Leddy, J.J. Foy, Charles Doherty, and Robert Manion attest,[13] Irish Catholics could be found as elected representatives of the Conservative party, they still had to stare down members of the Loyal Orange Order, who were more numerous in the Conservative ranks, both in Parliament and at the polls. But the beating of the Lambeg drums did not keep Catholics from the mayor's chair in Halifax, the board rooms of Winnipeg and Calgary, or the barracks of local militia units in Ontario. No simplified Irish nationalist or Canadian assimilationist labels easily apply to the diverse communities of Irish Catholics in Canada on the eve of the Great War.

When I wrote *Waning of the Green* seventeen years ago, I tackled the tough questions of Toronto's Irish Catholics in terms of their multiple identities: as social and economic actors in the city; as Catholics; as Irish migrants and, mostly, descendants; as educators; and as engaged citizens in Canadian life. Despite my critics, the study was not intended to propose a formula for Irish assimilation into Canadian life,[14] nor was it a testament to a complete denial of their Irish heritage. It was simply a multi-layered social and historical examination of people who were more than just "political" and faced the challenges of finding homes, feeding their families, educating their children, adapting to the changing face of the Church, and living in peace with their non-Catholic and sometimes unsympathetic neighbours. Toronto does not represent all of Canada, nor was it a microcosm of Irish-Canadian Catholicism in the nineteenth and early twentieth centuries. And while new and exciting studies by Sherry Olson and Patricia Thornton on Montreal, Allan Rowe on the Prairies, William Jenkins on Buffalo and Toronto, and Patrick Mannion on Atlantic Canada and Portland, Maine, have demonstrated clear distinctions in the social and political life of Irish Catholics in the late Victorian and Edwardian periods, some similarities also emerge.[15] By 1914, each Irish-Canadian community had retained a sense of its Irishness, but this was just one among many competing identities, not the least of which were the daily challenges faced by the children and grandchildren of Irish immigrants to work and live as Canadians in Canada.

The study of Irish Catholic responses to the Great War in Canada helps to amplify how these various communities had evolved by 1914 and demonstrates how Irish, Canadian, and imperial self-identifications overlapped and superseded one another at times. There was no definitive Irish Catholic response to the War, but there was a general consensus across Irish Catholic communities in Canada that this war was theirs to engage in. Key to this response were local parish priests and bishops, who almost unanimously became supporters and spokespersons for recruitment, wartime fundraising, and, at times, less popular features of the federal government's wartime strategy. Irish Catholics were not unanimous in their support of conscription in 1917, although many bishops tacitly or publicly endorsed the implementation of the Military Service Act. Irish Catholics were far from united in their response to the Irish Republican Brotherhood, who violently seized central Dublin for a week in the name of creating an Irish Republic. The thought of such violence, which played to the physical force nationalist idea that "Britain's disadvantage [the war] was Ireland's advantage," was repugnant, treacherous, and stupid to many Irish Catholics in Canada and elsewhere in the Empire.[16] Even though most Irish Catholic Canadians in the years after the Easter Rising could agree that Ireland needed Home Rule, they could not agree upon what form that might take. For many Irish Catholics in Canada, constitutional Irish nationalism and fighting the war were two sides of the same coin. If war was justified to thwart Prussian militarism and allow small nations to be free, then Ireland was also a good test case for the principle of a just war. As the Reverend Captain (later Major) John J. O'Gorman of Ottawa stated explicitly and publicly, Irish Canadians bore a "double duty" to win the war for Canada and the Empire and then secure peace and Home Rule in Ireland.

Despite the inviting prospect of understanding the behaviour and engagement of Canada's Irish Catholics in the Great War, there has been little scholarship on Irish Catholics, or in fact any non-francophone Catholics, and the war. The engagement of Catholics in the war is generally seen through the response of the Quebec Church and the ongoing difficulties between its bishops and the populist nationalist movement led by Henri Bourassa, Olivar Asselin, and Armand Lavergne. Numerous authors have mapped out the conscription crisis as it pertained to Quebec and, by the war's end, had seriously divided Canada along linguistic and cultural lines.[17] Réné Durocher, in particular, has explored how the efforts of French Canadian Catholic bishops to rouse public support among Catholics for the imperial war effort were constantly undermined by Bourassa, his new paper, *Le Devoir*, and an associated chorus of nationalists who elected to fight the war on Quebec's terms only.[18] Central to the rift between francophone and anglophone Canada was the ongoing problem of Regulation 17 in Ontario, which effectively banned French-language education in the province beyond the second grade. Irish Catholics tended to support the provincial regulation in an effort to preserve the quality of the separate schools and assure themselves control of their own Church outside of Quebec.[19] As Olivar Asselin might comment, "The Prussians are not across the ocean, they are next door."[20] Missing from the record have been the Catholics who were not directly implicated in the conscription issue in mainstream historiography.

This book argues that, in general, Irish Catholics in Canada – led by their clergy, and as made manifest in their voluntary recruitment – supported the Canadian and imperial war effort. Although Bishop Michael Francis Fallon of London and Father Matthew Whelan of Ottawa might disagree on how the Borden government might effectively bring victory, they shared a belief in the justice of the war and a commitment to its successful conclusion. Similarly, while Charles Power of Quebec City might vehemently disagree with Robert Manion of Fort William across the floor of the House of Commons on Canada's conduct of the war, both men, of Irish Catholic descent, had shed khaki that had been stained with blood at the Front, in order to return home and win the war in a manner espoused by their respective political parties. No doubt the six daily Catholic newspapers feeding the Irish Catholic communities across the country varied in their positions on the war and the concurrent Irish question, and did so to such a degree that no historian could dare define the Irish Catholic position on the war exclusively through any single organ. Nevertheless, none of the editors, whether Irish or Canadian born, would retreat from two principles: the war must be fought and won, and Ireland must have Home Rule. The devil was in the details that lay between the extreme positions taken by Irish Catholics on both issues. All of this is to say, as St Augustine might have said, Irish Catholic Canadians were united on the most important issues, and took great liberties on those contingent features of each cause.

Although Irish Catholic positions on the war were nuanced, given local circumstances, by the end of the war the Catholic Church outside of francophone Quebec was remarkably more unified than it had been beforehand. Editors of Catholic newspapers were reading one another's columns, and laypersons became aware, regardless of their geographic location, of the thoughts and patriotic rhetoric of bishops in Canadian dioceses they might never visit. The ordeal of giving up loved ones to the Canadian army, the reports of the wounded, and the shared grief of the death of a father, son, husband, or brother, provided a common bond across the Canadian Catholic world as few other events in the country's past ever had. The unfortunate irony of the war as a binding agent among English-speaking Catholics of Irish birth or descent was that, as their communities grew more closely aligned, they themselves became increasingly alienated from francophone Catholic communities, who constituted the Catholic majority in Canada. The Great War serves as a centrifuge in Canadian Catholicism, separating French- and English-speaking Catholics on key issues and fracturing the Church seriously, but not fatally, along linguistic lines. The Church in Canada was no stranger to the politics of language; there had been battles over episcopal control, immigrant accommodation, education, and missions, all rooted in differing linguistic and cultural visions of the Canadian Church, long before the first German infantryman crossed the Belgian frontier. The Great War, with its issues of Empire, recruitment, and conscription, poured salt on existing wounds within the Church and plucked the scabs off old ones. For Irish Catholic Canadians, the war forced clerical and lay leaders to navigate a course that would preserve Catholic unity while distinguishing between attitudes that might be construed as purely cultural, with no reference whatsoever to the faith. This task was made far more difficult by the fact that the most public Irish Catholic leaders during the war were also those men viewed by French Canadians as having been hostile to the francophone Church before the war.

Methodologically, this book departs from many studies of the Irish and military histories that have come before it. Combining evidence gleaned from manuscript collections, newspapers, personnel files, and routinely generated records, it attempts to offer a glimpse of Irish Catholics and their Church both from the bottom up and from the top down. In many ways, this approach is similar to that used by Richard S. Grayson in his ground-breaking work, *Belfast Boys*, which explores the intersecting lives of Protestant and Catholic Irishmen from West Belfast who served in the British forces during the Great War. Combining data gleaned from wills, service files, and newspapers, Grayson claims that he has created "a socio-military history that begins in the street rather than the trench or the training ground."[21] *The Imperial Irish* is written with a similarly close focus on Irish Catholics, beginning in the pews, the streets, and the fields, rather than at the Front. Central to understanding the behaviours of the Irish Catholic Canadian population during the Great War is a detailed examination of the leaders and the rank and file in Canada's Roman Catholic Church.

The first chapter attempts to trace the progression of attitudes among Canada's Irish Catholic communities as war approached. For Irish Canadians, the outbreak of war in 1914 did not mark a sudden rupture from the past, nor was it the fulfilment of a singular linear progression from imperial migrant to imperial militant. The long road to war was filled with curves, gullies, and some dead ends as Canada's Irish Catholics, in their many community settings, negotiated the demands of their religious faith, their nostalgic ties to Ireland, and their embrace of life and work in Canada. As Irish Catholic communities in North America evolved over the generations from their pre- and post-Famine migrations, each had to confront the realities of living in territories in which they were either a linguistic minority, a religious minority, or both. Their journey was marked by periodic tensions, and sometimes violent clashes, with their Protestant neighbours and by an uneasy alliance with their French co-religionists. While the violence of the 1850s and 1860s between the proverbial Orange and Green began to shift into more subtle forms of discrimination, periodic anti-Catholic politicking, or, at times, purely rhetorical forms, tensions between the French and Irish heightened. Protestant–Catholic relations evolved at many levels: constitutional, political, social, and theological. Although the constitutional protection accorded Catholics since the Quebec Act of 1774 offered Irish Catholics security under the law, just as Section 93 of the British North America Act protected their schools in some provinces, Catholics could find themselves under duress in other areas as issues arose. And while there were sometimes tactical truces in the political arena, and social toleration between denominations, theological differences might always lurk, keeping Canada's religious solitudes apart. As Principal William Grant of Queen's University observed around the time of the South African conflict, "Even in the cities where there is the closest association of Protestant and Romanist in commercial, industrial and political life, the two currents of religious life flow side by side as distinct from each other as the St Lawrence and the Ottawa after their junction. But the two rivers eventually blend into one. The two currents of religious life do not."[22]

What Grant underestimated was the developing political and social consciousness in the Catholic "river." As Irish Catholics gained confidence in their home communities, despite their Protestant neighbours, so grew their resolve to lay claim to the management and control of the Church outside of Quebec. Issues concerning bilingual schools, the mother tongue of bishops, and the cultural characteristics of religious orders all pointed to a collision of Irish and French visions of the Church in Canada. In 1899, when the Canadian government resolved to send troops to South Africa to defend imperial interests, and as many Irish Catholic Canadians articulated their loyalty to the British Empire, one detects a significant step in defining a cultural divide between the charter linguistic groups in the Catholic Church. As the opposing rhetoric of Fitzpatrick and Cronin made clear, however, there was no unanimity of opinion among Irish Catholics on the Boer War, but the debate seems to have been a prelude to the decisions that would have to be made by Irish Catholics fifteen years hence. The Great War served to amplify the differences that lay between Irish and French Canadian Catholics, while at the same time providing greater opportunities for Protestant and Catholic unity among those who shared the English language. This book explores how these interfaith and intercultural relationships developed and disintegrated over the course of the war.

The second chapter picks up on the themes of faith and culture by examining the powerful embrace of the war effort by clerical and lay leaders in the Church. In the first two years of the conflict there was near-unanimity among anglophone Catholic bishops about the war's just cause. Leaders tapped into the imperialist rhetoric of the day, offered theological explanations that would foster recruitment, and often made public appearances in support of recruitment drives and other war-related initiatives. While the efforts of bishops, priests, leaders of lay associations, and editors might be lauded by Protestant contemporaries – leaders of the Orange Order excepted – Irish Catholic leaders had to make cautious efforts not to alienate their French Canadian confreres, who faced significant opposition to certain aspects of the war effort from nationalists headed by the devout Catholic editor and politician Henri Bourassa. Across Canada, a consensus emerged among leading Catholic prelates and laymen that the war effort must be pursued vigorously, while making certain the Church in Quebec was affirmed as an ally in the imperial quest, in spite of the contrarian rhetoric of Bourassa and his colleagues. By 1916, however, the actions of Quebec nationalists, when combined with developments both at the Front and in domestic recruitment, caused Irish Catholic editors and prelates to lose their patience with Bourassa's nationalists, creating a widening chasm between the two solitudes within Canadian Church.

Chapter three explores the participation in the war effort of ordinary Catholics, specifically the men and women who volunteered to serve in the various branches of the Canadian Expeditionary Force (CEF). The participation of young Irish Catholic men was truly national in scope and demonstrated that, regardless of their community of origin, or their rural or urban roots, Irish Catholic Canadians were prominent in their enlistment for overseas service. Catholic recruits came from all occupational groups and nearly every community in the country, and as many as half had already served in local militias. In this way, Irish Catholic recruits appeared little different from their Protestant counterparts, save for the fact that the Catholic recruits were overwhelmingly Canadian-born and did not reflect the general enlistment patterns of British expatriates, who flocked to local recruiting centres and then were transported to Valcartier, Quebec, for deployment back to the United Kingdom for service in the CEF.[23] Although a small minority of Irish Catholic recruits had been born in Ireland, the vast majority of nurses and soldiers were descended from parents and grandparents who had migrated to Canada. Although a myriad of reasons could account for why young Irish Catholics signed their names to the attestation papers that made them soldiers and nursing sisters, the case can be made that many enlisted under the prompting of family and parish, buoyed by experience in Canada's military traditions, and in spite of the fact that, after early 1915, safe and gainful employment was available to them at home.

When these recruits set out for training or arrived at the Front, the faith of their parents was not far behind. Chapter four grapples with the question of how Irish Catholics in the CEF embraced, tolerated, or were indifferent to their Catholic faith, the dictates of Catholic morality, and the instructions of the priests who served as their chaplains. The story of the evolution of the Canadian Chaplain Service is itself evidence of Protestants and Catholics working together with a common resolve, despite a rather rocky start. The problems within the Catholic chaplaincy, apart from its early dysfunctional and denominationally biased command structure, were problems of language and culture. The Great War rekindled the unease between French Canadian soldiers and padres on the one hand, and their Irish and Scottish co-religionists on the other. Here, Irish Catholic leaders emerged to resolve the denominational challenges, while making certain that the transplanted intercultural struggle endemic to the Canadian Church did not threaten the faith of Irish Catholic soldiers, or bring scandal to the Church in the eyes of the military establishment. At the same time, Catholic chaplains often faced an uphill battle keeping Irish Catholic soldiers spiritually disciplined and morally upright.

Such balancing acts were not simply matters for the Church overseas. At home, Irish Catholics faced plenty of criticism, mostly from the Orange *Sentinel* and its political allies on the question of Catholic loyalty. Protestant pundits and fire-breathing politicos pulled no punches when it came to challenging the alleged pro-German sympathies of Pope Benedict XV, the alleged statements of disloyalty from the Ukrainian Catholic Eparch of Canada, the revolutionaries who caused the destruction of central Dublin after Easter 1916, or the anti-war voices in Catholic Quebec. Irish Catholic leaders forced themselves to be accountable for fellow Catholics, without bringing scandal to the Church through open division and while maintaining the public appearance of their own loyalty to the Empire and their resolve to win the war.

Chapter five discusses how bishops, priests, and the editors of Catholic newspapers navigated their way through treacherous waters, voicing their commitment to the war effort while advocating for Home Rule in Ireland, Catholic unity in Canada, and exoneration of the Pope from the calumnies spread about him. Irish Catholic leaders and their flocks were by no means of one mind on issues such as conscription, and Catholic unity was severely strained, but the course charted in 1914 to support the war until its successful end was maintained.

The final chapter explores the bonds created between Catholics and Protestants in the final year of the war. Despite eruptions of Catholic–Protestant tension over questions concerning the application of the Military Service Act, Irish Catholics continued to pursue the war effort prominently, and in some cases with the praise and compliments of their Protestant countrymen. The same type of rapprochement did not characterize Irish–French relations in the Church, as each side became increasingly alienated on the issues of schools, conscription, and Irish control of the Church. But while Simon Jolivet's fascinating book *Le vert et le bleu* discusses in detail the reconciliation between local French Canadian nationalists and some Irish Catholic nationalists in the city of Montreal,[24] this was not the case nationally, particularly among clerical leaders, men in arms, and Catholic editors. Some Irish Catholics in Montreal found allies in Bourassa's nationalists as they made the case for Home Rule in Ireland, but most Irish Catholic Canadians elsewhere avoided open association with French Canadian nationalism. The Great War, and the events in the wake of the federal election of 1917, had merely worsened the deteriorating intercultural relations within the Canadian Catholic Church.

The Great War further estranged Irish Catholics from their Catholic cousins who spoke French. The war did not cause the trouble, but only made fractured relations worse – so much so that some French Canadians must have felt that the Irish "green" had developed more of an "orange" hue. The wounds opened by the struggle between the Irish and the French over new bishops for the Prairie West, the allegiance of the new Catholic immigrants, and French-language education, were made deeper over controversies surrounding recruitment and conscription. Many Irish Catholic leaders, both lay and clerical, found it difficult to defend or justify francophone resistance to enlisting in the CEF. The implementation of the Military Service Act and the federal election of 1917, followed by the Quebec riots of 1918, seriously fractured the Catholic community along linguistic lines but also created political fissures among Irish Catholics themselves. The Great War caused an open parting of the ways between the francophone and anglophone hierarchies with respect to national priorities, such that English-speaking Catholic leaders found more common ground with their non-Catholic contemporaries than with their French-Canadian co-religionists. Postwar efforts such as the Bonne Entente became as important to some Catholic bishops as it was to other non-Catholic Canadians. It was one thing to win the war and another to lose the peace within the Canadian Church. Perhaps a glimmer of hope in the dying months of the war came when the bishops formally petitioned Rome for the creation of what would become the military vicariate for Canada. The move to appoint an *episcopus castrensis* – a bishop in charge of army chaplains, or "bishop of the camp" – and the Holy See's designation of a moderate French Canadian prelate to that role, provided a hopeful sign that, despite the recriminations arising from the war, the cultural and linguistic tensions within the Church were not beyond hope of healing.

Despite the fact that the Great War exacerbated internal linguistic tensions in the Church, in some ways it may also have provided a cardinal moment for building bridges between Irish Catholic communities in Canada. By 1918, there had been increased inter-diocesan communication and coordination as in no time before. During the war, Canadian bishops were in regular contact with one another, coordinating positions on the war, mounting fundraising campaigns, and maintaining a fresh supply of priests to the Canadian Chaplain Service. Naturally, bishops in various regions had often been in correspondence in the past, but the Great War marked a time of closer and more frequent coordination between the ecclesiastical provinces of Canada, including those in Quebec, at a time when there was no national organization or conference of Catholic bishops.

Irish Catholic laypersons also came to know one another better during the Great War. Once again, Irish Catholics in their regional communities had contact with one another before the war, whether through the cementing of family networks, voluntary associations, religious pilgrimages and conferences, or internal migration of Catholics from one region of Canada to another. However, the war amplified the contact between these Irish populations. Although soldiers and nurses were raised within the context of local recruiting initiatives and within regional hospital training schools, they soon became integrated with other Irish Catholics from across the country. Men who volunteered in the Ottawa Valley, for example, saw their units merge with those from other parts of Ontario, the Prairies, and the Maritimes, giving a good many of them first contact with Catholic men from Halifax, Montreal, or Saskatoon. In similar fashion, priests, although initially assigned by their bishops to battalions from their home diocese, soon found themselves ministering to Catholics from across the country and, in the process, learned that the religious practices of Irish Catholics varied from region to region. The Great War forced Irish Catholics to travel greater distances than they had ever travelled in their lives, to visit communities on their way to departure points in Quebec and Nova Scotia, and to work, fight, and receive the sacraments with other Catholics with whom they forged bonds, as soldiers did. In some ways the war became a means of broadening the Irish Catholic world in Canada, not just at home, but through their experiences in England, France, Belgium, and Greece.

Wartime communications and the heightened activities of fraternal benevolent associations among Catholics also bound the Irish Catholic regions of Canada more closely together. The English-language Catholic weekly newspapers increasingly used one another's stories and challenged one another in their interpretations of the Catholic narrative of the war; the Knights of Columbus emerged as the premier Catholic men's fraternal organization, not only by virtue of its increased numbers and national scope, but also in its proven ability to serve the nation and the Church in its time of need. Although the Knights' administrative structure was grounded in regional "state" councils, as determined by provincial boundaries, the war brought these councils together to focus on national aims and objectives with respect to winning the war and enhancing Catholic respectability from coast to coast.[25] For fraternal associations such as the Knights of Columbus, and for newspaper editors from Winnipeg to Antigonish, it was not just a matter of all Catholics, including the Irish, "doing their bit" for the imperial war effort: it was also important that they be seen by non-Catholics as doing so. This matter of public perception would be a constant struggle for Irish Catholic advocates, who were often put on the defensive by the Orange *Sentinel*, anti-Catholic politicians, and the interpretations rendered by non-Catholics of the actions or inaction of Catholics both at home and abroad. Editors, priests, and lay leaders had to maintain a watchful eye to clarify the Catholic position on the war.

This being said, the Great War also marked the best of times and the worst of times in Catholic–Protestant relations. Although numerous cases of sectarianism were recorded, and the use of un-Christian rhetoric could be striking in specific contexts, particularly during the federal election of 1917, the war may have tipped the balance in the opposite direction. Padres from all denominations worked co-operatively at the Front and behind the lines; fundraising efforts were undertaken with an ecumenical spirit, long before the institutional Catholic Church recognized the potential of such inter-denominational engagements; Protestant and Catholic men enlisted together, served together, died together, and had their names etched in stone together, without reference to which Christian denomination they belonged. These lessons were not forgotten by those who returned, both lay and clerical, but it is somewhat paradoxical that, of all the Catholic priests who returned from service overseas, none was ever deemed "safe" enough to be appointed to the Catholic episcopacy after the war.

Finally, the Great War also brought to a head what O'Gorman might term the double duty of the Irish Catholic Canadian. From the time of their various arrivals in Canada, Irish Catholics were often beset by questions about their focus of loyalty. The question at the fore was whether it was possible for Irish Catholics to embrace the emerging state of Canada within a British imperial context and yet not surrender his or her affections, loyalties, and ties to Ireland.

Throughout the nineteenth century, Irish Catholics had found themselves at the centre of controversy – the Gourlay Shanty riots in Halifax, the Orange and Green riots in Saint John and Toronto, and the murder of Robert Corrigan, a Catholic farmer who had converted to Anglicanism, by a mob of Catholics outside of Montreal.[26] The perception had often been in the non-Catholic public mind that Irish Catholics could not have a primary focus of loyalty that was directed at Canada. Loyalty to the Pope or to Ireland appeared to come first. Such suspicions appeared confirmed when Fenians crossed the Niagara frontier in 1866 in a vain attempt to capture British North America and trade it for Ireland's freedom,[27] and when Hibernians marched in the streets of Toronto with pikes aloft, or Irish nationalists in several Canadian cities flocked to meetings featuring the latest in a litany of Irish "patriots" who had come to Canada to raise money for their cause, throughout the nineteenth century.[28] Similarly, the persistence of Catholic schools partly funded by the state in Ontario, the refusal of the Catholic Church to allow the excommunicated Joseph Guibord, a Montreal printer known for his liberal politics, to be buried in his own plot in a Catholic cemetery in Montreal, or the restoration of the Jesuits Estates in Quebec, offered some Protestant Canadians evidence that Catholics demanded and unfairly held special privileges. Catholic of all stripes had to face the call, "Equal rights for all, special privileges for none."[29]

Yet history is not so simple. Irish Catholics throughout the country, from the time of settlement long before the Great Famine, had engaged many pursuits, worn many hats, and held two loyalties at the same time. In their cultural dimorphism as Catholics living in Canada, yet of Irish birth or descent, they had become nimble in wearing the hat that best suited them when a situation presented itself. This is why they could be ardent supporters of three Home Rule bills for Ireland; they realized that what Ireland needed was what they themselves had come to enjoy in Canada: autonomy within the Empire and responsible government at home. Similarly, in 1899, it was not such a stretch for many Irish Catholics to see concepts of self-government and autonomy as being in jeopardy when the Empire was threatened both internally and externally. Irish Catholics from every province volunteered to fight for the security of the British Empire in South Africa and, fifteen years later, to defend that same Empire against

Prussian militarism. For many Irish Catholics, their quest for Home Rule in Ireland and their loyalty to Canada were two sides of the same coin, with obverse and reverse showing their distinctive faces at different times. Between 1914 and 1918, many Irish Catholics went to war believing that the war itself was fulfilling a double duty: the defence of Canada and the Empire on the one hand, and, on the other, the defense of principles that would assure self-determination for Ireland within an imperial context.

1

The Long Road to War

Winding its way from Lake Temiskaming to where it blends with the St Lawrence River near Montreal, the Ottawa River has been a magnet for settlement for centuries. Long before the arrival of French explorer Samuel de Champlain in the early seventeenth century, Anishinaabe peoples summered on its banks and defended the strategic channels that whirled around Grand Calumet and Alumette Islands. In the early nineteenth century, Irish, French-Canadian, and Scottish lumbermen harvested the pine of the valley, providing square timber for construction in Britain's growing cities and masts for its powerful Imperial Navy. With the woodsman came settlement, moving northwest beyond the extension of French-Canadian seigneurial tenure in the lower valley on what would become the Quebec bank of the river. Irish Catholics and Protestants pioneered up the Ottawa Valley, leaving a trail of settlements that bore the names of their ancestral homes: Antrim, Leitrim, Donegal, Mayo, Killaloe, Mount St Patrick, and Westmeath. Scottish and English settlers entered the region at the same time, inscribing the map with names that reflected their distinctive origins: Renfrew, Pembroke, Bristol, and Clarendon. Poles from the Kaszuby region near the Baltic Sea arrived in the late 1850s, carving out farms in the Bonnechere and Madawaska valleys and invoking their homeland with place names such as Wilno, Wadowice, and Kaszuby.[1] Germans soon found homes in the upper valley on either side of the river, to the west in Renfrew County and to the east in the Pontiac at villages such as Schwartz. The Valley became a multicultural, linguistically diverse region whose economy was based in lumbering, milling, farming, and mining.

The Whelan family is well known in the Ottawa Valley. Stephen Whelan, a native of county Carlow,[2] was one of over 109,000 refugees from the Irish Famine who ventured to British North America in 1847. Born in 1829, the third child of Thomas Whelan and Mary Kinsella, he survived the voyage to Quebec along with eight siblings. Having made it through the quarantine stations on Grosse Île and survived the fever sheds at Pointe-St-Charles at Montreal, Thomas and Mary must have been delighted to meet other Irish Catholics when they arrived in Renfrew County, where they eventually purchased land off the Opeongo Road near Shamrock.[3] The Valley had become home to thousands of Irish well before the potato blight of 1845 and the ensuing human devastation for the next half-dozen years in Ireland. In the newly opened farmlands of Admaston Township, the Whelans put down their roots. Stephen was restless and, as a young man, ventured to the gold fields of California and the promise of Australia before returning home to the Valley and building his own fortune. In his middle age, re-established in farming, Stephen married his beloved Hanna (Johanna) O'Gorman, a Canadian-born Irish Catholic twenty-one years his junior. Together they farmed in Admaston, attended Mass in the local parish at Douglas, and raised eleven children – six girls and five boys. By the time of his death in 1906, Stephen had served as reeve of Admaston Township for thirty-five years, and, beginning at its inception in 1888, was a major stakeholder in the Ottawa, Arnprior and Parry Sound Railway Company, which would link the CPR emanating from Ottawa to Georgian Bay.[4]

Stephen and Johannah's second last child, Monica Marian Whelan, was born in 1891,[5] nearly forty-four years after her father stepped off the "coffin ship" from Ireland. Mona, as she would call herself, never became a farm girl, but pursued nurse's training in Montreal. In June 1915, at the age of twenty-four, and having completed her three years of training, Mona enlisted in the Canadian Army Medical Corps as a nursing sister, fully intending to serve the men of the Canadian Expeditionary Force (CEF) now fighting for King and Country in Belgium and France. Perhaps like her father and her brother Peter, who had left for California years before, Mona had a curiosity about the world that lay beyond the farms and forests of her native Valley. The local paper kept track of her movements from the time of her recruitment to her arrival in England.[6] For Mona Whelan and her family, it had been a long road to the Great War. But her father's path from famine waif to prosperous farmer, entrepreneur, and politician seemed to mirror Irish Catholic lives elsewhere in Canada. And now Irish communities, each with its own stories and local circumstances, were coming to terms with an imperial war that marked but another milestone in the journey of migration and adaptation to Canada. Although Stephen was now in his grave (d. 1906), young Mona was about to take this Irish family's next step in this great adventure.

Perhaps there is little use in trying to describe a singular Irish Catholic Canadian pathway to 1914. Irish Catholic men and women in Canada did not form a cohesive ethnic community in 1914, but lived in a community of communities separated by geography yet symbolically bound by a common heritage and faith. These communities were diverse with respect to region; the timing of their settlement; social class; employment; family and gender relationships as shaped by their inner-city or rural agrarian settings; the availability of good-quality education; the disposition and engaged leadership of local priests and bishops; the multicultural flavour of their local churches and dioceses; and their levels of engagement with non-Catholics. Although their attestation papers showed names that might appear to hail from the "old sod" and a faith tied to the Pope in Rome, the Irish Catholic men and women who joined the CEF brought with them a mosaic of Canadian experiences and identities. Toronto, for instance, could no more be identified with the whole of Irish Canadian experience than could Halifax, Montreal, Winnipeg, or the farmsteads of the upper Ottawa Valley. But the events of 1914–18 drew these communities together, united by lay leaders, newspapermen, and an episcopal leadership that identified the war as theirs as much as any other Canadians'. As Neil McNeil – the archbishop of Toronto of Scottish and Irish descent – would later proclaim, regardless of all other factors "we are all involved in the same issue."[7]

The Irish Catholics of Canada were essentially a community of communities based on the diversity of the their counties of origin, the time of their migration, and the place of their settlement. Historical geographers Cecil Houston and William Smyth make a convincing case that Irish Catholics cannot be collectively defined in terms of behaviour within a single Irish Catholic community.[8] The Irish imprint on Canada varies from city to city and from region to region.

Within their local contexts, Irish Catholic communities evolved in distinctive ways that were influenced by specific internal dynamics, the style of episcopal leadership, and relations with other Catholics and Protestants. An Irish Catholic from Eganville, Ontario, might share the altar rail with Irish Canadians from Montreal, Halifax, or Calgary, but may well differ from his co-religionists with respect to politics, education, social expectations, or even attitudes toward the French Canadian praying at the same rail or the Presbyterian who passed by the Church, suspicious of the priestcraft going on inside. Irish Catholics were as much creatures of their locale as they were of any overarching Irish Catholic Canadian identity. Much of this could be tracked to their origins.

Although Newfoundland's Irish Catholics are not included in this study, save for where they appear in the CEF as recruits away from home, their experience as sojourners and settlers helps bring into relief the importance of the origins of Irish communities in Canada. If one excludes the small number of Irish, mostly from a military background, who settled and assimilated into life in New France, the Irish communities in Newfoundland can boast to be the oldest in British North America. Sailors and fishermen from Wexford, Waterford, Tipperary, Kilkenny, and eastern Cork had ventured to the cod-rich waters of the Grand Banks and travelled back and forth across the Atlantic, before it became evident that it would be easier to establish a seasonal dry fishery on the shores of Newfoundland.[9] As early as the 17th century, these Catholics from southeastern Ireland began to form settlements along the coasts of the Avalon Peninsula and in the plethora of coves, bays, and inlets that comprise Newfoundland's Atlantic shore. In time, and in spite of the British government's objections to building a colony around the fishery, Irish Catholics formed one of the principal communities in what has been termed "Britain's oldest colony."[10] Here the men and women of eastern Munster and southwest Leinster built homes, raised families, adapted their culture, customs and language, struggled for their rights with the English Protestants, and fought among themselves along battle lines based on their counties of origin. As geographer John Mannion has aptly demonstrated, these Irish communities were tightly knit and well connected with their ports of origin – so much so that most could claim heritage from within a sixty-mile radius of the River Suir estuary, which separates counties Waterford and Wexford.[11]

The only other British North American Irish Catholic community that came close to approximating the distinctive local characteristics of Newfoundland's Irish Catholics was that of their cousins in Halifax, Nova Scotia. As Britain's naval bastion in the western North Atlantic, Halifax had become a critical nexus for the British Navy in addition to being an important trade centre in Britain's North Atlantic triangle, linking her ports to those of British North America and the British Caribbean. The first Irish Catholics in Halifax worked on the fortifications of the new city as early as 1749, when Lord Cornwallis envisioned a British counterweight to the French port and fort at nearby Louisbourg on Cape Breton Island. The Halifax Irish were almost entirely composed of the descendants of pre-Famine Irish migrants who had come mostly between 1790 and 1840 from the same southeastern Irish counties as the Irish Newfoundlanders.[12] Ironically, these same Newfoundland cousins would come to settle in Halifax and Cape Breton when the fishery no longer provided them a steady income. Known as "two-boaters," these Newfoundland Irish Catholics would become a significant part of the Halifax Irish community, which was almost entirely Catholic and, by 1901, would constitute about a third of the city's population.[13]

The Irish Catholics of Halifax and Newfoundland would also share another characteristic: they would each have their own bishop, separate from the control and influence of the French-Canadian Catholic Church. In 1820, the Holy See had appointed Edmund Burke to lead the Catholics of what are now all three Maritime provinces. Burke and his successors faced many challenges: managing the sometimes tenuous relations with local Protestants; maintaining autonomy from the Diocese of Quebec; and keeping the distinctive Catholic ethnic communities from suffocating one another. In 1844, the Holy See considered it wise to ease the turbulent relations between the Scottish Catholics of eastern Nova Scotia and the Irish of Halifax by creating two new dioceses, one for the Irish in Halifax and another for the Scots at Arichat (later relocated to Antigonish). The power and influence of the Irish bishops in Halifax was further enhanced in 1852 when Rome elevated the city to archiepiscopal status, to the effect that it could claim ecclesiastical sovereignty over suffragan dioceses at Antigonish, Charlottetown, and Saint John, New Brunswick. The creation of the new Archdiocese of Halifax would provide at least the pretext for ecclesiastical intercourse between the Irish Catholics of

Nova Scotia and the neighbouring Maritime colonies – later provinces – which contained Irish Catholic communities of their own, each with distinctive origins.[14]

In New Brunswick, for instance, Irish Catholics could be found in two separate regions of the province: the Saint John River valley, anchored by the city of the same name, and the Miramichi Valley in the northeastern section of the province. Again, as in the other British Atlantic colonies, the Irish migrants came in the four decades before the Great Famine, with at least 65,000 landing in New Brunswick between 1827 and 1835. The Irish were such a dominant group in the period that it is not surprising that one possible name invoked for the province had been New Ireland.[15] However, unlike the prevailing dominance of the Roman Catholics among the Irish immigrant population of Newfoundland and Nova Scotia, the Irish of New Brunswick were almost evenly divided between Catholics and Protestants. The reason for this balance lay in the different ports of departure in Ireland that were linked to New Brunswick's chief port, Saint John. From the ports of Queenstown (now Cobh) in Cork and Derry/Londonderry in Ulster came Protestant migrants seeking a better life in the new world, fleeing agrarian violence in the southern counties, or escaping the declining weaving and linen industries in the north. In addition to what would eventually become a distinctive Irish demographic in the region, pregnant with the troubles that arise from sectarianism, there were pockets of New Brunswick where Catholic Irish became dominant.[16] In the Miramichi Valley and along the coast of the Gulf of St Lawrence, Irish Catholic migrants were joined by Catholic two-boaters from Newfoundland, who were seeking employments in the farms, forests, and fishery of northern New Brunswick. Here, social relations would be defined less by rivalry between religious denominations within the Irish ethnic group, and more by competition between Irish and francophone Catholics for control of the local Catholic Church.[17]

In the southern section of New Brunswick, along the shores of the Bay of Fundy and where the Saint John River spills into the Atlantic, the Irish population elected either to find work in the port of Saint John and the surrounding area or to move on to the United States. In 1827, the free land grants in the province ceased. Irish who were unable to pay for available land in the interior of New Brunswick, or to navigate the bureaucracy of the incompetent Crown lands department, clustered in the port, making it one of the most Irish cities in British North America. In 1851, approximately 65 per cent of the city was Irish-born, and Irish Catholics comprised the largest minority group. However, many more Irish moved on to "the Boston States," as had Irish Newfoundlanders and Nova Scotians. It is estimated that, in the 1840s, between 50 and 80 per cent of the migrants who landed in Saint John or nearby St Andrew's departed to the United States. In the case of 4,168 migrants who landed in 1833, only 2 per cent could be found in the 1851 census.[18]

The Irish migrants to Prince Edward Island provided another contrast to the Irish in the other Atlantic colonies. Between 1767 and 1850, about 10,000 Irish migrated to this tiny island colony noted for its landlord-based system of land tenure and its fertile soils. These Irish settlers, almost entirely pre-Famine, were a much more eclectic mix than their neighbours across the Northumberland Strait. One group of Irish was comprised of two-boaters from Newfoundland, who brought with them the heritage of Waterford and Wexford; a second group was drawn from the counties adjacent to the ports of Limerick, Dublin, and Cork. The most distinctively regional group of Irish Catholics, however, numbering about 4,000, hailed from County Monaghan in Ulster. By mid-century, Irish Catholics comprised about one quarter of Prince Edward Island's population, the greatest concentration being located in Queen's County, in the central portion of the island, which included the capital of Charlottetown. Although most of the Irish Catholics in Prince Edward Island were English-speaking, a small group of migrants from Connaught, who settled in Lot 7 of the Tignish area, Prince County, spoke Irish. Much like their Irish cousins in the Miramichi, the principal rivals for the emergent Irish Catholic community were fellow Catholic islanders of Scottish and Acadian ancestry.[19] The former dominated the episcopal see of Charlottetown until the eve of the Great War. Their other struggles came when they attempted to break down the landlord–tenant system and demanded freehold tenure when lands became escheated.[20] Their social and cultural struggles had few parallels in the region.

Irish migration and settlement in the central Canadian colonies, Upper and Lower Canada, now Ontario and Quebec respectively, provide further evidence of the eclectic tapestry of Irish communities in British North America. In both colonies the primary period of Irish migration was prior to the Famine, between 1815 and 1845, with the port city of Quebec serving as the primary entrepôt for hundreds of thousands of British and European migrants.[21] Quebec had trading links with most Irish and major British ports, including Liverpool and Greenock, and so the mix of Irish migrants came not from specific regions, as had been the case in the Maritimes, but from all thirty-two Irish counties. There was one major exception to this rule in 1823 and 1825, when through the only government-financed migration scheme Upper Canadian Peter Robinson brought close to 2,000 Irish, most of whom were Catholic, to Upper Canada. The famous Peter Robinson settlers hailed from the Blackwater district of North Cork and South Tipperary, a region noted for its rural violence. The British government had hoped the planned migration would relieve tensions in the area. The Robinson migrants settled free lands in Peterborough County and what became Lanark and Carleton Counties in the Ottawa Valley area.[22] The Colonial Office was unwilling to replicate this expensive venture, however, and subsequent migrants from Ireland generally found their own means to settle in central British North America. Nevertheless, given the prominence of Irish migration to the Canadas before 1845, it comes as no surprise that, when the Whelans arrived in Renfrew in 1847, plenty of their countrymen were already there.

From 1846 to 1848, during the early years of the Irish Famine, over 250,000 Irish migrated to the British North American colonies, particularly New Brunswick, Canada East (now Quebec), and Canada West (now Ontario). All available historical evidence points to the fact that British North America was one of the primary receivers of Irish immigration in the earliest years of the Famine. Irish ports such as Derry, Cork, Limerick, and Dublin had well-established trade links with Quebec City and Saint John, as did the British port of Liverpool. In 1846 and 1847, fares to British North American ports were cheaper than those to the United States, and fewer restrictive head taxes were levied upon the poor and infirm entering British colonial seaports. In 1846, just over 43,000 Irish migrants ventured from United Kingdom ports to Britain's North American colonies; the number was over 200 per cent larger in 1847, when nearly 110,000 left Irish and British ports for Canada and the Maritime colonies.[23] Although this number would be slightly less than the total Irish migration to the United States that same year (119,000 persons), the total number of migrants to British North America in 1847 would prove to be the high-water mark of Irish migration to Canada to the present day[24] (table 1.1). The years 1848 to 1851 witnessed the arrival of little more than 30,000 Irish immigrants per year, and the year 1851 provided a brief anomaly, when the colonies received close to 43,000 Irish migrants.[25] Thereafter, with few exceptions until the creation of the Canadian confederation in 1867, Irish migration to British North America rarely surpassed 20,000 persons per year. Over the same period, levels of Irish migration to the United States were four to ten times higher than those for Irish migrants welcomed by their neighbours to the north (see table 1.2).

The arrival of Irish Famine migrants in British North America resulted in fairly consistent patterns of resettlement. Few Famine immigrants landed or settled in the colonies of Newfoundland, Prince Edward Island, or Nova Scotia. Halifax, British North America's largest port on the Atlantic, received only 2,000 Famine migrants in Black '47.[26] By contrast, in that same year Saint John, with its shipping connections to Cork and Derry,[27] proved to be the busiest entry point for Famine migrants. Nearly 17,000 arrived, most of whom stayed only a short time at its quarantine station at Partridge Island, as most refugees preferred to push on to the United States.[28] The United Province of Canada (Quebec and Ontario) was the largest receptor of Irish refugees, taking over 89,000 in 1847 alone. The new Irish arrivals would become aware that they were basically a continuation of an Irish migration chain that had been forged in the British North American colonies since the early nineteenth century.[29] Although a reasonable argument can be made that the Famine migration did not disrupt established Irish settlement patterns in Canada, it should be pointed out that cities such as Toronto and Hamilton experienced an upward spike in their Irish and Catholic populations over the course of the Famine. In Toronto, in 1847 alone, 38,000 migrants, most of whom were Irish, landed at Rees's Wharf to be received by a city population of less than 20,000. Although only 2,000 migrants would actually remain in the city, the city's Irish and Catholic population increased dramatically, from under 20 per cent to over 25 per cent by 1851.[30] Outside of the major cities, it appears that the recognizable impact of the Famine was negligible in the previously settled rural and agricultural hinterlands of Ontario.[31]

While tens of thousands of Irish elected to stay in what would eventually become the Dominion of Canada, thousands more continued

Table 1.1
Migration from the United Kingdom to British North America, 1843–48

Colony	*1843*	*1844*	*1845*	*1846*	*1847*	*1848*	*Total (%)*	
Prince Edward Island	529	257	242	286	536	59	1,909	(0.7)
Nova Scotia	1,203	747	615	698	2,000	702	5,965	(2.3)
New Brunswick	987	2,489	6,412	9,690	16,589	4,346	40,513	(15.4)
United Province of Canada	20,350	18,747	23,884	32,242	89,738	25,582	210,543	(80.2)
Newfoundland	448	684	618	523	993	343	3,609	(1.4)
Total	23,517	22,924	31,771	43,439	109,856	31,032	262,539	

Source: LAC, Colonial Office Papers, *Reports of the Colonial Land and Emigration Commissioners, 1845–1850*, CO 384/78-83.

Table 1.2
Irish migration to North America from all United Kingdom ports, 1846–56

Year	*To British North America, no. (%)*		*To the United States, no. (%)*		*Total*
1846	40,667	(37.2)	68,730	(62.8)	109,397
1847	104,518	(46.7)	119,314	(53.3)	223,832
1848	24,809	(13.6)	157,473	(86.4)	182,282
1849	33,392	(15.6)	181,011	(84.4)	214,403
1850	26,444	(12.6)	183,672	(87.4)	210,116
1851	31,709	(12.6)	219,453	(87.4)	251,162
1852	23,389	(10.7)	194,874	(89.3)	218,263
1853	22,391	(12.5)	156,970	(87.5)	179,361
1854	22,900	(17.1)	111,095	(82.9)	134,004
1855	6,106	(9.7)	57,164	(90.3)	63,270
1856	4,354	(6.9)	58,777	(93.1)	63,131

Source: Modified from Donald H. Akenson, *The Irish in Ontario: A Study in Rural History* (Montreal and Kingston: McGill-Queen's University Press, 1984), 32.

to travel in order to be reunited with friends and relatives in the cities of the United States or to procure cheap lands on the American frontier. The tightening of Canadian immigration laws in 1848 persuaded hundreds of thousands of Irish to migrate to the United States, where they built strong urban enclaves in eastern cities such as Boston, New York, and Philadelphia, or moved to cities further to west, such as Chicago, Buffalo, and Detroit.[32] After the spike in arrivals of Famine refugees to Canada in "Black '47", Irish migration from 1848 to 1856 slowed, and the preferred destination became "America," a republic where the Irish might be free of the sovereignty of the British, whom many of the refugees blamed for their plight (see table 1.2). From a time in the mid-1840s when Canada and the United States were comparable in the large numbers of Irish immigrants they received, the Canadian intake plummeted, by the mid-1850s, to almost one tenth of the numbers of Irish received by the United States. When one recognizes the enormity of this shift, both in percentages and in real numbers, it is not hard to grasp how "America" became the Irish place of refuge in the public consciousness, and how recognition of Canada's role in the Famine migration became eclipsed, if not forgotten, in the Irish mind. The massive Irish urban enclaves of the United States provided fertile ground for the dissemination of Irish nationalist writing and, not surprisingly, a cradle for the growth of Irish republican movements in "exile." By the weight of their numbers and their collective Famine experience, Irish Americans maintained strong ties with the "motherland."

In Canada, Irish Famine refugees were incorporated into an Irish population that had come by the hundreds of thousands before the Famine, and in many ways had acculturated to British colonial life on the North American frontier. Although there may have been some pockets of support for Irish republican causes in the British North American colonies, many Irish Canadians would generally embrace their citizenship in the British Empires.[33] While some Irish Canadians remembered the role of their adopted land during the Famine, the memory of Canada in Ireland itself was obscured by the numbers favouring America.

While Irish Catholics across British North America settled into a new life in the colonies and became absorbed in clearing land, raising families, starting businesses, and voicing their political opinions, they never entirely forgot their Irish roots. Much of the late nineteenth century witnessed Irish Catholics negotiating a new identity as British subjects and, for want of a better term, Canadian citizens, while making sure that the ongoing problems in Ireland were not forgotten. Buckets of ink have been spilled on the question of Irish Catholic loyalty in Canada and the place of Irish nationalism within various Irish-Canadian communities.[34] Without retracing all of these studies, what needs to be stated about the prelude to the Great War is that Irish Catholics were in a state of evolution with respect to their focus of identity and that the emphasis of their loyalties often varied from place to place. Canada's Irish Catholics were by no means united on such highly politicized issues as the question of Irish Home Rule. From the mid-nineteenth century onward, Irish Catholics found themselves split between constitutional nationalist and radical nationalist camps regarding the maintenance of the Acts of Union between Ireland and Great Britain.[35] In the press, on school boards, and in churches there was a strong sense that Ireland should have, at the very least, the constitutional status that had been accorded to Canada – in essence, self-government within the Empire. "If Canada is loyal today," argued the Liberal Party–leaning *Catholic Record*, "it is because she has enjoyed self-government, and if Ireland enjoyed the same, it would earnestly uphold the honour of the British Empire and the flag."[36] Sir Frank Smith, a Conservative Senator and Irish-born Catholic, agreed: "We love the old country ... we love our own too; and we also see the beneficial results Home Rule would apply to the whole Empire."[37]

Some Irish Catholic radicals thought this was clearly not enough and that monetary and military support ought to be given to movements espousing complete independence. As early as the 1860s, as the Irish Republican Brotherhood (Fenian Brotherhood) planned an invasion of Canada from the United States using demobilized Irish veterans of the American Civil War, Canadians watched in horror, fearing that their Irish Catholic neighbours might be closet Fenians ready to murder them in their beds. Indeed, small cells of Fenians in the towns of Canada West, in Montreal, and in Saint John, New Brunswick, along with the Hibernian Benevolent Society in Toronto, may have served as a screen for some Fenian sympathizers. Patrick Boyle's *Irish Canadian*, published in Toronto, served as an unofficial organ for the Hibernians,[38] and Boyle himself was incarcerated during the aftermath of the Fenian victory over the militia at Ridgeway, near Fort Erie and the Niagara River.[39] Nevertheless, the Catholic Church, through the words of Toronto's bishop, John Joseph Lynch,[40] and Irish Canadian politicians such as Thomas D'Arcy McGee, denounced the Fenians and violence, thus representing a majority of Irish Catholics in British North America who preferred constitutional remedies to end Ireland's union with Great Britain. In fact, Catholics were notable among the ranks of militia units raised to fight the Fenian menace should it ever come.[41] After Ridgeway, Fenian raids on Quebec, New Brunswick, and potentially the Red River Colony (now Manitoba) amounted to little more than comedies of error. Tragically, his denunciation of the Fenians would cost McGee his life. In 1868, this fervently Catholic member of Sir John A. Macdonald's governing Liberal-Conservatives would be felled by an assassin with Fenian connections.[42]

McGee's "new nationality" embodied an alternative approach for Catholics who wished for a Canada that was autonomous yet still within the imperial family. In his famous "Shield of Achilles" speech, McGee appeared to presage contemporary Canadian multiculturalism, as he called for a unity of the diverse peoples of the country under the Crown. "I look to the future of my adopted country with hope ... I see it quartered into many communities – each disposing of its internal affairs – but all bound together by free intercourse, and free commerce ... I see a generation of industrious, contented, moral men, free in name and in fact, – men capable of maintaining in peace and in war, a Constitution worthy of such a country."[43] He had departed the United States in 1857, regarding the country as anti-Catholic and seeking the greater freedom accorded his faith in Canada.[44] His legacy of constitutional nationalism was embraced by other Irish Canadians who regarded themselves as Canadian but also as members of the Empire and, as citizens of both, concerned about the Irish relationship to the Crown. Irish Catholics demonstrated support for the Irish National Land League when its emissaries came on fundraising and speaking tours of Canada and the United States. When Gladstone introduced Home Rule bills for Ireland in 1886 and 1893, Irish Catholics in Canada and other parts of the Empire supported his position and assisted the federal Parliament in Ottawa in passing a resolution endorsing Irish Home Rule.[45] For constitutional nationalists in Canada, it was a simple notion to award Ireland the type of legislative autonomy already evident in Canada. In the 1890s, Irish Catholics in Canada also sent delegates to the Irish Race Convention and demonstrated ongoing support for the Irish Parliamentary Party and its Home Rule agenda as espoused by leaders Charles Stewart Parnell, John Dillon, and John Redmond.[46]

Canada's Irish Catholics' support of Redmond and his Irish Party became even stronger with the introduction of the third Home Rule bill in 1912. Once again, the Canadian arguments were a hybrid of a home-grown sense of the suitability of the Canadian model of governance and a deep conviction that Ireland deserved similar Dominion status. Redmond himself had a vigorous correspondence with key Irish Catholic leaders in Canada, Wilfrid Laurier, and other Canadian politicians. Once again, Redmond leaned on Canadian expertise as he strived to put a Home Rule system in place that might imitate what the Canadian Irish had already attained since 1867.[47] When the Liberal government of Herbert Asquith passed the bill, with the support of Redmond's Irish Parliamentary Party, Canada's Irish Catholics were jubilant, citing the new Government of Ireland Act as a just solution to the generations-old Irish question.[48] According to the *New Freeman* in Saint John, "Premier Asquith has kept faith with the Irish people ... The present bill empowers the Irish people to legislate for themselves on many things of local importance, while it fully safeguards the religious rights of the minority."[49] On this latter point, there was a proviso that the bill would not become law for two years. This was intended to allow for a cooling-down and an accommodation of the Ulster Unionists and their Conservative supporters at Westminster, who considered Home Rule as little more than Rome rule. In 1913, groups of Ulster Protestants formed the Ulster Volunteer Force, armed themselves to the teeth, and threatened armed insurrection against the Crown to preserve their union with the Crown. In response, Home Rule supporters formed the Irish Volunteers, supported by Redmond, but whose ranks were infiltrated by members of the Irish Republican Brotherhood, who wished to use the crisis as a means of instigating more radical action to attain Irish independence. On the eve of the Great War, Ireland was a powder keg waiting to explode.[50]

Irish Catholics in Canada were well aware of the crisis through their newspapers and in the public press, where secular journalists weighed in on the pros and cons of the Government of Ireland Act. The *Casket* in Antigonish feared outright civil war in Ireland, and condemned Sir Edward Carson's Unionists and their attempt to thwart democratic rights in Ireland.[51] Carson had led the movement of 400,000 Ulstermen and 250,000 Ulsterwomen to sign the Solemn League of the Covenant, denouncing Home Rule and promising to defend Ulster at all costs.[52] The crisis threatened the peace of the Empire, the security of a fellow-Catholic population,[53] and the sustainability of Home Rule for the Irish people – and thus was of triple concern to observers in Irish Catholic communities in Canada. Catholics across the country stepped up their public support for Redmond and Home Rule, including rallies by the Ancient Order of Hibernians, an enthusiastic welcome for Redmond when he visited Canada in March 1914,[54] and a continuous barrage of criticism of the Unionist side from the English-speaking Catholic press.[55] The coming of the war in August 1914 and attendant promise from Asquith that the Government of Ireland Act would be delayed in its implementation until the successful completion of the struggle with Germany, prompted the cooling of tensions and the flow of Ulster Volunteer Force members and a majority of the Irish Volunteers into the British Expeditionary Force. The objective now clearly evident to Irish Catholics on both sides of the Atlantic was to win the war, and thus guarantee Home Rule.[56]

Such demonstrations of support for Irish Home Rule by constitutional means represented neither a preoccupation with all things

Irish, nor a retreat of Irish Catholics from their loyalty to the British Empire. As second- and third-generation Canadians, Irish Catholics were developing deep roots in Canada and cultivating an identity that recognized the importance of an independent Canada, under the Crown, in formal partnership with other territories in the British Empire. The Catholic school curriculum began to reflect a greater sense of Canadian identity, Catholic newspapers refocused their attention on Canadian issues, and Catholic politicians came to be integrated into all major Canadian political parties, both federally and provincially. While Catholics might disagree with the political activities and skulduggery evident at Westminster, they in no way regarded this as tainting the Crown or as a reason to lessen their loyalty to the Queen. Although born in Ireland, Patrick F. Cronin, editor of the *Catholic Register* in Toronto, alerted readers to this new sense of Catholic identity in 1901:

> Canada is a colony now growing to be a fine young lady ... she is no longer an infant and the time has passed when every inhabitant of this land must refer to some old country centre as his birthplace. The majority of the people of this grand country were born right here; in very many cases their parents are natives of this land too. ... The majority of people are proud to acknowledge Canada as their native land, and while they always shall have a warm spot in their hearts towards the home of their forefathers, nevertheless there can never be the same feeling in that way there was some fifty years ago. Canada is rapidly becoming a land of Canadians; of Canadians who know no other love than that towards their glorious country.[57]

With Queen Victoria's death in 1901, even the hardened veteran of the Fenian events, Patrick Boyle, offered no editorial comment other than to cite Father Francis Ryan's eulogy at St Michael's Cathedral, Toronto, in which he referred to the late monarch as "a good mother, a model mother."[58] Thus, for many Irish Catholic Canadian leaders, a loyalty to Canada was paramount and a loyalty to the Crown of the country became integral to this sense of citizenship. With the assent given to the Government of Ireland Act months before the outbreak of war, Toronto's *Catholic Register* under editor Father Alfred E. Burke, himself a Prince Edward Islander and a member of the Conservative Party, offered its view that imperialism was not to be equated with Orangeism, but was a movement that "appealed to Canadians of all political and religious beliefs."[59]

English-language Catholic weekly newspapers became a primary means of Irish Catholic expression and political opinion and may have been one of the few links that attempted to bind diverse Irish Catholic communities together. Regional papers frequently shared stories, copied one another's news items, and went head to head with one another on the pressing issues of Church and state. Although newspapers are highly problematic sources, given their circulation and presumed readership, they provide at least a modest articulation of male Irish Catholic opinion, both clerical and lay, and suggest the manner in which readers might approach certain political and social issues of the day. On the eve of the Great War there were six weekly Catholic newspapers in Canada, either edited or owned by Irish-born Catholics or those of Irish descent: the *Casket* (Antigonish, Nova Scotia); the *Freeman/New Freeman* (Saint John, New Brunswick); the *Canadian Freeman* (Kingston, Ontario); the *Catholic Register* (Toronto, Ontario); the *Catholic Record* (London, Ontario), and the *Northwest Review* (Winnipeg, Manitoba). The *B.C. Catholic* had been publishing intermittently, but did not appear during the war years. Each paper was different with respect to the level of clerical interference over editorial policy, its neutrality in politics or partisanship, and its preference in covering local stories and events over issues and events germane to Canada as a whole and the rest of the world. These papers tended to share stories among themselves (since only the *Register* and *Record* were in direct completion), and none claimed to be "Irish" per say, even though the writers and many of their readers could claim Irish birth or heritage. The circulation varied from paper to paper, but it should be noted that such papers were not likely substitutes for the daily secular papers available wherever Irish Catholics lived. Unfortunately, there is no available documentary evidence to suggest which particular secular dailies were favoured among Irish Catholics from Halifax to Victoria.

Timothy Warren Anglin had made the *Freeman* one of the most respected Catholic weeklies in the Maritimes in the 19th century. After his departure to Ontario, the paper failed and was reconstituted under the same name in 1900. The name changed again to the *New*

Freeman just before the Great War under Father C.J. McLaughlin, its locally born editor. Although much of its news was focused on New Brunswick and, in particular, the Saint John area, its pages included news and commentary from the other Maritime provinces, Ireland, the British Empire, and Canada, along with religious items of interest to its Catholic readers.[60] In 1915, McLaughlin was clear to readers about the mission of his paper: "We have always felt that a journal such as the *New Freeman* was needed in these Maritime Provinces to express the thought and feeling of a large and representative portion of our maritime population."[61] In the years leading up to the war and throughout the conflict, the *New Freeman* remained moderate in its opinions regarding Irish affairs, a champion of the British imperial war effort, and a dedicated reporter of local Catholic news.

The *New Freeman*'s Maritime counterpart, the *Casket*, was slightly different in its approach. Although its editor and manager during the war period, Michael Donovan, was under the watchful eye of the bishop of Antigonish, his paper both served the interests of the Church and provided news to broad local readership – Scots, Acadian, and Irish from the Antigonish area, the eastern counties of Nova Scotia, Cape Breton Island, and beyond. It consistently branded itself as a "Catholic Journal Non-Partisan in Politics."[62] Donovan expressed his opinions editorially on a variety of issues, both religious and secular, but kept within the bounds of episcopal approval whenever possible and rejected support to either the local Liberal or Conservative parties. In terms of the main imperial issues of the early twentieth century, the Boer War and the Great War, the paper variously supported and challenged issues specific to each conflict, but never from a partisan perspective.

The same could not be said of the three weeklies that competed for Irish Catholic readers in Ontario. The *Canadian Freeman* was never far from controversy. Circulated in eastern Ontario, western Quebec, Montreal, and parts of the upper Ottawa Valley, its news was primarily focused on Kingston and area and consistently gave Irish news a high priority, particularly in the early twentieth century during the lead-up to the third Home Rule bill. The paper claimed to be run by "representative men" with the approval of Archbishop Michael Joseph Spratt, who publicly endorsed the paper in early 1914 as one that was "practically under Episcopal supervision, and [in which] the personal opinions of subscribers, in matters political, will be respected."[63]

Again, like the Maritime weeklies, the *Canadian Freeman* promised to be both Catholic and non-partisan. It would also be in constant financial trouble – so much so that the priests of the Archdiocese of Kingston assumed ownership and directorship of the paper in 1915. Within a few months they appointed the "Irish born and Canadian bred" Father D.A. Casey to edit the paper. Casey had previously served on the editorial staff of the *Catholic Record*.[64] Under Casey, greater attention was paid to international news, particularly stories about Ireland and the Empire, and the paper would evolve into one of the country's most pronounced advocates for radical change in the governance of Ireland.

In Casey's old employer, the *Catholic Record*, Irish Catholics were treated to a paper that was Catholic in character, national and international in its coverage, and Liberal in its political sympathies. Its publisher and co-editor was lawyer and Liberal party stalwart, Thomas Coffey. As early as the 1890s the paper had announced its support of the Ontario Liberal Party, under Oliver Mowat, and of Wilfrid Laurier's federal Liberals; its columns put a positive spin on the policies of the Liberal government in Ottawa between 1896 and 1911, and then during the years of the Liberal's Official Opposition status in the next decade. Laurier's gratitude was palpable; in 1903 he appointed Coffey to the Senate.[65] James T. Foley, H.F. MacIntosh, and the aforementioned Father D.A. Casey shared editorial duties with Coffey.[66] The *Record* had the largest circulation of all the Irish Catholic weeklies with a circulation, in 1909, of about 18,883.[67] This number had jumped to over 31,000 ten years later.[68] Although about 90 per cent of its subscribers lived in Ontario, readers could be found across Canada, which accounted for its lack of emphasis on local news and its moderate positions on both political and Irish-related issues.[69] By 1915, its editor J.T. Foley boasted that there were as many subscribers in St John's, Newfoundland, as there were London, Ontario, and that there were over 1,500 subscribers in the United States. The latter readers may have been Canadian Catholics from western Ontario who sought employment in Michigan, Ohio, and the American Midwest before the war.[70] Even with five other rivals across the country, one might claim that the *Record* was the closest to being Canada's national English-speaking Catholic weekly.

Staff at Toronto's *Catholic Register and Canadian Extension* would disagree. Founded in 1892, with Archbishop John Walsh forcing a marriage of the *Irish Canadian* and the *Catholic Weekly Review*, the *Catholic Register* served anglophone Catholics in Toronto, Hamilton, Niagara, and the rest of central Ontario. Its subscription rates were modest, hovering around 5,000 in the 1890s and dropping as low as 3,000 by 1905.[71] The *Register*'s editor during much of this period, Patrick F. Cronin, offered readers a mixed fare of local and national news and perspectives on the challenges facing the Catholic Church internationally. The prominent Irish nationalism of its parent publication, the *Irish Canadian*, did not feature prominently in the *Register*, nor did the paper include the high culture of the *Catholic Weekly Review*. Cronin did manage to retain the conservative and Catholic sympathies of the *Review*, while not hesitating to speak out politically, but in a non-partisan way, in tones as sharp as those of the *Irish Canadian*'s former editor Patrick Boyle.[72] Boyle's effort to resuscitate the *Irish Canadian*, in 1900, however, ended in failure, which perhaps suggests that there was little interest in the area for an Irish nationalist organ. In 1908, the *Register* was purchased by the Catholic Church Extension Society and placed in the editorial hands of Alfred Burke, the president of the society, from 1908 until 1915. Because of the national character of the Extension Society and its intention to solicit funds for the Catholic home missions, Burke transformed the new *Catholic Register and Canadian Extension* into a national newspaper and doubled its circulation to nearly 6,000 in 1909 and more than doubled it again to 13,000 by 1919. Burke's Conservative partisanship, imperialist credentials, and bombastic style made the *Register* a natural rival for the *Record* that presented an alternative Catholic viewpoint on a variety of issues.

Further indication of the diversity of Catholic newspapers is found in the *Northwest Review* in Winnipeg, which served Catholics on the Prairies and eventually the Pacific slope. Founded in 1885, with Irish-born J.J. Chaddock as its first editor, the *Review* promised to be "conspicuously independent of politics … except when Catholic interests are at stake and in the cause of good government."[73] Like the Catholic tribunes of the east, Chaddock and his successors at the *Review* offered local Catholic news from across western Canada, Catholic literature, and international Catholic news, in the hope that the paper's "weekly appearance will be anxiously looked for."[74] It served as a source of information for Catholic immigrants newly arrived in Winnipeg and quickly became an ardent supporter of Home Rule for Ireland, on the grounds that Ireland should enjoy "the same legislative privileges as Canada."[75] During the Great War the editor was Irish-born Patrick Henry, who continued the paper's interest in Home Rule, Canadian labour issues, and news from the Church, locally, nationally, and internationally.[76] In time Henry would steer the paper in more radical directions regarding the independence of Ireland and the assertion of Canadian priorities and "ideals" over those of the British Empire.[77] Also akin to its eastern collaborators in the Catholic press, the *Northwest Review* was an ever-vigilant mouthpiece denouncing anti-Catholic behaviour whenever it might arise.[78] At times, aside from the words and actions of local clergy, the Catholic newspapers were the most vigilant and effective voices defending the Catholic community from the criticism and perceived aggression of non-Catholic neighbours.

Relations between Irish Catholics and their Protestant neighbours were variable according to time of settlement, specific political and social issues, class alignment, and region. There is no easy way to classify or categorize these denominational relationships, given the fact that each Irish Catholic community experienced their neighbours differently across the regions, rural areas, and cities of Canada. In the colonial period, Catholics in Upper and Lower Canada had voting rights and the liberty to sit in elected assemblies because of the collective rights for Catholics included in the Quebec Act of 1774. Catholics in the Atlantic colonies remained subject to the Test Acts, which discriminated against Catholics in public life, until the Catholic Relief Act (known popularly as Catholic Emancipation) was passed in 1829.[79] Nevertheless, the absorption of Cape Breton Island into the colony of Nova Scotia in 1820 resulted in an Irish Catholic sitting in the Legislative Assembly of the newly amalgamated province, which prompted a local deviation from the strictest interpretation of Catholics being forced to take the oath against belief in the doctrine of Transubstantiation.[80] By 1830, Catholics were of equal standing before the law in all the British North American colonies, so that, as far as the state was concerned, all male citizens, regardless of denominational affiliation, were accorded full civil and legal rights under the Crown.

While day-to-day relations between Irish Catholics and their Protestant neighbours might vary in cordiality from place to place and time to time, in the mid-nineteenth century episodes of sectarian violence erupted with greater frequency in each colony: the Gourlay Shanty riots near Halifax, the Orange and Green riots in Saint John, and the St Patrick's Day riots in Toronto in 1858.[81] These outbreaks of violence were sparked by local issues and sometimes vented a general feeling in the Protestant community that Irish Catholics and their co-religionists were part of a greater "papal aggression" that was hell bent on propagating the paganisms of Rome while obliterating Protestant religious freedom and the principle of an open Bible that could be read and interpreted by believers without the interference or censorship of priests and popes. In Upper Canada, later Ontario, sectarian peace was often disrupted by ritualized violence only on St Patrick's Day, the 12th of July (the anniversary of William of Orange's victory over James II at the Boyne River), or Guy Fawkes Day. In 1875, a parade celebrating the Jubilee of Pope Pius IX was attacked by Protestant mobs as the celebration wound its way through Toronto's inner city. But even the Jubilee Riots have to be placed within their context and not serve as a lens through which all Protestant–Catholic relations might be characterized across Canada in the half-century following Confederation.[82]

Sectarian hostility was often witnessed when the issue of publicly funded separate Catholic schools was raised. With the precedent of collective rights for Roman Catholics introduced by the Quebec Act in 1774, and with Catholic Emancipation across the Empire in 1829, British North American Catholics sought state support for distinctive Catholic schools. As early as the 1830s in Upper Canada, Bishop Alexander Macdonell of Kingston had successfully petitioned Lord Bathurst to issue annual stipends to his school teachers, who also happened to be priests. In 1841, under the Day Act in the United Province of Canada, minority ratepayers in either section of the province (Canada East and Canada West) could establish a separate Protestant or Catholic elementary school and request government funds to support it. These separate schools for each religious minority – Catholics in Ontario and Protestants in Quebec – were established in law, confirmed by the Taché Act of 1855 and the Scott Act of 1863, and then constitutionally protected in Section 93 of the British North America Act in 1867.[83] In New Brunswick and Nova Scotia, Catholic schools were established by gentleman's agreement, not in law, and were therefore not secured by Section 93. In 1871, a Protestant-dominated legislative assembly in New Brunswick abolished Catholic schools, setting off a wave of sectarian bitterness in the province, along with fears elsewhere that Catholic schools might be under siege. In 1870, under the terms of the Manitoba Act, publicly funded schools were guaranteed to the Catholic and Protestant minorities in the new province. Twenty years later, the tiny Catholic minority, mostly francophone, Métis, and Irish, were deprived of their Catholic schools under the Manitoba Schools Act. This action precipitated a six-year battle that culminated in the Laurier–Greenway compromise of 1897, which permitted Catholic instruction in Manitoba's public schools only after school hours.[84]

The ongoing battle between Catholics and Protestants over separate schools in Ontario, Manitoba, New Brunswick, and, after the 1880s, those portions of the Northwest Territories that would become Alberta and Saskatchewan, placed Irish Catholics on the front lines of sectarian politics. In Ontario, Irish Catholic laymen, clergy, and bishops lobbied successive provincial governments for equitable school funding, access to business and corporate taxation, and the extension of separate school funding to secondary schools. When issues pertaining to any extension of rights or privileges to Catholic schools were debated in the public square, a predictable and vociferous opposition rose up from the Loyal Orange Lodges, the Protestant Protective Association, the Equal Rights Association, and a host of Protestant clergy and politicians. Their battle anthem was "equal rights for all, special privileges for none," and their aim was the abolition of all separate schools across the province.[85] Irish Catholic papers and leaders were constantly on the defensive, trying to protect their underfunded school system. On the eve of the Great War, the Catholic bishops of Ontario were in negotiation with the Conservative government of James Pliny Whitney to ameliorate the financial situation of Catholic schools, and had made significant progress in their negotiations with what had been their political arch-nemesis (the Conservative Party) on the school issue. While the bishops would not sacrifice the Catholicity of the schools, the proposed textbooks reflected the Canadian patriotism and imperial sentiment that had been the hallmark of the *Canadian Catholic Readers* series compiled in 1899 by Father John Teefy, CSB, of St Michael's College in Toronto. In Ontario, the Catholic school curriculum was developing a distinctive ethos that combined the essentials of the faith with the inculcation of British Canadian values and citizenship.[86]

In 1900, the Holy See requested a unique survey of all the Canadian dioceses to ascertain the state of Protestant–Roman Catholic relations, and in particular, whether Protestants were engaged in any proselytization. Diomede Falconio had barely been in his position as apostolic delegate to Canada for a year when he was charged with administering both this survey and one on the state of Catholic education in Canada.[87] Over the next few months almost every bishop from across Canada reported on relations between his flock and neighbouring Protestants. The contents of their reports demonstrate once again that it is difficult to make blanket statements about Catholics as a national community when lived Catholicism had so many local and regional variations. Although the Quebec bishops, buoyed by their majority Catholic numbers in French Canada, reported no difficulties,[88] English-speaking bishops elsewhere were by no means unanimous in their assessment of Catholic–Protestant relations in the decade leading up to the Great War. The ten questions posed to the bishops in the survey included direct questions on the nature and degree of Protestant proselytization, the religious "disposition" of the Catholics in their dioceses, and an assessment of Catholic life in a non-Catholic environment. The Vatican wanted to assess how Protestant influence might be witnessed in such practices as mixed religious marriage. What is most interesting is that, in response to questions about Protestant proselytization and anti-Catholic activities by the state, the bishops were almost unanimous in their assessment that neither the Protestant churches nor the Canadian state appeared to present any direct danger to the Catholic faith. Although there was some anxiety about Protestant influences in public schools, particularly west of the Ottawa River, the episcopal reports generally confirmed that Catholics, including the Irish, were not hampered in practising their faith freely in Canada. By 1900, the characterization of certain Canadian centres as being the "Belfast" or "Derry" of North America was greatly exaggerated.[89]

What is most striking about the reports on Catholic–Protestant relations is the regional character of denominational engagement in Canada. In the Maritime provinces, where Catholics, particularly of Irish origin, made up a substantial minority of the general population and certainly dominated the Catholic Church in Saint John, Halifax and sections of Prince Edward Island, Archbishop Cornelius O'Brien of Halifax and his suffragans across the region reported neither any organized Protestant proselytism nor any overt hostility emanating from the Protestant majority.[90] Much the same could be said of the reports made by the Catholic bishops of eastern Ontario, as typified by the comments of Bishop Alexander Macdonell (namesake and kinsman of the first bishop of Upper Canada), who reported, "A spirit of toleration prevails between Catholics and their Protestant neighbors [sic]; they dwell together peaceably as citizens."[91] Back in Admaston, Stephen Whelan could not have maintained his thirty-five year tenure as reeve without an entente between Catholic and Protestant voters.

The rather irenic mood struck by bishops in Eastern Ontario and the Maritimes stood in sharp contrast to the views of their episcopal colleagues in Western Ontario and the Prairies. Archbishop Denis O'Connor of Toronto, Fergus Patrick McEvay of London, and Thomas Dowling, the Irish-born bishop of Hamilton, expressed concerns about Methodist Sunday schools, the dissemination of Protestant tracts, rural associations where Protestants and Catholics mingled, mixed marriages, and occasional anti-Catholic public lectures that stigmatized the Catholic population of their dioceses.[92] At the best of times, Denis O'Connor would have preferred greater isolation of his flock from Protestants, whom he saw as a veritable threat to the Faith in even the simplest facets of everyday life:

> Few perversions occur as the result of direct proselytism ... [A] greater number is due to mixed marriages, public schools, newspapers and protestant [sic] company. Those causes produce tepid Catholics, who without living as Catholic, like to die as such. The number who die perverts is, thank God, relatively small ... Protestant company is sought after by some Catholics because it commonly constitutes what is called good society. Other Catholics in country districts have few or no neighbours that are not protestants [sic]. Forced to associate with them, they accept little by little their notions, go to their churches and neglect their own which are frequently far distant, intermarry with them and their children are generally protestant. We have lost much in this way in country places and there are many, very many protestants [sic] with names of undoubted Catholic origin.[93]

However exaggerated O'Connor's claims may have been, perhaps to alarm Vatican officials, his words reveal a growing and living rapprochement among the laity of Ontario's Christian denominations.

Perhaps this was the daily peace that might be interrupted only by incendiary issues of language, the extension of separate school rights, or suggestions of Irish independence from Britain.

According to the Prairie bishops, however, the Church in Canada's west was in the midst of a denominational war. Much of this battle for souls was focused on recent Catholic immigrants from eastern and central Europe, and not on Irish Catholics, who were not numerous west of Winnipeg or outside of major cities such as Saskatoon, Calgary, and Edmonton. French Canadian, First Nation, German, Polish, and Ukrainian Catholics were the principal Catholic communities in the Prairie West, and all appeared vulnerable to the work of Presbyterian, Anglican, and Methodist missionaries, who used a variety of itinerant preaching methods, specialized "immigrant Churches," and schools to recruit new Canadian Catholics to Protestantism. Bishops cited frequent social interaction between Catholics and Protestants in the cities, a shortage of Catholic priests, and a dearth of Catholic schools as reasons for the potential apostasy of their flocks.[94] At St Boniface, the archiepiscopal command centre for the Church on the Prairies, Archbishop Adélard Langevin told Falconio that for "10,000 francs" per year he "could do wonders for separate schools" and thereby preserve the faith of the immigrants flocking to his and other western dioceses.[95]

Within the coming decade, however, it was the Irish Catholic presence in the west that the primarily francophone Catholic episcopate came to fear more than the Protestant missionaries. In 1908, Archbishop Fergus Patrick McEvay of Toronto, Father Burke of Prince Edward Island, Father Alfred Sinnott (also of Prince Edward Island), the secretary to the apostolic delegate, and Sir Charles Fitzpatrick, chief justice of the Supreme Court, among others, established the previously mentioned Catholic Church Extension Society of Canada, which was to become the primary agency for supplying buildings, financial assistance, educational materials, and clerical personnel for the Catholic home missions, the majority of which were west of Ontario.[96] Despite some French Canadian representation on its board of governors, the francophone bishops of the Prairies soon became concerned that the Extension Society was essentially a vehicle not only for preserving the Catholic faith of immigrants, but also for making certain that they were formally aligned with the English-speaking wing of the Church.[97] Adélard Langevin did not mince words, referring to the Extension Society as essentially a ploy by "*les maudits Irlandais*" to assume control of the Church in the west.[98] Langevin claimed that *les Irlandais* were brandishing their own form of imperialism over the Church in western Canada, while spreading their "anti-French rage and Francophobia" from Ontario to the west.[99] The Extension Society had both publicly and privately indicated that if priests for the home missions could not speak the languages of the immigrants, English should be the medium of Church life.[100] When combined with the anglophone hierarchy's growing opposition to bilingual schools in Ontario, and the apparent struggle for control of the episcopal sees of the West, it appears as though the francophone-led Church west of Kenora was doomed to be assimilated not by the Protestants but by Irish Catholics from the east.

The struggle for control of the episcopal sees in the Canadian West not only became evidence of the linguistic warfare erupting in the Catholic Church on the eve of the Great War, but was equally indicative of Irish Catholic determination to contain French Canadian influence in the Church within the boundaries of the province of Quebec. In French Canadian eyes, their Irish Catholic brothers and sisters were being aided and abetted by the English hierarchy in Great Britain – and by the Vatican itself, through the agency of the apostolic delegate. In the years leading up to the war, Delegate Donato Sbaretti, who had succeeded Diomede Falconio, actively sought to appoint anglophone bishops to western sees, believing that the future of the Church in Canada lay in the medium of the English language. In 1910, Cardinal Bourne, the archbishop of Westminster, proclaimed to a Canadian audience that the future of the Church in Canada was to be secured through the English language, a comment rejected by the French clergy and not forgotten by outspoken journalists and politicians such as Henri Bourassa. In the first fifteen years of the twentieth century the anglophone dominance was becoming clearer in the West. In 1909, the Holy See appointed Cape Breton academic Alexander "Sandy" MacDonald to the See of Victoria, which had formerly been held by Belgian-born bishops and other francophones. One year later, Neil McNeil, a fellow native of Mabou and cousin to MacDonald, was transferred from the Diocese of St George's, Newfoundland, to the Archdiocese of Vancouver, a former stronghold of francophone members of the Oblates of Mary Immaculate. In 1912, James T. McNally, a Prince Edward Islander, was named the first bishop of Calgary and, three years later, a fellow Islander, Alfred A. Sinnott, who was well placed as secretary to the apostolic delegate in Ottawa, was appointed as the first archbishop of Winnipeg, just across the river from St Boniface. Langevin, who died six months before the erection of Sinnott's new diocese, would have seen this as confirming his suspicions that the Irish were on the move. The only French victory came when, in 1911, the Holy See appointed Olivier-Elzéar Mathieu as its first archbishop.[101]

Irish Catholic aggression, as it was interpreted by French Canadian Catholics, descended into some of its ugliest expressions during the schools controversy in Ontario. The separate Catholic schools in the province were shared by the Irish, French, and other Catholic groups, although many of these schools, in counties highly populated by francophones, had developed into bilingual institutions where French was the primary language of instruction. Thus, when these schools, which were growing in number, and two thirds of which were Catholic separate schools, were challenged by government inspectors in 1911 as inferior, francophone and anglophone Catholics drew battle lines over whether to retain these schools. Bishop Michael Francis Fallon of London, the son of Irish immigrants, was determined to rid his diocese, which had a large and vocal French Catholic minority, of these schools.[102] While Fallon argued that it was entirely a matter of making sure that Catholic children were educated to the same standard as their non-Catholic neighbours, his francophone detractors suspected that something deeper lay behind Fallon's motives. Earlier in the century, while serving as a professor at the bilingual University of Ottawa, Fallon had been the champion of the failed anglicization of that pontifical institution, and French Catholics never forgot how *les Irlandais* attempted to seize control of Catholic higher education in the province.[103]

The troubles within the Church would deepen. In 1910, while the largely Irish contingent of Catholic bishops negotiated with the Ontario government for increased financing for Catholic schools, concessions for special Catholic textbooks, and the inclusion of Catholic schools as recipients of a proportional share of corporate tax revenues, the French Catholics went on the counter-offensive.[104] At a well-attended congress on education in Ottawa, which attracted even the talents of Wilfrid Laurier, the prime minister, the French Catholic faction requested that their educational rights be confirmed and extended in Ontario. Protestant Ontario was aghast at this audacious request. When the Orange caucus in Ontario's government demanded an end to bilingual schools, Premier James Pliny Whitney broke off his negotiations with the Catholic bishops. Feeling that all of the province's anglophone Catholics had been unfairly treated, the angry contingent of English-speaking bishops distanced themselves from the educational claims of their co-religionists. When, in 1912, Whitney's government enacted Regulation 17, which would effectively prohibit French-language education in the province after the second grade, the Irish bishops supported the government's action on grounds that it would improve the quality of education and make Catholic students better prepared for the modern society in which they would eventually seek employment.

The bilingual schools issue, however, also appeared to signal that the Irish bishops would seek to consolidate their control of the Church west of Quebec.[105] This strategy would become evident as episcopal sees with a high percentage of francophone Catholics – Sault Ste-Marie, Ottawa, and London – would witness Rome's appointment of anglophone bishops.[106] In 1909, Michael Francis Fallon was appointed bishop of London, much to the horror of French Canadian Catholics. Both the apostolic delegate to Canada, Donato Sbarretti, and the Vatican's secretary of state, Rafael Merry Del Val, took personal interest in all the episcopal appointments, sharing the belief that English was the language of the future in North America, and that it would be through the vehicle of the English language, and its Irish faithful, that Catholicism would spread throughout the continent.[107]

In the decade leading up to the Great War, the Catholic Church in Canada was bitterly divided between its two largest charter groups: French Canadians and Irish Catholics. Immigration, education, and episcopal politics were all fields of battle within the Church, although there was an effort to keep such controversies under carefully guarded discretion, lest non-Catholics formulated the impression that the Church was at war with itself. What appeared evident to the francophone Catholic leadership was the drift of their Irish Catholic co-religionists toward opinions, political positions, and ethnocentrisms that shared more with Canada's Protestants than with Canada's French Catholics. As we have noted, the Irish Catholic community was not homogenous in its public identifications and loyalties. There were great variations in attachment to a sense of Irishness, Britishness, or

Canadian-ness from region to region and between rural and urban areas within those regions. As John Moir recounted in his landmark essay in 1971, English-speaking Catholics found themselves to be in a "double minority" situation in Canada.[108] On the one hand, they were a religious minority amid the anglophone Protestant majority in Canada, and on the other hand they were a linguistic minority in their own Church. In cities such as Montreal and Ottawa, the Irish Catholic community found themselves precisely in this double minority situation, sandwiched between large and powerful French Catholic and English-speaking Protestant groups. In New Brunswick this situation was writ large because of the linguistic and religious demography of the province. In such situations, Irishness could be worn as a badge of distinction from the other two majority groups. In Toronto, Halifax, or Kingston, the double minority pressures were less evident; in these cities, it is notable how the Irish Catholic community, while remaining steadfast to their faith, came to accept the political, cultural, and imperial norms embraced by the charter Protestant groups.

At the intersection between Catholic–Protestant tension and Irish–French troubles was the issue of mixed marriage: that is, interdenominational marriages between Catholics and Protestants. Although language provided a sufficient barrier to a profusion of such marriages, the Holy See's issuing of the *Ne Temere* decree in 1908 enflamed sectarian relations when Quebec decided to incorporate the decree's mandates into provincial civil law.[109] The decree sought to regularize marriages under the auspices of the Church, outlining that valid marriage between two Catholic parties was to be officiated by a priest and attended by two witnesses. Mixed marriages, unless approved formally by a dispensation from the local bishop and performed before a priest, were considered invalid. In Protestant Canada, this decree was interpreted as an easy way for Catholic men to leave their Protestant wives high and dry on the pretext that their marriage contracted under civil law was invalid in the eyes of the Church. The Hébert case, which lingered before the civil courts as late as 1911, suggested to Protestant Canadians that families might be torn asunder and that the children of interdenominational marriages would become illegitimate under the law.[110] In 1912, Protestant fears that *Ne Temere* threatened Canadian families and civil marriage, prompted the introduction of the Lancaster Bill in the House of Commons in Ottawa, which sought to standardize marriages across the country and prevent the dissolution of mixed marriages.[111] In June 1912, in a nearly unanimous decision, the Supreme Court of Canada (including Irish-Canadian Catholic judges Frank Anglin and Charles Fitzpatrick), struck down the Lancaster Act as *ultra vires* the federal Parliament, since the solemnization of marriage was constitutionally a provincial matter and the law of Quebec still provided for civil marriages, the key element being the mutual consent of the parties engaged, not the religious affiliation of the presider.[112] Nevertheless, the *Ne Temere* decree had rekindled old Protestant–Catholic bigotries, which became focused on the alleged power of the Pope over civil marriage in Canada.

That being said, in the decade leading up to the Great War the question of mixed marriage was equally perplexing to Irish Catholics in Canada, but for other reasons. Increasing numbers of mixed marriages appeared to fulfill the worst fears of several bishops, who reported to Falconio that too-frequent social interactions between Catholics and their Protestant neighbours would lead to mixed marriages. In 1911, the *Catholic Register* recognized the failure of the *Ne Temere* decree in so far as the "number [of interdenominational marriages] is much larger than we would wish to see it."[113] In the major cities and towns of central Canada and the west, rates of marriage between Catholics and Protestants was viewed as a rising problem. In the Archdiocese of Toronto, Archbishop Denis O'Connor had tried to stem the rise of mixed marriage by refusing dispensations. Although the number of officially solemnized mixed marriages dropped, the number of civil unions of Catholics and Protestants actually increased. By 1905, civic and ecclesiastical records reveal that the total number of mixed marriages in the city was nearly double that of ten years before, and over 90 per cent were of couples wed before a justice of the peace or a Protestant minister.[114] The prohibitions against mixed marriage were loosened by O'Connor's successor bishops, Fergus Patrick McEvay and Neil McNeil, after which the total number of solemnized mixed marriages in the city rose to over 24 per cent by 1916.[115] That same year, in the province of Ontario, mixed marriages accounted for nearly one in every four marriages involving Catholics.[116] In the Diocese of Peterborough, Bishop Michael O'Brien asked his clergy to be particularly vigilant. Father F.J. O'Sullivan of Port Hope reported back to his bishop that he had twenty-two such unions in his parish, and "it is not the more staunch Catholics that marry Protestants but the lukewarm ones who are not apt to be steadfast under unfavorable circumstances."[117] In Calgary and Regina, bishops Légal and Mathieu, respectively, issued circular letters warning against mixed marriages, which appeared to be very popular in their dioceses.[118] French Canadian polemicists such as Albert Foisy, editor of *Le Droit*, openly accused his Irish co-religionists of endangering the faith because of their "deplorable" rate of mixed marriages, which only served as further proof that Irish Catholics and Protestants were a "community of language, of sentiments, of patriotism and ideas."[119]

In retrospect, Foisy may have only had to reflect on the Boer War (1899–1902) to confirm his belief that Irish Catholics and the Anglo-Protestant population were moving closer together. The experience in South Africa provided evidence that Canada's Irish Catholic communities were developing an interest in the affairs of the Empire and a sense of duty to the Crown as citizens of that Empire. Carman Miller describes this conflict as the "most significant public event" in the perception of Canadians in the twentieth century until the Great War, and it is certainly interesting to consider how one of Canada's largest religious and cultural minority groups responded to events unfolding in the Cape Colony.[120] For Canada's Irish Catholics, the path to the imperialist camp was slow and circuitous, negotiated with caution, and marked by struggles over communal and individual self-identification. In this context, the easy and more comfortable "Paddy" images are of little help as a means to understand Irish Catholic behaviour during the South African conflict. In 1899, Canada's Catholics of Irish birth or descent did not approach this war as a united group, nor did they speak as one body through a single bishop, politician, or newspaper. The Irish Catholic response to the war varied according to one's position in the Church, political affiliation, and region of origin, and by the unfolding of events. Lay leaders and the press sent out a variety of conflicting messages to their constituents, while the bishops offered few hints as to where the Church stood officially on the issue of sending Canadian troops to South Africa. Amid this lack of clarity from on high, rank-and-file Irish Catholics – whether out of loyalty to the Empire, a sense of adventure, or the allure of a steady paycheque – signed up in the Queen's service to preserve the rights of British subjects in South Africa.

By the war's end in 1902, however, Irish Catholics across Canada appeared to identify themselves more clearly with the imperial cause of "One Flag, One Fleet, One Throne."[121] The ambiguity of 1899 had been replaced by a greater sense of what Canada's role in the Empire was to be, and how Catholics were to view their citizenship as Canadians and British subjects. Eventually, Canada's Irish Catholics would write the Boer War experience into their own story of Canadian Irish Catholic loyalty to the Empire and its principles of justice and "the right." By 1914, the imperial views of Fitzpatrick had become more commonly held by Catholics of Irish descent as they faced the challenges brought by the Great War.

At the turn of the twentieth century, there were over half a million non–French-speaking Catholics in Canada's provinces and territories, comprising just over 10 per cent of Canada's people.[122] Most Catholics who spoke English were of Irish descent, and although estimates are difficult given the nature of the reporting of religion and ethnicity in the Canadian census, these Irish may have numbered as many as 480,000.[123] Among the non-francophone Catholic group, the Irish were joined by clusters of Scottish Highlanders in Cape Breton, Prince Edward Island, and eastern Ontario. Other tiny minorities included Catholics of English descent, converts from Protestantism, German settlers, Italians, Poles, and several First Nations bands. Those of the Irish majority were bound together by an institutional Church that was growing increasingly Irish in leadership, providing spiritual, educational, health care, and social services across the country. Irish Catholics could be found in all twenty-seven Canadian dioceses and apostolic vicariates, although Catholics living in Ontario and the Maritime provinces would be the only ones administered by bishops of either Scottish or Irish descent.[124] Moreover, Irish Catholics living west of the Manitoba–Ontario boundary were a tiny minority. Of great interest to observers of religion in 1901, however, was the fact that Irish Catholics across Canada displayed strong rates of regular church attendance, ranging from 73 per cent in Charlotte County, New Brunswick, to 85 per cent in Halifax, to allegedly 99 per cent in Hamilton, Ontario.[125] This strength of affiliation confirms local churches as community centres, and local church leaders as significant in the lives of Canada's Irish Catholic communities.

The newspapers and literature generated in their centres of settlement also indicate that Canadians of Irish Catholic descent were in a transitional period when the Boer War erupted. Political rhetoric, speeches by community leaders, and editorials in Catholic periodicals suggest that many Irish Catholics in Canada were still concerned about politics in Ireland, particularly the century-old struggle for the restoration of an autonomous Irish provincial parliament. Interestingly, the support of Irish-Canadian Catholics for Irish Home Rule stimulated their own reflections on the nature and current state of Canadian institutions and, in the process, nurtured a profound attachment to the Dominion's semi-autonomous status within the British Empire. Canada's Irish Catholics came to believe that Ireland ought to enjoy Canadian-style responsible self-government.

Not surprisingly, such comparisons became evident as Irish Catholic leaders expressed their affection for Canada, their gratitude for the rights enjoyed by Catholics in Canada, an appreciation of a neutral Crown, and their commitment to Canada's responsibilities within the Empire.[126] In 1898, the *Catholic Record* called upon English-speaking Catholics to be active in the exercise of their patriotic duties:

> Every Catholic, we think should take practical interest in live questions – that is questions which concern them temporally, or spiritually ... We do not insinuate for one instant that our taking part in public questions should make us aggressive in a way that would be calculated to arouse the enmity of our separated brethren ... We should take our stand as Canadians interested in the welfare and progress of our country. It might get us out of the rut or the "don't care" habit, and might also convince us that we are not serfs but citizens.[127]

In a similar spirit, in 1896, *Walsh's Magazine* (Toronto) discussed the Empire's involvement in South Africa, singling out Cecil Rhodes as "the greatest among energetic figures."[128] Membership in the Empire was a topic of discussion and one that raised serious questions of Canada's responsibilities, military and otherwise.

One might expect, given the hierarchical structure of the Catholic Church, that the bishops of English Canada might have offered public comment, whether negative or positive, on Catholic participation in the war. Given their outspoken positions on political and religious issues such as denominational schools in the west and the Jesuits Estates question in the east, few bishops made public statements concerning British activities in South Africa, the recruitment of a Canadian contingent, or the cultural politics at play in Laurier's caucus and in the press. The silence of the hierarchy might be explained, in part, by the fact that between 1899 and 1902 the Catholic hierarchy was in a time of transition. Bishops in a position to wave the flag or condemn the British war effort were hamstrung by a number of considerations. Many were young, inexperienced, and overly cautious about entering the public square with their guns blazing. Suffragan bishops and auxiliary bishops rarely took the lead in public debates without testing the waters first with their archbishop. In the case of Ontario, Denis O'Connor, appointed archbishop of Toronto in 1899, rarely made public appearances and eschewed any relations with politicians, although he was considered by many to have Tory sympathies.[129] It is not surprising, then, that O'Connor's suffragan bishops in Hamilton and London, the latter of whom was the newly appointed Fergus Patrick McEvay, balked at any public comment on political matters not directly related to the Church. Ontario's other metropolitan archbishop, Charles Hugh Gauthier of Kingston, who was less than a year in his position when the war erupted, preferred private negotiations and deal-making to public interventions on matters that did not relate directly to the faith or to Catholic moral life.[130] For many in the episcopacy, if a political issue did not offend the faith and morals of the Church, silence was to be interpreted as consent.

Some bishops, however, possessed a high public profile and a personality suited to political engagement. This certainly appears to be the case in Halifax, where the metropolitan archbishop Cornelius O'Brien was a noted Tory and a member of the Imperial Federation League.[131] Even if O'Brien's suffragan bishops in Saint John, Bathurst, Antigonish, and Charlottetown had opposed the war effort privately, which in a few cases seemed unlikely given their political sympathies, they would not have been prepared to cross O'Brien, who took an active interest in all his dioceses.[132] Soon after the outbreak of hostilities in South Africa, O'Brien issued a pastoral letter clearly stating his support for the "noble and just" imperial war effort.[133] His suffragans were silent in their support for or opposition of O'Brien's statement. Bishops John Sweeny of Saint John and James Rogers of Bathurst were both elderly and inactive by 1899, and their auxiliaries, given the nature of their subordinate positions, would not make public interventions of a political nature unless doing so would be directly relevant to the life of the local Church. In another case, Bishop John

Cameron of Antigonish was reluctant to enter the political arena, given the fact that Rome had severely reprimanded him for his partisan involvement on behalf of the Liberal-Conservative Party in the election of 1896.[134]

Curiously, two French Canadian archbishops, Joseph-Thomas Duhamel of Ottawa and Louis-Nazaire Bégin of Quebec City, who was also Primate of Canada, publicly endorsed the war effort in late 1899.[135] Likewise, Archbishop Paul Bruchési of Montreal, in his New Year's Eve address, said he regretted that the year 1900 could not begin in peace but hoped for a speedy end to the war "with the triumph of our great country."[136] Clearly, these public statements came at a time when Canadians were already actively engaged on the veldt and in the wake of the "Black Week" when the British forces suffered several setbacks at the hands of the Boers. Despite the large numbers of Irish Catholics in each diocese, the francophone archbishops' action appeared to be motivated more out of concern for the French-Canadian Catholic majority. Opposition to the war within the Liberal caucus (which including public expressions of dissent by members Dominique Monet, Henri Bourassa, and Laurier stalwart, Joseph Israël Tarte), in addition to anti-war sentiment in the French Canadian daily press, put the Church in an awkward position.[137] Since 1775, French-Canadian bishops had been visibly loyal to the British Crown in time of war. The angry reaction of many Anglo-Canadians to Bourassa and his colleagues necessitated that the Church in Quebec take a clear stand on the war and assert its loyalty. By contrast, there appeared to be no urgency stemming from charges of disloyalty to prompt prelates of Irish or Scottish descent to do the same.

Not necessarily constrained by the canons and protocols of episcopal office, many Catholic laypersons and some priests of Irish descent were less constrained in their support or opposition to the war. Charles Fitzpatrick, a Catholic MP of Irish descent from Quebec City and Laurier's Solicitor General, was an outspoken advocate of Canadian participation in the pacification of the Boer republics. Fitzpatrick had solid credentials both nationally and in Quebec; in 1885, he had been one of Louis Riel's counsels, and as an MP had worked hard to secure economic development in Quebec City. While respectful of the right of his French-Canadian Liberal colleagues to dissent from his position, as some did, Fitzpatrick nonetheless boldly laid out his reasons for his support in public addresses and in the House of

Commons, condemning Boer injustices against British citizens in South Africa, and hinting that fulfilling one's imperial responsibilities would send a powerful message to Britain's European rivals:

> I say that the time had come, not only because of what was going on in South Africa ... but because of mutterings on the continent for British subjects the world over to prove once and for all that the British Empire is no mere geographical expression for a number of sundered and disunited provinces – the time had come when it was necessary for the whelps of the lion to rally to the defence of the old land. The time had come when every man must be made to understand whether on the European continent or in South Africa, that blow for blow whensoever the blow might come, must be struck back by the British, and would be struck as freely from Australasia and Canada as from the heart of the Empire itself.[138]

No doubt Fitzpatrick was applauded by fellow jurist William Wilfred Sullivan, Chief Justice of Prince Edward Island, who cheered the departure of Islanders in 1899 as they sailed off to do their duty for "the Great motherland,"[139] and by Senator Lawrence Geoffrey Power of Nova Scotia who, as early as October 1899, publicly endorsed sending a second contingent to the war.[140]

Power's elder Irish Catholic colleague in the senate, Ottawa's Sir Richard Scott, was not so ardent. A veteran legislator who cut his political teeth on the bitter sectarianism of the 1850s and 1860s, Scott saw Canadian participation in South Africa as part of some jingoistic conspiracy hatched by Joseph Chamberlain and his Canadian supporters. As Secretary of State, Scott jousted with Sir Edward Thomas Henry Hutton, General Officer Commanding of the Canadian militia, over the latter's misplaced belief that he was to serve the British government first and the Canadian government second. While never as outspoken as Fitzpatrick was – certainly in deference to Laurier – Scott remained suspicious of Canadian participation in the imperialist adventure.[141] Scott's attempt to secure a pro-Boer resolution from the Irish Literary Society of Ottawa was defeated, indicating that not all of the veteran statesman's colleagues shared his views, and clearly underscoring the lack of an Irish Catholic consensus in the initial stages of the Boer War.[142]

Although Scott appeared atypical in his opinions he was by no means an isolated "Irish" voice. Fragmentary evidence suggests that other Irish Catholics suspected imperialist conspiracies or voiced outright opposition to British policies. At least one report of a pro-Boer resolution was passed by the Ancient Order of Hibernians in Montreal (AOH),[143] although this action appeared uncharacteristic of the behaviour of Catholic associations across the country.[144] There is no evidence to suggest that other branches of the AOH echoed the anti-Britishness of the Montreal group, nor did the larger Catholic men's associations – the Catholic Mutual Benefit Association, the St Patrick's Society, the Young Irishman's Literary and Benefit Society, the Holy Name Society, and the Knights of Columbus – make any significant public statements for or against the war effort. The behaviour of the Montreal branch of the AOH, however, confirms the presence of an ultra-Irishness in Montreal, a city where Irish Catholics were, religiously and linguistically, a double minority and tended to wear their Irishness as their principal badge of identity. As had been the case in the early nineteenth century, this double minority status made its imprint on recent Irish Catholic immigrants drawn to Montreal's buoyant economy and, as a result, several vociferous Irish nationalist factions emerged in Montreal's anglophone parishes. But neither Montreal, nor Toronto, nor Halifax for that matter, epitomized the Irish Catholic experience in all of Canada. Finally, there was some concern in "intelligence" circles in Ottawa, that Irish republican agents, operating from the United States, might use the war, to commit acts of sabotage on British military installations and strategic locations in Canada. In April, 1900, in fact, two American "Fenians" inflicted minor damage to Lock 24 on the Welland Canal, when they tried to dynamite it under cover of darkness. Although the perpetrators were arrested and imprisoned, the Canadian military had been placed on alert about prospective Irish radicals.[145]

The mixed reaction of Catholic lay leaders to the Boer conflict was also evident in the largest of Canada's English-language Catholic weekly newspapers: London's *Catholic Record*; Toronto's *Catholic Register*, both of which had a national readership; and New Brunswick's *Freeman* and Nova Scotia's *Casket*, two weeklies that served regional subscribers. In the fall of 1899, no Catholic weekly in Canada offered a ringing endorsement of imperial policy in South Africa or supported unconditionally the sending of Canadian troops. In fact, it was reported that the small *Canadian Freeman* of Kingston, Ontario, a paper sometimes at odds with Irish Catholic attitudes elsewhere in the country, was openly hostile to British actions against the Boer Republics.[146] Several of the papers even expressed a grudging admiration for the rugged Boer farmers and their considerable ability to carve out a homeland for themselves in the African interior.

Patrick Cronin of the *Catholic Register* was suspicious that this was an unnecessary military action hatched by Joseph Chamberlain and Canadian "jingos."[147] Most disturbing to the editor of Toronto's Catholic weekly was the fact that Parliament had not been called to decide upon the participation of a Canadian contingent. "There is a deeper Canadian loyalty than assuming the bloody shirt of the jingo and yelling for imperialism," wrote Cronin. "[T]he men who ignore our institutions of responsible government are necessarily the disloyal ones, if there be any disloyal ones among us."[148] As noted earlier, in addition to being critical of Laurier for circumventing Parliament on the question, the *Register* also aimed barbs at Charles Fitzpatrick and Father Francis Ryan, rector of St Michael's Cathedral in Toronto, both of whom had offered enthusiastic support for the British war effort and the recruitment of the Canadian contingent, justifying their positions with claims that the Boers had trampled on the civil rights of British subjects and upon the religious rights of Catholics in the Transvaal and the Orange Free State. Cronin eschewed any connection between jingoism and Catholicism, and went so far as to support Henri Bourassa's position that Parliament should decide.[149]

Although he expressed misgivings about military action against the Boers, Thomas Coffey, editor of the *Catholic Record*, was far more guarded in his criticism of Laurier. The *Record* had traditionally been sympathetic toward the Liberal Party, and Coffey had been instrumental in recent efforts to rally Ontario's Irish Catholics to the Liberal Party banner.[150] Coffey was put in the dangerous position of criticizing the most vociferous advocates of Canadian intervention, while avoiding anything that smacked of overt criticism of the Laurier government and ministers of the Crown such as Charles Fitzpatrick. Even Chamberlain was given the benefit of the doubt as the *Record* described his actions more as losing high-stakes "international poker" with Paul Kruger, the Boer president, as opposed to being at the heart of an imperialist conspiracy. Although Coffey labelled the Boers as "unprogressive" and "intolerant" of Catholics in South Africa,[151] he also displayed admiration for the "stubborn pluck and unquestionable courage" of Britain's foe in the Transvaal.[152] Nevertheless, the paper stood by earlier claims that "[l]oyalty is better proved by acts than words," and so in times of emergency Catholics could be counted upon to rally to the defence of the Empire.[153]

The *Casket* disagreed. Under the editorship of Michael Donovan, this paper shared the *Register*'s suspicion of Chamberlain and the imperialist lobby and regarded the war as needless. Donovan was careful to point out that Britain's claims on the Boer Republics were dubious under international agreements, and that any difficulties between the British and the Boers could have been worked out without bloodshed.[154] To his credit, Donovan printed critiques of his paper's position, including readers who thought it in poor taste for the paper to withhold support for the war effort, particularly given the alleged Boer persecution of Catholics.[155] In the early stages of the conflict, Donovan maintained his paper's non-partisan policy and refused to endorse the British position, but editorialized that he did not support the Boers, either.[156] Donovan bristled at the suggestion that his paper was "anti-British"; in his eyes, the *Casket* had only doubted the Cecil Rhodes' claims of justly defending the political rights of Uitlanders, suggesting the war was merely another of his "money-grabbing" schemes and contrary to the principles of the Empire.[157]

If one were to limit oneself to just this snapshot of several Catholic weeklies in 1899, Canadian Irish Catholic opinion on the war could be characterized in several ways: restrained support; hostility; suspicion; and ambiguity. Over time, however, the press slowly reversed its initial position on Canadian participation in the war, offering glowing tributes to Canada's troops that became even more enthusiastic as the imperial forces gained the upper hand. The *Record*, tied as it was to Laurier, continually defended the principle of a Canadian voluntary force and even defended the confiscations of Boer property by British troops.[158] The *Register*'s conversion to open support of the war effort came in late 1899 and early 1900. Cronin and his staff became increasingly concerned that the war might drive a wedge between the French and English population of the country.[159] As had been the case in the immediate past and would be the case in the next thirty years, Irish Catholics, torn by competing linguistic, religious, and cultural affiliations, feared being caught in the crossfire between Canada's two cultural solitudes. The *Register* urged peace between the "races," admonishing editors on both sides of the war question that, whether English or French, they had a "duty to Canada, and to Canadian people as a whole ... To go to stir up strife and racial differences, or hatred in a country where so many nationalities have to live together and work out their joint destiny does seem to us to be an overwise [sic] policy."[160] The transformation of the *Register* came in the wake of "Black Week" – a series of embarrassing military setbacks to the Boers – when any further criticism of the British effort might appear to more ardent imperialists as an expression of grave disloyalty in Britain's time of need. Likewise, the *Casket* reiterated its loyalty and eventually softened its stance, offering plenty of war news by 1900 and following the actions of the Canadian contingent with some measure of pride.[161]

It is within this context that the comments of the *Freeman* in Saint John are best understood. Re-established in January 1900 with a new editor, William K. Reynolds, the *Freeman* endorsed the war effort, repeating the claims of Boer oppression and anti-Catholicism, offering profiles of local Catholic heroes, giving laud to Archbishop Cornelius O'Brien and his imperialist affiliations, and suggesting that the port of Saint John should be more aggressive in its participation as a transportation centre for the war, lest Halifax monopolize the provisioning and outfitting of Canadian troop ships.[162] Reynold's staff kept local Catholics well informed about the recruitment and deployment of New Brunswick's Catholic volunteers; in the case of Harry Phillips, a local member of the AOH, the paper reported his enthusiastic "send off" and added: "He goes to join the 8,000 Irish Catholic soldiers who are fighting under the British flag in South Africa."[163] There was little doubt as to the imperial sympathies of the *Freeman* when, on Queen Victoria's death, the front-page headline boldly announced above her photo: "Demise of England's Greatest Constitutional Ruler, Her Gracious Majesty Queen Victoria."[164]

Perhaps the engagement of Canadian troops forced the hand of the Catholic weeklies, which in no way wanted to appear disloyal to the Canadians laying their lives on the line in South Africa. After 1900, and significantly after the Canadian heroics at Paardeberg, the *Register, Casket,* and *Record* joined the *Freeman* as enthusiastic boosters of the Canadian effort, highlighting in particular the role of Catholic heroes such as Archibald H. Macdonell, James H. Elmsley, James C. Mason, and the courageous and much respected Father Peter O'Leary, a Catholic chaplain from Quebec City serving with the Canadian contingent.[165] These men were promoted as examples of Catholic manhood and symbols of Catholic loyalty. The *Register* was quick to remind its detractors that its initial criticism of the Canadian war effort was centred on Laurier's circumvention of Parliament and was not to be interpreted as an expression of disloyalty to the Nation or the Empire.[166] All Catholic weeklies covered the war extensively until the end of the principal engagements, concluding with the capture of Pretoria, and expressed all the while a loyalty that wished to affirm imperial needs while respecting Canada's Parliamentary institutions. This was a war, commented one editor, in which Canada "did herself proud."[167]

The effect the journals had on forming the minds of their English-speaking Catholic readers, or how closely they reflected the views of their readers, is difficult to determine. One way of measuring the Irish Catholic response to the South African War is to evaluate the rate of Irish Catholic recruitment and the characteristics of the recruits themselves. The work of Carman Miller in analyzing the available files of 5,825 volunteers has not only made an enormous contribution to our understanding of the men who wore the Maple Leaf insignia in South Africa, but has also provided a model for the study of other such routinely generated records.[168] At a general level, the linguistic and religious analysis of the Canadian contingent, 1899–1902, reveals the extent of recruitment among Canadian Catholics of Irish descent. According to Miller's calculations, approximately 12.2 per cent of the contingent were Roman Catholic. When one subtracts from this figure the roughly 3 per cent of soldiers who were French Canadian, it leaves a non–French-speaking Catholic total of 9.2 per cent of the entire contingent, or perhaps as many as 536 men, among those whose files are preserved. These numbers suggest that English-speaking Catholics in khaki, mostly of Irish, Scottish, and English descent, were well represented in the South African contingents, although their numbers were slightly lower than their roughly 10.7 per cent share of the entire Canadian population, as was the case with several rival Christian denominations.[169] The following analysis is based on a sample of 234 of these men (extracted from 2,496 scanned files), or just under 44 per cent of the non-francophone Catholic recruits. Of this number, the analysis will focus directly on a sample of 165 Catholic recruits of Irish birth or Irish descent.[170]

Table 1.3
Distribution of Irish Catholic sample (n = 165) among Canadian recruits in the Boer War

Units	*Irish Catholic sample, no. (%)*	*Total Canadian contingent,* no. (%)*	*Irish Catholics, Halifax*
Royal Canadian Regiment	36 (21.8)	1019 (17.5)	15
Royal Canadian Dragoons	11 (6.7)		
Strathcona Horse	2 (1.2)	519 (8.9)	0
Royal Canadian Field Artillery	13 (7.9)		0
1st CMR†	6 (3.6)	1125 (19.3)	2
Yeomanry	17 (10.3)		
2nd CMR†	6 (3.6)	911 (15.6)	24
3rd CMR	13 (7.9)	477 (8.2)	
4th CMR	22 (13.3)	474 (8.1)	
5th CMR	12 (7.3)	522 (8.9)	
6th CMR	25 (15.2)	486 (8.3)	
Other/unknown	2 (1.2)	292 (5.1)	1
Total	165 (100)	5825	42

CMR = Canadian Mounted Rifles
* N = 5825
† The 1st CMR consisted of three distinctive units: two squadrons of Mounted Rifles (from which the 2nd CMR became a separate unit), the Royal Canadian Dragoons, and the Royal Canadian Field Artillery. The Irish Catholic sample was collectively 30 for the 1st CMR (18.8 per cent), and therefore was closely comparable to the general recruitment for the battalion. The Yeomanry was renamed the 2nd CMR, taking the name of a previously recruited unit; therefore, the Irish Catholic total for the 2nd CMR is 23 (13.9 per cent), again comparable to the percentage of the entire contingent.
Source: Carman Miller, *Painting the Map Red: Canada and the South African War, 1899–1902* (Montreal and Kingston: Canadian War Museum & McGill Queen's University Press, 1993), 393–5; Carman Miller, "A Preliminary Analysis of the Socio-economic Composition of Canada's South African War Contingents," *Histoire sociale / Social History* 8 (novembre/November 1975), 230–2.

The most striking feature of this sample group of Irish Catholic troops is that they were closely comparable to the general occupational and regional composition of the entire contingent. Irish Catholics were present in all phases of recruitment, with at least 20 per cent of their number included in the first Canadian contingent in 1899, close to 19 per cent among the second contingent, and almost 14 per cent in the 2nd Regiment of Canadian Mounted Rifles (see table 1.3). Given the paucity of Irish Catholic settlement west of the Ontario–

Manitoba border, the number of recruits in Lord Strathcona's Horse and the 5th Canadian Mounted Rifles was light, amounting to only 8 per cent of the total Irish Catholic enlistment. In fact, the western provinces and territories accounted for only 16 per cent of all Irish Catholic recruits in this sample. The other notable difference between the Irish Catholics who departed Halifax and their Protestant colleagues was the fact that 77 per cent of the Irish had been born in Canada, as compared with the contingent's 63.7 per cent.[171] Most Irish Catholic recruits – nearly 45 per cent – were born in southern Ontario and Nova Scotia, which by coincidence were the two areas of strongest recruitment for the entire force. About 22 per cent of recruits had been born in Quebec or New Brunswick. None of this should come as a surprise, given the fact that Halifax, Montreal, the Miramichi, Saint John, and southern Ontario were the principal foci of Irish Catholic settlement in the early nineteenth century. No doubt, high recruitment among Haligonian Irish would have been influenced by the positive disposition toward the Empire by Archbishop O'Brien, strong Catholic participation in local militia units, and, perhaps, by the enticement and pride of being attached to the uniformed columns of Canadian men streaming in and out of the port of Halifax. Overall, the Canadian nativity of Irish Catholics in the sample group supports the historiographical contention that Canada's Irish Catholics experienced little demographic growth by means of immigration after 1850[172] (see table 1.4).

The Irish Catholic sample also suggests that the idea of a "vertical mosaic," when applied to Irish Catholics in the Canadian social spectrum, may have been overplayed by historians.[173] Although, perhaps as a result of urban recruiting patterns in eastern Canada, the number of blue-collar recruits was higher than the national average (40.6 per cent to 29.2 per cent), it should be noted that the Irish Catholic percentage of white collar workers was practically identical to the national average (22.4 per cent to 22.9 per cent), while the percentage of Irish Catholic recruits employed in the service sector was actually higher than the number for all of the contingents (20.6 per cent to 16.3 per cent). The one significant difference with respect to occupation was that few Irish Catholics recruits had been employed in primary industries when compared with the rest of the members of the contingents (13.9 per cent to 27.4 per cent).[174] (See table 1.5.) Again, the low recruitment of Catholics from western Canada and its fron-

Table 1.4
Irish Catholic recruits to the Boer War, by place of birth (n = 165)

Birthplace	*Irish Catholics, no. (%)*	*Total Canadian contingent,* no. (%)*
Prince Edward Island	13 (7.9)	139 (2.4)
Nova Scotia	35 (21.2)	435 (7.5)
New Brunswick	16 (9.7)	353 (6.1)
Quebec	21 (12.7)	484 (8.3)
Ontario	39 (23.6)	2110 (36.2)
Manitoba/Northwest Territories	3 (1.8)	147 (2.5)
British Columbia	0 (0.0)	42 (0.7)
Canada total	127 (77.0)	3710 (63.7)
Other British Empire	33 (20.0)	1710 (29.4)
Other	5 (3.0)	159 (2.7)

* N = 5825
Source: Carman Miller, "A Preliminary Analysis of the Socio-economic Composition of Canada's South African War Contingents," *Histoire sociale / Social History* 8 (novembre/November 1975): 221. The data represent 5579 of 5825 (95.8%) for whom nativity could be identified.

tier economy helps to account for this significant discrepancy in recruits coming from ranching, lumbering, and mining. It appeared that what Irish Catholics lacked in terms of their participation in the manual tasks of the primary industries of the west, they compensated for in their blue-collar work in the cities of the east. Overall, the sample does reveal clearly that the Irish Catholics serving in the South African contingents could not be stereotyped simply as "feckless paddies and navvies" searching for steady work. In fact, if they had chosen to do so, Irish Catholics could have found abundant, gainful, and safe employment in Halifax, given its strong wartime economy,[175] rather than herding aboard the troop ships bound for the Cape Colony. Irish Catholics appeared eager to enlist less for want of work than for want of adventure.

Nor could Irish Catholics be regarded as newcomers to khaki or as averse to Canadian military traditions. The Irish Catholic sample indicates that 62.4 per cent of recruits had some military or militia background before enlistment; such a high number of men with experience challenges the impression that Irish Catholics had only loose ties to the militia tradition in English Canada.[176] Some Irish Catholic

Table 1.5
Irish Catholic Canadian recruits to the Boer War, by occupation (n = 165)

Occupation	*Irish Catholic, no. (%)*	*Percentage of total Canadian contingent**	*Difference*
White collar	37 (22.4)	22.9	−0.5
Blue collar	67 (40.6)	29.2	11.4
Service	34 (20.6)	16.3	4.3
Primary	23 (13.9)	27.4	−13.5
Unknown	4 (2.4)	4.2	−1.8

* N = 5825

White collar: *Professional*: student, teacher, doctor, law student, professional engineer, dentist, medical student
Proprietorial: merchant, gentleman, owner/florist/outfitter, hotel/restaurant keeper, business owner manager
Sales/Clerical: salesman, travelling salesman, clerk, store clerk, traveller, bookkeeper, commercial traveller, chemist, messenger, bank clerk, druggist, merchant tailor, draughtsman, inspector, bill collector, grocer, agent/life insurance, surveyor, stenographer, law clerk, agent, civil servant, accountant

Blue collar: *Skilled*: artisan, baker, printer, cooper, miller, butcher, saddler, electrician, plumber, brickmaker, machinist, stone mason, shoe smith, painter, photographer, tailor, glass worker, cheese maker, black/tinsmith, carpenter, book binder, marble polisher, mechanic, brewer, wheel wright, watch maker
Un/semi-skilled: factory worker, labourer, stevedore, cotton worker, mill hand, bridge worker, packer

Service: *Protective*: soldier, police, fireman
Transportation/communication: conductor, line/brake/trainman, coachman, driver, telephone/telegraph
Personal: gardener/servant, waiter/barman, janitor, cook
Miscellaneous: barber, reporter, horse trainer, actor/artist, jockey, veterinarian

Primary: *Agriculture*: farmer, farm labourer, rancher, ranch labourer/cattleman/cowboy, stablehand, dairy man
Mining: miner, prospector
Fishing: sailor, mariner
Trapping: hunter/trapper
Lumber: lumberjack, shanty man, teamster

Source: Adapted from Carman Miller, "A Preliminary Analysis of the Socio-economic Composition of Canada's South African War Contingents," *Histoire sociale / Social History* 8 (novembre/November 1975), 230–2.

recruits enlisted with long-standing service to local militia units, while others, once the war had begun, joined the militia units so that they might be enlisted directly into the second contingent. In fact, the Irish Catholic soldiers in this sample appear more experienced than their Scottish co-religionists, whom historians have memorialized for their military traditions.[177]

The Irish Catholics of Halifax provide an interesting micro-study of Irish Catholic recruitment. The random sample of forty-two Irish Catholic recruits from the city reveals a local reflection of national trends and some characteristics of a more local flavour. The majority of the recruits (80.9 per cent) were born in Canada, and almost all of these were Nova Scotian. The high proportion of blue-collar workers in the Halifax sample was also similar to that in the Irish Catholic sample nationally, most likely because their abilities as skilled workers, drivers, and blacksmiths in Halifax were much sought after by the army, particularly for the cavalry units that set sail from that port. Over half the Halifax sample had served previously in the militia, which should come as no surprise, since the Charitable Irish Society of Halifax had supported at least two militia units and had many members serving in them before the war.[178] Also interesting is that about 36 per cent of the sample served in the first wave of volunteers, the Royal Canadian Regiment, and over 50 per cent volunteered for mounted units later in the war when there was a renewed call for volunteers. These trends appeared to mirror national trends for all volunteers and those among the Irish Catholic volunteers generally across Canada. It should also be emphasized that over half (55 per cent) of the recruits had deep roots in the Halifax Irish community. The database of burials for the Holy Cross Catholic Cemetery in downtown Halifax reveals that the men of the sample came from families with long-standing connections in the region, whether locally born, Irish-born, or two-boater Newfoundland migrants, who committed their deceased family members to eternal slumber in this sacred space. Boer War volunteers bearing names such as Rolfe, Fitzgerald, Fleming, Fogarty, O'Brien, Tierney, Conway, or Ryan could all find memorials to parents, aunts and uncles, siblings, and cousins at Holy Cross. The Irish sample indicates clearly that some communities of Irish Catholics in Canada embraced the imperial conflict in South Africa as their own and, furthermore, that they did not sever their attachment to the Empire thereafter. Of the thirty-nine men in the sample who lived through the Boer War, one third volunteered for service just over a decade later when the CEF called for volunteers.[179]

When Irish Catholic participation in the Boer War is situated within the broad context of the evolution of Irish Catholic communities in Canada, it appears less a radical point of departure in terms of Irish Catholic loyalty and participation in the Canadian imperial story. One could make a case that it was one more step – an important step – in the Irish Catholic's positive engagement with the mainstream of English Canadian life. The Boer War challenged Canada's Catholics of Irish birth and descent to define more clearly their focus of political loyalty and, should their decision veer in an imperial-national direction, to place themselves in the service of Queen, country, and Empire – and not always in that order. The Catholic elementary schools had already moved their curriculum in this imperial direction both in Ontario and in the northwest. One inspector at St Mary's School in Calgary, in 1900, when treated to a concert that included a patriotic rendition of "The Rose, the Shamrock, and the Thistle," exclaimed that "[n]othing could be more admirable than the sight of those manly little fellows, pupils in a Roman Catholic school, looking you squarely in the eyes and singing a patriotic British song with all the enthusiasm imaginable."[180] The concert, while obviously an effort by the teachers to pander to the inspector, was nonetheless symptomatic of much broader changes in the civil indoctrination of Catholic youth.[181]

Similarly, as the press and clerical leaders lined up behind the war effort after the arrival of Canadian troops on the veldt, the question of Canada's role in the Empire came to the fore for many Irish Catholic adults. Here, the Catholic press, at least in central Canada, advocated a vision of Canada as an equal partner in the British Empire.[182] There was little difficulty for Irish Catholics to identify with Canada as a player in the Empire, provided it was clear that, to echo the sentiment of Kipling's "Our Lady of the Snows," Canada would be mistress in her own house. Such ideas would permeate Irish Catholic communities and foster enthusiastic support for Canada's participation in the Great War – and, later, equally strong levels of Irish Catholic recruitment in the Canadian Expeditionary Force after 1914.

It is not surprising that, imbued with this sense of "national" purpose, Catholic veterans of the veldt emerged as leaders during World War I: Captain Charles McGee of Ottawa, Generals J.H. Elmsley and A.H. Macdonell of Toronto, William Donovan of Quebec, Corporal Edward "Ned" Murray of Pembroke and later Alberta, and Margaret C. MacDonald of Bailey's Brook, Nova Scotia, who went from nursing sister in South Africa to matron-in-chief of the CEF.[183] The fearless and beloved Father Peter O'Leary of Quebec City, renowned for his service in South Africa, volunteered again for the Canadian Chaplain Service in the Great War, and although he was physically and mentally a mere shadow of his former self and had to be discharged, his heroics during the Boer War became the rod by which all Catholic chaplains would be required to measure themselves.[184] Although not all of these returning veterans were of Irish descent, as a group they became identified by anglophone Catholics as powerful symbols and models of Catholic service and "undoubted" loyalty.[185]

The legacy of the Boer War and Irish Catholic participation in it was absorbed by the next generation of English-speaking Catholics, whose links to Ireland would be far weaker than those of their parents and grandparents. This was particularly true in the publicly funded Catholic schools of Ontario, where Catholic children drank deeply from the imperial sentiments of textbooks, young boys shouldered mock rifles and marched in school cadet corps, and girls and boys celebrated the imperial connection in poetry, art, and song on Empire Day each year.[186] After 1907, across the country, English-speaking Catholic youth joined the burgeoning Scout movement, founded by Lord Robert Baden Powell, the veteran of the siege of Mafeking and commander of the South African Constabulary. For Catholic youth in English Canada, the Boer War would form part of a much larger imperial tapestry in which Canada was perceived to play, according to Catholic Senator A.C. Macdonell, the role of "bridge" between the Great Anglo-Saxon peoples of America and Britain.[187] It would be these youth, nurtured on such memories, who would form the English-speaking Catholic contribution to the CEF from 1914 to 1918. Back in Admaston Township, Mona Whelan's brothers never volunteered, but as farmers in the upper Ottawa Valley, their priorities would have been focused on the success of the family farm and feeding a country doing its imperial duty.

Thus, the story of the Irish Catholics and the Boer War is really two stories. Situated within the time of the conflict itself, it is a story of indecision, ambiguity, and a people searching for a clearer understanding of their loyalties. In Fitzpatrick's words – words not unanimously received by his own constituency at the time – Catholics of Irish descent may have been "whelps of the lion" but they were truly "whelps," scampering about, playing with ideas, and tumbling over one another. By the end of the Boer War, their own service done and their dead buried, the Irish Catholic leadership appeared more clearly focused on Canada's role in the Empire and their role within Canada. Even the *Catholic Register* eventually praised Fitzpatrick's patriotism, recognizing in him a man who "commands the respect of all

Canadians."[188] In the decade that followed, Catholics of Irish descent created a new narrative. This story drew on a selected memory of South Africa, unencumbered by the ambiguities evident in 1899; it arose in a context of the passing of the sons and daughters of mid-nineteenth-century immigrants and the rise of a new generation, who appeared to have a greater distance between themselves and memories of migration, Famine, and Fenianism; it was a story composed in an environment in which Irish descendants were forced to redefine who they were relative to the thousands of new Catholics migrating to Canada from southern and eastern Europe. And, equally as influential on the tone of the story, were the ongoing conflicts in the Canadian Church between Quebecois, Franco-Ontarians, and Acadians on the one side and *les maudits Irlandais* on the other. Although there were many regional variations in Irish Catholic life from Halifax to Vancouver, this second story was the one that propelled Canada's Catholics of Irish descent into World War I. The once-separated communities of Irish Catholics were becoming more tightly bound by an assertive anglophone hierarchy, regular co-operation among regional Catholic weeklies, a nascent sense of Empire brought to the fore in South Africa, and a sense of distinctiveness, if not defiant autonomy, from French Canadian Catholics. In 1914, the Irish Catholic Canadian whelps of the lion appeared to be ready to take their place in the imperial pride.

2

"Let All Come to the Battle"

Catholics Embrace the Imperial War

The Imperial Theatre in Saint John, New Brunswick, was a busy place in 1914 and 1915. As one of the largest public venues in the city, it had become a hive of activity where local politicians and clergy of all religious stripes called on the citizens of the province to join in the Empire's war. The city's Irish Catholic priests were frequent visitors to the stage, and their message was clear: it was a Catholic citizen's duty to assist Great Britain in her time of need. Led by Bishop Edward Alfred LeBlanc's stirring appeal in November 1914 to defend the "civil and religious liberties of the Empire," priest after priest from the diocese walked the stage of the Imperial, rousing the crowds to support the war effort and urging young men to enlist.[1] One of the most poignant speeches was made sixteen months into the war by Father John E. Burke. A native of Saint John and a member of the Paulist order, whose members were known for their skill in oration and effective communication of the faith, Burke did not disappoint. On the first Sunday of January 1916, Burke managed to pack the theatre with a "large and enthusiastic audience." Flanked by Major W.R. Brown and Mayor James H. Frink, Burke retold the story of the Apostle Paul's incarceration in Jerusalem and the plans by authorities to scourge him for his alleged attempt to stir up the local Jewish population. Burke, with the audience in the palm of his hand, then offered Paul's admonishment to the police: "Is it permissible for thee to scourge a man who is a Roman citizen?"[2]

Burke then announced that he had something in common with Paul that evening, and something in common with the audience. Although he could not claim Paul's sanctity, he said, he did share with him a pride in citizenship:

> I feel that I am a citizen of the great Dominion. I am a native of this good old city. I hold a heritage which is dearer than life itself. I hold something in common with you that an army would rise to defend. I hold a heritage in common with you. Shall I name it? I am a British subject. The very years of British citizenship have given us a feeling of security. Our forefathers were people who struggled for self-government and now have the best government, the best in liberty."[3]

His oration went on to extol the strength of the British Navy, British principles, and the British resolve to stop the rise of Germany, "a nation which was conceived in sin and begotten in sin." Rising to an even higher rhetorical plateau, Burke claimed that now standing shoulder to shoulder with Britain were her Dominions and, particularly, those peoples who bore such names of "Kelly, Burke, and Shea." Recounting the proud heritage of Catholics in that city by recounting his visit to the Cathedral of the Immaculate Conception in Saint John, Burke then took up an analogy to another great metaphorical Cathedral: "It had been builded [sic] for the great principles of human liberty. There rich and poor came, bond and free and worshipped alike ... The British Empire is the name of that Temple." Then, pointing to the crowd, he implored them to "lay low the felon who would wipe from the face of the earth, this God-like building, this temple dedicated to human rights and the British Empire."

Amid the roar of approval from the crowd that evening, it could not have been lost, even on the most dispassionate of witnesses, that here was an Irish Catholic priest extolling the virtues of the British Empire. On 4 August 1914, the British Empire had declared war on the German Empire and its allies; although the previous decade had witnessed a fierce arms race among competing European imperial powers, and the political machinations that underscored these international rivalries,[4] the British went to war officially because of the German invasion of Belgium, whose neutrality had been guaranteed by a treaty signed by the major European powers in the 1830s. Under the current constitutional arrangement, when Great Britain was at war so were Canada and other dominions and colonies of the Empire. Within two days of the war's declaration, the Canadian government had offered the motherland one infantry division.[5] Within weeks, thousands of English, Scottish, and Irish expatriates rushed to recruiting stations to serve the Empire in its time of need.[6] Catholics were among them, and bishops and laypeople reflected the enthusiasm offered by clergy like Burke that night in Saint John. Anglophone Catholics in Canada had many reasons to support the British declaration of war against Germany. Clergy and community leaders would claim that the war was to be fought for the Christian values that they perceived as the foundations of modern civilization. Irish Canadian Catholics would also claim that the Belgian people required support against the oppressors from Germany; akin to the recently promise of Home Rule for Ireland, small nations must be free. Within some Catholic circles, it was believed that Germany itself and the propagation of its *Kultur* had to be stopped for the sake of civilization. The Catholic Church had to be careful not to be too zealous in its negative characterizations of Germans, however, since there were sizeable German Catholic minorities in the Ottawa Valley, southwestern Ontario, and Saskatchewan. By far the most overwhelming reason for going to war, for Irish Catholic Canadian bishops, priests, politicians, newspaper editors, and lay leaders was that the Empire's war was their war. Like Burke, they were proud of their imperial citizenship.

From the onset of hostilities, and continuously through the phases of voluntary recruitment, the Irish and Scottish Catholic bishops of Canada were unequivocal in their support for the Empire's war. In some ways this was a twentieth-century incarnation of the loyalty professed in the eighteenth century by bishops Jean-Olivier Briand and Joseph-Octave Plessis of Quebec. In the wake of the British conquest of 1760, their openly declared allegiance to Britain's Protestant monarch facilitated the granting of rights to Canadian Catholics that were virtually unheard of in other parts of the Empire.[7] Episcopal loyalty, based in a strict reading of Paul to the Romans, eventually provided for Catholics voting rights, property rights, and rights of assembly and representation that would not be granted to Catholics in other parts of the Empire until after 1829. Thereafter, the Catholic Church, although it might disagree with the policies of individual governments, and despite the fact that individual bishops might at times dissent from specific government actions, had maintained a public loyalty to the Crown. These historical factors were treated neither as historical artifacts nor as empty words by clerical Catholic leaders. In Ottawa's Glebe neighbourhood, Father John J. O'Gorman of Blessed Sacrament Parish recalled the tradition of Catholic loyalty to the

Crown during Pontiac's rebellion in 1763, the American Revolution, and the War of 1812. "Bishop Briand," O'Gorman preached, "told his people it was their duty as Catholics to obey the lawfully constituted authority of Great Britain."[8] The Church in Canada had established clear historical precedents from which it would not stray; it would do its duty.

The imperial rhetoric used by Catholics implied that rallying to the Empire was something they had always been prepared to do. For several Catholic commentators, the Catholic participation in the Canadian voluntary enlistment for the Boer War was recalled as a precedent for the current struggle and a capstone for the historic rapprochement between the Catholic hierarchy and the Crown. Indeed, in the decade and a half that separated the Boer War from the Great War, Canadian Catholics of Irish descent incorporated the South African experience into the story of their own contribution to Canada and the Empire. In the period immediately leading up to August 1914, and throughout the first months of the Great War, Catholic leaders across the country would reminisce proudly about Catholic loyalty during the Boer crisis. In Saint John, the *New Freeman* reported on the stirring remarks of Father O'Gorman, including his contention that, as in South Africa, Britain's engagement in the Great War was just and honourable.[9] In Winnipeg, the *Northwest Review* was even more open in its imperial sentiment, claiming that Canadians were "loyal to the Motherland. The spirit that animated their forefathers a century ago when invasion threatened this infant nation, the spirit which impelled her sons to brave the dangers of the African veldt – that spirit, the surest defence against aggression, animates them still."[10] In a similar fashion, T.W. McGarry, the Irish Catholic member and Cabinet minister representing Renfrew South in the Ontario legislature, addressed the departing second contingent from Renfrew, reminding them that they would bring honour to Canada, just as had the troops who had ventured to South Africa.[11]

The most notable rhetorical justification for going to war offered by bishops, clergy, and lay leaders was the necessity to defend the British Empire in its time of need. Although many reasons were offered for complete engagement by Catholics in the war effort, English-speaking Catholic leaders, most of whom were of Irish birth or descent, were adamant that Canada was a part of a vast Empire worthy of defence. This imperialist language was not particular to any part of the country, but was featured in the statements of bishops from Nova Scotia to British Columbia. The imperial language was no stronger among bishops of Scottish descent, such as James Morrison of Antigonish and Alexander MacDonald of Victoria, than it was among the Irish cohort, who included such episcopal extroverts as Timothy Casey of Vancouver, James McNally of Calgary, Alfred Sinnott of Winnipeg, and Michael Fallon of London. Hybrid Celts such as Neil McNeil of Toronto, whose father was of Scottish descent and mother was a Meagher with deep family roots in Kilkenny, took no back seat to his colleagues when it came to imperialist pronouncements. McNeil set the template for Catholic support in English Canada early in the war and reaffirmed it often. In August 1914 he issued a circular letter to his diocese, the largest outside of Quebec:

> There are duties to our fellow-men in general and to our country in particular which events press upon us, and to which I call your attention. The first duty is prayer to God for peace …You do not need to be reminded of the duty of patriotism. You are as ready as any to defend your country and share in the burdens of Empire. But those of us who are remote from the scene of conflict, and cannot leave Canada, may be tempted to think that our part is simply that of interested spectators. It is not. We can all help, and therefore should all help, by taking care to stop all unnecessary expenses in our homes and in our daily lives. It is no time for luxuries or festivities when millions of men are in mortal combat, and the poor everywhere are likely to need all we can spare.[12]

McNeil's template was replicated, with variations, by other bishops across Canada. Invocations for prayer, service to country and the Empire, the necessity of recruitment, the duties of all Catholics to support the war on the home front, and the call to hear the cry of the poor, both at home and abroad, became integral to the bishops' support of the war effort.

In 1914 there were ten archdioceses and twenty-eight dioceses in the Canadian Catholic Church, serving about 40 per cent of Canada's population. At least sixteen of the thirty-eight diocesan divisions were under the control of bishops of Scottish or Irish descent. In 1915 the Holy See created the Archdiocese of Winnipeg with no suffragan sees and appointed a Prince Edward Islander of Irish descent in charge.

Francophones might argue that Charles Hugh Gauthier, who presided over the bilingual Archdiocese of Ottawa, was essentially Scottish in his approach to life, preferring his matrilineal over his patrilineal blood line. By 1916 the bishops within the ecclesiastical provinces of Halifax, Toronto, Kingston, and Vancouver presided over 780,000 Catholic faithful and 771 priests.[13] Of the 17 English-speaking Catholic bishops, only three were identified as Scots and only two – Thomas Joseph Dowling of Hamilton and Patrick Ryan of Pembroke – were born in Ireland. Almost all of this anglophone subset of bishops were born in Canada and were of Irish descent.[14] Most had been educated in Canada and were inculcated with a sense of their Canadian citizenship within the larger British Empire.

These bishops were also new and relatively inexperienced. Only four of the sixteen had ever served as bishop of another diocese or as an auxiliary bishop before being named to their current see. Two of these veterans – Dowling, born in 1840, and McNeil, born in 1851 – were among the oldest bishops in a group whose average age was fifty-four years and nine months. Eight of the bishops had less than five years' experience in their role when the war was in its initial stages. In short, the English-speaking Catholic bishops of Canada who faced the war were, by and large, young, inexperienced, and Canadian in their education and pastoral experience. It is not surprising that many of them would look to senior members of the episcopal club, particularly McNeil, for guidance and leadership as the war progressed. McNeil was an obvious choice. He had served as bishop in St George's on the west coast of Newfoundland and later in Vancouver, had led St Francis Xavier University, and was using his seminary, St Augustine's in Toronto, as an educational centre for seminarians from across Canada.[15] Although normally the archbishops – including McNeil, Edward McCarthy of Halifax, Michael Spratt of Kingston, Timothy Casey of Vancouver, and eventually Alfred Sinnott of Winnipeg – provided canonical leadership for all the Canadian bishops, over the course of the war the much-respected McNeil was exceptional in his public presence and was a voice for Catholics beyond his diocesan boundaries.

Loyalty to the Empire was the primary theme of the early episcopal calls for Catholic support for the war effort. In Calgary, Bishop James McNally, born in Prince Edward Island, made service to the Empire a centerpiece of his appeal to Catholics in southern Alberta, considering it his episcopal duty to take to any public platform to rally his flock to the imperial banner:

> Surely in such circumstances it may be permitted to one in my position to strive, not only by earnest prayers and exhortation, but also by example to exalt loyalty and love of our country and of our Empire, in whose greatness from our childhood we have cherished such legitimate pride and confidence and in whose prestige we have often found practical protection that the greatness and prestige of that Empire may be maintained undiminished and that all her sons may in the time of trial show towards her every interest, the unbounded generosity which unselfish patriotism and unselfish love should inspire.[16]

Bishop James Morrison agreed, claiming that Canadians must stand "shoulder to shoulder" with Englishmen, Irishmen, and Scots in Belgium to "defend the integrity of the Empire."[17] In Victoria, Cape Breton–born Alexander "Sandy" MacDonald was clear that, as British subjects, all Canadians are "under manifold obligation to the Motherland."[18] Michael Francis Fallon, the controversial bishop of London, Ontario, issued a circular letter on August 28 that was to be read from every pulpit. In it he raised the stakes, implying that failure to come to the defence of the Empire in its time of need posed a risk to civilization itself: "Every sentiment of loyalty to our King and country, as well as love for our very homes, prompts us to turn to God and seek from Him the blessed gifts of peace and security for the Empire, that will mean the freedom and welfare of the world."[19] Fallon would take to both the pulpit and the public recruiting platform to reiterate and strengthen his support for the war effort. In a similar vein, so would Archbishop Timothy Casey of Vancouver, who though still bristling from his transfer from his native New Brunswick, became passionate about Catholics doing their part and found justification for doing so in scripture. Citing 1 Maccabees 5:42, he urged: "Suffer no man to stay behind, but let all come to the battle."[20]

Bishops in English Canada would return to this theme frequently over the next eighteen months. It was the Catholic practice to pray for peace and to demonstrate loyalty to Canada as a member of the British Empire. The Irish-Canadian bishops clearly articulated the necessity of every Catholic to profess both piety and patriotism[21] in the Empire's time of need. It appeared equally as clear that the laity expected no less patriotism from the episcopacy. When, in 1915, Alfred A. Sinnott was appointed the first archbishop of Winnipeg, the *Northwest Review* proclaimed him a true patriot, "Canadian to the core, and staunch defender and upholder of British institutions." The paper promised that Sinnott would be prepared to "advance every cause which will elevate the standard of British citizenship."[22]

Catholic newspapers across Canada quickly fell in line with the bishops. Within a week of the declaration of war, the *Casket* in Antigonish was unequivocal in its support of the Empire, citing Bishop Morrison's appeal verbatim.[23] The paper also quoted liberally from the statements of other Canadian bishops and added, for its own part, the view that "[t]he British colonial policy of 'the square deal' has given the King an Empire bound together by nothing but the wish to be and to stand together. And is not that the firmest of all bonds?"[24] Further to this sentiment, *Casket* editor Michael Donovan wrote: "It is our deliberate conviction that the smashing up of the British Empire would be a tremendous blow to the welfare of mankind."[25] In a "no-holds-barred" approach, he challenged support of Ulster in the days leading up to the war as nothing less than support for Germany against the Crown. Moreover, disavowing any position that the current conflict was not Canada's war, the *Casket* boldly proclaimed that "Canada's future is, at the moment, being fought for on the banks of French rivers, and Canada's safety was fought for, to some extent, last week, off the coast of Chile." Quite simply, the Empire's war was Canada's war.

Toronto's *Catholic Register* sounded an even stronger note of imperial sentiment, one certainly in keeping with the tone set by McNeil in his many speeches in 1914. The *Register*'s editor, Father Alfred E. Burke, was a native of Prince Edward Island and a supporter of the Conservative Party, and years earlier had addressed the Empire Club on the role of the Catholic Church in the Empire. With these facts in mind, his readers would not have been surprised by the papers' imperialist tones. The *Register* had a paid circulation of about 13,000 during the war period and, given its affiliation with the Catholic Church Extension Society, had a nationwide audience and influence.[26] In early September the *Register* editorialized:

> It will be for us beyond peradventure that we as Canadians are Britishers to the core and that Britain's troubles are our troubles,

> Britain's shield our safety. We must sacrifice something for this protection. Where would we be today but for the Empire's Navy and the Empire's men? Our part is to give generously what is our honest toll, whether it be for the army and the navy ... what we need is to finish the work effectually – so effectually that Pax Britannica may rejoice the world for another half century. The God of Armies is great and wonderful in his dispensations.[27]

The *Register* never wavered in its support for the war effort, and the rhetorical flourishes of the editors, even after Burke's departure for the Front in 1915, were often laced with imperialist vocabulary.[28] Canadian Catholics were reminded by the *Register* that they had duties to the British Empire and that they should take pride in this fact. "We are as British as we always have been," argued the paper, "and will, please God, always be."[29] In its support for the Empire's war, the paper could be most forgiving of Orange "enemies" such as Colonel Sam Hughes, now minister of militia and defence, whom the *Register* defended against his critics regarding the chaos at Valcartier, the training camp for the CEF. Burke actually visited the camp outside Quebec City and returned to Toronto, vindicating Hughes and the basic training of the recruits and confidently adding that this will continue in so far as "Our men will go to good hands for preparation in Britain."[30]

London's *Catholic Record*, although the principal rival of the *Catholic Register* in Ontario, delivered similar rhetorical flourishes on imperial duty, but in a nuanced fashion. Because the *Record* had been closely aligned with the Canadian Liberal party through its proprietor Senator Thomas James Coffey, its editor, Father James T. Foley, was careful not to state anything that might reflect badly on from Sir Wilfrid Laurier, who now sat as leader of the Opposition to Robert Borden's Conservative government.[31] Like most Catholic papers, the *Record* was skilful in trying not to work at cross purposes with its local bishop, in this case the controversial Michael Francis Fallon, but Foley acknowledged that his paper had a national readership and would attempt to reflect national, not local, Catholic concerns.[32] With a paid circulation reaching over 31,000 by 1919,[33] the *Record* remained Canada's largest English-speaking Catholic weekly and was therefore significant in the reach of its commentary on the war. At times the *Record* appeared more cautious than the *Register* about who should fight the war, considering that Parliament had the ultimate say as to whether the militia, volunteers, or any other type of military service was warranted.[34] Nevertheless, the editors were clear that Canadian Catholics must do their duty and come to the assistance of the British Empire in its time of need. For one correspondent, this Catholic duty was unequivocal: "We will suffer no aspersions on our allegiance to the flag," wrote a columnist known only under the pseudonym "Columba." "NO man dare forbid us 'God bless the Pope,' but because of that 'God save the King' loses none of its significance when uttered by Catholic lips."[35] Foley was adamant: "[E]very Canadian should contribute his quota of self-sacrifice to the conservation of the Empire."[36] Later, while commenting on high levels of Catholic recruits, particularly in Nova Scotia, the *Record* employed a clear imperial tack: "We have realized that the British Empire is a Commonwealth and that the duties of patriotism are commensurate with the needs of Empire."[37]

Central Ontario Catholic weeklies were not alone in expressing pride in the Empire and the necessity of Catholic Canadians doing their duty. Donovan's *Casket* became the chief exponent of the imperial war effort among Catholics in eastern Nova Scotia. In the early stages of the war it republished the speeches of Canada's bishops, particularly those of Cape Breton roots, and the local ordinary, James Morrison, who were frequently invited to public gatherings to raise material support for the war and recruits for the CEF.[38] It also culled war news and opinion from Canadian secular dailies.[39] The paper itself, however, was not shy in its own use of imperial language in justifying the war and rallying Canadians to the cause: "It is our deliberate conviction that the smashing up of the British Empire would be a tremendous blow to the welfare of mankind. That may seem a cold-blooded way to state the case, but ... the interests not only of Canada but the world, require the preservation of this Empire; and when we say "interests" we do not mean merely sordid money-making interests; but larger matters which go to the make up of what we call social and political freedom."[40] Much of the same could be said for the *New Freeman*, which reprinted speeches from Bishop LeBlanc and the steady stream of priests who used the stage at the Imperial Theatre to rouse the local population – Catholic and non-Catholic – to the imperial cause.[41] After LeBlanc's first public address on the war, editor C.J. McLaughlin took time to praise every aspect of the bishop's speech, particularly the invocation to fight for the "civil and religious liberties of the Empire."[42] The *New Freeman*'s coverage included much of the

Maritimes and even reported on priests in Halifax, chiming its endorsement of imperial support preached by St Mary's Cathedral rector, Dr. Foley, who described the British Empire as "the embodiment of liberty and upholder of justice."[43]

The imperial language used by Catholics in actively endorsing the war effort was not restricted to the higher clergy and Catholic newspapers. Politicians and parish priests often employed such language or appealed to Catholic citizenship in the Empire to rouse supporters and parishioners to make material contributions to the war effort. Politicians such as Conservative Cabinet minister Charles J. Doherty of Montreal and former Liberal privy councillor and Chief Justice of Canada, Sir Charles Fitzpatrick, unsurprisingly invoked the glory of the Empire in their speeches.[44] Parish priests, however, might seem less likely to use such rhetoric, given the historical cautions against using the pulpit for political ends. Not so, however, for many Catholic priests across all regions in Canada during the first eighteen months of the war, for whom the call of the Empire was urgent and pressing. In Assiniboia, Saskatchewan, for example, Father A. Sammut, a recent immigrant from Malta, held patriotic services in his parish to "help assert in this hour of trial our boundless loyalty and sincere fidelity to our august King and our Great Empire."[45] In Sydney, Nova Scotia, Father John O'Reilly, an associate editor of the *New Freeman*, called upon local parishioners to pray for "the success of the arms of Great Britain and her allies," particularly "heroic" Belgium.[46] In Fredericton, Father F.L. Carney took to the stage at a recruitment meeting to say that, although the British Empire was peace-loving, all should contribute to the war effort because "the very existence of our country is at stake."[47] In concluding his speech, Carney did not mince words: "This war is the war of every person under the British flag and particularly Canada's war. If Britain goes down to defeat, Canada will be the first prize for Germany."[48] In the example of Carney, rank-and-file Irish Catholic clergy – whether Carney in Fredericton, Father J.P. Cummings in Walkerton, Ontario, Father J.A. Meehan in Morrisburg, Ontario, or O'Gorman in Ottawa – were never far from a recruiting platform during the phases of voluntary enlistment. They spoke; they invoked the Empire; and they became the visible presence of the Catholic Church's support for the Empire's war across all regions.[49]

O'Gorman's patriotic verve was notable. Born in Ottawa in 1884 and raised in St Patrick's parish,[50] O'Gorman was educated at the University of Ottawa (where he earned both a BA and a B.Phil.), at the Grand Seminaire in Montreal, and in Catholic institutes in Germany, Belgium, and Rome. He was a multilingual, nimble intellectual and one of the most energetic priests of his generation.[51] He would engage with local French Canadians in the struggle over bilingual schools in the Ottawa Separate School Board, and soon became noted as an unrepentant advocate for anglophone Catholic rights. His clashes with the French Canadian clergy and the Franco-Ontarian organ *Le Droit* became so heated that Archbishop Charles Hugh Gauthier banned all clerical combatants, including O'Gorman, from publishing or speaking on subjects related to Catholic schools.[52] When the war broke out, O'Gorman, from his pulpit at Blessed Sacrament, a parish he had founded, became a passionate advocate for material and military support for the Empire's war. After the joint pastoral letter issued by the archbishops of Quebec, Montreal, and Ottawa in October 1914, O'Gorman delivered a powerful sermon reiterating the points made by French Canada's leading metropolitans on the necessity of Catholics doing their duty as citizens of the British Empire, claiming that it was not just a patriotic but a religious duty for Catholics to "fight with the Empire." This facet of patriotism would become a constant theme in O'Gorman's rhetoric throughout the Great War. His views infuriated Henri Bourassa at *Le Devoir*, who wrote to Gauthier protesting the historical and theological errors perpetrated by a priest of his diocese. Gauthier permitted O'Gorman to respond – which he did, refuting Bourassa point by point on the historical issues and then accusing Bourassa of making a veiled attack on the Quebec Pastoral Letter and its authors.[53]

O'Gorman's tour de force on the war was yet to come, but once again he was mired in controversy with his bishop, who was trying to keep the peace and maintain the fragile linguistic balance in his archdiocese. In 1915, O'Gorman's pulpit and platform presentations on the war culminated in the preparation of a pamphlet based on his lectures and sermons: *Render unto Caesar*. Shortly after he delivered the final sermon on 2 January 1916, he submitted the text to Archbishop Gauthier for his imprimatur.[54] Gauthier refused, stating that the diocesan censor had found it to contain "unsound moral doctrine."[55] O'Gorman, undaunted, re-edited the text, which soon appeared with the title *Canadians to Arms!* under the imprimatur of Neil McNeil, archbishop of Toronto.[56]

O'Gorman's pamphlet began with an unquestioning affirmation of the British Empire: "An unprejudiced study of the relations between the Mother Country and Canada proves, that ... Britain has ever been the benefactor, and Canada the beneficiary."[57] O'Gorman then argued that no apology was needed "for a sermon on Canada's duty in the present crisis," and he proceeded to defend the Quebec bishops' support for the war, offering a veiled attack against his arch-nemesis, Henri Bourassa. Having expounded upon the duty of each Catholic to be loyal to his country, he took the next step, claiming that since "the safety of the State is the supreme law" it follows that "the able-bodied Canadian citizen who is not detained by a more urgent duty is in conscience bound to enlist."[58] To those he considered to be shirkers, he proclaimed that every "Catholic in that number will be a scandal to the Church."[59] Making good on this idea, he himself enlisted to serve in the Canadian Chaplain Service, just prior to the pamphlet's publication. O'Gorman's unequivocal message to serve King and country received great praise from both the *Catholic Register* and the *Catholic Record*.[60] The secular *Canadian Annual Review* for 1916 highlighted his address and his subsequent challenge to the Knights of Columbus that, should members fail in their patriotic duty, they should be expelled from the order, or the name "Knights" be dropped from the organization.[61] Given O'Gorman's tone and categorical denunciation of men who would shirk their duty, it is understandable why Archbishop Gauthier balked at this Irish Catholic priest's hymn to Empire. The majority of Gauthier's flock were French Canadian, and many lived in the eastern portions of the diocese on the Quebec side of the Ottawa River, where the arguments of Bourassa, not O'Gorman, held sway.

The heavy emphasis on joining the fight because of imperial duty was not unique to Canada's Irish Catholics. The imperialist statements made by bishops, clergy, politicians, and Catholic newspapermen were very much in keeping with the general response by journalists in English Canada in the first years of the war. According to Matt Bray's study of English-language dailies in Canada, only two newspapers, the Toronto *Globe*, and the *Manitoba Free Press*, took the position that the war was Canada's war and was being fought in Canada's own right for liberty and democracy.[62] Although, as it has been noted, Irish Canadian Catholics did recognize Canada's duty to support the war effort, in the first two years of the war this duty was almost always expressed within the context of Empire and Canada's obligations as a British dominion.[63] As the war dragged on, the Irish Catholic press and some leaders began to place more emphasis on Canada's obligation to the war, irrespective of membership in the Empire. With the admission of Sir Robert Borden into the Imperial War Cabinet[64] and the sacrifice of Canadians at St Julien in the Second Battle of Ypres in April 1915, there appeared to be a new exploration of Canada's duty to fight the war. In the wake of the Easter Rising in Dublin in April 1916, this sense of a specific Canadian obligation may have been heightened by the way in which Irish Catholic leaders and pundits held up Canadian autonomy as the model for Irish Home Rule. The search for a flexible imperial solution to the Irish question may have helped Irish Catholic Canadians develop a clearer sense of Canada's autonomous place in the Empire and a place that carried with others a responsibility for maintaining liberty in the world.

There was only one exception to the unwavering imperial rhetoric among Canada's English-language Catholic papers in the early stages of the war. The *Catholic Record*, with its ties to the Liberal party still intact, appeared to reassess Canada's role in the world and in the Empire. In February 1915, even before the 1st Canadian Division saw action in Belgium, the Liberal editors at the *Record* were musing about how the war might affect Canada's identity on the international stage:

> Canada is now at the parting of the ways ... Either we set up for ourselves as a self-governing nation in reality, or we enter into a full partnership with a partner's rights and duties as responsibilities. This we take to be the great political question confronting Canadians in the very near future. One need not be an "Imperialist" in any sense of the word, good or bad, to look upon it as the most vital political questions since Confederation ... The war has not changed our relations to the Empire; it has only revealed in a striking manner how anomalous they are.[65]

Certainly, staff at the *Record* would have been well aware of Borden's and Sam Hughes' battles with the British military authorities to retain the independence of the Canadian battalions, the principle of Canadian officers commanding Canadian troops, and the distinctiveness of practices in branches such as the Canadian Chaplaincy Service. In the process, a distinction was being made between fighting alongside the Empire as a subordinate and as an ally, and it appeared that the *Record* aspired to the latter, knowing full well that the cost of materials and men by Canada required a full voice at the table of the Empire. No other Catholic newspapers appeared to have arrived at these hypotheses so early in the war. As the war dragged on, however, suggestions that Canada might be fighting as an ally grew among some of the staff at the *Record*'s competing Catholic weeklies.

Perhaps the second most notable reason articulated by Irish Canadian Catholics for going to war was the religious imperative to defend Christian principles. Indeed, from the onset of the war, the Catholic bishops and clergy made regular appeals to Catholics for prayers and novenas for world peace. This appeal emanated from Pope Pius X himself, whose death shortly after the war's declaration was popularly blamed on his sorrow that he had failed to mediate a peace between the great imperial powers.[66] Prayers for peace were common from the pulpit across Catholic Canada,[67] but added to this were the spiritual terms in which priests and bishops framed a Christian's duty to go to war. First, the war was caused by humanity's sinfulness and abandonment of the Divine law; with this in mind, pastors and pundits described the struggle as a defensive war of the Christian community against Germany. Second, in this righteous war, Christians must be prepared to make sacrifices. One who dies while fighting a just war might be considered a martyr. Third, because patriotism was a Christian virtue, Christian men ought not to fail in their duty to defend the Empire.

This view of the war as the product of sin became widely articulated in Catholic circles by commentators ranging from parish priests to student editors and general readers. Father Matthew Whelan at St Patrick's in Ottawa considered the outbreak of war to be God's chastisement of humankind for turning away from Him.[68] For Jesuit Father William Drummond in Edmonton, the war was another example of human suffering and a means of teaching every person that the road to heaven is filled with trials and tribulations.[69] Such thoughts were echoed in the 1915 issue of the *Ontario Catholic Yearbook*, prepared by the Paulist Fathers in Toronto, which reprinted the *Catholic World*'s view that "[i]f the habitual neglect of His law begets injustice and war upon the earth, it is, we say, blasphemy to attribute the result to God. War and its horrors are the direct outcome of man's efforts and plans. That the just may be attacked and compelled to suffer, is due to the fact that there exist those who are unjust."[70] In Toronto, Marjorie Power, editor of *St Joseph's Lilies*, the student publication of St Joseph's Academy (secondary school), agreed in principle, observing that war emerged from the nature of man, whom she described as a "fighting animal and vicious." An advocate for peace, the young Power was not beyond pinpointing the injustice as caused directly by the Serb who killed Archduke Franz Ferdinand and the "years of hatred and injustice and cruelty between the contestants."[71] A letter-writer to the Antigonish *Casket* would agree with other commentators that sin lay at the root of the war, but he attributed some responsibility to the world's Protestants, who had failed to heed the Pope's invitation to unite for peace.[72]

As consensus about war's origin in sin became established, the next step was to pinpoint why the chief sinner, Germany, had to be stopped. The Catholic position was nuanced in that clerics and lay leaders did not condemn the German people outright, nor did they vilify them with dehumanizing adjectives or ethnic pejoratives. Catholic leaders knew well that not all Germans were to blame and that there were significant German Catholic populations in Saskatchewan, southwestern Ontario, and in the Upper Ottawa valley that need not be alienated, nor be left exposed to harassment from ultra-patriots. Quite clearly, the Catholic press and clerics made clear distinctions between German leaders and their militarism, who were responsible for the war, and the German people, who were oppressed by their leaders. Editors at the *Canadian Freeman* in Kingston made their view clear within days of the declaration of war that Germany had been the aggressor, as it had been in Morocco and South Africa before the war. "There can be no peace in Europe," they argued, "no rest until this madman is deposed and his Empire dismembered."[73] Striking a similar note, Archbishop Timothy Casey in Vancouver regarded the elimination of German autocracy, which had its roots in the "blood and iron" policies of Otto Von Bismarck in the nineteenth century, only to be refined by Kaiser Wilhelm, as the greatest danger to the world.[74] Likewise, when greeting the New Year in January 1915, the *Catholic Record* made clear this distinction when its editors announced: "We would free the German people, free Europe from the tyranny of German militarism."[75] The agents of the latter were described as vandals who had laid "poor" Belgium waste and dared to impose its *Kultur* on the world to replace Christianity. Germany must be defeated – yet, as the *Record* cautioned, that blatant militarism ought not to be answered with even greater militarism. The war was to be fought, but "the way to peace is through humility and penance."[76] Such was the Christian way to answer German militarism.

The rejection of German *Kultur* was made explicit by both Bishop Fallon, who kept a watchful eye on the *Record*, which was located in his diocese, and by Father O'Gorman in Ottawa. Both Fallon and O'Gorman had been students in German universities before the war and regarded themselves as experts on the conduct of German teachers and the flawed ideas that were artificially bound together in the intellectual straw man referred to as *Kultur.* In the first few weeks of the war Fallon reflected on his student days in Germany; as he told an audience in London, "The war comes as no surprise to me. Twenty-not [sic.] years ago I went to school in Germany and even then the young men of the nation were filled with war fury. They were determined that the British Empire should go down."[77] He would repeat these words to the local councils of the Knights of Columbus within the month, adding that Germany could be defeated only by the "British Empire which guaranteed the liberties of all."[78] Perhaps Fallon's greatest fear concerned the *Kultur* that underlay German militarism, a force that he described as having been influential on the training of Canadian and American professors. *Kultur* included a misshaped theology resembling the modernist heresies that had been condemned by Pope Pius X in the years before the war. German professors, according to Fallon, had taught that "Jesus was a myth, a fakir, a lunatic, and that of the whole Bible there was not one page that had not been annulled by German universities."[79] Similarly, O'Gorman used his own experience as a student to describe *Kultur* as "un-Christian," but pointed out that the Catholics of Germany and many of its Protestants had battled against the imposition of such ideas. Therefore, remarked O'Gorman, on the Christian principle of hating the sin while loving the sinner, Germany must be defeated, but the German people must not be annihilated. He asked his listeners and readers to pray for Germany's conversion.[80] For its part, the *Canadian Freeman* advocated preventative precautions, advising that Canadian graduate and medical students refrain from continuing their education in Germany and remain in Canada.[81]

The question still remains, however, as to whether such finely tuned assessments of German philosophy, militarism, and *Kultur* as agents of the war were received by rank and file Irish Catholics and their parish priests. Preliminary investigations appear to confirm that most Canadian Catholics of Irish birth or descent believed the danger of German militarism, but there is only fragmentary evidence to suggest that they understood the *Kultur* arguments that raised the objective of defeating Germany to a higher philosophical or theological plane. In 1917, young Beauford Nally, a student at St Ann's Catholic School in Hamilton, Ontario, won the Gold Medal from the local Canadian Club for his essay "In Freedom's Cause." In it Nally argued that "[i]n a word, we are fighting for the rights of human liberty – a desire for which Almighty God has infused into the soul of every man, and which has been usurped by a monster who places himself on par with his Creator, and who … has decreed that liberty of life and conscience must be subordinated to militarism."[82] Nally reiterates what several clergy and newspaper men were saying: that the Kaiser and his Germany must be brought down by the Empire and the principles for which it stands. It is impossible to know whether this Catholic school student had arrived at these conclusions by absorbing them at home, or in the Catholic school classroom in the new war-related curriculum,[83] or through his own independent reading. *St Joseph's Lilies* published several essays on the war, religion, and morality by F.B. Fenton, a returned veteran who had been wounded at Givenchy. Fenton referred to the war as a means of vanquishing Satan and claimed that the greater the religious conviction of those who fight the enemy, the greater the morale.[84] Earlier he had written that it was a moral imperative to overthrow "the dominion of mere militarism, as embodied by Teutonism."[85] Parish priests continued to vilify Prussian militarism throughout the war, particularly when standing on the recruiting platform. As late as September 1916, when making the final enlistment push for the 199th Battalion Irish Rangers in Montreal, Father John Brophy talked about there being "nothing sacred to a German." In perhaps one of the most outrageous condemnations of Germans by a Roman Catholic priest in Canada during the war, Brophy[86] proclaimed: "This is a war of the German people, and behind it every man, woman and child in Germany, ready to back up and fight for their century-old idea of establishing military domination of the world."[87] There was no nuance here, just the blunt observations of the necessity to defeat the German aggressor and its "military junta."[88]

Having identified the justice of the cause, the depravity of the Kaiser, and the defensive nature of the Empire's wars, Catholic clerics unpacked a theology of sacrifice that would provide a spiritual dimension, if not a Divine justification, to enlist in the fight. In the first weeks of the war, Monsignor Burke at the *Register* had stated: "The God of Armies is great and wonderful in His dispensations." He would later add that Christ would crown the "military valour" of a soldier who died in the just cause.[89] The *Register* also cited Cardinal Desiré Mercier of Malines, Belgium, who claimed that "Christ assures the safety of that man's soul" who dies in military valour.[90] Michael Spratt, the archbishop of Kingston, developed the notion of sacrifice further during his second Lenten pastoral letter of the war, which coincided with a huge push in voluntary recruitment. While attempting to pull the young men of their diocese from their pews and send them to the CEF, Spratt wrapped enlistment in a spirituality of sacrifice:

> The Man, who, from supernatural motives, leaves house or brethren, or sisters, or father, or mother, or wife, or children, or lands, and goes into a far off country, to offer himself a victim for immolation upon the altar of his country, in defense of the weak and in behalf of his fellow men, without doubt acquires the title to the promised hundred-fold and life everlasting. This is the supreme act of self-denial and the plenitude of the virtue of penance.[91]

Both Spratt and Burke constructed an analogy of *imitatio Christi*, comparing the sacrifice of Christ for the sins of humankind and the sacrifice made on the battlefield for the just cause. One knows little more of Spratt's means of unpacking this theology or how far he would carry the analogy. Almost all of his papers were burned after his death in 1938.

One of the clearest and most widely publicized theological justifications for Catholic participation in the war was included in Father O'Gorman's *Canadians to Arms!* Employing his advanced theological training, O'Gorman devoted one section of his treatise to the issue of sacrifice and detailed Spratt's suggestion that the soldier who takes up the cause is imitating Christ:

> Enlisting for Overseas Service means a sacrifice. This very fact should be an additional motive to urge us on: for there is nothing so essentially Christian as sacrifice. Every man who is about to enlist should count the cost of the sacrifice and see whether he have the wherewith to complete it. Only he loves his neighbor, who is willing when necessary to lay down his life for him. Without obedience and without love, there is no Christianity. 'For the definition of Christianity is the imitation of Christ.[92]

O'Gorman outlined three levels of "imitation" under such circumstances: in the first, sacrifice is lovingly undertaken when it is one's duty; in the second, sacrifice is indifferent to pleasure or suffering in carrying out the will of God; in the third and most perfect form of sacrifice, men enlist despite all "privations and sufferings" and risk their lives for love of God and neighbour. Citing examples from both history and Biblical texts relating to the Maccabean rebels of the second century BCE, O'Gorman brought theological muscle to his call for Canadians to do their duty. Although his own archbishop declined to endorse anything in the pamphlet, Neil McNeil, himself an accomplished academic and former president of St Francis Xavier University, gave O'Gorman his approval.

A final element of the Catholic spirituality revealed by the onset of the war involved multiple expressions regarding the Catholic virtue of patriotism. Numerous clergy, publishers, and politicians all trumpeted the fact that Catholics would by definition be patriotic. When citing Bishop M.F. Power of St George's, Newfoundland, the *New Freeman* gave front-page attention to his contention that "[f]aith and love of Fatherland are twin virtues, that Catholicism and Patriotism – love of God and love of Country – cannot be separated."[93] This point was drilled home many times and, as in the *Casket* in 1915, was used to remind non-Catholics that patriotism was a Catholic principle and that Catholics would be second to none in doing their duty during the current crisis.[94] In Ottawa, O'Gorman made similar associations between loyalty, patriotism, and faith, as did Irish-born Father Thomas O'Donnell in Toronto.[95]

In time, the coupling of the virtue of patriotism with the Catholic faith would allow for Irish and Scottish Catholic Canadians to extricate themselves from guilt by association if Catholics elsewhere in Canada, Australia, America, or Europe opposed some aspect of the war. The fact that patriotism flowed from Catholic thought itself, and was not contingent on language, culture, or partisanship, would allow Irish Catholic leaders to pinpoint what might be "racial" arguments against the war, but not "Catholic" arguments. Thus, the tripartite theological justification was complete: the war was fought in defense against evil; Christians are called to imitate Christ and serve their suffering neighbour; and patriotism is a virtue. Even if political and imperial arguments for the war became problematic, Irish Catholics might still return to spiritual principles that lifted participation in the Great War to a higher plane.

Complementary to spiritual ideas of self-sacrifice and uplifting the oppressed was the Irish Catholic appreciation of those for whom they would be making themselves martyrs. Catholic leaders were able to rouse support for the war effort by putting forward the case of tiny Belgium, whose neutrality had been violated and whose people were oppressed by the Kaiser's army. For Catholics in Canada, Belgium was presented not only as violated and spoiled by war, but as a Catholic country whose pluck and determination against a much larger aggressor was worthy of praise and defence. The speech of Father John O'Reilly in Sydney, Nova Scotia, in January 1915, typified the Irish Catholic clerical response to the Belgian situation, beginning with the acknowledgement that Prussian militarism caused the war and Belgium was the victim. The *New Freeman* described O'Reilly's oration to the potential recruits:

> He eulogized the noble Belgians for their heroic defence, and declared that King Albert, who is sharing the fortunes of his soldiers on the field and in the trenches, will go down in history as Albert the Great. He will be in a class with Brian of Ireland and Bruce of Scotland. Belgian resistance to the German military machine was perhaps the most noble sacrifice in all the world's history.[96]

Despite the hyperbole of dramatic speeches, the respect, admiration, and pity heaped on the Belgians by Canadian Catholics for the purposes of rousing the Catholic population to war should not to be underestimated. References to Belgian gallantry and "martyrdom" laced the speeches of bishops, priests, and politicians, and became common in the columns of Catholic editors across the country. In Winnipeg, the *Northwest Review* described the "revolting cruelty" of the German invaders" that made "civilized humanity" shudder.[97] Archbishop McNeil of Toronto went so far as to announce: "I am prepared to defend the cause of right, the cause of Britain and Belgium, with my life."[98]

One tangible means of supporting the Belgian cause was through monetary donations to the Belgian Relief Fund. Across Canada, bishops and politicians of all religions and party colours campaigned for Belgian relief. In Antigonish, Bishop James Morrison issued a circular advocating Catholic generosity in coming to Belgium's relief, while in Peterborough, Ontario, Bishop Michael O'Brien advised local Catholics to make their donations to Belgium through the local Children's Aid Society.[99] The Belgian Relief effort spanned Catholic Canada including the Prairie West: St Mary's Academy in Winnipeg raised funds for Belgium, as did Catholic parishes in Saskatoon.[100] The press republished the appeals made by Cardinal Mercier, the senior Belgian prelate and Catholic philosopher who, in exile from his diocese of Malines, was touring allied Europe in search of funds to assist the homeless and hungry refugees from the German occupied zone. Mercier became a popular figure among Catholics in Allied Nations. He symbolized the suffering of the Belgian people at the hands of Germany, and therein the oppression of Catholics in Germany's occupied territories.[101] Canada's Catholics watched in horror as Belgians made sacrifices for their faith and freedom, of which the words and deeds of travelling Cardinal Mercier were a constant reminder. Mercier's appeals and his reprinted pastoral letter on patriotism were directed right at the heart of the Catholic world, not only as a means of raising funds but in an effort to provide a practical, personal application of a Catholic theology that upholds the virtue of patriotism. According to the *Catholic Record*, Mercier was "the patriot who consciously [gave] his life for his country, by that very act secure[d] the salvation of his soul."[102] In Mercier, the sacrifice of Catholic Belgium became not only something that inspired Canadian Catholics to charity, but was also a demonstration to Canadian Catholics of how they must exercise the same virtue in the hope of winning the war. Mercier was not unaware of the Canadian efforts for Belgian relief, and sometimes acknowledged Catholic generosity with personal letters to individual bishops. Addressing Bishop O'Brien of Peterborough, Mercier wrote: "Racial affinities and a common faith further deepened their sympathy for our cause."[103]

In a similar fashion, as Belgium became symbolic of Catholic patriotism and duty, Irish Catholic Canadian leaders also hoped that the example of Ireland in the war would inspire the same sense of duty among the Canadian faithful. The press and the prelates made it well known that the Irish Volunteers under parliamentary leader John Redmond were recruiting in vast numbers to the British army.[104] Furthermore, in the common cause against Germany, Irish Catholics and Protestant Unionists set aside their differences, averted civil war, and joined the British Expeditionary Force. Once again, it was Bishop Fallon who pointed out this rapprochement eloquently when he spoke to the Middlesex Patriotic Fund, meeting at the London Masonic Temple, where normally a Catholic prelate would never set foot:

> We have had our differences [in Ireland] in the past, and it was said that we were on the verge of civil war, but when Germany spoke, Irish Nationalist and Unionist alike said "Take away your troops from our shores, and we together will defend here." It has been said that Britain's difficulty was Ireland's opportunity, and it has been, because it gave Ireland a chance to show what she thought of the British Empire.[105]

Some papers could not help but comment on the irony of the Unionists under Sir Edward Carson, who since 1913 had purchased 20,000 Mauser rifles and two million rounds of ammunition[106] from the German militarists for the Ulster Volunteer Force and were now marshalling themselves against the Kaiser in the common defense of the Empire.[107] English-language Catholic newspapers and bishops frequently offered examples of Irish recruitment, service on the battlefield, and the stirring patriotic oratory of Redmond, in an effort to goad Canada's Irish to similar action.[108] Ireland, so leaders conjectured, had made a decision to join the Empire in securing the rights of small nations to be free, in return for the British government's pledge that Ireland would join Canada, Australia, and New Zealand as a self-governing part of the Empire when the war was won. Hopefully, for Canadian Catholic leaders, the example of Ireland would be further incentive to join the war effort.

Ordinary Catholic citizens appeared to respond to the call of their leaders to win the war in a variety of ways. One manifestation of support for the war and obedience to Church leaders was the high level of Irish Catholic recruitment, which will be discussed at length in the next chapter. For those who were ineligible to enlist, or who were employed in meaningful and essential industries in support of Canada's growing military machine, there were ways in which the war could be supported at home. One of the earliest and most tangible forms of such support was to contribute to the Canadian Patriotic Fund, which was designed to assist the families of the men who had enlisted in the CEF. Once again, the Catholic bishops took the lead in promoting the Fund, and the English-language Catholic weeklies followed suit. In Toronto, Archbishop Neil McNeil backed up his own circular appealing for donations to the Patriotic Fund with a personal pledge of $5,000.[109] To ensure that his parish priests also set an example, he mandated that each pastor would donate $40 every six months until each had donated $200 to the Fund. McNeil argued that "all the people of Toronto watch us to see whether our professions of patriotism are genuine ... let us show the public that we mean what we say."[110]

McNeil's request brought out the best in Toronto's Catholic community, and not just the Irish: substantial donations came from the Maronite-Syrian Catholic community and the Italian National Club.[111] Alderman John O'Neill and brewer Eugene O'Keefe, one of the leading Irish Catholic philanthropists in the city, offered $1000 each, immediately after the distribution of McNeil's circular.[112] The clergy took the lead elsewhere in Canada, notably the dioceses of London, Peterborough, Kingston, Ottawa, Montreal, Quebec, Nicolet, Trois Rivières, Sherbrooke, and Antigonish, while newspapers published full-page advertisements soliciting donations to the fund.[113] In Whitby, Ontario, local parish priest Father William Joseph Ryan sat on the finance committee for the local Patriotic Fund.[114] Lists of donors across the country read very much like the one in Walkerton, Ontario, where Catholics and non-Catholics gave what they could to the cause. For brothers Jack and Andrew O'Neill, farmers in Brant Township near Walkerton, that amount was three dollars (a value of $63.60 in 2015).[115] As for most Catholic Canadians, any donation, however modest, was an affirmation of support for the country in its time of need.[116]

Rank-and-file Catholics had many financial options at their disposal to support the war effort. In addition to the Canadian Patriotic Fund and the Belgian Relief Fund, Catholics donated to the Red Cross and the Polish Relief Fund, and purchased Victory Bonds from the federal government to assist in underwriting the costs of the war.[117] Local churches also made distinctive contributions to funds that appealed to the culture, occupation, or location of these Catholic communities. In Prince Edward Island, for example, Bishop Henry Joseph O'Leary spoke eloquently when assisting in recruiting efforts and promoting local Catholics to donate to the British Sailor's Relief Fund.[118] The Catholics of the Diocese of Pembroke, where there was a multicultural Catholic population, made pointed efforts to relieve the misery of the Polish people whose lands, not yet a country, had been occupied and ravaged by German, Austrian, and Russian armies. This financial campaign resonated in the Madawaska Valley, where there were hundreds of descendants of the Kaszub Poles who had immigrated there from the shores of the Baltic Sea as early as the 1850s.[119] In Hamilton, Catholics often used the traditional charitable agency, the St Vincent de Paul Society, to channel funds into war-related charitable projects.[120] At St John's Parish in east Toronto, parishioners formed their own "Soldiers Aid" society to send money directly to local men who were fighting overseas.[121] In a different type of donation, the Congregation of the Sisters of St Joseph, in Toronto, used the services of the Women's Patriotic League to send Christmas gifts to "our brave soldiers" overseas and offered concerts for soldiers invaliding in the city.[122] Thus, while Catholics participated in national fundraising efforts to support the war effort, they also devised projects that gave their war contributions particular relevance to local interests.

These local diocesan and parish-based initiatives to support the war effort were not simply financial in nature. Parishioners, particularly women, many of whom had husbands or sons in the CEF, formed a variety of committees to provide material aid to the CEF. In Antigonish, Nova Scotia, Catholic women of Irish and Scottish descent joined with local Protestant women in the Auxiliary of the Antigonish Red Cross. In 1917 alone, they knitted 1,975 pairs of socks and 26 suits of pajamas.[123] In the west end of Toronto, the women of St

Helen's Parish formed the St Helen's Women's Patriotic League. This parish-based service society was a complement to the hundreds of young men who had left the parish to fight in the CEF. The group met every Thursday at St Helen's Catholic school and commenced sewing, knitting, and raising funds for the purchase of wool for knitted goods and cotton for socks and shirts. Similar committees were established at St Mary's Parish and at Our Lady of Lourdes Parish, where Patriotic Association Secretary Eleanor Moore reported that the women knitted 662 pairs of socks in 1916–17.[124] In 1916, Toronto's Rosary Hall, a Catholic hostel for single working women, prepared 1,975 pieces of clothing for the Belgian Relief, 2,424 "comforts" for soldiers, 2,800 pairs of socks, 35,072 surgical supplies, and $1,346 in cash for the war effort.[125] Such local efforts were typical across Catholic Canada.[126] In Pembroke, for example, newly appointed bishop Patrick Ryan insisted that, because of the war, no money be channelled into his episcopal installation. Money was needed elsewhere.[127] Fraternal benevolent associations like the Knights of Columbus offered to maintain life insurance policies for any members who enlisted.[128] In Brandon, Manitoba, the State Convention of the Knights in Saskatchewan and Manitoba pledged funds for Polish relief and assistance with CEF recruitment drives. Similar support for the war effort was offered by the Knights in New Brunswick and Toronto.[129]

While many of these local initiatives, undertaken within the "limina" of the Catholic community, might have gone unnoticed by the general public, there were two unmistakable public signs that local Irish Catholics were enthusiastically supporting the imperial war effort. Concert suppers and recruiting meetings were forums whose attendees often came from a wider catchment area than the parish, in terms of both geography and religious affiliation. As with the concert held by the Sisters of St Joseph in Toronto, parishes across the country held public dinners and concerts to raise funds, entertain the troops, and assist wounded soldiers in their rehabilitation into Canadian life. In her journals for 1915, Ottawa Catholic socialite Ethel Chadwick reflected on one "Soldiers' Supper" held at St Patrick's Hall, adjacent to the parish of the same name in centretown Ottawa. Chadwick was a parishioner at St Joseph's in Sandy Hill, to the east of Parliament Hill and part of the neighbourhood where notables such as Sir Wilfrid Laurier resided. Chadwick's parish had a distinguished record of recruitment to the CEF that included her brother Frank and friends Jack Woods, Alex Farer, and Charles and Frank McGee. Frank McGee was a national celebrity as an all-star hockey player for the Ottawa Silver Seven; his record for number of goals in a Stanley Cup game has never been replicated. For Ethel's part, she wrote voluminously to her friends and brother, took part in special Masses for the intentions of the war, and worked with the local Red Cross. The Soldiers' Supper on 8 June 1915 drew huge crowds for the support of the war effort, including six cars of soldiers from the Rockliffe Military Base, Charles J. Doherty (the minister of justice), Charles Fitzpatrick (chief justice of the Supreme Court), and numerous officers of all denominations. Catholic priests and politicians spoke, and Chadwick hailed the event a great success.[130] Events like this one reaffirmed for Catholics themselves the importance of working to win the war on the home front and maintaining morale, but also showcased to the non-Catholic community the front-and-centre patriotism of the Catholic Church, particularly its members of Irish descent.

A second public affirmation of popular support for the war was the visible presence of Catholics, particularly clergy, at recruiting rallies. The appearances of Father John Burke and Bishop LeBlanc at rallies at the Imperial Theatre in Saint John, for instance, were not isolated examples either locally or nationally. Even Catholic businessman could be found making public gestures of patriotism. Because of the outspoken support for the war effort by bishops in English Canada, priests felt liberated to show up on the recruiting platform to deliver a mixture of imperialist rhetoric and Christian theology. Whether the meetings were in Ste Anne-des-Chênes, Manitoba, or Renfrew, Ontario, or in Toronto or Saint John, the Church made its presence seen and its word felt. Given the sometimes troubled history between Christian denominations in Canada, particularly between Irish Catholics and the Loyal Orange Lodge, this was a prudent policy on the part of the Catholic Church.[131] In Vancouver, millionaire Patrick Burns made a huge cash donation, the largest in this particular case, to help underwrite the expenses of the Princess Patricia's Canadian Light Infantry, the first Canadian unit to see action with the British Expeditionary Force.[132] It was one thing to support the war, but it was as important for the Catholic Church to be seen, and seen often, undertaking patriotic exercises.

There were Catholic voices, however, that were, allegedly or overtly, firmly against the war effort. These voices were few and faint amid the roar to support the Empire, free Belgium, and destroy Prussian militarism and German *Kultur.* Early in the war, the Canadian government feared incursions of anti-British Irish, Austrian, and German Americans, whose sympathetic position toward the central powers might provoke acts of sabotage on the Welland Canal, border towns, railways, bridges, and other key communications and military targets. As has been demonstrated in chapter 1, a minor act of sabotage was committed by Irish American physical force nationalists on the Welland Canal during the Boer War. The Boer War incident conjured up fears of Fenian-type raids and reminiscences of the Fenian invasion at Ridgeway on the Niagara peninsula in 1866 in the minds of nervous militia officials.[133] During the war, however, Canada's Irish Catholics demanded that the anti-British and pro-German propaganda in publications such as the *American Hibernian* and *Irish World* be blocked from distribution in Canada.[134] As for actual border attacks, the Catholic press reported on isolated incidents, such as the capture of German spies at Kingston's Fort Henry, or an alleged German attempt to destroy the CPR bridge on the St Croix River between New Brunswick and Maine, but no Catholics were ever implicated in the failed mission.[135] During the war, allegations were made that several priests, including five in the diocese of Victoria, were pro-German, and that several seminarians at St Augustine's in Toronto were "disloyal," but these stories never gained much traction, likely because the bishops in both dioceses, Alexander MacDonald and Neil McNeil, respectively, were such ardent supporters of the Canadian and imperial war effort.[136] Perhaps, aside from the comments made by Ukrainian Catholic Eparch Nykyta Budka before the war and the subsequent incarceration of some "enemy aliens" from among his flock (see chapter 4), Catholics generally presented no public resistance to the war effort. Notable by their silence were any Irish Catholics harbouring extremist views with regard to the liberation of Ireland. If they existed in Canada – and no doubt there were some members of the Irish Republican Brotherhood – they remained remarkably silent during the first eighteen months of the war.

Perhaps the greatest challenge facing Canada's Irish Catholics and their leaders, however, was the maintenance of solidarity with French Canadian Catholics, the majority partner in Canada's Catholic Church. As we have seen, when war was declared in 1914 all of Canada's Catholic bishops, regardless of language, were supportive of the imperial war effort.[137] Despite the differences between the major linguistic groups within the Church, there was a great show of solidarity in the early months of the war. The English-language Catholic press reported positively on the work of the bishops on behalf of the war effort, and particular note was taken of French-Canadian recruitment to the CEF.[138] Even the outspoken French Canadian nationalist Henri Bourassa received fair reporting on his support for a Canadian contribution to the European struggle.[139] The *Northwest Review* defended his right to free speech, even though it might not agree with him.[140] The *Casket* went so far as to publicly defend Bourassa for statements he made questioning the extent of Canada's contributions to the war effort. Refuting the Orange mayor of Toronto, Horatio Hocken, and others who essentially branded Bourassa at traitor, the *Casket*'s editor, Michael Donovan, carefully distanced his paper from Bourassa's argument while hammering away at his fire-breathing detractors: "It is beyond question that Canada shares the Empire's peril," Donovan corrected Bourassa. "This is, therefore, not to balance constitutional accounts with Great Britain; nor to do or say anything that might even indirectly prevent one single recruit from volunteering his services for the allies." Once having crafted this polite rebuttal, the paper then took Hocken, *Globe* editor John S. Willison, and company to task for their support of Sir Edward Carson's near-rebellion in Ulster just months before. Bourassa, Donovan claimed, was no traitor; in fact, he continued, "Henri Bourassa is worth a thousand such hypocrites to the citizenship of their country."[141]

Privately, however, some Catholic leaders were not impressed by Bourassa's public stance on the war or his criticism of the Quebec bishops' pastoral letter and its claims that it was the historic position of the Church to defend the Empire. While the anglophone Catholic media, clergy, and bishops were trying to maintain the Irish–French Catholic solidarity publicly, Bourassa was being attacked behind the scenes in letters that never saw the light of day, lest scandal erupt. Archbishop McNeil lambasted Bourassa for his disrespectful stance toward the Quebec bishops and defended England's right to ask for Canadian assistance in the war. Pulling no punches, McNeil set the record straight in terms of the importance of unity:

> Canada is a vast country and we [bishops] could not meet for the purpose of issuing a collective letter; but we are at one with the

> Bishops of Quebec in patriotism and in the advice given to our people in regard to the war. By means of your journal, le Devoir, you have raised a barrier between the Province of Quebec and the other Provinces of Canada; but you cannot succeed in building a barrier between the Bishops of Quebec and the Bishops of Canada. On the contrary, we are grateful to them for having forestalled the danger by which your policy threatened the national unity of Canada.[142]

Bourassa also engaged in a heated behind-the-scenes exchange with Father O'Gorman, concerning whose sermons on the war Bourassa protested to Charles Gauthier, O'Gorman's bishop in Ottawa. Having received Bourassa's critique from Gauthier, O'Gorman, in his typical style, dissected the letter point by point and returned a complete refutation to the Montreal editor. In reporting back to Gauthier, O'Gorman scoffed "His final word to the bishops is as stupid a piece of anticlerical nationalism as the editor of *Le Devoir* has ever penned."[143]

The anglophone Catholic public defence of Bourassa and his French Canadian nationalist allies, however, did not last long into 1915. As Bourassa's oppositional voice became sharper on issues such as recruitment, the bishops' support for the war, and whether this was actually Canada's war, Irish Catholic Canadian leaders and their newspapers had to carefully nuance their criticism of the French Canadian politician, lest the Church be viewed by the public at large as divided at a time of national crisis. Bishops and editors had to devise defences to the critique of Catholic Quebec "shirking its duties" by making certain their responses carefully extricated the bishops and clergy from the rhetoric and actions of the French Canadian nationalists, while carefully identifying the problems arising in Quebec as not emerging from anything particularly Catholic, but, rather, as by-products of excited expressions rooted in language and culture or, as described at the time, race. In Toronto, having earlier labelled Bourassa as a traitor,[144] editors at the *Catholic Register* did not mince words: "It is most gratifying to observe that the madness of two or three megalomaniacs among the Nationalist party in Quebec is being repudiated by their fellow Canadians of French origin."[145] In the same breath, Quebec's bishops were praised for their support of the war effort. The once nuanced *Casket* pulled off its gloves and refused to defend Bourassa any longer: "Mr. Bourassa is not Quebec and *Le Devoir* is not the journalism of Quebec."[146] The paper was equally critical of nationalist politician Armand Lavergne, who believed Canada had no duty to participate in any war in which she had no say.[147] The paper was quick to point out that Lavergne's ideas were rejected publicly by such notable French Canadians as Wilfrid Laurier, Adolphe Lemieux, and Louis-Alexandre Taschereau, and by senators J.P.B. Casgrain, Napoléon Belcourt, and Raoul Dandurand.[148] Thus the *Casket* exemplified the shifting English-speaking Catholic position, which entailed criticizing the Bourassa nationalists while defending the efforts of the Church in Quebec and of, in their estimation, the majority of Quebec's population.

To save Catholic unity while criticising Bourassa, the anglophone Catholic Press continued to call attention to the patriotic actions of the Quebec bishops and even the recruitment of French Canadians to the CEF. Shortly after the publication of the Quebec bishops' pastoral letter endorsing the imperial war effort, the *Casket* made a point of highlighting the glowing praise of the bishops' position offered by the Duke of Connaught, Governor General of Canada.[149] Similarly, the patriotic speeches of Archbishop Paul Bruchési were translated and quoted verbatim in several Catholic newspapers. Of particular note was the praise given by the *Canadian Freeman*, a publication sometimes noted for its salty critiques of British policy, to an address delivered by Bruchési at Laval University on the subject of Canadian obligations to the British Crown:

> It is the solemn duty of every Canadian citizen, to the utmost limit of his force, to stand side-by-side with the Motherland in her heroic effort to crush the tyrant who wishes to trample small nations and states beneath his iron heel. What fate would be ours if the Germans obtained a foothold here? Were Great Britain defeated, Germany would secure domination on the St Lawrence … French Canadian countrymen, I for one, do not want to be a German citizen.[150]

The speech was an indisputable refutation of Bourassa's ongoing argument that Canada was not under German threat. Bruchési's oration was also quoted on the front page of the *New Freeman* and referenced in O'Gorman's well-known pamphlet *Canadians to Arms!*[151] For its part, the *Northwest Review* analysed Quebec recruiting and argued that, as a primarily rural province, much like parts of Prince Edward Island and Ontario, Quebec was naturally experiencing slow recruitment. The paper added that local military authorities had cited Catholic priests as having been "at our disposal" and that they "have taken an actual part in our recruiting meetings held in their parishes."[152] The strategy of criticizing the opinions of Bourassa and the nationalists as contrary to the loyalty of the Catholic Church in Quebec emerged as the unofficial primary strategy of Catholic clergy and editors to maintain a semblance of Catholic unity in Canada while competing factions with extreme positions were pushing the nation toward disunity and, potentially, civil strife.

Less is known about how rank and file Irish Catholics saw the French Canadian question regarding the war. At least one student commentator, James Day, writing in *St Joseph's Lilies*, offered an olive branch to counter what he regarded as "an insidious jealousy … springing up in some quarters between the British and French in Canada."[153] He affirmed that, in Canada, "British free institutions" were creating a united people, and chastised those quick to judge the French Canadian participation in the war effort. His essay provided an apology for the contributions of French Catholics to Canada: "the first Catholic pioneers, the fighting race, the enduring race, the knightly race, whose explorer's daring first opened up this land, whose valour conquered it … whose endurance held it."[154] His was an obvious attempt to place French Canadian Catholics in a larger perspective, and although Day does not mention Bourassa by name, his essay follows in the strategy displayed by editors and bishops in the first year of the war: to isolate the noisy elements of French Canadian nationalism from the idea of the Catholic Church's legacy of loyalty and civility in Quebec. Although only one example, Day's essay is evidence that the ideas of Irish Catholic elites were influencing adolescents in Catholic schools and were being affirmed in a student publication overseen by the Congregation of the Sisters of St Joseph.

Behind the scenes, anglophone Catholic leaders were constantly trying to assist francophone bishops to manage the public perception of the French-Canadian war effort, while navigating the shoals around the bilingual schools problem, among other issues. Chief Justice Charles Fitzpatrick wrote privately to Archbishop Louis-Nazaire Bégin of Quebec to get his assurance that Bégin's clergy were not blocking recruitment. For his part, Bégin told Fitzpatrick that his priests were loyal, but that excellent French Canadian officers had been mistreated by their anglophone counterparts in the army.[155] Publicly, Bégin, the Primate of Canada, continued his public support for the war effort and particularly the Red Cross.[156] McNeil kept in constant contact with Archbishop Paul Bruchési of Montreal, encouraging Catholic representation on the entirely Protestant Social Service Council and helping to recruit balanced individuals, both French and English, to resolve the fighting over the bilingual schools.[157] In 1916, the Pope had issued a circular letter to the Canadian bishops to solve the internecine struggle over schools, and in January the Ontario bishops, including three French Canadians, published a circular promoting "civil and religious peace and harmony" in the Catholic community. The bishops claimed that Regulation 17 had been misunderstood due to its "obscure language" and had not completely proscribed French-language education.[158] What was clearly underlining the request for peace in the mind of the bishops was that open warfare among Catholics only obscured the general Catholic will to win the war. McNeil expressed real fear that, as Bourassa's comments were translated into English and increasingly reprinted in Canada's daily newspapers, this discord "could bring disaster" for the Church outside of Quebec.[159]

The early years of the war marked a time in which the diverse communities of Irish Catholics in Canada began to articulate common positions through their bishops and lay leaders. The newspapers provided a connecting link between rural and urban Catholics, Irish Catholics on each coast and in between, and sometimes between parishes within single dioceses, which themselves were culturally and occupationally diverse. The content shared between Irish Catholic centres was key to the emergence of a "Catholic voice," and this content was more often than not generated by the Catholic bishops themselves. By 1916, few Irish Catholics in the Prairies or New Brunswick would be unfamiliar with the words and actions of Neil McNeil or Michael Fallon. Similarly, Catholics in central Canada became increasingly familiar with the rhetoric of Casey in Vancouver, McNally in Calgary, O'Leary in Charlottetown, and Morrison in Antigonish. Although these disparate Irish Catholic communities were still distinguishable in ways already discussed, common ideas were being expressed by Catholic leaders, clerical and lay, and they were becoming better known by the best means of communication for that day.

In fact, the war and the need for frequent patriotic communication that it occasioned, was helping to unite Canadian Irish Catholic communities in a new way.

By mid-1916, however, the public entente between French and Irish Catholics in Canada was beginning to fray. The evident lack of recruits from Quebec during the phases of voluntary enlistment was becoming more difficult to nuance for the anglophone Catholic press, as was the continued agitation over the lack of English-speaking Catholic support for bilingual schools in Ontario. The Orange *Sentinel* and its supporters continued to hammer away at the Catholic Church, blaming it for tepid recruitment in Quebec and Ireland, although their facts in the latter case left much to be desired.[160] The Catholic hierarchy, clergy, press, and politicians had claimed a high profile in support for the war in its first twenty months, but by mid-1916 events out of the control of the Irish Catholic hierarchy would demand constant attention from Catholic leaders. Dissent in Quebec, the challenge posed by enemy Catholic aliens in Canada, the neutrality of Pope Benedict XV, and rebellion in Dublin would return Irish Catholic leaders in Canada to a defensive position on the war, and a sense that perhaps their patriotic rhetoric and high levels of recruitment had not made an impact on their Anglo-Protestant neighbours. Sectarian catcalls and public agitation from the usual anti-Catholic suspects, notably the Orange order, would escalate. Perhaps the best testament to the loyalty of Irish Catholics to the war effort would be found not in the words of bishops, priests, and pundits, but in the numbers of recruits who willingly left their homes, farms, factories, and schools and heeded the call to arms placed before them by secular and spiritual leaders.

3

Ned Murray's War

Canada's Irish Catholics and the Call to Serve

Ned Murray was the pride of one of the Ottawa Valley's most prominent and influential Irish Catholic families. His half-brother, J.L. Murray, was soon to become State Deputy of the Knights of Columbus; his uncle, the Reverend W.L. Murray, was a chaplain in the Canadian Expeditionary Force (CEF); and his siblings were settled in successful marriages or religious life. Ned – christened Edward Francis – was born in Pembroke on 27 March 1880, the son of Margaret Foran and William Murray, a local merchant.[1] He was educated at the Classical College in Rigaud, and later at the Military Academy of St Jean. For seven years he served as a lieutenant in the 42nd Regiment of the Renfrew and Lanark Highlanders, based in Smiths Falls and Renfrew.[2] During the South African War, he enlisted in the 2nd Canadian Mounted Rifles. While he was fighting at Harts River, his horse was shot from under him. On his return to Canada he decided, like many young men from the Valley, to move to the Prairies, where he took up sheep farming. When war was declared in 1914 he enlisted like many of his generation, and in view of his Boer War experience placed himself on the officer's list. By January 1916 he had grown impatient waiting for his call-up, and so re-enlisted as a private in the 138th Battalion in Edmonton.[3] He was wounded by shrapnel at Passchendaele in 1917, returned to his unit, and was subsequently shot at the Somme in February 1918. Again he returned to the line, and was killed in action near Amiens, during the last major Canadian offensive in the summer of 1918.[4] What was said of Ned Murray after he died might well have applied to other Irish Catholic men who took up the King's cause in the Great War: "He has been a true soldier, ready always to take up arms and enter the fray, and now has sacrificed all his future prospects and given his life in the great cause which he crossed the ocean to champion."[5]

Seen within the context of the Irish Catholic men and women of his generation who joined the CEF, the story of Ned Murray does not seem unusual. Most recruits were Canadian-born; most appeared to be the product of upwardly mobile families with respect to occupation, and many had seen previous service in local militia units and regiments. The story of Irish Catholic recruitment, in fact, appears to mirror the general patterns of voluntary recruitment across the country regardless of religious denomination. Irish Catholic men were prominent at the local voluntary enlistment depots in 1915 and 1916, but like other Canadian-born recruits, they appeared to be less represented in the initial wave of voluntary enlistment in 1914, which tended to be dominated by the British-, Welsh-, and Scottish-born immigrants who were eager to return home and take up the King's good cause. When asked to sign registration cards during the period of National Registration in 1916, they followed the encouragement and direction of their priests and bishops in participating in the program, and thus were among the first to be conscripted in 1918 under the terms of the Military Service Act. However, the conscripts of Irish Cath-olic descent appeared to be little different from conscripts of other faiths and ethnicities; many were engaged in agriculture or lumbering or were single men in blue-collar occupations. Any suggestion that Irish Catholic recruits balked at national service because of the "Irish Question" after the Easter Rising of 1916 does not bear up to empirical scrutiny. In fact, the evidence supports the claims of Catholic bishops that English-speaking Catholics were second to none in the performance of their duty. Although there may have been dissent over some political and religious issues among Irish Catholics, these individuals did not represent the majority within the new generations of Irish Catholic Canadians.

As was the case for other Canadians, a range of motivations compelled Irish Catholics to enlist in the CEF. Many, inspired by patriotism and strongly cultivated imperial loyalties, responded to the calls made in the press and by the leading politicians of the day. Others were members of militia units, which in the second phase of recruitment (in 1914 and 1915) became the primary source of men to form battalions for the second and third contingents. Families also provided a nursery for soldiers: brothers frequently enlisted together – or in succession as younger siblings came of age. Given the unemployment levels in 1913 and 1914 in many of Canada's major cities, many Irish Catholics facing underemployment or unemployment were attracted by the $1.10 daily pay for private soldiers and the early prognostications of victory by Christmas. No doubt, many young men were also attracted by the romance and adventure associated with donning khaki and travelling to parts of the world they might otherwise never see. There were many reasons why a man might elect to serve or to stay behind, but most left no lasting record of how they came to their decision. It is left to historians to piece together inferences and hypotheses as to why so many chose to enlist. For those like Ned Murray, who never lived to tell his tale, one can only suspect that his education, military background, sense of duty, and perhaps even his Catholicism prompted his efforts to join the CEF.

There were three phases of voluntary enlistment in Canada during the Great War. In the initial phase, between August and October 1914, thousands of men enlisted locally across Canada and then travelled to Valcartier, Quebec, where the Canadian Department of Militia and Defence organized the recruits into the First Canadian Contingent. The second phase, from October 1914 to September 1915, was coordinated by the dozens of militia units across the country, which became recruiting centres for battalions that would eventually form parts of the Second and Third Divisions. In the final phase of voluntary recruitment, from October 1915 to October 1917, militia units were joined by clubs, organizations, and associations that recruited their own specialty battalions. Many of these units were eventually disbanded in Britain and their recruits dispersed to reinforce the existing battalions of the five Canadian divisions.[6] By the end of June 1917, during the third phase of voluntary recruitment, Roman Catholics accounted for 51,426 recruits, or about 14 per cent of the total. Among Canada's principal Christian denominations, Catholics ranked behind Anglicans (46.8 per cent of the total force) and Presbyterians (19.7 per cent), but ahead of the Methodists (just over 10 per cent).[7] (See table 3.1.)

Table 3.1
Voluntary recruitment in the Canadian Expeditionary Force, by religion, to 1 June 1917

Denomination	*No. of volunteers*	*Percentage of* CEF	*No. in in general population*	*Percentage of general population*
Anglican	165,145	46.8	1,043,017	14.5
Presbyterian	70,671	19.7	1,115,324	15.5
Roman Catholic	51,426	14.2	2,833,041	39.3
Methodist	35,908	10.2	1,079,892	15.0
Baptist	18,458	5.2	382,666	5.3
Jewish	851	0.2	74,564	1.0
Other	12,409	3.8	–	–

Source: LAC, RG 9 III, Department of Militia and Defence Records, vol. 4652, "Establishments #8," Voluntary Enlistments to 1 June 1917

Recruitment throughout the voluntary phases was affected by a number of factors, including country of birth, level of patriotic fervour, previous engagement in the militia, familial and social pressures, and economic circumstance. In the earliest phase of enlistment most recruits were young men born in the British Isles who had only recently emigrated to Canada for work. English and Scottish volunteers dominated the early drafts of men at Valcartier in 1914, although Canadian-born recruits increased relative to the size of the CEF as the war dragged into 1915 and 1916.[8] Employment status also was a significant variable. Because war was declared in August, agricultural workers were less likely to enlist, knowing that the autumn harvest would soon be upon them. For urban blue-collar workers, however, the story was different. For unskilled and semi-skilled workers in Canada's major cities, during the aforementioned recession, the army's wage of one dollar per day plus a field allowance of ten cents looked like a much more viable option to either unemployment or seasonal work that would dry up in the winter months.[9] In Halifax, in May 1914, some skilled jobs were available, as was some unskilled work in the building of ocean terminals, but manufacturing was flat and "all along the waterfront also conditions were quiet."[10] By September, Fredericton and Moncton were experiencing "fairly active" levels of employment in all sectors, unencumbered by the war.[11] In Toronto, on the other hand, unemployment levels were high across both skilled and unskilled occupations, and in Ottawa close to four thousand men were out of work. The nation's leading manufacturer of agricultural implements, Massey-Harris, was forced to close plants across Ontario because of the loss of European contracts when war erupted.[12] Unemployment was the mother of an army.

Yet, as the economy gave to the CEF, it could also take away. In 1915–16 the economy began to heat up because of war contracts and special orders from the Shell Committee, which was primarily responsible for the government's tendering process. As more skilled and unskilled jobs opened up, there was far less incentive for workers to leave their secure and well-paying positions only to be shot at in the mud baths of Belgium by the Kaiser's legions. Voluntary enlistment had transformed from a constant flow to a trickle by mid-1916. In September 1916, the *Labour Gazette* reported that there was full employment in Regina and that farmers in the province were fully occupied. In fact, soldiers on leave were assisting with the harvest, while the forest industry complained of worker shortages.[13] In Edmonton there was a pronounced lack of workers, and in Vancouver the building trades and garment industries were booming, which was also contributing to a rise in real estate prices.[14] In Ottawa there was a demand for men in the building trades, and farms desperately needed workers for the harvest; meanwhile, Toronto was experiencing "a shortage in all classes of labour."[15] In Canada's largest city, Montreal, all sectors of labour were active, and women were employed in large numbers. However, there were complaints of a shortage of good skilled labour.[16] In Halifax, the trends noted two years earlier had reversed themselves; all sectors reported high activity, and the workforce included women, who were prominent in the confectionary and biscuit-making industries. Rural Nova Scotia, however, was plagued by a labour shortage, and some farmers were offering three to four dollars a day to any man who could help.[17] Together, all of these developments by September 1916 resulted in a reduced incentive to enlist across all classes, ethnicities, and religions.

Throughout the war, however, pundits and politicians hostile toward the Catholic Church repeatedly pointed out that Catholic recruitment was very low in proportion to the percentage of Catholics in the entire population, which stood at roughly 40 per cent according to the census of 1911.[18] In response, Father John J. O'Gorman, who had been wounded at the front and was convalescing in

Ottawa with plenty of time on his hands, took a closer look at the numbers. What he presented to the Department of Militia and Defence was a finely grained analysis of Catholic recruitment that demonstrated that, when the French Canadian Catholics were removed from the count, there remained 36,512 Catholics of Irish and Scottish descent. This group of English-speaking Catholics, argued O'Gorman, was second only to the Anglicans in terms of their proportion of the general population.[19] What the padre's subtext pointed to was the strong recruitment of Irish Catholics and the weak recruitment among French Canadians, who were the overwhelming majority within the Canadian Catholic Church. If O'Gorman's calculations are to be trusted – and the numbers have been substantiated in other Militia and Defence records – it is clear that Irish Catholics in Canada recruited strongly during the voluntary phases of enlistment. What remains less clear is how it was they came to be well represented in the CEF both before and after Conscription.

The data generated by the Department of Militia and Defence regarding the voluntary enlistment of men and women by religious denomination is fragmentary and, at times, contradictory. From 1915, when the first comprehensive records become available on religious enlistment, until the end of voluntary enlistment in the autumn of 1917, the numbers are fairly consistent with regard to Catholic volunteers. In each report Catholics rank third, at between 12 and 15 per cent of recruits, well behind Anglicans and Presbyterians, and ahead of the Methodists. The pattern set in the reports of 1915 never appears to have varied from year to year.[20] The department sought to update the figures regularly to ascertain the allocation of chaplains to brigades and divisions. There was significant pressure from the Canadian churches to make certain that there was adequate coverage of their troops, even at the battalion level. Catholics were particularly vociferous, fearing that the Anglican priest who headed the Canadian Chaplain Service in the early years of the war was not responsive to the needs of Roman Catholic troops and therefore parsimonious in his allocation of Catholic padres.[21] Catholic recruitment also varied from region to region. By December 1916, Military District (MD) 5 (Quebec), MD 4 (Montreal), MD 6 (Halifax), and MD 3 (Ottawa) ranked as the regions with the highest percentages of Catholic recruits. In both Halifax and Montreal, Catholics formed over 27 per cent of recruits, coming a close second in each case to the Anglicans. As noted, MD 6 incorporated all of the Maritime provinces, where Catholics formed a significant proportion of the population. Much the same could be said in Montreal, where Catholics, both French and Irish, constituted the majority. Catholics comprised 55 per cent of the recruits in Quebec, where French Canadians were overwhelmingly the majority. In Ottawa and the surrounding counties of eastern Ontario and the Ottawa Valley, Catholic recruitment levels reflected the large Catholic population in the region. In the rest of the Canadian military districts, Catholic recruitment ranged between 8 and 10 percent, again reflecting a lower proportion of Catholics in the general population. It should be noted that in each of these districts, all of which were west of Ottawa, Methodists, supported by their higher percentage of the general population, were more numerous than Catholics.[22]

The role of the Catholic clergy in recruiting parishioners from the pews should not be underestimated as one of the "push" factors in leading young men and women into the CEF. As we have seen, bishops and priests from across Canada had distinguished themselves in the patriotic fervour from the outset of the war. Their ongoing support of the Canadian and imperial war effort, particularly on the part of English-speaking Catholic clergy outside of Quebec, was manifest in recruiting committees and on the platforms of the mass rallies that would come to characterize Canadian recruitment schemes from 1914 to 1917. Just as the long-held principle of Canadian Catholic loyalty to the state had been espoused consistently by the bishops since the time of Briand and Plessis in the eighteenth century, so the bishops and clergy of the Great War period used pulpit and platform to proclaim that it was a young Catholic man's duty to serve. In 1916, Father O'Gorman in Ottawa preached three recruitment sermons just before his own enlistment as a chaplain. For O'Gorman, a Catholic's duty was clear: "[H]e who is disloyal to his country is disloyal to the Church … For the shirker the whole world is a prison … Canada's first line of defence is Flanders."[23] In O'Gorman's opinion, enlisting was an act of patriotic and religious duty. In a similar vein, at a public recruiting meeting held in Walkerton, Ontario, parish priest Father J.P. Cummings called on "all eligible men to act as true Canadian citizens and British subjects and do their duty." In response, eleven volunteers came forward in this mostly rural community populated by Irish and German Catholic farmers and factory workers.[24]

Given the clerical control and the rigidity of the hierarchical leadership in the Catholic Church at the time, these rank and file priests would not have been so bold in their recruiting efforts had they feared offending their local bishop. Indeed, the bishops themselves were notable for their activities on the recruiting front. In Antigonish, Nova Scotia, Bishop James Morrison appeared on the recruiting platforms to implore Irish and Scottish men to serve.[25] In his circular on enlisting, in 1916, Morrison proclaimed that he had "the fullest confidence that our Catholic young men will maintain the excellent record of the already large number of their brethren in faith, who have enlisted for overseas service."[26] In Manitoba and Alberta, priests took the lead from Archbishops Alfred Sinnott of Winnipeg and Emile Légal of Edmonton (St Albert) in stirring up patriotism publicly to encourage recruitment.[27] In Toronto, Archbishop Neil McNeil spoke at numerous rallies, offered CEF units billeting in his parishes with the opportunity to recruit locally, and even personally endorsed the efforts of the 198th Battalion (Canadian Buffs) to recruit young Catholic men as signallers, scouts, transport drivers, machine gunners, bombers, and snipers. In handbills that clearly claimed McNeil's blessing of the unit, Catholic men were invited to "Come Along! Join the Buffs and Hunt the Huns!"[28]

The work of the clergy was one of many variables that would push young Irish Catholic men and women into the ranks. The parish and the diocese remained as focal points for Catholic enlistment in the manner in which clergy and leading laity acted as recruiters; in the way parish societies and clubs promoted service and supported the troops with assistance and packages from home during the war; and in the manner in which the parish rallied around families grieving the loss of a son or father, who typically would be memorialized both in print and on honour rolls in the local church. In the parish, as previously indicated, the role of the priest was central to all parochial activities, including recruitment. If a priest viewed the war effort unfavourably, chances are that recruitment levels would be low. In Cape Breton, for instance, Bishop Morrison noted that enlistments within Acadian parishes increased when French Canadian priests were replaced with locally born francophones.[29] In Bruce County, Ontario, local Irish and German Catholic priests, and Jesuits at the Cape Croker Reserve were notable in their abilities to promote the war effort in their parishes, the outcome of which was a strong presence of Catholic recruits – Irish,

German, and Ojibwa – in locally raised infantry units, including the 160th Bruce Battalion.[30]

Parishes also provided the locus of Catholic family life away from the hearth. Notable among the sample prepared for this study were the numbers of brothers who followed one another into the service. For their part, those other family members who remained in Canada assisted with the war on the home front, which included parochial organizations that raised money for war bonds, prepared special food and clothing packages for the soldiers overseas, or voted in their fraternal associations, such as the Knights of Columbus or the Catholic Mutual Benevolent Association, to waive insurance fees or promise to honour life insurance policies for the soldiers, even if they were killed in action.[31] Parish activities related to recruitment were picked up by the local Catholic and non-Catholic press, and specific parishes were singled out from time to time for their distinguished levels of recruitment. In Calgary, St Mary's Cathedral became the key contact for administrators in MD 13 when it came to managing the Catholic troops.[32] The parish was notable for its recruits – and equally notable as the primary place of dispersion for Alberta Catholics upon demobilization in 1919. To the north, in the Edmonton neighbourhood of Grandin, Father Reynolds at St Joachim's Parish rallied parishioners, asserting that the Church teaches loyalty and thus Catholics must obey and "are obliged, according to their means to support and lend assistance, to their country."[33] In Winnipeg, Immaculate Conception parish in the western section of the city was singled out by the *Northwest Review* in 1917 when it unveiled its honour roll of 118 volunteers, most of whom were Irish Canadians, and of whom 12 had been killed and 15 wounded.[34] In Kingston, Ontario, the *Canadian Freeman* trumpeted the patriotism of local Catholic parishes and published lists of recruits and wounded, particularly from St Mary's Cathedral parish, on a regular basis. The editors of the *Freeman* were crystal clear in pronouncing why such publicity for Catholic recruitment was necessary: "It is precisely because Catholics are so loyal to the Church that they invariably loyal to the State. A good Catholic must necessarily be a good citizen … The Honour Roll of Kingston Catholics, which we publish in this issue, bears eloquent testimony to the practical loyalty of the Empire's Catholic citizens. Catholics are not much given to flag waving, but when the flag is in danger they are there with the goods."[35] Similarly, in 1917, the Catholic press in

Fredericton praised the small parish of St Dunstan, which had sent seventy recruits, of whom only five were conscripts. Conscious of the "anti-Catholic" rhetoric afoot, the editors of the *New Freeman* issued a challenge: "How many non-Catholic congregations have done as well, proportionally?"[36]

Perhaps the most publicized parish effort in Catholic Canada was that of St Patrick's Church in Ottawa. Founded in 1855 and located on Kent Street in centretown, St Pat's long held the distinction of being the Irish counterweight in the city to the basilica parish of Notre Dame, the archdiocesan cathedral. By the end of voluntary recruitment in 1918, St Patrick's had offered 25 per cent of its male population between the ages of 18 and 50, comprising about 7 per cent of the entire parish population.[37] At that time, thirty-two men from the parish had died. Excluded from the parish tally were any men who were of foreign birth and had no family ties in the parish. A memorial held for the dead in December 1917 focused specifically on the all-Canadian contribution of the parish.[38] By war's end, fifty-nine men who made the supreme sacrifice were memorialized by a massive painting placed inside the front doors of the Church.[39] For Father Matthew Whelan, long-time pastor, controversial proponent of English-speaking Catholic rights in the Church, and an Irish nationalist, claimed his parish's level of voluntarism gainsaid the advocates of conscription. When noting Whalen's addresses to the parish, the Winnipeg-based *Northwest Review* boasted: "What a magnificent display of patriotism! … The boys of Father Whelan's parish need no spur to awaken them to a sense of duty. When the call went forth they instinctively flocked to the colours."[40] Perhaps significant is not only the manner in which this Ottawa parish's example was picked up by Catholic papers across the country, but also the manner in which the local priest, despite his curmudgeonly reputation, was seen as a key player in the parish's successful war effort.

The parish community was not alone in its central role as a recruiter of young Catholic men. In Antigonish, where the proverbial "town met the gown," the efforts of St Ninian's Cathedral Parish are hard to extricate from the recruitment push stimulated by its next-door neighbour, St Francis Xavier University, local voluntary associations, and the efforts of specific regiments working in tandem with municipal authorities. On 15 October 1915, the "patriotic event" held at Antigonish's Celtic Hall exemplified how the Catholic parish became part of a complex local network of like-minded organizations. The crowds in the hall that evening were joined by soldiers in the Antigonish-Guysborough Platoon of the 85th Battalion, members of the local branch of the Red Cross, professors from the university, local politicians, and clergy from the local Protestant and Catholic churches. Catholic priests and Protestant ministers had an opportunity to address the crowd on their common concern for increased local recruitment. "Each speaker," the *Casket* reported, "complimented the young men, urged them to be ever faithful to their God as well as their king, [and] assured them that their movements and actions would be followed by deep interest by those they are leaving behind."[41] In Antigonish, as in other eastern Nova Scotian communities, Catholics were joined in their recruitment efforts by non-Catholics and representatives of secular institutions. Given such parish- and community- based efforts, it is not surprising that Irish, Scottish, and Acadian Catholics were prominent in enlistment from their towns and villages in the Diocese of Antigonish. By the end of the war, this diocese, with a population of about 87,000, had produced 4,791 volunteers, including 5 chaplains, and had witnessed 558 killed and 691 wounded.[42] Although there were many reasons for these men to enlist, the role of the parish within the greater community is not to be underestimated as an agent of recruitment.

Within the parish, the stimulus to enlist often came from within the recruit's own family. In large Catholic families, one son might enlist, followed in short order by younger siblings. Here the spirit of patriotism, or adventure-lust, or the frustration of underemployment may have touched one child, only to have a ripple effect through a family, which was already softened to the war effort by a persistent priest or activist patriotic bishop. In the parish of St Helen's, in the Junction neighbourhood of west Toronto where railway lines and major intersections converge, 183 men appeared on the congregation's honour roll, prepared in 1917. Twenty-six families in the parish sent two or more men to the CEF, which accounted for approximately one third of the recruits in the congregation.[43] One widow, Mary-Anne Cooney, saw four of her sons, aged nineteen to twenty-eight, join the colours. Her eldest boy, James, died of wounds sustained in battle; two younger sons were also wounded in action but recovered. One of the wounded brothers, John Thomas, was buried alive by a shell and remained traumatized thereafter "by loud noises."[44] For parishioners like the Mulhollands of Symington Avenue, the war also became a family affair. The Cork-born John Joseph Mulholland, a labourer, was over-age when he enlisted in September 1914 and was eventually placed in the 17th Battalion.[45] He had served in the British Army in India, Egypt, and South Africa before his emigration to Canada in 1910. In March, his twenty-year-old son, John Patrick Mulholland, also born in Ireland, enlisted in the Canadian Engineers.[46] To be closer to her family, and to her son John Patrick, who had been gassed at Ypres, Mary Alice Mulholland left Toronto and resettled some of the family in Cork and, later, London for the remainder of the war. When it was discovered he had lied about his age and was too old to serve, John senior was reassigned to England to work as a blacksmith in the CEF reserves.[47]

The Mulholland and Cooney family sagas were played out in similar ways in families in Catholic parishes across the county, whether by the four Cosgrove brothers of St Alphonsus Parish, on Alumette Island, Quebec, or the sons of J.P. O'Leary of Saskatoon, three of whom enlisted by autumn 1915. The *Northwest Review* used such families as the O'Learys to highlight demonstrations of Catholic duty to the war effort. "The timely enlistment of his three sons," reported the Catholic weekly, "all of them who [are] representing their Church and Country in the thickest of the fight, [are] thereby demonstrating to the world the fact that Catholics not only can be, but are just as patriotic as any of their separated brethren."[48] Privately, however, families may have had more reservations about war service than Catholic pundits led the public to believe. At St Helen's in Toronto, Berta Wadham was guarded in her enthusiasm as her husband and her eldest son, Elmer, went off to war. In a rare glimpse into the thoughts of a Catholic mother, Berta wrote to a family friend, Archbishop Charles Hugh Gauthier of Ottawa, that "[t]his war is making a lot of terrible trouble, and it is so hard for mothers to give up their sons even though it is for a just cause."[49]

Locally, families were supported by parish and community networks, which themselves were part of the recruitment process. Catholic colleges and universities were unanimous in providing recruits to the CEF from among their students. St Francis Xavier University drew Catholic men and women from across Canada. In February 1916, the university provided its own military hospital, No. 9 Stationary Hospital, becoming the second Catholic university, after

Laval, to donate a medical unit staffed with students and local recruits for the CEF. The unit initially established itself as a stationary hospital near Boulogne in 1917, but was quickly converted to a casualty clearing station to provide immediate medical aid at the front.[50] The university also established a Canadian Officers Training Corps (COTC), which provided one of the few ways in which Catholic men with no militia experience could be groomed for roles as officers in the CEF. The university also publicized the hundreds of names of its Irish, Scottish, and Acadian students who had volunteered for duty.[51] In Montreal, the Jesuit-run Loyola College saw much of its student body enlist in a variety of units, including the 199th Irish Canadian Rangers.[52] As a result of this support from young men hailing from middle-class and professional Irish Canadian homes, the graduation pictures for the years of the war and those immediately thereafter are noted by the paucity of students.[53]

St Michael's College in Toronto mirrored its collegial cousins to the east with a robust COTC program and dozens of enlistments in both the CEF and the American Expeditionary Force (related in large part to the high numbers of American-born students at the college). The leading scholar and former rector of St Michael's, Oshawa native Father Henry Carr, CSB, confessed that recruitment in 1914 had been slow and that "pro-German" sentiment had been uttered by some staff.[54] By 1915, however, thirty-six young men of the St Mike's COTC formed their own company in the larger University of Toronto student recruitment program.[55] The St Michael's honour roll for 1916 included the names of 96 students, most of whom were of Irish Catholic descent.[56] By war's end the St Michael's College yearbook published the names of 240 students who had volunteered for the CEF.[57] Robert Falconer, president of the University of Toronto, paid high tribute to the students of St Michael's when he observed: "I believe that St Michael's stands for sacrifice. You have the emblem of sacrifice upon your buildings, and those who teach you aim to have it also engraved on your character."[58]

For Catholic men unable to attend college or who were wedded to work that did not require post-secondary education, Catholic clubs and fraternal organizations offered their members incentives to join the CEF. One of leading proponents of the war effort was the Knights of Columbus, a fraternal insurance association for Catholic men founded in 1882 by Father Michael McGivney, a parish priest in New

Haven, Connecticut. McGivney wanted to assist blue-collar workers and their families by creating a Catholic benevolent association that would provide affordable life insurance benefits to families in the event of the loss of their primary breadwinner through illness or industrial accident.[59] The "order," based upon principles of charity, unity, and fraternity, spread quickly throughout the eastern United States, and by 1897 its 284th council had been established in Montreal, making it the first in Canada. By 1911, and the end of episcopal resistance to what some conservative Catholics thought might be a "secret society" prohibited by the Church or, worse, a Catholic version of the Freemasons, Council 1388 had been established in Toronto. The Toronto council demonstrated that the Knights attracted a constituency beyond its original designation for working-class Catholic families: of the its 131 charter members, most were Irish Catholic and most were white-collar workers or professionals.[60] Quite simply, the Knights became the fastest-growing Catholic association in Canada. By 1922, there were 138 councils representing every Canadian province.[61] Their unconditional support for the war effort was well articulated, and men from their ranks jumped into the fray, joining rifle clubs, local battalions, and a variety of war services – all of which would be supported, near the end of the war, by the Knights-sponsored recreational Army Huts.[62] For the Knights, Catholic participation in the war was both a demonstration of loyalty to the Crown and a refutation of sectarian animosity directed toward Catholics historically: "[T]he Knights of Columbus were afforded the opportunity of putting fully into practice their two-fold obligation to God and Country … No class or creed can justly claim a monopoly of Patriotism; whether we happen to be Catholics or Protestants, we are all Canadians – and 'Canadians first.'"[63]

The patriotic ethos of other Catholic clubs, organizations, and schools also created a fertile environment for recruitment. Catholic high schools, particularly in Toronto and Saint John, prepared adolescent men for military service by permitting school Cadet Corps to shoulder wooden replica rifles and practice drills on the playgrounds.[64] In Ottawa, Charles Murphy, the Liberal MP for Russell, commented to the parishioners in his home parish of St Theresa, near the Rideau Canal in centretown, that the alumni of the local boys' separate school had produced 150 recruits.[65] Catholic boys' clubs across the country encouraged members who were of age to enlist. In

1917, the Winnipeg Catholic Club published a list of dozens of recruits from among its ranks, most of whom bore either Irish or French Canadian surnames.[66] In Saint John, a staggering two thirds of the young men enrolled in the St Peter's Young Men's Association, or approximately 131 of the 196 members, had volunteered for duty. By December 1917, ten had been killed in action and twenty-five had been wounded. The *New Freeman* boasted that nineteen other club members volunteered but were turned away for medical reasons, which meant that closer to 80 per cent of the club's members had either enlisted or had attempted to join the CEF. The honour roll for the association was conspicuous in its confirmations that many families had sent two or more sons. Perhaps as its own affirmation, within the context of the conscription debate, that Catholics were distinguished by their voluntarism, the paper was compelled to comment that "[i]t is doubtful if there is another society in Canada, in proportion to its numbers that has done more in the matter of war response under the voluntary recruitment system."[67] Finally, it should be noted that Canada's largest fraternal insurance association, the Catholic Mutual Benefit Association,[68] assured its members of continued insurance protection if they enlisted, while the Holy Name Society of Toronto, with over 2,800 members, had a recruitment rate of 47 per cent by 1917.[69] All of these examples provide insight into ways in which Catholic institutions, imbued with notions of loyalty, social obligation, and family security, would encourage and recruit young men and women to serve their country formally in its armed forces.

Beyond local communities, but not detached from them, the Department of Militia and Defence had an eye to encouraging both Irish Catholic and Irish Protestant recruits by permitting the creation of distinctive Irish Battalions during the second phase of voluntary recruitment. The precedent for distinctive Irish units had been set early in the war, when the British Expeditionary Force included three Irish Divisions within its complement: the 10th Irish, 16th Irish, and the 36th Ulster Divisions.[70] In Vancouver in 1915, the 11th Regiment of Militia, or the Canadian Irish Fusiliers, began to send drafts of its Irish Catholic and Protestant recruits to the 121st Battalion.[71] Although not officially an Irish Canadian Battalion, the 121st was popularly known as the "Western Irish"; like many battalions raised after the four combat divisions were at full strength, it was merged into the 16th and 2nd Reserve battalions, in 1916, and eventually reinforced the 7th Battalion (British Columbia).[72] In Montreal in 1914, the Irish Catholics and Protestants of Montreal raised the 55th Regiment of Canadian Irish Rangers, which by 1915 sent a draft of men overseas with the 60th Battalion. In early 1916, the Rangers would be granted status for service overseas as the 199th Battalion. Eventually, after a good-will tour of Ireland in January 1917 that was marked by an enthusiastic reception by the Irish people, the Battalion was merged with the 22nd and 23rd Reserve Battalions.[73] In February 1916, Lieutenant-Colonel J.W.H. McKinery began to recruit men for Edmonton's 218th Battalion, nicknamed the "Irish Guards." It took a year before the 634 recruits sailed from Halifax, after having been converted to a railway and construction battalion. In March 1917 they were merged with the 211th Battalion and became the 8th Canadian Railway Troops.[74] Finally, early in the war the Toronto Irish Club and the Toronto Rifle Club formed the 110th Irish Regiment, which by February 1916 provided the foundation for the 208th Battalion or Irish Regiment of Canada. Like the 199th, it first became part of the 5th Canadian Division, in reserve in England, but it too was broken up in January 1918 to help reinforce existing battalions at the front.[75]

Of the aforementioned battalions, the Toronto and Montreal Battalions were the best known among Irish Canadians, who were recruited both from within these cities in addition to adjoining counties and regions. O'Gorman, soon to be a CEF Chaplain, was the chief recruiting agent for the 199th in the nation's capital.[76] In Montreal itself, recruiting was a loud and public effort. In May 1916, the Montreal Battalion held a massive recruitment rally that included speeches from Sir Charles Fitzpatrick, the Quebec-born Chief Justice of Canada, Father William Hingston, a Jesuit and chaplain to the 199th, and the Reverend C.A. Williams of St James Methodist Church.[77] The tone of the rally was as patriotic as it was ecumenical. It should be remembered that John Moir's idea of a "double minority" probably fit Montreal's Irish Catholic community more than any other in Canada. As a linguistic minority in their own Church, and a religious minority within their own language group, Montreal's Irish Catholics were vociferously Irish as a means of asserting community identity. This may help to account for the acute local disappointment when the 199th, like so many other units in a critical phase of battalion redeployment in 1917, were broken up and never fought as a unit. The disappointment in Montreal was palpable, and the accusation, how-

Table 3.2
The 208th Toronto Irish Battalion, by religion and previous service (N = 658)

Denomination	*Total recruits, no. (%)*	*Recruits with previous service, no. (%)**	*Denominational representation among those claiming previous service, no. (%)*
Irish Catholic	84 (12.8)	27 (32.1)	27 (14.5)
Other Catholic	15 (2.3)	2 (13.3)	2 (1.1)
Church of England	235 (35.7)	78 (33.5)	78 (41.9)
Presbyterian	143 (21.7)	43 (30.1)	43 (23.1)
Methodist	89 (13.5)	22 (24.7)	22 (11.8)
Baptist	24 (3.7)	4 (16.7)	4 (2.2)
Eastern Orthodox	19 (2.9)	0 (0.0)	0 (0.0)
Other Christian	19 (2.9)	6 (31.6)	6 (3.3)
Jewish	3 (0.5)	1 (33.3)	1 (0.5)
Unknown	27 (4.1)	3 (11.1)	3 (1.6)
Total	658 (100.0)	186 (28.3)	186 (100.0)

*Percentages in this column are calculated using the total number in each religious category.
Source: LAC, RG 9 II-B-3, vol. 80. Canadian Expeditionary Force, 208th Battalion, Nominal Roll of Officers, Non-Commissioned Officers and Men, Embarkation, Halifax N.S., "S.S. Justicia," 3 May 1917. My thanks to the students of SMC 385H (fall 2014), "Numbers and Humanities," at St Michael's College, University of Toronto, for their assistance in researching the data for this table as part of their course work.

ever questionable, flew that they were decommissioned because they were Irish.[78]

In Toronto, although it had a more pronounced Protestant flavour than its Montreal counterpart (the padre was Methodist),[79] the 208th was reported to have attracted "one hundred fair Irish colleens," primarily Catholic women to act as recruiting sergeants on St Patrick's Day, 1916.[80] The active presence of Irish Catholics in the formation of the 208th obscures the fact that Catholics constituted around 15 per cent of the battalion's strength, the rest being members of Toronto's four principal Protestant denominations. Of the ninety-nine Catholics in the unit, about eighty-four, or 12.8 per cent of the battalion, were of Irish birth or descent (table 3.2). The 208th also published its own magazine, the *Irish Canadian*, which featured photographs of the officers, group shots of each platoon in each company, a nominal roll, poetry, and maxims on the war. Most interesting are the many pages of business advertisements in the magazine – a testament to both community support and the hard work of local Irish Catholic women who offered volunteer and financial support to the battalion, including Roman Catholic philanthropist Teresa Korman Small (wife of the notorious Ambrose Small, a local theatre owner, and herself, the heiress to Korman's brewery).[81] Known as the "fairy godmother of the battalion," Small donated $5000 of the $7000 raised for the 208th's recruitment drive.[82] The 208th Battalion appeared as the great irony of the alleged "Belfast of Canada": a largely Protestant and Irish Battalion underwritten with the money and hard work of Irish Catholic women.

The specialty Irish battalions themselves appeared to reflect patterns and trends in Irish Catholic male recruitment that were evident across Canada. In all units, the Irish Catholic recruits were primarily Canadian-born, constituting close to 70 per cent of the random samples displayed in table 3.3. Of the foreign-born, almost 15 per cent were from Ireland, the remainder being from other parts of the United Kingdom, the United States, and other sections of the Empire. The recruits came from a spectrum of occupations, and much like the pattern set elsewhere in Canada, the majority were blue-collar workers. Although occupational records in the Department of Militia and Defence are fragmentary, the records that do exist from mid-1916 suggest the percentage of men engaged in clerical occupations (just under 19 per cent) was lower than the national average in the same category (13.3 per cent). In addition, the Irish Catholic sample in table 3.3 shows that these Irish battalions had a lower proportion of blue-collar workers in their ranks (65.6 percent) than the national average (75.5 per cent). There were almost equal numbers of men formerly employed in agriculture and the lumber industry, the Irish sample having 6.9 per cent these industries, as compared with 6 per cent nationally.[83] Clearly, neither the Montreal nor the Toronto sample included men from agriculture or logging, given the urban focus of the recruitment, but since the 121st had focused its recruiting in both Vancouver and Prince Rupert, it is not surprising to find some Irish Catholic farmers and lumberjacks in the ranks.[84] Finally, over half of the sample indicated that they had militia or other military experience before enlistment. Although this signals that Irish Catholics were not inhibited in their participation within English Canada's militia culture before the war, it should be remembered that these specialty units drew directly from militia units formed as a precursor to the battalion itself. In the 208th, for example, levels of Irish Catholic military service before enlistment was comparable to both the Anglican and Presbyterians levels (table 3.2). It should also be noted that although the prior militia experience claimed by a sizeable proportion of Irish Catholics in the 199th confirms the importance of the 55th Regiment as a training ground for the Irish Canadian Rangers of Montreal, it does not necessarily represent a deeply rooted militia experience among Montreal's Irish Catholics that predated 1914.

Perhaps the most interesting feature of the men included in the samples of the Irish units was the timing of their enlistment. It has been contended by several contemporary observers that the inability of the 199th Battalion to fill its ranks may have had something to do with the Rising in Dublin on 24 April 1916 and the subsequent summary execution of the rebel leaders by Sir John Maxwell and the British Army. As will be discussed later, the Easter Rising did have a negative effect on some Canadian Irish Catholics, but to assume that it caused the decline of Irish Catholic recruitment may be a case of falling into the historical brambles of *post hoc ergo propter hoc*.[85] First, the numbers in the sample in table 3.3 do not bear out this hypothesis. Although the 121st should be excluded from the question because its recruitment was completed by the spring 1916, in the other three Irish battalions over 40 per cent of the recruits came in May 1916 or later. Moreover, there was a general drop in recruitment right across Canada because of the heating-up of the war economy and the shortage of skilled labour. This was a considerable deterrent to enlistment, particularly when one could earn more than a dollar a day in a safer environment, without leaving Canada and the comforts of home and a loving family.[86] Finally, the suggestion that the dismantling of these Irish units implied an anti-Irish or anti-Catholic action, and therefore discouraged further Irish Catholic recruitment, also misses the mark.[87] Most units raised in 1916, regardless of designation, were broken up in England to fill the insatiable need for men to reinforce the divisions on the front lines. High casualty rates meant that battalions that had been deployed in the field since the Second Battle of Ypres in 1915 were drastically reduced in manpower, and this required that new units be broken up and added to old units. By the end of 1916, casualty reports, lists of the dead, reports of battlefield conditions, and the booming economy at home were significant disincentives to enlistment.

Table 3.3
Designated Irish units, recruitment and social characteristics (N = 142)*

	Recruits, no. (%)				
	121st Vancouver (no. = 24)	*199th Montreal (no. = 49)*	*208th Toronto (no. = 29)*	*218th Edmonton (no. = 40)*	*Total†*
Attestation					
Before 30 April 1916	20 (83.3)	24 (49.0)	16 (55.2)	23 (57.5)	83 (58.5)
Before 1 May 1916	4 (16.7)	25 (51.0)	13 (44.8)	17 (42.5)	59 (41.5)
Birthplace					
Canada	9 (37.5)	39 (79.6)	22 (75.9)	23 (57.5)	93 (65.5)
Ireland	7 (29.2)	6 (12.3)	2 (6.9)	11 (7.5)	26 (18.3)
Britain	5 (20.8)	2 (5.0)	2 (6.9)	3 (7.5)	12 (8.5)
United States	2 (8.3)	1 (2.5)	2 (6.9)	3 (7.7)	8 (5.6)
Other	1 (4.1)	1 (2.5)	1 (3.4)	0 (0.0)	3 (2.1)
Marital status					
Married	5 (20.8)	7 (14.3)	8 (27.6)	8 (20.0)	28 (19.7)
Occupation					
Professional	1 (4.2)	1 (2.1)	0 (0.0)	4 (10.0)	6 (4.2)
Business	0 (0.0)	5 (10.2)	2 (6.9)	5 (12.5)	12 (8.5)
Clerical/supervisory	1 (4.2)	11 (22.5)	7 (24.1)	4 (10.0)	23 (16.2)
Skilled worker	4 (16.7)	9 (18.4)	6 (20.7)	6 (15.0)	25 (17.6)
Semi-skilled	3 (12.5)	7 (14.3)	3 (10.4)	5 (12.5)	18 (12.7)
Unskilled	8 (33.3)	16 (32.7)	11 (37.9)	6 (15.0)	41 (28.9)

Agriculture/forestry	7 (29.2)	0 (0.0)	0 (0.0)	8 (20.0)	15 (10.6)
Other	–	–	–	2 (5.0)	2 (1.4)
Military service					
Officer	0 (0.0)	0 (0.0)	2 (6.9)	8 (20.0)	10 (7.0)
Previous service	9 (37.5)	40 (81.6)	8 (27.6)	18 (45.0)	75 (52.8)

* Unless stated otherwise, percentages are calculated using the number from the sample in each battalion.

† N = 142

Source: LAC, RG 9 II-B-3, vol. 80, Nominal Rolls of Officers, Non-Commissioned Officers and Men, 121st, 199th, 208th, and 218th Battalions, CEF.

A special comment ought to be made about the Edmonton "Irish Guards" or 218th Battalion. This unit was perhaps the most anomalous of the designated Irish units in the CEF, and for a number of reasons. First, although intended to recruit Irish Canadians and the Irish born, which it did, it was a unit far more notable for its foreign-born population than its Irish. By the time of sailing in 1917, the 218th could count 37 of its men as Irish-born, both Protestant and Catholic, accounting for only 5.8 per cent of its total strength. Russian-born members of the unit accounted for 159 of the men aboard the SS *Southland*, or a whopping 25.1 per cent – one in every four men of the unit.[88] Based on birth alone, the 218th ought to have been renamed the "Slavic Guards" with its huge numbers of Russian, Polish, Serbian, and Montenegran immigrants returning to Europe to fight the Central Powers who were at war with their homelands. Among the selected sample of forty Irish Catholics serving in the battalion, a higher proportion were Irish-born relative to the urban battalions raised in Montreal and Toronto. Interestingly, most of the Canadian-born Irish Catholic recruits hailed from Ontario and Quebec. Quite simply, the 218th Battalion resembled the pre-war migrations patterns of Irish- and Canadian-born Catholics who were seeking opportunities in the Prairie West, much like Ned Murray, who had gravitated to Edmonton. Naturally, the 218th also differed from its fellow Irish battalions in the high numbers of farmers represented in its ranks. These birth and occupational demographics of the 218th reinforce the notion that, even when examining Irish units themselves, it is risky to make generalizations about Irish Catholics; the Irish battalions resemble much of their local and regional contexts. Finally, and perhaps yet another indicator of how well the actions of the Irish Republican Brotherhood/Volunteers were perceived by the Irish in Canada, four of the Irish-born recruits actually enlisted after the insurrection in Dublin. It would appear that Irish-born soldiers, with the most immediate ties to Ireland, regarded the execution of Patrick Pearse and his companions as insufficient cause to ignore the pleas of CEF recruiters.

Quite simply, most Irish Catholic men did not require a specialty battalion that pandered to their Irishness and, instead, choose to join units that were close to home, or in which friends and family members could already be found. One only need look in the regular battalions raised across the country to find most of the Irish Catholic volunteers, and often in very high numbers, depending upon the region of the battalion's origin. As suggested earlier, battalions raised in Nova Scotia and New Brunswick had a high proportion of Catholics of French and Irish descent. In the second division's fifth brigade, three of the four battalions (the 25th Nova Scotia, the 26th New Brunswick, and the 22nd Quebec) had high numbers of Catholics, warranting the army to consider at least two brigade Catholic chaplains, one francophone and the other anglophone.[89] Battalions raised in Montreal, the Ottawa Valley, and sections of southern Ontario also attracted high numbers of Irish Catholics because of their large numbers in cities such as Pembroke, Ottawa, Kingston, Peterborough, Hamilton, and Toronto. The *Catholic Register* boasted that its city's parishes had raised over three thousand men, enough to outfit three battalions.[90] Most Ontario units witnessed rates of Catholic recruitment of between 10 and 15 per cent of all ranks. In eastern Ontario, Catholic recruitment could be higher due to the large Catholic population. The 154th Battalion, raised in Stormont and Glengarry Counties, for example, attracted high numbers of the Scottish Catholics who lived in this section of eastern Ontario, and who had been prominent in public life there since the early nineteenth century when their forefathers in the Glengarry Fencibles had been given land north of the St Lawrence and west of the Ottawa.[91] Farther to the north, the Lanark and Renfrew Highlanders 130th Battalion would attract many Irish Catholic men from the farms and town of the upper Ottawa Valley. The overtly "Scots" designation of the 130th in no way deterred the Irish from enlisting. The battalion had deep local roots and was aggressive in its recruitment from Pembroke to Perth.

Strong Irish Catholic recruitment in regional battalions is particularly evident in the 25th and 40th Infantry Battalions raised in Halifax during the first two years of the war. It is clear from data extracted from the sailing lists of both units that Irish Catholic men were among the largest single groups accounted for in the ranks. The 25th, which began recruiting in the autumn of 1914, drew men from all over Nova Scotia. The unit remained intact for the duration of the war, and over 5,500 men passed through the battalion, which needed constant replenishment because of the heavy casualties it endured. Between 1914 and 1918, approximately 3,497 officers and enlisted men in the battalion were killed, wounded, or declared missing in action and presumed dead.[92] Table 3.4 contains data derived from 131 Haligonian recruits, which formed part of the initial complement of

Table 3.4
25th Battalion, Canadian Expeditionary Force, Halifax recruits by religion, birthplace, and military service (N = 131)

	*Birthplace and previous service: no. (%)**					
Denomination	*Canada*	*United Kingdom*	*Other*	*Unknown*	*Militia/military service*	*Total†*
Anglican	33 (61.1)	19 (35.2)	2 (3.7)	0 (0.0)	39 (72.2)	54 (41.2)
Presbyterian	11 (64.7)	6 (35.3)	0 (0.0)	0 (0.0)	13 (76.5)	17 (13.0)
Wesleyan/ Methodist	10 (71.4)	2 (14.3)	1 (7.1)	1 (7.1)	7 (50.0)	14 (10.7)
Baptist	2 (66.7)	1 (33.3)	0 (0.0)	0 (0.0)	2 (66.7)	3 (2.3)
Irish Catholic	31 (91.2)	3 (8.8)	0 (0.0)	(0.0)	23 (67.6)	34 (26.0)
Other Catholic	1 (100.0)	0 (0.0)	0 (0.0)	(0.0)	0 (0.0)	1 (0.7)
Unknown	3 (37.5)	1 (12.5)	0 (0.0)	4 (50.0)	3 (35.7)	8 (6.1)
Total	91 (69.5)	32 (26.5)	3 (2.3)	5 (3.8)	87 (66.4)	131 (100.0)

* Percentages are calculated using the total number in each religious category.

† N = 131

Source: LAC, RG 9 III-B-3, vol. 79, Canadian Expeditionary Force, 25th Battalion, Nominal Roll of Officers, Non-Commissioned Officers and Men.

LAC, Soldiers of the Great War database, www.bac-lac.gc.ca/eng/discover/military-heritage/first-world-war/first-world-war-1914-1918-cef/Pages/canadian-expeditionary-force.aspx

nearly 1,100 volunteers in preparation for the sailing of a second Canadian contingent.[93] In examining the place of birth, religious configuration, occupational profile, and previous military/militia service of these 131 Halifax men, it is interesting that Irish Catholics in these units confirm the characteristics of Irish Catholic engagement in the local militia traditions, their likelihood of being native Haligonians, and their concentration in blue collar occupations at rates similar to their non-Catholic comrades in the 25th.

Irish Catholic recruits in the 25th Battalion reflected a group of men who were overwhelmingly Canadian-born and whose families were deeply rooted in Halifax. The recruits appeared to need no ethnic enticement or Irish symbolism to convince them to enlist in the 25th. The fact that it was a local battalion, drawn from among friends and neighbours regardless of background seemed incentive enough. Their presence was not token. No other denomination demonstrated recruitment so indigenously Haligonian as the Irish Catholic group. In the major Protestant denominations, recruits born in the United Kingdom or another part of the Empire amounted to over a third of the total. This high number of non-Canadian born recruits among Protestant Haligonians reflected national trends of recruitment in the first two years of the war. Until 1916, across Canada, British-born men dominated enlistment, given the fact that so many had emigrated to Canada during the boom years of migration to Canada from 1900 to 1914.[94] It should be mentioned, however, that Halifax's Protestant churches sent proportionally fewer British-born recruits than their counterparts in Ontario and western Canada, perhaps because the focus of the new immigration was less on the Maritimes and more on the industrial cities of central Canada and the growing communities in the Prairies. Demographically, Halifax had fewer British migrants in its pool for recruitment than other provinces of Canada to the west, particularly Ontario and Manitoba.[95]

The indigenous character of Irish Catholic recruitment in the 25th Battalion was also a feature of the 40th Battalion (Halifax Rifles), which contained far more recruits with Halifax addresses than the men of the 25th. The 40th Battalion began recruiting in May 1915 from its home base in Aldershot, Nova Scotia. Under the command of Lieutenant-Colonel A.G. Vincent, a first draft of 250 men and five officers was sent to England for basic training in June 1915. The main body of the battalion followed them to England in late October 1915,

Table 3.5
40th Battalion, Canadian Expeditionary Force, Halifax recruits by religion and place of birth (N = 211)

	*Birthplace, no. (%)**								
Denomination	*Halifax*	*Nova Scotia*	*Canada*	*Great Britain*	*Ireland*	*Newfoundland*	*Other*	*Unknown*	*Total†*
Anglican	36 (51.4)	7 (10.0)	–	23 (39.2)	1 (1.4)	2 (2.8)	1 (1.4)	–	70 (33.2)
Presbyterian	11 (61.1)	1 (5.6)	–	3 (16.7)	2 (11.1)	0 (0.0)	1 (5.6)	–	18 (8.5)
Wesleyan/ Methodist	8 (61.5)	1 (7.7)	1 (7.7	1 (7.7)	–	2 (15.4)	–	–	13 (6.2)
Baptist	3 (37.5)	3 (37.5)	1 (12.5)		–	–	1 (12.5)	–	8 (3.8)
Irish Catholic	70 (90.9)	2 (2.6)	–	3 (3.9)	–	2 (2.6)	–	–	77 (36.5)
Other Catholic	7 (50.0)	4 (28.7)	3 (21.4)	– –	–		–	–	14 (6.6)
Other	–	–	–	2(100.0)	–	–	–	–	2 (0.9)
Unknown	2 (22.2)	1 (11.1)	4 (44.4)	1 (11.1)	–	–	–	1 (11.1)	9 (4.3)
Total	132 (62.6)	19 (9.0)	9 (4.3)	33 (15.6)	3 (1.4)	6 (2.8)	3 (1.4)	1 (0.5)	211(100.0)

* Percentages are calculated using the total number in each religious category.

† N = 211

Source: LAC, RG 9 III-B-3, vol. 79, Canadian Expeditionary Force, 40th Battalion, Nominal Roll of Officers, Non-Commissioned Officers and Men, October 14, 1915; June 15, 1915; October 9 1915. LAC, Soldiers of the Great War database, www.bac-lac.gc.ca/eng/discover/military-heritage/first-world-war/first-world-war-1914-1918-cef/Pages/canadian-expeditionary-force.aspx

on board the S.S. *Caledonia*, and it is from among these 1,100 men that a sample of 211 with Halifax addresses was drawn.[96] Although the battalion was raised among Nova Scotians, when it was decommissioned in 1917 most of its men and officers were absorbed by the 26th Battalion from New Brunswick, a long-serving battalion of the 5th Brigade, which also claimed the reinforced 25th Battalion.[97] Not only did Irish Catholics comprise the largest religious group among the Halifax residents of the 40th Battalion, but almost 91 per cent of the Irish Catholics claimed Halifax as their place of birth. No other religious group came close to this rate of familial attachment to the city; the next closest denominations, the Presbyterians and Methodists, claimed just 61 per cent of their recruits as native Haligonians (see table 3.5). Only five Irish Catholic recruits claimed birth outside of Canada; two of these were from Newfoundland (which remained a separate British Dominion until 1949). As was the case with the 25th Battalion, the Anglicans of the 40th were a large group, ranking second among the denominations, with over 40 per cent of their number claiming birth in either Britain or Ireland. The presence of so many British-born among those who followed the "King's religion" merely confirmed the national trends, although it should be borne in mind that the rates of Canadian-born recruits in the Halifax area were higher across all denominations relative to battalions elsewhere in Canada.[98]

The analysis of the Halifax residents of the 25th and 40th Battalions also provides a glimpse into the depth of the attachment of Irish Catholic men to the military culture of the city, historically Britain's most important naval installation in the northwestern Atlantic. Irish Catholics had been represented in the ranks of the 63rd and 66th militia units in Halifax. It is not surprising, then, to find men with long-standing service and participation in these units among the recruits in these two battalions (table 3.6). In the 40th Battalion, the levels of militia experience were lower than the 25th across the denominations, but considering that the unit was raised six months after the formation of the 25th, and given the frenzied level of recruitment early in the war, it is not surprising that the pool of militia-based recruits had dried up somewhat. Still, nearly six of every ten Anglican recruits, among whom a high proportion were British-born, had seen previous militia or other military experience – a level twice that of the Irish Catholics. Most of this militia experience had been gleaned in the

Table 3.6
40th Battalion, Canadian Expeditionary Force, by religion and militia regiment (N = 211)

	*Military service: no. (%)**						
Denomination	*Previous service*	*66th*	*63rd*	*Other Canada*	*Imperial*	*Other*	*Total†*
Anglican	40 (57.1)	11 (15.7)	10 (14.3)	10 (14.3)	7 (10.0)	2 (2.9)	70 (33.2)
Presbyterian	15 (83.3)		8 (44.4)	5 (27.8)	2 (11.1)	–	18 (8.5)
Wesleyan/Methodist	7 (53.9)	2 (15.4)	5 (38.5)	0 (0.0)	–	–	13 (6.2)
Baptist	5 (62.9)	2 (25.0)	1 (12.5)	1 (12.5)	–	1 (12.5)	8 (3.8)
Irish Catholic	22 (28.6)	10 (13.0)	8 (10.4)	4 (5.2)	–	–	77 (36.5)
Other Catholic	8 (57.1)	2 (14.3)		5 (35.7)	–	1 (7.1)	14 (6.6)
Other	–	–	–	–	–	–	2 (0.9)
Unknown	4 (44.4)	–	3 (33.3)	1 (11.1)	–	–	9 (4.3)
Total	101 (47.9)	27 (12.8)	35 (16.6)	26 (12.3)	9 (4.3)	4 (1.9)	211 (100.0)

* Percentages are calculated using the total number in each religious category.

† N = 211

Source: LAC, RG 9 III-B-3, vol. 79, Canadian Expeditionary Force, 40th Battalion, Nominal Roll of Officers, Non-Commissioned Officers and Men, 14 October 1915; 15 June 1915; 9 October 1915. LAC, Soldiers of the Great War database, www.bac-lac.gc.ca/eng/discover/military-heritage/first-world-war/first-world-war-1914-1918-cef/Pages/canadian-expeditionary-force.aspx

63rd Halifax Rifles and the 66th Princess Louise Regiment, confirming that these units were among the best sources for officers and men from all denominations, who appeared to have incorporated this type of service into the norms of their community life in Halifax. Catholics were not excluded from this service: within the 40th Battalion, thirty out of ninety-one Haligonian Catholic volunteers, or nearly one third, claimed previous service; of these, twenty had served in local militia units.

Certainly, one could question whether patriotism was as fundamental a motivation to enlist as were the conditions of the local labour market in Halifax. Although in other areas of Canada, particularly in urban centres still reeling from the recession of 1913–14, a soldier's daily pay might have been sufficient incentive to sign up, this may not have been the case in Halifax.[99] Issues of the *Labour Gazette* for the early years of the war indicate that the Halifax labour market was humming well, particularly for the unskilled workers who might be engaged along the piers and dockyards of the harbour. Even though manufacturing establishments were slow on the eve of the war, "the ocean terminals provided plenty of work for unskilled labour."[100] In fact, by September, 1914, the *Labour Gazette* reported that, despite a high level of anticipated work on the docks, over three hundred longshoremen had opted to enlist in the CEF.[101] Most trades appeared brisk during the first two years of the war, except for those connected with building, which slowed in the winter of 1914–15, although a local correspondent predicted a pick-up in construction in the spring, coincidental to the mobilization of the 40th Battalion.[102] Despite the demands for local labour, there appeared to be no shortage of men, both Catholic and non-Catholic, who found their way to the recruiting officers of the 25th and 40th Battalions. Based on the sample, approximately 60 per cent of the Halifax recruits to each battalion were men unskilled or semi-skilled labourers, who would have been in demand at the time of their recruitment (table 3.7, table 3.8). What is surprising is that skilled workers, particularly those in the construction trades, were the most underemployed group in the city, and yet they were also less represented in the battalions. Skilled workers, it appears, were more willing to wait out the lull in the labour market than to sign on for duty overseas. At the other end of the blue-collar spectrum, Irish Catholics appear to have been over-represented in semi-skilled and unskilled occupations in comparison with non-

Catholic recruits. In both data sets, however, the numbers of Methodists and Presbyterians are small, and their combined totals on both units were less – sometimes considerably less – than for Anglicans and Irish Catholics. Presbyterians and Methodists tended to cluster in the skilled trades and in clerical and supervisory occupations. Since the battalions were dominated by Anglicans and Irish Catholics, their numbers bear closer scrutiny. In both denominations, in excess of two thirds were blue collar workers. Among Anglicans recruits, more than 50 per cent in each battalion were unskilled or semi-skilled workers; the corresponding rate among Irish Catholics was 70 per cent. Many of the Catholic workers appear to have worked around the harbour as teamsters, porters, stevedores, longshoremen, and labourers, and to have lived within walking distance of the harbour, between Holy Cross Cemetery and the harbour, or further north in St Patrick's parish.

Although Irish Catholic recruitment appeared robust, primarily as a result of the historical engagement of Catholics in the military traditions of the city, this pattern of recruitment cannot be extrapolated to the entire country. That the one area of potential weakness in Irish Catholic recruitment was in western Canada should come as no surprise. In MD 10 and MD 13, comprising Manitoba, Saskatchewan, Alberta, and a portion of northwestern Ontario, the proportion of Catholics in the ranks was tiny in comparison with other religious groups, often amounting to between 5 and 9 per cent, although the proportion of Catholics in some Edmonton-based battalions was as high as 12 per cent.[103] Migration to the "Last Best West" had been strong since the 1890s, but Irish Catholics were under-represented in the Catholic population of the West and were far less numerous than Catholic Poles, Ukrainians of the Eastern Rite (Ruthenians), Hungarians, Germans, Métis, and French Canadians. There were pockets of Irish Catholic settlement in the major cities, notably Winnipeg, Calgary, Edmonton, Saskatoon, and Vancouver, but Irish Catholics were not well represented in rural areas.[104] The Church itself acknowledged the minority status of Irish Catholics when, in 1911, through the lobbying of the hierarchy in Quebec, Rome appointed French Canadian Olivier-Elzéar Mathieu archbishop of Regina. Despite the lobbying of the English-speaking Catholic hierarchy, the apostolic selegate recognized that the French and immigrant communities were the dominant Catholic presence on the prairies. According to Arch-

Table 3.7
25th Battalion, Canadian Expeditionary Force, Halifax recruits by religion and occupation (N = 131)

	Occupation: no. (%)*								
Denomination	*Private*	*Professional*	*Business*	*Clerical*	*Skilled*	*Semi-skilled*	*Unskilled*	*Unknown*	*Total†*
Anglican	–	1 (1.9)	1 (1.9)	10 (19.0)	4 (7.4)	14 (25.9)	23 (42.6)	1 (1.9)	54 (41.2)
Presbyterian	–	2 (11.8)	–	5 (29.4)	3 (17.6)	4 (23.5)	3 (17.6)	–	17 (13.0)
Wesleyan/Methodist	–	1 (7.1)	1 (7.1)	4 (28.4)	1 (7.1)	2 (14.2)	4 (28.4)	1 (7.1)	14 (10.7)
Baptist	–	1 (33.3)	1 (33.3)	1 (33.3)	–	–	–	–	3 (2.3)
Irish Catholic	1 (2.9)	1 (2.9)	–	3 (8.8)	4 (11.8)	9 (26.5)	16 (47.1)	–	34 (26.0)
Other Catholic	–	–	–	–	–	1(100.0)	–	–	1 (0.7)
Unknown	–	–	–	1 (12.5)	–	2 (25.0)	2 (25.0)	3 (37.5)	8 (6.1)
Total	1 (0.8)	6 (4.6)	3 (2.3)	24 (18.3)	12 (9.2)	32 (22.4)	48 (36.6)	5 (3.8)	131(100.0)

* Percentages are calculated using the total number in each religious category.

† N = 131

Source: LAC, RG 9 III-B-3, vol. 79, Canadian Expeditionary Force, 25th Battalion, Nominal Roll of Officers, Non-Commissioned Officers and Men. LAC, Soldiers of the Great War database, www.bac-lac.gc.ca/eng/discover/military-heritage/first-world-war/first-world-war-1914-1918-cef/Pages/canadian-expeditionary-force.aspx. Occupational categories based on Mark G. McGowan, *The Waning of the Green: Catholics, the Irish, and Identity in Toronto, 1887–1922* (Montreal and Kingston: McGill-Queen's University Press, 1999), Appendix A.

Table 3.8
40th Battalion, Canadian Expeditionary Force, Halifax recruits by religion and occupation (N = 211)

	*Occupation: no. (%)**								
Denomination	*Private*	*Professional*	*Business*	*Clerical*	*Skilled*	*Semi-skilled*	*Unskilled*	*Unknown*	*Total†*
Anglican	–	3 (4.3)	3 (4.3)	13 (18.6)	13 (18.6)	6 (8.6)	32 (45.7)	–	70 (33.2)
Presbyterian	–	4 (22.2)	1 (5.6)	7 (38.9)	1 (5.6)	2 (11.1)	3 (16.7)	–	18 (8.5)
Wesleyan/ Methodist	–	1 (7.7)	–	1 (7.7)	5 (38.5)	4 (30.8)	2 (15.4)	–	13 (6.2)
Baptist	–	–	–	4 (50.0)	3 (37.5)	–	1 (12.5)	–	8 (3.8)
Irish Catholic	–	2 (2.6)	3 (3.9)	12 (15.6)	3 (3.9)	18 (23.4)	39 (50.7)	–	77 (36.6)
Other Catholic	–	–	–	1 (7.1)	1 (7.1)	4 (28.6)	8 (57.1)	–	14 (6.6)
Other	–	–	–	1 (50.0)	–	–	1 (50.0)	–	2 (0.9)
Unknown	–	–	–	–	–	–	3 (33.3)	6 (66.7)	9 (4.3)
Total	–	10 (4.7)	7 (3.3)	39 (18.5)	26 (12.3)	34 (16.1)	89 (42.2)	6 (2.8)	211 (100.0)

* Percentages are calculated using the total number in each religious category.

† N = 211

Source: LAC, RG 9 III-B-3, vol. 79, Canadian Expeditionary Force, 40th Battalion, Nominal Roll of Officers, Non-Commissioned Officers and Men, 14 October 1915; 15 June 1915; 9 October 1915. LAC, Soldiers of the Great War database, www.bac-lac.gc.ca/eng/discover/military-heritage/first-world-war/first-world-war-1914-1918-cef/Pages/canadian-expeditionary-force.aspx. Occupational categories based on Mark G. McGowan, *The Waning of the Green: Catholics, the Irish, and Identity in Toronto, 1887–1922* (Montreal and Kingston: McGill-Queen's University Press, 1999), Appendix A.

bishop Adélard Langevin of St Boniface, this did not stop *les maudits Irlandais* from trying to dominate the positions of leadership in the Church west of Ontario.[105] Ned Murray, however, appeared typical of the kind of Irish recruit one might find in western Canada. In a random sample[106] of forty Irish surnames from Murray's 138th Battalion, raised in Edmonton in 1916, the vast majority of men, both Catholic and Protestant, claimed a birthplace outside of the western provinces. Murray and others were primarily transplanted easterners, seeking better economic circumstances and bringing with them the cultural baggage of the east.[107] This characteristic of Irish Catholic settlement in the west may also account for the paucity of Irish relative to other recruits to Edmonton's 218th Irish Guards.

The records of the CEF battalions raised during the periods of voluntary enlistment allow one to reconstruct a profile of the Irish Catholic volunteers. One has to be mindful, however, that these records reflect the efforts of militia units working aggressively in local recruitment with the help of both civic and religious authorities, at a time when the Canadian economy was slowly pulling itself out of a recession. Most of these battalions respected the articles of enlistment as laid down by Sam Hughes' Department of Militia and Defence. Irish Catholics, like all other recruits during the period of voluntary enlistment, had to meet the following criteria: they had to between 18 and 45 years of age, with a minimum chest measurement of 33 inches if they were under 30, and 34 inches if they were over thirty; they had to be at least 5' 2" tall; and they were not permitted to be flat footed, lest they be unable to sustain long marches carrying heavy gear.[108] In the earliest phase of recruitment, married men were allowed to enlist only if they had written permission from their wives. By mid-1915, this marital provision was eliminated as the need for recruits became more pressing, particularly after the shocking Canadian losses at the Second Battle of Ypres that spring.[109]

As several of the previous tables indicate, Irish Catholic troops had distinguishing features as well characteristics similar to those of their non-Catholic co-combatants. All of the sample units shown in the tables were raised during the second phase of voluntary recruitment in 1915 and 1916; therefore, most of the Irish Catholics enlisted before 1 May 1916, as was the case with the non-Catholic majorities in each of these battalions. In each of these units, the Irish Catholics were most distinguished by the fact that they were overwhelmingly

Canadian-born, at a level of 71.1 per cent. The corresponding proportion was even higher in battalions raised in the Maritimes, where there had been less immigration from the British Isles immediately before the war. With the exception of several Ontario-based battalions, where Irish- and British-born Catholics constituted about 25 per cent of the Catholic strength, Irish Catholics were Canadian-born at a rate of over 80 per cent. This figure distinguishes them from the general trends in voluntary recruitment, wherein English- and Scottish-born troops were the majority in the CEF. Data collected in 1915 and 1916 by the Department of Militia and Defence show that Canadian-born troops across the corps were nearly 40 per cent Canadian-born, with higher percentages noted in the Maritimes, Quebec, and Eastern Ontario.[110] From the information gleaned from these sample battalions, representing six provinces, it appears that Irish Catholics did not seem to use the excuse that their Canadian rootedness, by means of the birth, deterred them from thinking that this was their war to fight.

Table 3.9 also captures the occupational status of these Irish Catholic volunteers. As we might expect, given the state of the economy, there was a heavy proportion of blue-collar workers among these recruits. As was noted with the Irish-based specialty battalions, this trend does not differ significantly from the aggregate breakdown of occupations among all of the volunteers in this period of enlistment. What is striking about the battalions raised in Prince Edward Island, Manitoba, and Saskatchewan is the evidence of higher numbers of volunteers drawn from agriculture and the lumber industry – something not evident in the three Irish Battalions raised in primarily urban areas. Unlike the volunteers in the ethnically Irish-based battalions, the rank-and-file Irish Catholics tended to be more occupationally diverse, reflecting a recruitment catchment area that spanned rural and urban areas; the battalions represented in table 3.9 thus resembled the national trends in their enlistment of clerical and supervisory workers at a rate of a little more than 14 per cent. The battalion data on Irish Catholic recruits also confirms the finding in the Irish and Halifax units that many of these Irish Catholic men had either a long-standing relationship with militia units or had quickly discovered that joining a militia unit was an effective conduit to full membership in an overseas battalion. Of the 356 men in this sample, over 40 per cent claimed some previous military service. It should be noted, however, that this service did not appear to produce many Irish Catholic commissioned officers, with a rate of 3 per cent – far lower than the Irish Catholic percentage within the entire military population. Clearly, Irish Catholics had some relationship with the militia traditions of the Dominion, but not in a capacity that would produce a distinctive officer class, as was the case among Anglicans and Presbyterians. Even Ned Murray, with his excellent education, Boer War service, and seven years in the 42nd Regiment, was frustrated in acquiring a commission and settled for a field promotion to corporal.[111] Whether this signals some anti-Catholic behaviour in the military establishment remains unknown for lack of hard evidence, although Catholic chaplains did comment on a general lack of sympathy for Catholics within the administration of their own service.

The examination of Irish Catholic soldiers by means of the specialty units and the volunteer battalions, however, still does not provide a complete picture of Irish Catholic recruitment. Not captured in these methods of exploration are the men who volunteered in the last period of voluntary recruitment, those who were conscripted under the Military Service Act in late 1917 and throughout 1918, or those who left to serve either in the American Army, after the United States joined the allies in 1917, or who ventured to the British Isles early in the war to enlist, or those who were seconded to the Royal Flying Corps in Canada or in England. Sometimes parish honour rolls, public memorials to the dead, and demobilization information provided by the Department of Militia and Defence help to fill in the gaps. Since the parish was critical in recruiting young Catholic men, printed honour rolls along with artistic sculptures, paintings, and bronze plaques provide a valuable record of recruits – regardless of place of birth, blind to whether they were volunteers or conscripts, and often distinguishing between parishioners who survived and those who made the supreme sacrifice. A few caveats should be applied to these repositories of information, however. First, not all parishes placed honour rolls in their church, for reasons undocumented, and some that had existed were removed, lost, or destroyed during the architectural and artistic transformation of Catholic churches after the Second Vatican Council in the early 1960s. Finally, some honour rolls were restricted to the dead, which effectively becomes a testament to volunteers who enlisted early in the war or those of frequent service at the front who, the odds being what they were, were more likely to

Table 3.9
Recruitment and social characteristics of Irish Catholics in regional battalions (N = 356)

	Battalion, no. of recruits							
	Nova Scotia 25th & 85th	*Prince Edward Island 105th*	*New Brunswick 26th & 132nd*	*Ontario 38th, 77th, 160th, 240th*	*Ontario 75th*	*Manitoba 100th*	*Saskatchewan 68th*	*Total (%)*
Sample size	57	16	60	109	70	19	25	356 (100)
Attestation								
Before 30 April 1916	57	15	60	94	70	19	25	340 (95.5)
After 1 May 1916	0	1	0	11	0	0	0	12 (3.4)
MSA conscript	NA	NA	NA	4	NA	NA	NA	4 (1.1)
Birthplace								
Canada	47	16	52	80	43	9	6	253 (71.1)
Ireland	2	0	7	11	12	6	11	49 (13.8)
Britain	3	0	1	15	12	4	8	43 (12.1)
United States	0	0	0	1	2	0	0	3 (0.8)
Other	5	0	0	2	1	0	0	8 (2.5)
Marital status								
Married	10	0	11	12	2	3	4	42 (11.8)
Occupation								
Professional	0	1	1	12	0	0	0	14 (3.9)
Business	0	0	3	0	3	1	1	8 (2.3)

Clerical/supervisory	6	2	4	20	9	9	3	53 (14.9)
Skilled worker	3	4	7	20	19	1	1	55 (15.5)
Semi-skilled	11	0	5	13	11	0	5	45 (12.6)
Unskilled	33	0	34	29	27	4	5	132 (37.1)
Agriculture/forestry	4	9	6	15	1	4	10	49 (13.8)
Military service								
Officer	0	1	1	3	2	2	1	10 (2.8)
Previous service	16	13	35	29	27	12	11	143 (40.2)

NA = not applicable

Source: RG 9, II-B-3, vol. 80, Nominal Rolls of Officers, Non-Commissioned Officers and Men; LAC, Soldiers of the Great War database, www.bac-lac.gc.ca/eng/discover/military-heritage/first-world-war/first-world-war-1914-1918-cef/Pages/canadian-expeditionary-force.aspx

be killed. Thus. honour rolls are helpful but by no means perfect tools in furthering our understanding of the Irish Catholic recruits.

The data in table 3.10 add another layer to our portrait of the Irish Catholic men who joined the CEF. The data derived from the personnel records of the men listed on honour roles reveal that few were employed in agriculture or logging and that there were few conscripts. The lack of conscripts is not surprising given that, by the later years of the war, there was almost full employment in urban industries necessary to the war effort and the government wished to avoid creating a shortage of needed labour both skilled and unskilled. The characteristics captured in table 3.10 are consistent with, and sometimes amplify, the patterns evident in the other surveys of specialty battalions and the second phase of voluntary enlistment. Again, Irish Catholic recruits were overwhelmingly Canadian-born, at just over 75 per cent of the total. In addition, a familiar pattern appears to emerge with regard to Irish Catholic nativity; as one moves from the Atlantic to the Pacific, the proportion of Irish Catholic men born in Canada declines, to the point where in the small sample from Victoria it is only 50 per cent. As indicated earlier, the numbers of Irish Catholic recruits in western Canada essentially reflected the low percentage of Irish Catholics in the population west of the Great Lakes. With regard to occupation, what becomes clearer is the white-collar recruitment of Irish Catholics in Canada's major cities. Clerical and supervisory workers made up at least one in every four Irish Catholic recruits. Similarly, the rate of blue-collar engagement, on an aggregate level at around 57 per cent, is slightly lower than the level of blue-collar workers reported across the CEF. The parish data also confirm a high level of military participation prior to enlistment: one in every three recruits declared some type of militia or other military experience. The honour rolls also reveal a higher number of Irish Catholic officers in the CEF – over twice that revealed in the random samples of the battalion survey.

The Irish Catholic soldier in the CEF is not easily defined. He hailed from every region of the country and from across the occupational spectrum. Corporal William O'Brien was a law student and a third-generation Irish Canadian from Peterborough who joined the 23rd Battery, Royal Canadian Artillery, in the Second Division. O'Brien kept a diary of his war experiences in which he commented on matters spiritual, political, and practical, excitedly noting on 4 May 1916 that his "first open air bath" in weeks was "a dandy." Bill lived to tell his tales and circulated his diary among his children and grandchildren.[112] Henry Dunlap, an engineering student at Queen's University in Kingston, was a long way from his Cape Breton home when he enlisted in 1917. Dunlap would earn the Military Medal for bravery and receive a Mention in Despatches. Young William Meagher of Lindsay, Ontario, was not so lucky. Like Ned Murray before him, Meagher had moved west, in his case to Manitoba, where he worked as a machinist, and enlisted at Camp Sewell in that province. He was wounded playing with a grenade among friends in the 10th Canadian Machine Gun Company. He was later killed in the action leading up to the victory at Vimy Ridge in April 1917.[113] Private Frank Joseph McCarthy, a moulder from Saint John, also never returned home. He left his foundry job in Stratford, Ontario, joined the first contingent, and saw action at Festubert, Givenchy, Ypres, St Julien, and Mount Sorrel, where he was killed in 1916.[114] Finally, also among this interesting mix was Ottawa's Frank McGee, one of the fledgling NHL's stars; he had scored a record fourteen goals in a single Stanley Cup game for his Ottawa Silver Seven. A hockey accident had earned him the nickname "one-eyed Frank," which should have made him ineligible for service. Nevertheless, this scion of St Joseph's Parish in Ottawa memorized the eye chart, enlisted, and served on the front line with distinction, until he, too, was killed in action.[115] A machinist, shepherd, law student, engineer, moulder, and hockey player appear as the tip of the iceberg of diversity among Irish Catholic volunteers.

In sum, if one were to try to answer the question "What manner of Irish Catholic men were these soldiers?" one should say quite comfortably that, like most Canadian recruits, they came from all walks of life, with strong representation from clerical and supervisory occupations. This perhaps revealed the growing presence of an educated, literate, and upwardly mobile generation of Irish Catholic leaders in Canada, who had embraced the importance of rallying to the imperial colours when called. The Irish Catholic Canadian soldier was also a blue-collar worker, often coming from skilled and semi-skilled trades, belying the oft-held stereotype of the Irishman as unskilled navvy or feckless Paddy. Far from it: when the skilled workers are blended with the white-collar workers, the emergence of an Irish Catholic Canadian middle class about the time of the Great War becomes clear. Nor were these men divorced from the imperial forces

Table 3.10
Irish Catholics on parish honour rolls (N=497)

	City, no. on parish honour roll									
	Sydney	*Halifax*	*Montreal*	*Ottawa*	*Toronto*	*Winnipeg*	*Calgary*	*Victoria*	*Total (%)*	
Sample size	40	39	52	115	154	54	32	11	497	(100.0)
Attestation										
Before 30 April 1916	27	32	37	57	121	45	21	7	347	(69.8)
After 1 May 1916	10	7	11	47	28	9	9	2	123	(24.8)
MSA conscript	1	0	3	11	5	0	2	0	22	(4.4)
Other/unknown	2	0	1	0	0	0	0	2	5	(1.0)
Birthplace										
Canada	35	38	40	104	116	26	11	5	375	(75.5)
Ireland	0	0	5	2	16	12	6	2	43	(8.7)
Britain	0	0	3	7	14	15	8	3	50	(10.1)
United States	2	0	2	2	6	0	6	0	18	(3.6)
Other/unknown	3	1	2	0	2	1	1	1	11	(2.2)
Married	5	11	11	13	39	17	11	1	108	(21.7)
Occupation										
Professional	4	0	3	22	4	0	3	2	38	(7.7)
Business	1	1	3	6	4	2	0	1	18	(3.6)
Clerical/supervisory	8	10	10	42	29	21	5	3	128	(25.8)
Skilled worker	8	7	12	14	51	11	6	0	109	(21.9)
Semi-skilled	6	8	9	10	23	7	7	0	70	(14.1)

Unskilled	11	10	14	15	40	9	4	3	106	(21.3)
Agriculture/forestry	0	1	0	5	2	3	7	0	18	(3.6)
Other/unknown	2	2	1	1	1	1	0	2	10	(2.0)
Military service										
Officer	2	1	7	16	1	1	3	5	40	(8.1)
Previous service	16	20	26	39	40	25	7	7	180	(36.2)

Sources: *Catholics of the Diocese of Antigonish, Nova Scotia, and the War, 1914–1919* (Antigonish: St Francis Xavier University Press, c. 1919) for the Honour Rolls for Holy Redeemer, Sacred Heart, and St Mary's Parishes; Honour Roll, St Mary's Cathedral, Halifax; Honour Roll, St Patrick's Parish, Montreal; Honour Rolls, S. Paul and St Helen's Parishes, Toronto; Honour Roll, St Patrick and St Joseph Parishes, Ottawa; Honour Roll, St Mary's Parish, Winnipeg; Honour Roll, St Mary's Cathedral, Calgary; Honour Roll, St Andrew's Cathedral, Victoria.

swirling about them; many, like Ned Murray, had been active in the militia culture of the day. Moreover, the fact that so many married men rallied to the war effort further testifies to the readiness of Irish Catholic men to "do their duty."

Often forgotten in the contemporary accounts of Canada's recruits during the Great War is the contribution made by hundreds of Canadian women who served in the Canadian Army Medical Corps as nursing sisters. Building on the experience of the South African War, when nurses were first attached to Canadian units, some 2,845 nurses served in the CEF, the majority of whom hailed from Ontario, Quebec, and Nova Scotia.[116] These women were well educated and had typically completed programs in practical nursing in American and Canadian hospitals. They served with distinction in hospitals in England, Canada, and France; some were close to the front in Casualty Clearing Stations, where they were under shell fire and at risk of their lives. Forty-seven nurses were killed, and numerous others were injured in action or suffered long-term psychological trauma as a result of their service. Fourteen nurses were drowned in 1918, when the Germans torpedoed a Hospital Ship, the *Llandovery Castle*, off the coast of Ireland;[117] among the victims was nursing sister Christina Campbell, a Catholic of Scottish descent from Victoria.

Catholic women were, in fact, prominent among the nursing sisters. The head of the Nursing Corps was Major Margaret Macdonald, a Catholic of Scottish descent from Bailey's Brook in the Diocese of Antigonish. Macdonald was an accomplished military nurse who had trained in New York and first served with the American Army during the Spanish–American War. During the South African War she joined the First Contingent of Canadian volunteers and ended up doing two tours of duty in South Africa. After the war, she studied in New York and served with the American Army in Panama, where her chief enemies were mosquitoes carrying malaria and yellow fever. Her subsequent enlistment in the Queen Alexandra Imperial Nursing Service and her study of medical administration in the United Kingdom provided sufficiently strong credentials for her to lead the nurses as matron-in-chief in the First Canadian Contingent when war broke out in 1914.[118] Macdonald was clear about the historic significance of women playing such a prominent role in the war effort. "The numbers of nurses employed in the combined theatres of the war," she asserted, "totalled a colossal figure. It seems almost incredible that such vast organizations, imposed entirely of women, governed by women, should during a crisis extending over four and a half years present an unbroken line. In the Nursing Service not a weak spot, not even the semblance of a breakdown was found."[119]

As a practising Roman Catholic,[120] Macdonald would not be alone in what one might consider a Protestant-dominated service. She was joined by many Catholic women of Irish, French, and Scottish descent from across the country who shared her dedication to medical service in the cause of the imperial struggle against Germany. The enlistment pattern of nurses mirrored that of the CEF generally, Catholic women constituting just under 14 per cent of the Nursing Service, behind the Presbyterians and Anglicans, but ahead of the Methodists.[121] As the sample of ninety-one, [122] or roughly 23 per cent, of the Catholic nurses described in table 3.11 indicates, Canada's Irish Catholic nursing sisters had a great deal in common with the other nursing sisters in the CEF. Close to 90 per cent were born in Canada, the majority in Ontario. As we might expect given the high proportion of Catholics in the Maritime population, Irish Catholic nurses were well represented from Nova Scotia and New Brunswick. The Quebec total appears to be much lower than the national average, but this is easily explained by the prominence in the Quebec totals of both French Canadian Catholic nurses, drawn from the province's majority, and a high number of Anglo-Protestant nurses who enlisted in the Montreal region. This sample offers no nurses from western Canada, although this may be deceptive. Although the table lists place of birth, it does not account for several nurses who were born in Ontario but were living in Alberta, British Columbia, Manitoba, or the United States at the time of their enlistment. In addition, the table does not account for the numbers of Irish Catholic Canadian women who, studying in the United States or nursing there, as was the case for a number of women from Prince Edward Island, opted to join the medical corps in the American Army.[123]

Also notable among the Irish Catholic nurses was their life experience before enlistment. Close to 60 per cent of the Irish Catholic nurses declared at the time of attestation that they had served in the military previously. Often, this accounted for a brief training period in Canada before enlistment, or actual service in hospitals related to the war effort. To take one example, before she enlisted in the CAMC, Florence Kelly of Summerside, Prince Edward Island, had served in the

Table 3.11
Irish Catholic Canadian nurses: recruitment and social characteristics, 1914–18 (N = 91)

Characteristic	*Irish Catholic Canadian nurses, no. (%)*	*Total nursing service, no. (%)*
Attestation		
Before 30 April 1916	36 (39.6)	
After 1 May 1916	55 (60.4)	
Birthplace		
Canada	81 (89.0)	
Ireland	7 (7.7)	
Britain	1 (1.1)	
United States	1 (1.1)	
Other	1 (1.1)	
Previous occupation		
Nurse	91 (100.0)	
Canadian birth		
Canada total	81 (100.0)	2,499 (100.0)
Nova Scotia	16 (19.8)	268 (10.7)
New Brunswick	12 (14.8)	37 (1.5)
Prince Edward Island	1 (1.2)	With Nova Scotia
Quebec	5 (6.2)	572 (22.9)
Ontario	47 (58.0)	1,115 (44.6)
Manitoba	0 (0.0)	171 (6.8)
Saskatchewan	0 (0.0)	30 (1.2)
Alberta	0 (0.0)	123 (4.9)
British Columbia	0 (0.0)	143 (5.7)
Military service		
Previous service	54 (59.3)	

Source: LAC, Soldiers of the Great War database, www.collectionscanada.gc.ca/databases/cef/index-e.html; C.A. Sharpe, "Enlistment in the Canadian Expeditionary Force 1914–1918: A Regional Analysis," *Journal of Canadian Studies* 18, no. 4 (Winter 1983–84): 17.

US Army Medical Corps during the Spanish–American War and had worked as a public health nurse in New York City. She had also been a roommate to Margaret MacDonald when they trained at Mount St Vincent Academy in Halifax.[124] Not as well connected as Kelly, Nora Gilbert, a native of Halifax who actually enlisted in Calgary, began her service as a military nurse in September 1914 but did not formally apply for overseas service until 1917.[125] Like all of her colleagues in the sample, Nora listed her occupation before the war as a nurse and was single. Another characteristic shared between Nora and 60 per cent of her Irish Catholic colleagues was that her formal enlistment for service overseas came after May 1916. On the one hand, this can be accounted for by the increased demand for medical personnel as the CEF accumulated more wounded and convalescent patients as the war dragged on. Yet it also provides more evidence to contradict the notion that the Easter Rising of 1916 and the summary execution of its leaders dampened the imperial spirits of Irish Catholics.[126] This is not to suggest that these well-educated Irish Catholic women had no interest in Irish affairs, but should make us consider that, even among women with nationalist sentiments, the strong emotional pull of Irish nationalism was insufficient to keep them from serving King and country.

As for Catholic men who enlisted, the clergy and leading laymen may have been influential in promoting the enlistment of Catholic women in the nursing service. In April 1915, just prior to the Second Battle of Ypres, when Canadian heroism would dramatically escalate recruitment at home, Toronto's archbishop and leading physicians took an active role in the commissioning of nursing sisters from St Michael's Hospital. In an address to the ten nursing recruits, Dr. Robert Joseph Dwyer emphasized the anti-Christian influences that had brought the enemy to start this conflict. At a special Mass in the hospital chapel, Archbishop McNeil not only congratulated the women for their patriotism but also stressed that their role in assisting the wounded and dying was not just medical but also spiritual. "I feel deeply grateful," preached McNeil, "and we should all feel grateful, to the Canadians who have volunteered in defence of their country, and to you we also owe gratitude … but I want you to remember that not only to the body you can give assistance, but the soul as well. To the dying soldier – non-Catholic as well as Catholic – you can suggest ejaculations that will excite sorrow for sin … Short acts of Faith, Hope, and Love. The prayer need not be long."[127] Once again, as had been the case in the drawing of young men to the colours, the clergy were rarely far away, prompting the laity to perform their patriotic and spiritual duties.

Apart from Cynthia Toman's recent monograph, little has been written on the experiences of nurses in the field, although the personnel records of these women attest to the fact that they endured hardship and injury commensurate with their duties at the front. Irene Brady and her younger sister Leila, from St Joseph's Parish in Ottawa, both suffered from "nervous disability" after their experiences in the nursing service. One physician ascribed Irene's illness to being "rundown" after air raids and loss of sleep in France. Leila, who was awarded the Royal Red Cross for her distinguished service in the field and was mentioned in dispatches, was hospitalized in 1918 for tremors and nervous tension resulting from sleep loss and "trench fever." Although she was demobilized to Canada, her trauma continued with fits of hysterical laughter, crying, suicide threats, and physical attacks on a nurse, which included biting her arm. She was committed to the sanitarium in Guelph after the war. In addition to physical and emotional collapse, several Irish Catholic nurses became victims of the influenza epidemic, and Dorothy Smith of Ottawa had to be demobilized after suffering from breast cancer and undergoing a mastectomy in 1917.[128]

Mona Whelan, the daughter of the famine migrant and Ottawa Valley farmer in (whom we met in chapter 1) had a much less dramatic war experience. She had enlisted in the Canadian Army Corps in Montreal in May 1915, and was assigned to the West Cliff Hospital in Folkstone, England, just before Christmas that same year. Mona never left England to work in the hospitals or Casualty Clearing Stations near the Front. In fact, she was admitted to hospital herself in the autumn of 1916 with bronchitis and, later, influenza. It was clear that, by 1917, her attending physicians were concerned about her lungs, given her family history, which included her father Stephen's death from pneumonia in 1908 and that fact that one of her brothers had died of tuberculosis. In August 1918, Mona was permitted to resign for health reasons and she was demobilized to Canada.[129] Her war was over. It certainly had not been a tale that would have attracted Hollywood's attention. There is no evidence to suggest that she returned to the Ottawa Valley. Whelan's story was perhaps typical of the life of most nursing sisters, particularly the many who never served in France or Belgium but worked diligently and without renown among the wounded and mutilated who arrived daily in England from the Front. Their work was important, but like the work of all women in the CEF has received scant attention.[130]

The examination of Irish Catholic male and female recruitment in aggregate terms appears to be a rather artificial exercise conceived by administrators in the CEF and historians thereafter. In reality, men and women enlisted within specific contexts influenced by their families, their communities, what they read in the newspapers, and what they heard from the pulpit. One can garner a more realistic appreciation of recruitment, perhaps, by starting on the ground where recruitment actually took place: in places of social interaction in the farms, villages, and cities of Canada. Robert Rutherdale has done a credible job of trying to capture the home front in his microstudies of Trois Rivières, Quebec, Stratford, Ontario, and Lethbridge, Alberta.[131] Here one discovers the local circumstances within which the war was communicated, and how young men and women negotiated their roles in the war while weighing in the balance social expectations, the local economy, and any ideas they might have of doing their duty. At war's end, in most Canadian communities, the issues that may have divided those who opted to serve are forgotten but what is remembered in stone or bronze is simply the sacrifice or service they shared. Often the only distinguishing feature on a war monument is whether one paid the "supreme sacrifice" or not. Unknown to the viewer is whether the person whose name is etched for posterity was Catholic or Protestant, volunteer or conscript, officer or NCO, wounded or unscathed, a toiler in the trenches or a worker behind the scenes. A monument brings together all of these things and reinforces the sense that the entire community served and sacrificed. On the other hand, a community-based or regional approach to reconstructing the history of recruitment might allow one to garner a better appreciation of what who these Irish Catholics were, within the context of all who served from their home communities. For the present discussion, a closer look at the rural areas and small towns of the Ottawa Valley offers a perspective that straddles two provinces and also provides a useful comparison to the largely urban-based regional analysis already evident in this chapter.

In 1914, the Ottawa Valley provided an interesting witness to the growing human mosaic that had settled the shores and hinterland of the great river named in Ojibwa of its first inhabitants. The upper valley north of Ottawa consisted of two counties, Renfrew in Ontario and Pontiac in Quebec, which were separated by the Ottawa River and dozens of islands that created numerous channels and rapids as the river pushed its volume out of Lake Temiskaming and its watershed. The upper valley was home to a variety of peoples, including the original Ojibwa inhabitants who were clustered on reserves around Golden Lake and Round Lake in Renfrew County, and the Algonquins for whom the Maniwaki area was their home territory. A traveller in the region might be astonished to find, in addition to English Methodists and Anglicans and French Canadian Roman Catholics, Polish Kaszubs, who emigrated from the Baltic region as early as the 1850s, German Lutherans, Highland and Lowland Scots, Anglo-Americans, British immigrants, Irish Protestants, and Irish Catholics. Roman Catholics formed a sizable minority in the region, although on the Quebec side of the river, in Pontiac, English-speaking Protestants were the majority. The early pioneers of Clarendon Township, for example, had been exclusively Protestant, and the township became a bastion of the Loyal Orange Order in western Quebec. The names of settlements signalled their Britishness: Shawville, Bristol, Ladysmith, and Campbell's Bay. Likewise, on the Ontario side of the River, distinctive Irish Catholic enclaves were found at Donegal, Eganville, Shamrock, Mount St Patrick, and Westmeath. In the midst of Irish and Scottish settlements, however, one might find Wilno, named after Vilnius (now Lithuania), and the site of Canada's oldest Polish Catholic church. For Catholics of any language, the upper valley was bound together in a single diocese whose seat was Pembroke. When the war began, Narcisse-Zephérin Lorraine, a native of Laval, Quebec, was bishop. Upon his death in 1916 he was succeeded by Patrick Thomas Ryan, a native of Curragh, County Kildare, whose appointment signalled a shift in power from the French Canadian leadership of the diocese to that of the Irish, who were an imposing presence on both sides of the river.

Like much of Canada before 1931, the upper Ottawa Valley was rural farm country. For generations the inhabitants of Renfrew and Pontiac cleared the forests in the winter, rode their timber down the great river in the spring, planted crops on the cleared land, and in autumn sold their harvests in the market towns of Pembroke, Renfrew, Arnprior, and Eganville on the Ontario side of the river, and on the Quebec side, in Shawville. The city of Ottawa retained a metropolitan influence over the region as the seat of national government, the heart of the lumber industry, the media centre and transportation hub, and the home of higher education. The Ottawa, Arnprior and Parry Sound Railway provided a steel spine linking Ottawa to the Valley towns, on the Ontario side of the River, while the Pontiac & Pacific Junction Railway snaked up the Quebec side of the river, beginning in Aylmer, Quebec, until it terminated in the timber town of Pembroke, Ontario. Younger sons, unable to inherit the family farm or dreaming of a new life entirely, sought their fortunes on the railway as construction workers, linemen, engineers, bridge builders, or skilled tradesmen. As rural depopulation became a common feature of early twentieth-century Ontario, young people from the Valley made Ottawa their new home, or, as in Ned Murray's case, left for the promise of the Prairie West.

When war broke out in August 1914, life in the Valley continued as it had for generations: crops needed harvesting, sawmills continued to carve up the spoils of the great pine forests, and town life barely skipped a beat.[132] There seemed to be no sense of urgency to enlist, and judging from the names inscribed on local war memorials, few men from the Valley could be found in the initial regiments and, later, battalions that constituted the 1st Division of the CEF at Valcartier. Beginning in 1915, however, numerous units from Ottawa, Kingston, Port Hope, Brockville, and Montreal began penetrating the Valley on both sides of the river, holding monster meetings in Renfrew, Shawville, Fort Coulonge, and Pembroke in search of recruits.[133] When, in December 1915, the representatives of the 77th Battalion arrived in Shawville there was great excitement. "When eight o'clock, the opening of the proceedings arrived," reported the *Equity*, "every seat in the lecture hall was full, and many people were standing in the intervening spaces, an evidence indeed that more than ordinary interest had been awakened in the residents of the village and surroundings."[134] The Ottawa-based battalion picked up eight more recruits that evening. As in Shawville, other Valley towns became electrified, and by war's end hundreds of men and women had come forward to serve. After the armistice, a somber *Renfrew Mercury* published the names of 148 men from Renfrew County who were either killed or listed as missing in action, and invited the public to submit names that the editors may have missed.[135]

Shaken by their losses, the residents of towns and villages on both sides of the Ottawa River built monuments to the dead in the years after the war. Eighteen public memorials and plaques were erected in the Valley, stretching across a geographic arc beginning with the tall stone plinth at Arnprior, Ontario, and then curving north through Pembroke, with its large memorial of a soldier vigilant in battle. After

Pembroke, one crosses the Ottawa River, entering Quebec near Chapeau, with its monuments adjacent to the local Catholic Church, and finally curving south along the Quebec side of the Ottawa to Quyon, with its stone monuments guarded by decommissioned military hardware. From the hundreds of names on these memorials, which include in most cases all service personnel, and not only those killed in action, 470 names were correctly identified by means of the Library and Archives Canada online database and the census of 1911.[136] The process of analyzing war memorials and their inscribed names is by no means a research project situated in a proverbial clean laboratory. The communities responsible for the names on monuments often misspelled them, or included men known locally by their nicknames, or omitted Valley men and women who were working or living elsewhere when they enlisted. Mona Whelan was not included on the Douglas monument; she had moved away to study. Dozens of files could not be located because of these problems, but the 470 files that were identified contain the names of recruits and conscripts, men and women, and representing all religions and ethnic groups in the Ottawa Valley (table 3.12). In stone and bronze they help provide a portrait of the communities within which Irish Catholics found themselves to be integral members.

In the sample, Roman Catholics constituted 43 per cent of the recruits and conscripts (see table 3.12). Only the Presbyterian group constituted a higher proportion than the Irish Catholics. French Canadian Catholics had the fourth highest number of names memorialized. Census data show them to have had the highest proportion of conscripts under the Military Service Act among all religious groups in the sample: almost one third of the French Canadian Catholics were conscripted, and over half of the conscripts were farmers. This Ottawa Valley sample, therefore, appears to confirm the prevailing wisdom that French Canadians were less interested in enlisting during the first three stages of voluntary enlistment; it also suggests that one of the reasons for this lack of interest may have been their commitment to work on the family farm, which might be seen as an indirect means of supporting the war effort. Irish Catholics in the sample had slightly higher proportions of conscripts in comparison with their Protestant neighbours and with the overall average for the entire sample of about 17.7 per cent. About 20 per cent of the Irish Catholic sample were conscripts, over one third of whom were

Table 3.12
Characteristics of Ottawa Valley recruits, by religious group (N = 470)

Characteristic	*Irish Catholic*	*French Catholic*	*Other Catholic*	*Church of England*	*Presbyterian*	*Methodist*	*Baptist*	*Other*	*No record*	*Total*
Birthplace										
Canada	112	62	22	60	116	52	8	1	6	439
Britain	4	0	0	11	8	2	1	0	0	26
United States	0	0	0	0	0	0	0	0	1	1
Ireland	1	0	0	2	0	0	0	0	0	3
Other	0	0	1	0	0	0	0	0	0	1
Total	117	62	23	73	124	54	9	1	7	470
Percentage	24.9	13.2	4.9	15.5	26.4	11.5	1.9	0.2	1.5	100.0
Marital status										
Married	6	5	0	5	6	5	1	1	2	31
Recruitment										
MSA	23	20	4	10	18	8	0	0	0	83
MSA: farming/forestry	9	11	2	7	14	8	0	0	0	51
After May 1916	30									
Military service										
Previous service	18	4	4	17	34	12	5	1	2	97

Source: LAC, RG 150, 1992-93.166 LAC, Soldiers of the Great War database, www.bac-lac.gc.ca/eng/discover/military-heritage/first-world-war/first-world-war-1914-1918-cef/Pages/canadian-expeditionary-force.aspx

farmers and the rest mostly unskilled and semi-skilled labourers. (See tables 3.13 to 3.15.)

As in other places in Canada, the parish was a crucible of recruitment in the Ottawa Valley, but there is little evidence of how parishes viewed the militarization of their youth. Newspapers provided only limited coverage of parish events, and parish bulletins have not been well archived for the war period. The village of Mount St Patrick, in Renfrew County, however, suggests that Irish Catholics in the "Valley" were very public in the reception of their soldiers, regardless of religious affiliation. Mount St Patrick is about as demonstrably and visibly Irish and Catholic as any other settlement in Canada. Nestled in the Calabogie Hills about twenty miles inland from the Ottawa River, Mount St Patrick and its church were founded in 1843 by pre-Famine Irish settlers. Shortly thereafter, famine migrants emigrated to nearby Admaston Township,[137] and more Irish settlers poured into the southern portion of the county when the government of Canada opened the Opeongo settlement road, stretching from Castleford on the Ottawa River through the town of Renfrew and eventually terminating in what is now Algonquin Park. St Patrick's Parish featured a stone church in the heart of the village, a cemetery in which graves were adorned by large Celtic crosses, and a Holy Well, which became a site of local pilgrimage. In 1917, a local company of the 240th Battalion trained and bivouacked along Constant Creek, which meanders through the village, and officers were billeted at local homes. Locals saw the visit as so important that all the men of the parish gathered in their finest in front of the church to have their photograph taken with the men of the battalion. Photographs also survive of young boys in the parish wearing their own imitation khaki kit, thereby emulating the recruits.[138] The local separate school at Ashdad boasted at least fifteen recruits, all Irish Catholics, two of whom were killed in action.[139] At war's end, the parish erected an honour roll to commemorate the four men of the parish who had been killed overseas.

While the experience of one parish does not make a "rule," the example of the very "Irish" community of Mount St Patrick suggests that the nationalist rhetoric of the Irish Republican Brotherhood (IRB) and Sinn Fein did not resonate strongly here. Events in Ireland would have been known to the locals, had they read either the Liberal-Unionist *Renfrew Mercury* or the Liberal and pro-Catholic *Eganville Leader*.[140] Knowledge of events in Ireland did not stop them from con-

Table 3.13
Characteristics of Ottawa Valley recruits, by religious group: percentages (N = 470)

Characteristic	*Irish Catholic*	*French Catholic*	*Other Catholic*	*Church of England*	*Presbyterian*	*Methodist*	*Baptist*	*Other*	*No record*	*Total*
Birthplace										
Canada	95.7	100.0	95.6	82.2	93.5	96.3	88.9	100.0	85.7	93.4
Britain	3.4	0.0	0.0	15.1	6.5	3.7	11.1	0.0	0.0	5.5
United States	0.0	0.0	0.0	0.0	0.0	0.0	0.0	0.0	14.3	0.2
Ireland	0.9	0.0	0.0	2.7	0.0	0.0	0.0	0.0	0.0	0.6
Other	0.0	0.0	4.4	0.0	0.0	0.0	0.0	0.0	0.0	0.2
Marital status										
Married	5.1	8.1	0.0	6.8	4.8	9.3	11.1	100.0	28.6	6.6
Military service										
MSA	19.7	32.3	17.4	13.7	14.5	14.8	0.0	0.0	0.0	17.7
MSA: farm/forestry	7.7	17.7	8.7	9.6	11.3	14.8	0.0	0.0	0.0	10.9
Previous service	15.4	6.5	17.4	23.3	27.4	22.2	55.6	100.0	28.6	20.6

Source: War memorials of the Ottawa Valley, and LAC, Soldiers of the Great War database, www.bac-lac.gc.ca/eng/discover/military-heritage/first-world-war/first-world-war-1914-1918-cef/Pages/canadian-expeditionary-force.aspx.

Table 3.14
Occupational classifications of Ottawa Valley recruits, by religious group (N = 470)

Characteristic	*Irish Catholic*	*French Catholic*	*Other Catholic*	*Church of England*	*Presbyterian*	*Methodist*	*Baptist*	*Other*	*No record*	*Total*
Farmer	21	15	5	15	34	19	2	0	2	113
Forester	8	8	2	1	4	3	1	0	0	27
Unskilled	29	20	12	17	15	8	1	0	1	103
Semi-skilled	27	7	1	7	8	6	0	0	0	56
Skilled	13	8	3	9	17	9	0	0	0	59
Clerical	7	2	0	13	27	4	2	1	1	57
Business	2	0	0	4	5	0	0	0	2	13
Professional	10	1	0	6	12	5	3	0	0	37
Other	0	0	0	0	0	0	0	0	0	0
No record	0	1	0	1	2	0	0	0	1	5
Total	117	62	23	73	124	54	9	1	7	470

Source: War memorials of the Ottawa Valley, and LAC, Soldiers of the Great War database, www.bac-lac.gc.ca/eng/discover/military-heritage/first-world-war/first-world-war-1914-1918-cef/Pages/canadian-expeditionary-force.aspx

Table 3.15
Occupational classifications of Ottawa Valley recruits, by religious group: percentages (N = 470)

Characteristic	*Irish Catholic*	*French Catholic*	*Other Catholic*	*Church of England*	*Presbyterian*	*Methodist*	*Baptist*	*Other*	*No record*	*Total*
Farmer	18.0	24.2	21.7	20.5	27.4	35.2	22.2	0.0	28.6	24.0
Forester	6.8	12.9	8.7	1.4	3.2	5.6	11.1	0.0	0.0	5.7
Unskilled	24.8	32.3	52.2	23.2	12.1	14.8	11.1	0.0	14.3	21.9
Semi-skilled	23.1	11.3	4.4	9.6	6.5	4.8	0.0	0.0	0.0	11.9
Skilled	11.1	12.9	13.0	12.3	13.7	16.7	0.0	0.0	0.0	12.6
Clerical	6.0	3.2	0.0	17.8	21.8	7.4	22.2	100.0	14.3	12.1
Business	1.7	0.0	0.0	5.5	4.0	0.0	0.0	0.0	28.6	2.8
Professional	8.5	1.6	0.0	8.2	9.7	9.3	33.3	0.0	0.0	7.9
No record	0.0	1.6	0.0	1.4	1.6	0.0	0.0	0.0	14.3	1.1
Total	100.0	100.0	100.0	100.0	100.0	100.0	100.0	100.0	100.0	100.0

Source: War memorials of the Ottawa Valley, and LAC, Soldiers of the Great War database, www.bac-lac.gc.ca/eng/discover/military-heritage/first-world-war/first-world-war-1914-1918-cef/Pages/canadian-expeditionary-force.aspx

tributing young men to the imperial cause, including the local 130th Battalion (in the case of the soon-to-be-deceased Patrick Scully and James Dwyer), nor did it stop the parish from welcoming all ranks of a local battalion company and proudly appearing with them to be immortalized in a portrait. Indeed, grumblers might have stayed home and been inhospitable, but that was not the case in Mount St Patrick. Perhaps these Irish Catholics knew that their primary investment as Catholics and citizens was to be made in the best interests of their community in Canada. Realistically, although there may have been survivors of the migration generation still living in the village and adjoining townships, most of the inhabitants would have been second- and third-generation Irish Catholics, born and raised in Canada, moving to the annual rhythms of agricultural life in the Valley. While likely fluent in the stories of the *auld country* and of the loggers, farmers, and pioneer women who carved out homesteads in and around Calabogie, there seemed little doubt that Mount St Patrick, and perhaps other settlements in the Valley, claimed this war as their own, regardless of the Rising in Dublin.

Like Ned Murray before them, the 42nd Regiment of Lanark and Renfrew Highlanders had been a popular militia unit among both the Catholic and non-Catholic recruits in the Valley.[141] Approximately 57 (12.1 per cent) of the 470 recruits in the sample joined, of whom 31 were Catholic and 26 were Protestants. Organized in November 1915 and authorized to recruit by the Militia Department the following month, the 130th Battalion was led by Lieutenant Colonel J.E. de Hertel. Mobilized at Perth in Lanark County, it drew a strong cross-section of volunteers from across the Ottawa Valley, including numerous French Canadian Catholics from areas north of Pembroke.[142] The battalion recruited quickly and sailed in November 1916. Like most of the Battalions raised during the spring of that year, as was the case with the Irish specialty battalions, the 130th was placed in reserve in England and then broken up to renew battalions already in the field, such as the 38th Battalion of Ottawa. What is important to understand is that the Irish Catholics of the upper Valley continued to serve as part of companies and drafts of neighbours and colleagues from all walks of life and faiths from their home parts of the province.

The microstudy of the Valley's Irish Catholics helps to amplify the manner in which Irish Catholic recruitment, and the Irish Catholic community for that matter, could not be seen in isolation from the social, political, and economic world in which they earned their daily bread. In the CEF, as in life, Irish Catholics were part of a multi-faith and multicultural community consisting of Scots, English, Poles, German, and Ojibwa neighbours. Local newspapers published stories of the fallen and letters from the Front regardless of the religious affiliation of the soldier or his family.[143] It was ever thus in the army as well, where the sons of farmers and shopkeepers, students and miners, raw recruits and experienced militia veterans joined together and fought for a common cause. As for Irish Catholics, their occupational profiles did not deviate significantly from the non-Catholics with whom they were memorialized, although there was a larger number of unskilled labourers among the Irish group (tables 3.14 and 3.15). These men would have been factory hands in the Valley towns, miners, railway workers, and farm hands. One striking feature of the regional study was how, consistent with the other regions of Canada where Irish Catholics were recruited, over 95 per cent of Irish Catholic recruits inscribed on the Ottawa Valley memorials were Canadian-born (table 3.13). Although, as has been noted in this chapter, such high levels of Canadian birth were not seen in other groups of recruits, non-Irish and non-Catholic recruits from the Valley had similarly high levels of Canadian nativity. The average rate of Canadian birth for all the groups represented was over 93 per cent. In the farms and towns of the Valley, less affected by the recent immigration waves of the Laurier–Borden years, recruiting officers discovered that the men signing their attestation papers, regardless of creed or culture, were men rooted in the region, often second- or third-generation Canadians.

Regional studies of Irish Catholic recruitment offer a nuanced understanding of how Irish Catholic men came to enlist for the Empire's war. For instance, a comparison of the recruitment patterns of Irish Catholics in the largely rural Ottawa Valley with those in the aforementioned 25th and 40th Battalions in urban Halifax shows obvious differences but also certain similarities. In both Halifax and the Ottawa Valley one discovers a mix of Catholics across occupational boundaries, with, of course, concentrations in the harbour-related occupations in the port of Halifax, and in agriculture and logging in the Ottawa Valley. Another similarity is that each group was overwhelmingly Canadian by birth, a characteristic that in the case of Halifax (and other Irish Catholic parishes across Canada) differed significantly from their Protestant neighbours. In the Ottawa Valley, which was less touched by recent immigration, Irish Catholics differed very little in this respect from non-Irish Catholics. The Valley Irish and Haligonian Irish Catholic groups demonstrated significant levels of previous military service, but more so in Halifax, where the Irish Catholic population, as supported by the patriotic work of the Charitable Irish Society, was visibly present in great numbers in local militia units. Similar rates of previous service were found among Irish Catholics across the country, whether they were identified by their parishes or by their battalions of initial enlistment. Although nothing can be said definitively about why individual Irish Catholic men signed their attestation papers, the data reveal that employment considerations did not appear to factor heavily. Given their strong numbers, previous experience, and similarity of occupational circumstance to the major Protestant denominations, that Irish Catholics, ordinary men and women, took common cause with their neighbours to fight for King and Canada.

When Ned Murray was laid to rest in the Rosiers Communal Cemetery Extension in France in 1918, he represented a generation of Irish Catholic Canadians who embraced the war effort as their own.[144] Well educated, sufficiently interested in the military to have volunteered to serve in South Africa, Murray probably exceeded the military qualifications of his Catholic peers. Nevertheless, he was symbolic of a change taking place in the Irish Catholic community, where professions of loyalty to the Empire were perhaps more demonstrable than they had been in the past. His own varied career, from student to shepherd, stretched the gamut of occupations among his co-religionists, and his wandering to the west to pursue the latter vocation was typical of many in his generation. When he died at Amiens in August 1918 he left a balance of $490.96 in unused military pay, which was sent to Pembroke for his sister, Mary Elizabeth Donahue.[145] The money was likely meaningless to the grieving Murray and Donahue families. For Mary and for the rest of the Murray clan, Ned's sacrifice had not been in vain, nor had it dampened the family's contributions to win the war and defend the Faith in the process from any gainsayers who would deny Catholics their due. His brother, J.L. Murray, would see to that.

4

Irreligion, Immorality, and Blasphemy

Faith at the Front

In November 1917, as the men of the 5th Brigade advanced against the Germans in the sea of mud that was Passchendaele, Father Ronald MacGillivray scratched out a note to his superiors, reporting on the state of the Faith at the front. The battle-hardened Cape Bretoner was frank and reflective about his role as a chaplain. In the events that had taken him from Vimy to Belgium, he had witnessed some of the fiercest fighting of the war. The second battle of Passchendaele was raging, and Catholic men were waiting in a church behind the lines to offer their confession and receive the padre's absolution. MacGillivray had just finished hearing the confessions of his "boys" when he was approached by the officer who had brought the men to the church. The officer said he wanted to talk but requested no confession, since he had not been a practising Catholic for years. MacGillivray continued his report: "I asked him if he knew what prompted him [to have the chat;] he replied in the negative and added 'It is a whim I suppose.' I then told him it was undoubtedly his mother's prayers. With this he remained silent for a while and then said: 'She sent me a Sacred Heart Badge last night and I know she always prays for me. Father I will go to Confession.'" In the hours that followed the encounter, MacGillivray was responsible for helping move the wounded to the rear and collecting the bodies of the fallen. Among the dead, he discovered the officer he had seen shortly before. He covered him with a blanket and said a "little prayer to St Monica," whose prayers had brought her wayward son, the future St Augustine, into the fold of the Church. It was experiences like this – witnessing men's faith and devotion in the face of death – that caused him to remark how necessary and rewarding his presence was among the men at the front. "I would not exchange those few hours in the mud and cold," he wrote, "for years of peaceful parish work."[1]

MacGillivray's report touches on two dimensions of the religious experience of Catholics in the CEF during the Great War. First, it suggests an awareness by the Canadian churches of the importance of a religious presence among the men and women in active military service and a sense of the importance of this spiritual role among the chaplains themselves. From the onset of hostilities in August 1914, organized Canadian religious groups, regardless of denomination, fully expected that the CEF would reflect Canadian values in general and would make accommodations for an institutionalized religious component for those serving their country and the Empire. It was anticipated by most churches that there would be a need for a chaplaincy and, moreover, that the men would want it. Chaplaincy within the CEF has left a good paper trail that has been followed by various historians, official and unofficial, over the past century. The opinions of chaplains, the structure of the Canadian Chaplain Service (CCS), and the trials and tribulations of its leadership have been well documented in a number of studies.[2] But the reports of clergy and the expectations of religious leaders at home give a limited perspective on the state of the Faith among lay soldiers at the front. The gap between pulpit and pew is often wide, as is the distance between what is preached and what is actually practised.

It is even more difficult to uncover the second dimension of religious experience in the CEF, as epitomized by MacGillivray's officer: faith as it was lived in the ranks. To adopt a biblical analogy, portrayals of piety and devotion at the front are like bricks made without straw: the bricks can be made, but the product is unreliable – or, in this case, speculative. Padres reported what they saw through their own particular lenses; for the pharisaics among them, the men could never be good enough; for battle-hardened soldier-priests, on the other hand, the men were engaged in an ongoing process of conversion in the face of adversity. One suspects that the reality of spiritual life fell somewhere between these two interpretations. Since few men offered spiritual reflections on their war experience in letters or diaries, and those who did so were typically cryptic or brief, there are only fragments of evidence on which to build a case for grassroots piety or a lack thereof. Of little help are the memoirs of veterans such as Charles Harrison and Will Bird, for whom the soldiers were "godless, cynical and profane" and the chaplains "irrelevant."[3] With such opinions as the stuff of popular reading from the Great War, it is little wonder that when historians discuss religious life they do so mainly from the chaplain's perspective or simply offer statistical tables showing a denominational breakdown of the troops.[4] In the case of Irish Catholics, a more finely grained discussion is made even more difficult by the fact that the padres themselves rarely distinguished one group of Catholics from another. Although one might argue that the confessional knows no language or race, there are hints from chaplains' reports that priests in the field were aware of differences between Catholic groups, and that the linguistic tensions between French- and English-speaking Catholics at home often resurfaced in the CEF overseas.

This chapter examines both sides of the religious coin: that is, both the official role of the Canadian Catholic Church through its chaplains, and the religious behaviour of Catholics, particularly Irish Catholics, who donned khaki and blue. We can gain some glimpses into the "lived religion" of men and women in the CEF through the comments of chaplains and in routinely generated records. On the assumption that a person's beliefs may be demonstrated by his or her actions, the personnel records of soldiers and nurses can help us gauge the gap between pew and pulpit and assess whether the adage "there are no atheists in foxholes" held true for Catholics at the front. It can be difficult to extricate the Irish Catholics from others, since the padres themselves do not always make the distinction. Sometimes the available evidence enables us to compare the behaviour of Irish Catholics to that of their French, Scottish, Chinese, and First Nations co-religionists. Irish Catholics were well represented among the over one hundred Catholic priests who served as chaplains between 1914 and 1918, and Irish Catholic soldiers were identified as approaching the sacraments, as did other Catholics under fire.[5] What is striking, though, is a pattern observed by padres, in which Catholic men who were only loosely affiliated with parishes at home, or did not practise their religion before the war, embraced the sacraments and devotions while in the thick of action, only to drift away from the Faith once the hostilities were over. What is clear from the evidence is that Irish Catholics, with some exceptions, practised their faith when a padre was available, but did not necessarily keep to a godly path otherwise

At the outset of hostilities in August 1914, the minister of militia and defence, Sam Hughes, himself a devout Protestant and member of the Orange Order, hurriedly allocated thirty-three chaplains to the First Contingent, although he did not formally establish the CCS until August 1915.[6] In 1914, he appointed his friend, the Reverend Richard H. Steacy, an Anglican minister, to serve as Honourary Major and Senior Chaplain, and later promoted him in the reorganized CCS to Honorary Colonel and Director of the Service;[7] after all, it seemed only appropriate that a representative of the King's church be the head of the religious arm of the King's forces in Canada, in which the overwhelming majority would be members of the Church of England. Hughes cared little about accommodating existing chaplains serving in the militia, but went about willy-nilly making his own appointments from his own sources.[8] In the early months of the war, Hughes contacted Catholic bishops directly to secure at least five padres for the 1st Division.[9] One means by which he did this was to seek out clergy who had already been affiliated with the military. Both Catholic and Protestant chaplains had accompanied the Canadian troops during the Boer War. As we might expect, some of the first recruits to the CCS were actually veteran clergy from that conflict. These veterans included Father Peter O'Leary of Quebec City, whose heroic exploits in the African veldts were the stuff of legend. O'Leary had been loved by Catholics and Protestants alike for his sense of humour and his willingness to make the marches and accompany the troops wherever the war led them. He was held up as the model priest for the new CCS,[10] and his style of engagement with his fighting flock would be emulated by Catholic clergy who enlisted from 1914 to 1918. Ironically, O'Leary's re-enlistment in 1914 did not go as planned. He was demobilized in 1917 at the age of 67: he could no longer to keep up the pace of a chaplain's duties, and it was alleged – with no hard evidence – that he was dependent on alcohol.[11]

Much of the original formation of the chaplain service was rather ad hoc on both sides of the Atlantic. For their part, Steacy and Hughes, who did not always agree with one another, resented the interference of the British Army and refused to have any but Canadian clergy serve in the CEF, despite the fact that a high percentage of volunteers in the early phases of the war were British-born. Steacy also objected when the British War Office wanted to restrict the number of Canadian padres attached to the First Division to five, to match the

British Army's standard allotment per division at the time.[12] The Canadians refused to comply, insisting that a Canadian-raised and Canadian-financed army should make its own decisions about the allocation of chaplains. Canon Frederick George Scott, the well-known poet and popular Anglican padre from the Quebec Diocese, made this case to the War Office, defending Canadian autonomy in these matters.[13] In the end, Steacy sent eleven chaplains to France with the First Division, most of whom were allocated to the hospital units, thus betraying a preference to keep the clergy out of the thick of front-line action. In some ways, Steacy had an embarrassment of riches in his thirty-three chaplains, but a shortage of Anglicans to serve the majority Anglican presence in the First Division.

The allocation of an appropriate number of chaplains to troops from different denominations was a source of controversy on the home front as well. In 1914–15 there was considerable anxiety among Catholic leaders that there were not enough priests for the Catholic recruits.[14] For the Catholic Church in Canada, it was absolutely necessary that men in arms have the services of a priest, particularly for the sacraments. Given a Roman Catholic's religious duty to receive the Eucharist (Holy Communion) on Sunday and other "days of obligation" and to regularly attend Confession, it became clear not only that Catholic priests would be required for the CEF, but also that their responsibility to administer the Sacraments would compel them to be as close to the troops as possible, even in the support trenches at the front. For Catholic recruits, the most poignant visible reminder of the Catholic faith was the presence of the Catholic chaplain. In the minds of ordinary Catholics and their leaders, the priest was "the first necessity of the Church."[15] Church leaders in Canada deemed it imperative that Catholic soldiers and nurses be able to continue their religious observances and obligations overseas, without hindrance or danger to their faith, and made every effort to place over one hundred priests in the CCS by the end of the war.[16]

So confident were the bishops that young Catholic men in Canada were ardent practitioners of the Faith, that they argued recruiting efforts among Catholics would be futile unless the men knew priests would be available to them in the service. In Antigonish, Bishop James Morrison was adamant that the lack of Catholic chaplains would be a "serious handicap" to recruitment and that provision had to be made for priests in battalions wherever the numbers of

Catholics justified it.[17] To this end, Morrison and other bishops in Maritime dioceses became actively involved in releasing one of their own diocesan priests to serve as a chaplain to a specific unit containing high numbers of Catholics. In Nova Scotia, for example, Morrison and Archbishop Edward McCarthy of Halifax unilaterally made appointments of priests to the 25th, 40th, and 85th Battalions. For Morrison, the case was clear: "It is unnecessary to say that Catholics are ready and willing to give their lives for their country, as they have been doing in good numbers, but their religious welfare should not be sacrificed through the unpatriotic indifference of those who control the chaplaincies; [this] is something we cannot stand for and of course will not stand for."[18] Similar efforts were made by other bishops in eastern Canada, where Catholic recruits were numerous. Catholics in the 22nd Battalion (Montreal), 25th Battalion (Nova Scotia), 185th Battalion (Cape Breton), 105th (Prince Edward Island) 199th Battalion (Montreal), and 132nd Battalion (New Brunswick), had a priest available to them throughout their basic training, and often until their arrival in England. Like Morrison, clergy in the rest of Canada and some Catholic officers explained to military authorities that, without the assurance that the spiritual welfare of Catholics would be taken care of by battalion chaplains, Catholic families would be reluctant to support the enlistment of their young men. By 1916, the Maritime bishops, led by McCarthy, pledged to coordinate their recruitment of priests with efforts being made by the Ontario bishops in recruiting chaplains from their own dioceses.[19]

Throughout much of the war, it was left to individual bishops to spearhead the recruitment and appointment of chaplains. There was no overarching canonical structure that brought all of Canada's bishops together into a conference, as would be the case in the 1940s. The best that could be done in the early years of the war was to recruit priests by means of the local coordination of bishops within their ecclesiastical province, which did not always jibe with the civil provincial boundaries of Canada. In Ontario, the bishops of the Archdiocese of Toronto (Toronto, Hamilton, London), the Archdiocese of Kingston (Kingston, Alexandria, Peterborough, Sault Ste. Marie), and Ottawa (Ottawa, Pembroke, Temiskaming) met to determine how priests would be allocated to the CCS. As in the Maritime dioceses, there was a critical shortage of priests in central and western Canada.[20] The newly minted archbishop of Winnipeg, Alfred A. Sinnott, was aware of the shortage of English-speaking priests at home when he told the CCS that "there is a consensus of opinion [among bishops] that [soldiers'] needs must be balanced with the needs at home."[21] Bishops had to determine how to serve the men and women at the front, while making sure there was an appropriate complement of priests to staff the domestic Church. In 1918, this situation worsened when many priests in Canada were stricken with influenza, thereby crippling some dioceses.[22]

In 1915, the Ontario bishops appointed the controversial Michael Francis Fallon, bishop of London, as their liaison between the Church and government on the issue of chaplains.[23] The fluently bilingual Fallon was politically well connected (leaning to the Liberals) but was reviled in French Canadian circles for his opposition to French-language education in Ontario schools. Although Fallon corresponded immediately with Sam Hughes, the Apostolic Delegate, and the anglophone hierarchy in Canada, it was debatable whether his authority in these matters extended outside of Ontario – or even into the Archdiocese of Ottawa, which straddled the Ottawa River and included huge sections of western Quebec.[24] Although Fallon recognized that his own authority was confined to English-speaking Catholics,[25] the chaplaincy question, with all of its denominational challenges, now became more complicated by his appointment and his evident unpopularity as a *maudit Irlandais* in French Catholic Canada.

The Catholic Church in British Columbia appeared to share many of the concerns expressed by bishops and priests to the east. The allocation of chaplains was left primarily to the archbishop of Vancouver, Timothy Casey, himself a recently transplanted prelate from Saint John, New Brunswick. Casey's assumptions about the need for and placement of Catholic chaplains seemed to be more or less what his colleagues Morrison and McCarthy assumed for their dioceses in Nova Scotia: battalions with high numbers of Catholics were to have their own padre. By 1915, however, this expectation was unrequited in British Columbia. Father Ambrose Madden, an Irish Catholic native of Winnipeg, but attached to the Oblates in British Columbia, had been stationed at the infantry training Camp in Vernon, British Columbia. He had reported to Casey on the good deportment of the Catholic men, but complained that nearly a thousand Catholic soldiers from the province had been shipped out without a chaplain – a role that he had expected to be his. He reported to his bishop that the camps in British Columbia were all in close proximity to local Catholic parish churches, and so the need for a priest in the camp was less urgent than the need to have a priest travelling with the troops. He pleaded with Casey to arrange for his transit with the next available battalion, likely the 54th, which presumably had a high number of Catholics.[26] Madden eventually arrived in Europe, not as a battalion padre, but as Catholic Brigade Chaplain to the 2nd Brigade, First Canadian Division.[27]

It was on this issue of the allocation of Catholic priests where the hierarchy met stiff resistance from Steacy and Hughes. The bishops' first obstacle with the CCS was the fact that, although they could nominate chaplains for specific units, Steacy and Hughes ultimately had the power officially to appoint the nominated chaplains – or, as the case may be, to delay appointments or ignore nominations.[28] By late 1915 it was becoming increasingly clear that neither Hughes nor Steacy thought there was any urgency to fill divisional vacancies with Catholic chaplains.[29] Moreover, Steacy and Hughes had worked out their own allocation policy, which was generally to appoint one chaplain per specific denomination per brigade, provided that the denomination in question accounted for one thousand or more troops in the brigade.[30] Each infantry brigade was comprised of four battalions of just over a thousand men each, in addition to a trench mortar battery. There was therefore almost no chance, given the numbers of Catholic recruits and the actual size of the battalions, that each battalion would be allocated its own priest.[31] The 185th Battalion of Nova Scotia Highlanders, of which over half were Roman Catholic – many of them Gaelic speakers[32] – were particularly indignant when their chaplain, Michael Gillis, was transferred because the CCS allowed for only one Catholic chaplain per brigade of four battalions.[33]

The best the Catholic bishops could hope for was one priest per brigade, three priests per division, and perhaps a few extra padres to cover the divisional field batteries, engineers, signals companies, machine gun corps, and hospitals. This was poor consolation for the Catholic bishops, who had hoped for better coverage, and who suspected that the official rationale for the allocation of priests masked a Protestant plot to curtail the Catholic clerical presence among the troops. Bishop Morrison was furious when he discovered there was no Catholic chaplain, but two Anglicans and a Baptist, administering to the 64th Battalion of Nova Scotia, of whom the majority were

Catholics of Irish and Scottish origin. He complained to Hughes in a registered letter: "That is all right, and I have nothing to say about it. But the wrong is that there is no Catholic chaplain there."[34] He was more blunt in his remarks to John J. O'Gorman, a politically well-connected chaplain from Ottawa, about "bigotry and a lack of efficiency in the D.C.S."[35]

The power struggle over the allocation of chaplains came to a head over the appointment of a Catholic chaplain to the 5th Infantry Brigade of the 2nd Canadian Division. This dispute, which tapped into sectarian rivalries as well as the tension between francophone and anglophone Catholics, lasted from early 1915 to late 1916. Throughout the war, only the 5th Brigade could be seen as predominantly Catholic, encompassing the 22nd Battalion ("Van Doos") from Quebec as well as the 24th (Montreal), 25th (Nova Scotia), and 26th (New Brunswick) Battalions. The numbers involved soon warranted the unprecedented appointment of a second Catholic chaplain to the brigade.[36] The 22nd Battalion was French-speaking, and its 1,100 men were almost all Roman Catholics. The 25th and 26th Battalions also had a high proportion of Catholic troops, but most were English speakers of Irish and Scottish descent. There were also Catholics in the Montreal Battalion, who were also largely anglophone Irish and Scots. In combination, these battalions presented the Church and the CCS with a dilemma.[37] There were approximately 1,792 Catholics in the 5th Brigade[38] – over 45 per cent of the brigade's strength – but only one Catholic chaplain was permitted per 1000 troops. In effect, this meant that the chaplain would be francophone and serving primarily the Van Doos. This was unacceptable to the Irish and Scottish Catholics, who wanted to receive the sacraments from someone who shared their culture and language. By their reckoning, two Catholic chaplains ought to be appointed to the brigade: one for the French speakers and one for the English speakers. The heads of the CCS, however, were unwilling to budge from the formula they had set to keep the peace between the denominations. As far as Steacy and Hughes were concerned, the 5th Brigade would have one chaplain, and that chaplain would be Captain Constant Victor Doyon of the Van Doos.

The situation was overwhelming for Doyon, who had limited English-language skills[39] and found it difficult to minister to all four battalions and the other units in the brigade. He admitted that anglophone troops were reluctant to approach him, which meant that nearly eight hundred Catholics in the brigade effectively had no priest. The Nova Scotia bishops were particularly vexed, because Bishop Morrison had arranged for Father Donald Macpherson to attend to the Irish and Scottish Catholics of the 25th Battalion. After the battalion arrived in England, Steacy had Macpherson shipped off to Thessalonika, in the Aegean theatre, in August 1915, where according to Macpherson's own account he was surrounded by Greek Orthodox, rather than Catholic, adherents and was tormented by disease-carrying flies and numerous outbreaks of dysentery.[40] Needless to say, Morrison was outraged by the arbitrary reassignment of his hand-picked chaplain, and by the fact that the 25th was now left with only the services of Doyon. Morrison, who called Hughes' position with regard to the 5th Brigade a "shameful deception," fought the military establishment for over a year to secure a chaplain for English-speaking Catholics.[41] His campaign included a frank appeal to Prime Minister Bordon in 1916: "[I]f such treatment is going to be handed out to our Catholic recruits, it is only fair that they should know it before offering to enlist ... [T]his utter disregard for the religious needs of our Nova Scotia Catholics is nothing short of a public outrage."[42]

The matter had become something of a public concern in September 1915 when the *Catholic Register* printed a letter written home by a soldier who complained that Irish and Scottish Catholics were without priests:

> I must say that it is simply rotten the way English-speaking Catholics are treated here. We are in danger of losing our lives, yet the officials are indifferent to our appeal for at least a chance to make our Easter duty ... Other creeds have their ministers here with them, who preach to their following at every opportunity. Now what do they think of us Catholic boys who never see a priest at all? I don't know if this letter will pass the censor, but if it does I and all the Catholic boys here on the firing line would like you to ask the question, "Why are we not supplied with a priest?"[43]

Indeed, how did the letter slip by the censors in the 5th Brigade, who typically were the chaplains, and in this case were the francophone Doyon and two Anglicans and one Baptist minister? The details of the letter dovetailed nicely with the anger festering among Catholic chaplains and within episcopal circles. Questions of the letter's authenticity aside, the message was clear: something was amiss in the 5th Brigade, something that may have been symptomatic of a greater malaise within the CCS when it came to just treatment for English-speaking Catholics.

In France, the battle over the Catholic allocation of chaplains to the 5th Brigade continued. Father MacGillivray weighed in on the practical pastoral crisis created by having only one priest for so many men. In January, he detailed the key issues to his bishop, Morrison:

> In our brigade there are over 1200 French Canadians and these fully occupy the time of Father Doyon, who by the way speaks but little English, besides there are about 1000 English speaking Catholics, the majority of them from Nova Scotia and New Brunswick. I understand that many of the boys have not been to confession since Fr Macpherson has gone to the East ... The boys I find are frank and manly and have a leaven of excellent fellows who do more good than a chaplain. They very often discuss religion and when these good Catholic boys get into difficulty they bring their man to the priest.[44]

McGillivray was by no means a disinterested observer. In October 1915, Morrison had appointed him to the 25th when Macpherson was transferred to Thessalonika. Morrison's appointment was allegedly made on Hughes' request, but it was then blocked by Steacy.[45] In 1916, Father Wolston Workman, a British Franciscan working with the Canadians and later to be Assistant Director of the CCS, had unsuccessfully tried to attach McGillivray to the 5th Brigade to relieve Doyon and to care for the Irish and Scots outside the Van Doos. The British Chaplaincy Service made the appointment, but again Steacy rescinded it, claiming that Catholics already received "too many favours," and that special concessions might also have to be offered to other denominations whom Steacy was already holding at bay.[46] For Workman, Steacy's head-counting was twaddle. Any numbers upon which allocations of chaplains are decided, asserted Workman, "should be based on the percentage of *Communicants*, for it is the *Communicant* that gives the real work."[47] As well as expressing his frustration with Steacy, Workman's comments may also hint at robust religious adherence among the Catholics of the 5th Brigade. One senses this also in McGillivray's comments about soldiers taking on pastoral duties themselves in the absence of an English-speaking chaplain. For Workman and other padres, this matter of allocating priests was more than a head count; it was an accounting of practising Catholic men. Shortly thereafter, the prime minister intervened, and McGillivray was permitted to visit the brigade, where he remained until he was replaced by Renfrew Ontario's Father Francis L. French in October 1916.[48]

The problem of the 5th Brigade revealed not only the ineffectiveness of decision-making in the Steacy-led CCS, but also the infighting between chaplains in the field and the obdurate leadership at the service's headquarters in London. The incident also reveals tensions within the Catholic ranks. It was well known that there were far fewer French Canadian Catholic recruits in the CEF than volunteers from among Irish and Scottish Catholics, which was reflected in the higher number of anglophone chaplains in the Catholic branch of the CCS. Even the prickly Monsignor Alfred E. Burke, the controversial Catholic chaplain allied with Hughes and Steacy, admitted to Canada's apostolic delegate that the flow of French Canadian priests to the "Service" should be reduced because "it is English-speaking chaplains we need. Besides some of these chaplains from Quebec do not know English well enough or wish to employ it if they do and there are complaints from our soldiers at the front on this account."[49] Burke's opponent on almost all matters with regard to the service agreed. Reverend Captain O'Gorman, responding to the possibility of a French Canadian priest being nominated to head the newly formed Catholic Branch of the CCS in Ottawa, argued strenuously against it, claiming that "[a] Frenchman will ruin us – the French anti-war, anti-enlist campaign being more than the country can stand."[50] It appears that even among Catholics in a time of war, Irish–French mistrust was not far from the surface.

An obvious question remains. Was the 5th Brigade controversy an example of Protestant senior chaplains discriminating against Roman Catholics? Although Steacy's rather pharisaic approach to the allocation numbers might cause one to hypothesize that he used his own protocols to foil Catholic ambitions in the corps, there is little evidence to bear this out. Both Steacy and Hughes were joined in their direction of the Catholic chaplains by Burke, who fancied himself the head of the Catholic chaplaincy overseas. Although Burke paraded around Europe with his delusions of grandeur – with neither the authorization nor the support of the Catholic hierarchy in Canada – he was a convenient shield for Steacy and the CCS against any accusations of anti-Catholic bigotry. Burke was a native of Georgetown, Prince Edward Island, where, as a priest, he had distinguished himself as a human whirlwind not only in his engagement in parish life and his involvement in provincial and national associations, including as the president of the Prince Edward Island's Fruit Growers' Association, vice-president of the Maritime Beekeepers Association, vice-president of the Canadian Forestry Association, grand trustee of the Catholic Mutual Benefit Association, and member of the Conservative Party.[51] An imperialist, he was close enough to Robert Borden, then the Conservative leader, to send him an intricate scheme to build a tunnel under the Northumberland Strait to link Prince Edward Island and the mainland. "Tunnel Burke," as he became known, vaulted onto the national ecclesial and political stage in 1908. As described in chapter 1, he became the first president of the Catholic Church Extension Society and editor of the *Catholic Register*.[52] The *Register* was Burke's bully pulpit from which he condemned anti-Catholicism, praised Canada's Imperial ambitions, fought for the rights of immigrants to Canada, and roused support for Canada's war effort in 1914. One of the most controversial Catholic figures of his generation, he was described by his former altar boy Father (later Bishop) Francis Clement Kelley[53] as follows: "Half his world swore by him and the other half at him."[54] In 1915 he secured an honorary rank of major, as a chaplain, through the intercession of his friend Senator James Lougheed. He travelled to the Vatican and met with Pope Benedict XV, and proceeded to London, proclaiming himself head of the Catholic chaplains.[55] His imperialist and Conservative credentials unassailable, Father Burke would help Steacy and his staff repel charges of anti-Catholicism while antagonizing both the Canadian Catholic chaplains in the field and their episcopal patrons at home.

Burke was unequivocal in his public refutation of reports that Catholic men in arms were poorly tended-to with respect to their spiritual duties. In November 1915 he made a tour of the Canadian Divisions in France and reported positively on the work of all the chaplains he met. His bottom line to CCS headquarters was clear: "[W]e shall have a sufficiency for all purposes and all that the Establishment rules allow us. This will be gratifying in view of the fact that a great many complaints were circulated as to the inadequacy of our chaplain service at the front. I may say that on investigation I found this to be without foundation, as where we had no priests of our own,

British priests saw that nobody went without the sacraments in necessity."[56] Burke conveyed these comments to the Canadian bishops,[57] to his fellow chaplains, in the Catholic press,[58] and even to Borden, to whom he wrote: "I have only to repeat what I said before to Sir George Perley, when he made the enquiry consequent upon the foolish letters of zealots and agitators, that not a single soldier's soul has suffered for the want of spiritual assistance."[59] At every turn, Burke backed Steacy and the CCS, therefore undercutting the criticisms coming from the Catholic chaplains and the Canadian bishops – presumably, Burke's "zealots and agitators."

By mid-1916, however, it appeared Burke had overplayed his hand and underestimated the desperation of his fellow chaplains to see justice done for Catholic soldiers. Bishop Morrison had little regard for Burke even before the war and had let his episcopal colleagues know that Burke was "totally unfitted" for the presidency of the Extension Society.[60] But, since Morrison was in Nova Scotia, away from the centre of the chaplaincy leadership and not as well connected politically as Burke, the self-designated padre-in-chief had plenty of room to manoeuvre. More difficult for Burke to handle were attacks from his colleagues, especially the outspoken O'Gorman who had initially described his relationship with Burke as "friendly ... over a period of ten years."[61] Burke's claims to Canadian bishops and the Canadian press had stunned O'Gorman, who was chafing at the bit to rebut them. Countering Burke's assessment, O'Gorman maintained that at least twelve English-speaking chaplains were needed, that the 4th Division in the field was also short of priests, and that the 5th Brigade question had not been solved satisfactorily. Offering Burke some collegial advice, the younger priest suggested: "Boost your fellow chaplains, don't knock them ... praise your fellow chaplains rather than blame them ... I don't know if you realize how angry many of the chaplains are with you."[62] Burke turned a deaf ear and lived to pay the price. He underestimated how effectively O'Gorman could gather a loyal opposition on the ground to what was seen as negligence at the heart of the CCS Headquarters.

Burke's authority as senior Catholic chaplain, which had often been questioned, became a major issue. In early 1916, Father Philippe Casgrain, a Canadian chaplain working as a Russian translator in the War Office,[63] told the apostolic delegate to Canada that Burke had "no special mission" from the bishops.[64] In mid-1916, O'Gorman launched an unsuccessful protest about the lack of Catholic chaplains to Steacy himself.[65] Later, O'Gorman was joined by Fathers Casgrain and Workman, Canon Ludger Adolph Sylvestre in Montreal, and Father Miles Tompkins of the Diocese of Antigonish in repeated letter campaigns to the Canadian bishops, leading members of the Cabinet, the apostolic delegate, and the Canadian military officials in London. Burke was described as a "joke"[66] and Steacy as an "Orange bigot."[67] Despite a rash of promotions in the chaplaincy service, no Catholics moved beyond the rank of captain – except for Burke, who became an honorary lieutenant colonel.[68] Burke continued to survive behind the shield of Hughes and Steacy[69] and within the gaps of Catholic authority: he was beyond the jurisdiction of the Canadian bishops and the reach of the cardinal archbishop of Westminster. By July, Bishop Fallon begged for action from the apostolic delegate, who was firm with the renegade monsignor: "One thing appears to be pretty certain that you have not convinced anyone on the sufficiency of the chaplain service ... This criticism and hostility has gone so far that I have actually received requests for your recall."[70] Knowing that the Delegate had no actual power to do so, since his was a military appointment, Burke simply deflected such criticism toward the "overzealous and busy-body clerics" in the CCS when he addressed his military superiors.[71] His Catholic colleagues in the CCS were aware of this; by August, all had signed a petition to the government "protesting against Mgr. Burke speaking in their name."[72]

As the war within the Catholic chaplaincy raged, O'Gorman was temporarily removed as one of the ringleaders of the revolt against Burke and Steacy. In September 1916, while serving with the 3rd Brigade at the rank of honorary major,[73] O'Gorman took charge of evacuating the wounded from "no man's land." While under the flag of the Red Cross, hauling bodies from the muck, he was struck by shrapnel from a German whiz-bang. The hot metal tore into his legs and shattered his left shoulder, elbow, and wrist. O'Gorman was evacuated through the hospital network that he once served, wracked with pain and later beset by repeated infections.[74] He was transported back to Canada, and if the leaders at the CCS thought they could breathe more easily, nothing was further from the truth. O'Gorman used his convalescence in Ottawa to wade deeply into the controversy plaguing the CCS and was able to access and alert cabinet members, particularly Charles J. Doherty, the minister of justice, about problems in the recruitment, allocation, and treatment of Catholic chaplains by their Protestant commanding officers. He gainsaid the positive reports sent by Burke and undercut Steacy, whom he claimed discriminated against Catholics by being indifferent to their problems and complaints.[75] O'Gorman recommended a shake-up in the CCS, which would involve the appointment of a new director (who would be a Protestant but not an Orangeman), and an assistant director (who would be in charge of the Catholic branch of the service). By March 1917, O'Gorman, who was also well-connected to fellow Ottawan Sir George Perley, the Canadian High Commissioner in London, had achieved his desired objectives.[76] Colonel John M. Almond, an Anglican minister and veteran of the Boer War, replaced Steacy as director, and Father Workman became the ADCS-Catholic.[77] Steacy could not count on Hughes' support: Borden had sacked his minister of militia and defence in November 1916.

In the end, O'Gorman's revolution not only brought about major changes in the structure of the CCS, but also spelled the end of Burke. Steacy had tried to protect him by recommending that he return to Canada to assist with recruiting – but to no avail.[78] The Ontario bishops had evidently been working through Minister of Justice Doherty, who told Sir George Perley in London that Burke's appointment to head the Catholic branch of the Chaplain Service would be opposed by the Canadian hierarchy and the apostolic delegate.[79] Burke, without allies, was at the mercy of Father Workman, who tried to assign him to a chaplain's position in France. Instead, Burke decided to continue his freelancing and assisted the Irish Parliamentary Party as they tried to rebuild after being blindsided by the Easter Rising.[80] Burke returned to Canada in July 1917,[81] but eventually went to the United States under the protection of Father Francis Clement Kelley, a friend, also an expatriate Prince Edward Islander, and president of the American Catholic Church Extension Society. Burke claimed he was going to the United States to help train military chaplains.

Finally, Canadian anglophone and francophone bishops came to a compromise on their own differences in August 1918 and successfully recommended the appointment of a bilingual bishop, Joseph-Medard Emard of Valleyfield, Quebec, as the first *episcopus castrensis*, or military bishop, to coordinate the appointment and management of chaplains on behalf of the entire Canadian Church.[82] It had taken the Church nearly two years to get its own house in order.[83]

Although these battles in the CCS might appear to have been remote from the Catholics at the front, they were important to what the priests considered their primary duty within the CEF. Chaplains such as Ambrose Madden and Miles Tompkins, both recipients of the Military Cross, knew, first, that their sacerdotal ministry made it absolutely necessary that they be with the troops on a daily basis and, second, that without adequate numbers of chaplains they could not properly administer the sacraments as they had been ordained to do. For priests at the front, the "numbers game" was no mere game. In MacGillivray's words:

> While in the trenches we can only attend to the wounded and bury the dead. It is while they are in reserve that we must administer the Sacraments. Now be the number of Catholics in each brigade, three hundred or three hundred thousand I hold that, from the nature of our ministry, the number of priests is inadequate. The men in reserve have numerous duties to perform and the hour, or very often, half hours allotted to hear their confessions is not sufficient ... As it is, in attending to the Infantry needs we must neglect the Artillery and other units, or vice-versa.[84]

Perhaps, in good faith to his allocation tables, Steacy could argue that Catholics troops had more than their fair share of chaplains,[85] although in reality Catholic padres knew that their ministry, by its very nature, required far more than just preaching, counselling, and church parades. Had Steacy or Burke spent any time doing work at the front or in reserve camps, they might have known better. As Tompkins wrote in disgust: "*The Front*. Why they never saw the front. They don't really know what the word front means."[86]

Once overseas, Catholic chaplains were stationed in most base camps, reserve units, and military hospitals, so the sacraments would be available as broadly as possible. As Catholic soldiers moved from "Blighty" to France and Flanders, they would have the opportunity to see the padre at base camps, casualty-clearing stations, and the front itself. Chaplains often complained, however, that they were responsible for too wide a district in England, too many hospitals, or too many combatants, to give each man the spiritual attention he deserved. What exacerbated their stress and overwork was the fact that non-Catholics appeared not to appreciate the fact that the sacerdotal nature of their ministry consumed most of their waking hours and left them precious little time to organize other activities or even censor the mail of the "other ranks."[87]

Awareness of the primary importance of the priest's sacerdotal ministry was intimately linked to the manner in which the Catholic men and women responded to the padres. In the popular lore of the Great War, one enduring myth is that Catholic padres were more popular among the men than their Protestant counterparts because priests were anxious to follow the men to the trenches.[88] In a minor way, the Catholic chaplains' sense of urgency to be on the firing line with the boys was a product of their patriotic fervour, and perhaps reflected a desire to emulate Father O'Leary, the celebrated veteran chaplain of the Boer War.[89] But it is more likely that Catholic padres were motivated by an understanding that their primary mission was to dispense the sacraments, those visible signs of God's grace, essential in Catholic belief for the salvation of souls. This was their calling as priests, regardless of risk to life and limb.[90] Many priests came to recognize that the dangerous work of anointing the mangled bodies of dying men at the front and comforting the wounded elsewhere was not only their duty, but the most rewarding pastoral work they had ever done. Tompkins, considered by some to be "the most popular chaplain at the front,"[91] was adamant about his responsibilities to the men and his need to be at the firing line: "[T]his is the very worst part in the whole British Front. If the Bishop calls me back, I suppose I shall have to go, but much against my will."[92]

Notable bravery arose from the need for Catholic chaplains to be close to their men in battle. Ambrose Madden garnered considerable attention and respect for all padres when he won the Military Cross for bravery in 1916, and then the Distinguished Service Order in August 1918 "for conspicuous gallantry" during the Canadian attack on Caix. In the latter action, Madden had rushed into the assault with the troops and cared for the wounded in the open field, where he was wounded himself. It was reported that "[t]he calmness of his demeanour, his disregard of his own safety, and his unflagging efforts were a very fine example to all."[93] Father Tompkins, Father Thomas McCarthy of London, Father R.A. Macdonell of Victoria, and Father MacGillivray also received the award for valour, and Father F.L. French of Renfrew was mentioned in despatches.[94] Canadian priests were not unique in this respect. Other Catholic priests in the British,

American, and Australian Expeditionary Forces disregarded personal safety, and sometimes orders, by ministering to their men in the line of fire.[95] Such risks could result in serious injuries. O'Gorman was seriously wounded at the front, as we have seen, as was Dublin-born Lorenzo Patrick Lowry, whose right thigh was ripped open by shrapnel at Passchendaele.[96] Numerous other Catholic padres were "hit," including Madden. The death of a padre in the heat of battle, however, brought to the fore the connectedness between the priest's sacerdotal role and the respect given the priest by Catholic soldiers. On 6 April 1918, 38-year-old Father Rosario Crochetière of Nicolet was blown to bits when serving at a first aid station about a thousand yards from the front line. Father Ewan MacDonald, who was first on the scene after the explosion, and who removed the Eucharist and holy oils from Crochetière's remains, eulogized his fallen comrade as "a priest who died doing a priest's work and no more need to be said." MacDonald added, nevertheless, that "[o]ne expression was used by many of his boys and may serve to show us as priests how our work is appreciated if done properly – 'He was a real Father to us' – 'he worked for us and we never had to go without Mass or the Sacraments.'"[97] Such thoughts were forthcoming from A.J. Lapointe, a signaller in the 22nd Battalion, for whom the death of his padre was "*une grande perte*." In his journal, Lapointe remembered Crochetière as *le Bon Pere* who risked his life to hear confessions during the heat of battle.[98] The wounded and those at "the hour of death" called for the priest, for absolution and the Viaticum; the presence of clergy offered peace of mind for the soldier and, perhaps, solace for the soldier's family; one of the dying told Father Benedict Murdoch to console his family by telling them that "[he] had the priest."[99]

Although the CCS appeared more stable in terms of its institutional structures as the war dragged on, there appears to have been less tranquility in the field. After only six months of service in the CEF as a chaplain, Father Bernard Stephen Doyle of Toronto was clearly unimpressed with the spiritual exercises of the men in his care. "I have become more firmly convinced," he wrote to Archbishop Neil McNeil, "that war and a soldier's life do not promote the welfare of religion. The ordinary man is not any more fervent out here than he was at home."[100] Doyle complained of fair-weather Catholics who seemed eager go to the sacraments before the heat of battle but "forgot their good resolutions afterwards." Soldiers, according to Doyle, were mired in irreligion, immorality, and blasphemy, and many were remiss in making their Easter duty during the war, continuing what seemed to be the bad habits they possessed well before they ever donned khaki. Such rotten fruit in "the red vineyard" was, in Doyle's mind, the harvest of a domestic Church that had failed to nurture young men in the Faith. His only words of hope came when he described Catholic youth from the Maritimes and the Ottawa Valley, most of whom would have been of Irish and Scottish descent.[101]

Doyle's negativity appears to refute some of the claims made by MacGillivray and other Catholic padres who took great satisfaction in their battlefield ministry. One might attribute Doyle's diatribe to his limited experience in the variety of postings typical of the life of a CEF chaplain.[102] Perhaps his observations were evidence of the disappointment and shock experienced by a zealous young priest who, ordained less than four years, received a strong dose of reality in his first significant pastoral assignment.[103] But whether or not his comments were coloured by the deflated expectations of an eager and committed priest, they prompt some rather significant questions about the spiritual life of priests and Catholic laity in the CEF. As was made clear by the battle over the allocation of Catholic clergy to the brigades in France, priests serving as chaplains had a very specific understanding of their ministry. Religious or not, Catholic soldiers were sufficiently affected by the horrors of the battlefield that they sought out the priest in moments of doubt, reflection, and terror. MacGillivray's "officer" was perhaps one of many who had strayed from the Faith of his childhood before the war, only to be drawn closer to it in the knowledge that death could come at any time. The priests appeared to respond in kind, creating a close bond between themselves and the men, bringing to the troops the sacraments Catholics believed were the key to salvation and everlasting life. And, because they were always close to the front, many Catholic priests attained a higher regard than their Protestant colleagues in the myth and lore of the soldiers themselves. Although assessing the "religiosity" of the Irish Catholic soldier might be about as easy as nailing jelly to a wall, one can at least measure the soldiers' religious practice as an indication that, at least on the surface, few were willing to pass on Pascal's wager.

In wartime, priests and laypersons in the CEF also had to adjust to celebrating the Mass in the difficult circumstances presented by the exigencies of war, the limited availability of chaplains, and the physical environment. At base camps and hospitals, men and women might attend weekly Mass in formal open-air church parades, in hastily arranged barracks, or in curtained-off areas of noisy canteens.[104] At the front, Catholics could hear Mass only when they had rotated out of front-line duty; Mass attendance might occur every two weeks, sometimes at a local French church, although Peterborough-born artillery officer William O'Brien noted that three months could go by between one opportunity to receive Communion and the next.[105] Priests' Mass kits included cruets, vestments, altar plate, candles, bells and other sacred items – keeping impractical and unnecessary items from having to be carried to the front.[106]At the front, they toted portable altars, complete with candles, altar plate, cruets, linens, and the bare minimum of vestments. Sometimes propped up on two bayonets, the improvised altar would be the focus of Mass in a barn, field, railway siding, burned-out building, hospital ward, old tent, or even a chalk cave carved out from under the lines of fire.[107] Priests and men were exempted from the required fast before Communion and, as was the case even at parade, the sermons were brief so that attention could be placed on the Eucharist.[108] We might surmise that the rank and file appreciated this efficient preaching, since relatively few Catholic soldiers were found "absent from parade" on the Sabbath.[109]

Evidence from Irish Catholic Canadian troops themselves relating to regular Mass attendance is fragmentary at best. Perhaps an exceptional case of a recorded testimony of individual religious practice was that of Flight Lieutenant Bernard Glynn of Hamilton, Ontario. The son of Patrick Glynn, who served as the secretary of the Separate School Board in Niagara Falls, Bernard was a medical student when he enlisted in August 1916. By 1917, he had volunteered to join the 34 Squadron of the Royal Flying Corps and so was normally located at an airfield, where religious services were readily available. In a letter written to his parents, to be opened only in the case of his death, Glynn wrote: "I go to Mass and Holy Communion every morning as possible, and my prayers are with all of you at home. When you get this letter I shall have passed into another world … After all dear parents, we are only placed here for a few years to do our duty to God and our country, and then be eternally happy forever with Him in Heaven … I just want you to say, 'God's will be done,' and go on caring for the rest."[110] Glynn was killed at the age of twenty in an air battle 29

May 1917. He was predeceased by his brother Ignatius.[111] Glynn was well educated, from a religious family, and in a position to receive the sacraments regularly. The language of his letter speaks of strong religious convictions, not just words to placate his grieving parents, who would likely have seen through the deception. Some characteristics of the Glynn story appear exceptional, although the available evidence suggests his practice may have been similar to others'.

In fact, chaplains' reports and religious statistics from individual units indicate that Mass attendance among Catholics in the CEF was high.[112] Although chaplains did not normally identify specific groups of Catholics by their language and culture, in some reports French Canadian Catholics and members of the Chinese Labour Corps were cited for their exemplary attendance. Bishop Fallon went so far as to comment on the high quality of the singing in the French Canadian congregations.[113] Private Arthur Lapointe consistently noted the high attendance levels of French Canadians at Sunday Mass and special feast days. Lapointe's memoirs also reveal his own religious discipline and devotion, which included participation in Sunday liturgies, attendance at Midnight Mass on Christmas Eve, and special visitations to the Eucharist (reserved in a chapel) when he was in need of spiritual and emotional strength – "*le courage de pouvoir supporter vaillamment toutes mes épreuves*."[114] He mentions nothing of the Irish or Scots, nor do the chaplains who served them, making only generic comments about the faithful attendance of their men at Mass when given the opportunity.[115] Sometimes, however, the Irish are singled out by others as shining examples of piety, in contrast to "careless Catholics" of unnamed ethnicity. Obviously stressed by the number of Catholics who "had passed through a period of religious neglect" before their arrival at West Sandling Camp, Father James Patrick Fallon noted that, by contrast, the "three hundred Catholic soldiers from the Diocese of Pembroke" (most of whom would have been Irish) were frequent communicants at Mass. "They caused me less work," wrote an exasperated Fallon, "than almost any other ten Catholics in the camp – the reason [being that the men from Pembroke] had never been neglected."[116] Fallon was implicitly weighing in on both some men's neglect of their religious duties at home, but certainly not in the diocese of Pembroke.

Notable in their ability to muster troops to Church parade and Mass were Catholic battalion officers and nursing sisters. In hospitals,

Catholic nursing sisters were praised for their diligence in preparing the spaces needed for the administration of the sacraments and for rounding up Catholic patients, whether they were inclined to celebrate the sacred mysteries or not.[117] Similarly, officers such as William O'Brien of the Royal Canadian Artillery gathered the men of his unit for Sunday service when out of the line, and personally attended Mass as often as he could, in addition to services on Good Friday, Easter Sunday, and Christmas Eve. However, on Easter Sunday, March 1918, O'Brien lamented in his diary that the guns "blazed" all day and "for the first time" he missed Easter Sunday Mass.[118] The son of a prominent Ontario Catholic school inspector, a promising law student, and the confidant of many priests and alumni of St Michael's College, O'Brien was one of a cadre of middle-class officers who offered themselves as examples of "practical" Catholics to the men in their units. Some lay officers were known to upbraid a priest if Mass had not been said in his unit or area for some time. In 1918, the efforts of padres and lay leaders appeared successful when Workman's subordinate Father Ludger Adolph Sylvestre, reported to the apostolic delegate that 90 per cent of Canadian soldiers received the sacraments regularly.[119] Other Catholic soldiers may have used the Mass as an opportunity to proselytize to their non-Catholic comrades in arms. One lad from St Mary's parish in Toronto reported to his mother that he was going to Mass at the base camp in England and that "Gordon Levy goes with me and he is taking instructions and will be a regular Mick in a few weeks."[120]

Each week, Catholic chaplains were required to fill out reports to be submitted to the chaplaincy service, and after March 1917 specifically to Father Workman, the assistant director Chaplaincy Service (Catholic) in England, and his assistants Fathers Sylvestre and F.L. French in France. In these reports, every sacrament administered, and every religious visit, Mass, and burial were listed by brigade. These records provide a snapshot of religious life and confirm the obvious in some cases. In any given week, the brigade with the most Masses (sometimes as many as four), high numbers of confessions, and the fewest burials were the ones in reserve behind the lines, while brigades "in the line" all week were lucky to have one Mass and only few consecrated burials.[121] These tallies were often accompanied by comments or actual written reports, which revealed more about religious practice and behaviour among the troops. On 9 July 1917, while serving with the 5th Brigade (as one of two Catholic chaplains now), MacGillivray wrote that he had to attend two executions; these were likely of deserters.[122] It is also clear from the reports that Catholic padres spent little time writing or censoring letters; when their men were in action there was little time. When a brigade was moved forward to the front, Catholic padres were far too busy hearing confessions, assisting at aid stations, and burying the dead. It was surprising that they had time to fill out the detailed reports required by the CCS. During the Vimy Ridge offensive in April 1917, for example, Father MacGillivray found himself being shelled in a dressing station, while anointing the sick, offering absolution, getting bodies ready for burial, and assisting in any way possible with the wounded – including German prisoners – until, after three days of non-stop labour, he was able to catch a morning's sleep.[123]

MacGillivray's colleagues would agree that their tasks in the front lines were varied, but perhaps the most time-consuming of these was the hearing of confessions, particularly on the eve of a units' departure to the trenches. Motivated by the fear of death and the desire for a clear conscience and absolution, Catholic soldiers made Confession the most frequented of the sacraments. At their own insistence men could confess anywhere: behind the lines, in the trenches, at the aid post, or, if they were fortunate enough to have the padre nearby, in the mud of the battlefield as life slipped away from them. The padres on the front lines could also offer the Viaticum – the consecrated hosts that many of them carried – and administer the last anointing (Extreme Unction, the last rites). To "have the priest" was to have the assurance that one was prepared to meet one's maker.[124]

During the Battle of Vimy Ridge, Father McCarthy[125] was stationed with the 7th Brigade and spent much of his time in the aid station hearing confessions – when he wasn't hauling in more wounded and writing letters to their kin.[126] That same day, Father Madden reported much the same, but this heroic padre, who had already earned the Military Cross, went so far as to wade into the wire of the battlefield, using German prisoners as stretcher bearers, to retrieve the Canadian wounded.[127] Father Tompkins, during his earlier experiences in Flanders in 1916, noted that General Absolution was the only way he could accommodate the masses of men who desired Confession. Even C.W. Gordon, the Presbyterian minister who wrote popular novels under the name Ralph Connor, remarked to Tompkins how moved he was to see Catholic men huddled around their padre in the dawn before battle, waiting for their confessions to be heard. For Tompkins, this was something that Protestant chaplains generally could not emulate because of their theology, although several "high" Anglicans were trying to hear confessions, but with a mixed reception. In this light Tompkins reported to Bishop Morrison that the Anglican Canon Scott "will be a Catholic before this war ends."[128]

Father Doyon reported that on one Saturday he heard 204 confessions between 4 p.m. and 10:15 p.m. – an average of one per minute and fifty-one seconds.[129] During the war, administering the sacrament of Confession before battle was made easier by the Vatican's permission to use General Absolution during the war. In times of great urgency, as Tompkins attested, crowds of soldiers could be absolved without having to bare their souls in private auricular confession. Thus, this expeditious form of the sacrament was popularly attended.[130] In March 1918, the Catholic chaplains had reported hearing 65,094 individual confessions in the previous nine months.[131]

Catholic soldiers could be particular about their confessors. Clearly, given the intimacy of the sacrament of Confession, when undertaken individually, men wanted to be heard, understood, and appreciated in their own tongue and within the context of their own culture. As we saw earlier, continual complaints from Irish and Scottish Catholics in the 5th Brigade about Father Doyon's poor command of English resulted in the appointment of an additional, anglophone, priest.[132] Conversely, French-Canadian Catholics in the 5th were angered when the CCS replaced their chaplain with Belgian-born Father Jules Pirot; despite his distinguished service in the missions on the Canadian prairies, his background was felt to be too remote from that of the French Canadians in the brigade. Perhaps the most articulate defense of providing French Canadian priests for French Canadian troops was made by Major J.A. Filiatrault of the 23rd Reserve Battalion:

> You know the great influence of the clergy on the population of the countryside in the province of Quebec. The curé there is not only the spiritual guide of the flock but also their counsellor paid attention to in all difficulties. It is [...] this spirit that our young soldiers [have] when they arrive ... It is necessary for us to have a chaplain who understands the French-Canadian mentalité, who speaks fluent French, who takes an active interest in the spiritual

> and material well-being of the men. I have nothing against Father Samon [Sammon] our current chaplain. But unfortunately he fulfills none of the conditions that I have enumerated above.[133]

O'Gorman suggested that the anglophone padres all be bilingual so that they could serve in any unit of the CEF, particularly since francophones would be a minority outside of the 5th Brigade.[134] Although bilingual priests appeared to be a suitable compromise to the Irish Catholic leaders, they were not seen that way by French Canadians. In a similar vein, some Scottish officers from Cape Breton demanded a Gaelic-speaking padre.[135] Such linguistic and cultural tensions persisted within the Catholic ranks throughout the war.[136]

In the absence of the priest, many Catholic soldiers carried with them tangible reminders of the faith. Chaplains reported that their supplies of prayer books, prayer cards, Sacred Heart badges, blessed medals, scapulars, and rosary beads were quickly exhausted.[137] Each of these items provided a sense of a sacred presence, offering spiritual comfort and, perhaps, a greater sense of security in the line of fire. Belief in the protective power of scapulars was fairly widespread in the popular Catholicism of the day, when stories abounded of men being saved from death by wearing these sacred emblems, sewn onto long strips of cloth, under their shirts.[138] For others, like gunner William O'Brien, reciting the rosary was a devotional substitute when action at the front precluded attendance at Mass.[139] In May 1917, Father Crochetière of the 150th Battalion, Father Ronald MacDonald of the 85th Nova Scotia Highlanders, and Father William H. Hingston, SJ of the 199th Irish Rangers gathered their Irish, Scots, and French Canadian men together in a joint service to be dedicated to the Sacred Heart of Jesus – a popular devotion in which the image of a flaming heart is a focal point for contemplating the burning love of Jesus for humanity. The men were given a Sacred Heart badge to wear as they proceeded to the Front.[140] Similarly, hundreds of Catholic soldiers also formed branches of the Holy Name Society, a fraternal devotional association dedicated to abstinence from blasphemy, profanity, and "lewd talk." Sir Arthur Currie, commander and chief of the Canadian Forces, was so impressed with the vision and effects of the Society that he wished membership personally, and commended the principles of the Holy Name Society to non-Catholic service personnel.[141]

The large numbers of soldiers thumbing their beads, carrying copies of *God's Armour Is Prayer*, a compact prayer book, in their breast pockets, and attending the sacraments, however, gives testimony to only one aspect of Catholic religious life in the CEF. Reports of chaplains, religious statistics generated by headquarters, and personnel records indicate that there were large pockets of dissent from the re-created Catholic culture in military life. Forestry units and companies of Railway Troops, composed of men accustomed to labouring in remote and rugged areas in Canada far from the reach of a priest, were noted for their "irreligion." Because labour battalions of loggers and navvies were stretched thinly from the front lines to the interior of France, or were employed in the forests of England and Scotland, the chaplains assigned to them found it difficult to make regular visits. On the rare occasion when they did, the priests were appalled at the irreligiosity of these labourers, whom they described as indifferent if not "impossible" soldiers led by officers who were openly hostile to the meddling of the chaplain.[142] In these forestry and railway companies, as well as in the base and reserve camps[143] and in the front lines, chaplains were horrified by the numbers of Catholics who had not made their "Easter duty," not just during wartime, but for long periods before the war. Perhaps, so far from the frontline action, these Catholics did not have an urgent sense that death awaited them and thus felt a less pressing need for the Faith and its priests. However, there were also numerous reports of young men, even behind the lines, who requested spiritual succour after a long absence from the Church. Some had drifted away from Catholicism after entering an interfaith marriage, or had never been confirmed or never made their First Communion. In rare cases, some men had never been baptized, even though they were raised as nominal Catholics.[144] To take a different example, a remorseful General A.C. "Batty Mac" Macdonell confided in "a heart to heart" with Bishop Fallon, during the bishop's tour of the front, that he had been baptized Catholic but raised Protestant.[145]

The "unchurched" soldiers excused their neglect of the Mass and the sacraments on the grounds that there were never any priests around.[146] This special pleading wore thin with the Catholic chaplains, particularly in the closing months of the war, when Catholic Army Huts were being built in England and France and the Catholic chaplaincy was well organized and exponentially larger than it had been in the early phases of the war. Facing the problem of the "unchurched" with the zeal of missionaries, Catholic padres used the dangerous context of war to reconcile lapsed Catholics to the Church. Father Benedict Murdoch, a priest of Irish descent from New Brunswick, likened this pastoring in the front lines to a labourer working in "the red vineyard," while another chaplain triumphantly spoke of bringing men back to the sacraments "after many years of estrangement from God."[147] During his visit to the front in May 1918, Bishop Fallon took the time to confirm three Catholic soldiers, who had obviously missed receiving the sacrament when they were adolescents in their home parishes.[148] This was not an isolated incident; in January that same year, Father A.B.W. Wood reported that he had taken seven men to London, England to be confirmed by Bishop Amigo of Southwark.[149]

The presence of the "unchurched" suggested to many chaplains, Doyle included, that serious problems existed in the domestic Church. Some young men were slipping through the care and shepherding of local pastors. This seemed to be happening all over Canada, but notably in some parts of Ontario and widely in the West.[150] During the demobilization process in 1918–19, chaplains attempted to place the boys back in their home parishes by means of a letter to their pastor. At St Mary's Cathedral in Calgary, where one of the only collections of these letters remains, it was clear that dozens of Catholic veterans were referred to the Cathedral parish because they could not identify either their parish of origin or even the name of a local priest.[151] This problem was not attributable only to the war; it was a signal, perhaps, of a deeper malaise within the Canadian church, particularly on the Prairies, where there had been a shortage of anglophone priests and churches. Murdoch was grateful that, although he encountered Catholic men from his home province of New Brunswick "who had passed long years away from the sacraments," they came to him and "had been reconciled after many years of estrangement from God."[152] Bishop Fallon was less charitable in his observations in 1918, but excused the Catholics in comparison with others: "I have been much consoled by the work of the Chaplains, by the Cath. Spirit of the men, and by evidences of faith and piety … Yet there is much carelessness among Cath. and no religion among the Protestants."[153]

Given that Irish Catholic troops were integrated into multidenominational units, serving alongside men of similar class backgrounds, but potentially different regional loyalties and life experience, and considering the shortage of Catholic priests and the many disruptions to the regular rhythms of Catholic religious life, it is to be expected that many Catholic soldiers became relaxed in their religious practice. For many, the ethos of male military culture replaced the norms and boundaries of their former life.[154]

What is clear is that the religiosity of the "churched" and the previously unchurched was continually challenged by the physical, emotional, and psychological stresses of trench warfare. Fidelity in receiving the sacraments did not always translate into moral behaviour that reflected the spirit and the letter of canon law. Although their prayer books and catechisms taught otherwise, high numbers of Catholic soldiers – Irish Canadians and others – went on report for drunken and disorderly behaviour, insolence toward superiors, disobedience of orders, and absence without leave.[155] Such misdemeanours were typical in military life and are unsurprising, given the brutal carnage witnessed by these young men, who on a daily basis watched friends and brothers torn to pieces by shrapnel or lost forever amid explosions, twisted wire, and the putrid ooze of the battlefield. When on leave or back in base camp they encountered many temptations to relieve the stress levels that sent numerous men into shell shock and drove others to risk the death sentence by deserting their posts.[156] Cases of drunkenness, insubordination, and being absent without leave were particularly high in French-Canadian Catholic units, where British military traditions were foreign, and where linguistic and cultural tensions seemed rather close to the surface. Members of the Van Doos and Olivar Asselin's 163rd Battalion fought with distinction, but nevertheless had high rates of infractions against military regulations.[157] Even their chaplain, Doyon, bickered with his Irish and English Catholic superiors who, at times, were perceived as unsympathetic to the special needs of francophone Catholic troops.[158]

Sometimes a diligent priest helped to avert the temptations of fighting, cussing, drinking, and riotous behaviour. When tired, bored, and fed-up Canadian troops awaiting demobilization rioted in Kinmel Park Camp at Rhyl, Wales in 1919, Catholics were conspicuously absent. Chaplain Ivor Daniel, an Oblate from Alberta, having noticed the ugly riot fomenting, gathered Catholics together for an Ash Wednesday service in the meeting hall, where they remained while the melee erupted all around them. Daniel reported how pleased he was by the Catholics' behaviour, particularly how the "[French Canadian] element" kept out of the fight. In fact, he boasted a record number of Communions that day.[159] Father Daniel was obviously aware of the many temptations to enlisted men that abounded in the camps and in areas frequented by men on leave. Whether his troops would have joined the fracas without his intervention remains a mystery.

Among Irish Catholics and fellow co-religionists there were some bright spots, where self-discipline, obedience to superiors, and high moral standards were evident. Hundreds of Catholics secured commendations for their "good character," and many earned good conduct badges. Most notable in this regard were Catholic nursing sisters, who under the command of chief matron Margaret C. Macdonald, a Catholic from the Diocese of Antigonish, had an exemplary record of service. Although German air raids, the spread of infectious disease, and the constant spectacle of wounded, mangled, and dying youth in their wards took their toll on many young women – leaving nerves worn thin and emotions close to the surface – the nursing sisters' records were exemplary. By war's end close to 25 per cent of the nurses sampled had been decorated for their efforts.[160] Elsewhere, the Ojibwa Catholics from the Cape Croker and Saugeen Reserves defied racist stereotypes of the "drunken Indian" that stigmatized them as they marched as recruits in the 160th Bruce Battalion through the towns and fields of western Ontario on route to war. Eight of the thirty First Nations recruits won good conduct badges and one earned the Military Medal for bravery; only one was ever cited for being intoxicated. The Jesuits who ministered to their reserve territories had encouraged recruitment and proudly reported the progress of their "warriors."[161]

One does get the impression that priests like Daniel, having heard so many confessions, was not under the illusion that Irish and Catholic soldiers were saints. They understood that Catholics who obeyed the first and second commandments could nonetheless be lax in honouring the sixth, among others. Manuals for confessors indicate an awareness that soldiers would be seeking absolution for every manner of sexual sin: "Have you made indecent actions? (a) Alone. (b) with men. (c) with women. (d) with animals. How many times?"[162] Sexual transgressions, it was believed, could leave long-lasting moral and physical damage. In 1918 the chaplains conferred with Bishop Fallon on the subject. They were perplexed by the spread of venereal disease (VD) among the Canadian troops and were particularly troubled by the finding that "the percentage of Catholics who have contracted the disease is as high as the general average."[163] Indeed, the CEF recorded the highest levels of venereal disease among all the Allied troops. In 1915 alone, 28.7 per cent of the men in the CEF had been diagnosed with gonorrhoea or syphilis. By war's end there were 66,083 cases – roughly 15.8 per cent of the men – of VD in the CEF.[164] Soldiers contracted the disease through sexual contact mainly with prostitutes while waiting for embarkation in Halifax, in the reserve camps in England, on furlough in London and Edinburgh, or on leave in France.[165] The various means of controlling the outbreak, such as clamping down on prostitution, providing "blue light stations" for prophylactic washes, and including prophylactic kits in a soldier's equipment did not arrest the Canadian pastime significantly. Treatment was uncomfortable and embarrassing, and men were not forthcoming with names of their partners.[166]

As was evidenced at the chaplains' meeting with Bishop Fallon, Catholics could not turn a blind eye to the problem or take comfort in the high numbers of men frequenting the sacraments. Among a sample of 1073 Catholic soldiers, derived from honour rolls and sailing lists (see tables 4.1 to 4.3), 15.8 per cent were diagnosed at least once with VD – a rate identical to that for the entire CEF. Some units, such as the 163rd battalion, which had been raised in Montreal and later merged with Van Doos, had a staggering infection rate of 24 per cent. Even the 5th Brigade, with its Catholic majority from Quebec, Nova Scotia, and New Brunswick, and under the watchful eyes of two priests, exceeded the CEF rate with rates of 18 and 16 per cent in the 22nd and 25th battalions respectively. Catholics became as conspicuous as their non-Catholic colleagues in what Fallon described as a nearly "hopeless" situation underscored by a "lack of the sense of the supernatural."[167] In an effort to address the VD plague and segregate the infected, the Canadian Army Medical Corps established a special Canadian VD hospital at Etchinghill in Kent in 1916, where a high percentage of Catholic soldiers, notably men from French-Canadian units, became patients in the last years of the war.[168]

Table 4.1
Venereal disease (VD) among Catholic soldiers, 1914–18: Irish Catholics predominant

Battalion/location	Province	N	VD cases, no. (%)	No. of Canadians in group	VD cases, no. (%)	Average age
105th Battalion	Prince Edward Island	28	2 (6.9)	28	2 (6.9)	25 y, 2 m
199th Battalion	Quebec	58	10 (17.5)	44	8 (18.2)	29 y, 6 m
240th Battalion	Ontario	33	6 (18.2)	28	6 (21.1)	24 y, 8 m
77th Battalion	Ontario	82	21 (25.6)	62	19 (30.7)	24 y, 11 m
121st Battalion	British Columbia	31	6 (19.4)	13	4 (30.8)	30 y, 8 m
68th Battalion	Saskatchewan	21	5 (23.8)	12	3 (25.0)	21 y, 10 m
100th Battalion	Manitoba	21	5 (23.8)	11	4 (36.4)	23 y, 8 m
St Patrick's Ottawa	Ontario	54	5 (9.3)	45	5 (11.1)	25 y, 10 m
St John's Toronto	Ontario	22	4 (18.2)	22	4 (18.2)	21 y, 3 m
St Helen's Toronto	Ontario	83	6 (7.2)	65	6 (9.2)	23 y, 11m
St Paul's Toronto	Ontario	55	2 (3.6)	42	2 (4.8)	22 y, 6 m

Source: LAC, National Personnel Records Centre, Ottawa, Confidential Personnel Files of Canadian Expeditionary Force Personnel.

Table 4.2
Venereal disease (VD) among Catholic soldiers, 1914–18: French Catholics predominant

Battalion/location	*Province*	*N*	*VD cases, no. (%)*	*No. of Canadians in group*	*VD cases, no. (%)*	*Average age*
22nd Battalion	Quebec	61	11 (18.0)	58	9 (15.5)	24 y, 4 m
163rd Battalion	Quebec	43	11 (25.6)	38	9 (23.7)	22 y, 10 m

Source: LAC, National Personnel Records Centre, Ottawa, Confidential Personnel Files of Canadian Expeditionary Force Personnel.

Evidence from personnel records (crossed referenced with parish honour rolls) shows that Canadian Catholic men in the CEF diagnosed with VD had clearly defined characteristics: they were usually between 18 and 24 years of age (and hence were younger than the average age of troops); 82 per cent were Canadian-born; they had little previous military experience; they came from all regions (although troops from the Prairies, Quebec, and the upper Ottawa Valley had the highest rates); many were unskilled labourers, forest workers, miners, and farm labourers, and those whose religious participation before the war was unconfirmed, had higher rates than those who appear to have been "churched," given the parish records. In the group associated with St Mary's Cathedral in Calgary, those recommended by the CCS to the pastor at the time of demobilization had a VD rate four times higher than that of soldiers whose names were entered on the parish roll of service during the war. Samples taken from parish lists across the country had much lower rates of VD than samples from battalion lists, where church participation was not a given. The VD rates appear to validate, in a small way, what chaplains were reporting about the practising Catholic soldier and the "careless Catholic." As tables 4.1 and 4.3 indicate, soldiers listed on parish honour rolls – presumably members of the congregation and known to the clergy as frequent receivers of Communion – had lower aggregate rates of VD than those Catholics sampled randomly from the battalions indicated. Attestation papers, upon which sailing lists of battalions were based, never indicated whether the professed Catholic had a parish of origin; nor, for that matter, did the military administration care. The Catholics listed in battalions probably rep-

Table 4.3
Venereal disease (VD) among Catholic soldiers, 1914–18: mixed ethnicities

Battalion/location	*Province*	*N*	*VD cases, no. (%)*	*No. of Canadians in group*	*VD cases, no. (%)*	*Average age*
25th Battalion	Nova Scotia	87	14 (16.1)	74	10 (13.5)	22 y, 5 m
85th Battalion	Nova Scotia	75	12 (16.0)	64	9 (14.1)	22 y, 9 m
26th Battalion	New Brunswick	54	5 (9.3)	47	5 (10.6)	20 y, 11 m
132nd Battalion	New Brunswick	75	15 (19.7)	71	15 (21.1)	22 y, 5 m
160th Battalion	Ontario	73	12 (16.4)	64	11 (17.2)	24 y, 1 m
Bruce-Grey	Ontario	15	2 (13.3)	15	2 (13.3)	26 y, 5 m
184th Manitoba	Manitoba	15	1 (6.7)	8	1 (12.5)	21 y, 0 m
46th Battalion	Saskatchewan	20	5 (25.0)	6	3 (50.0)	20 y, 9 m
St Mary's Calgary	Calgary, Alberta	67	10 (14.9)	26	2 (7.7)	28 y, 3 m
Cathedral roll	Alberta	24	2 (8.3)			
Demobilized list	Alberta	43	8 (19.0)			
Etchinghill VD hospital	United Kingdom			34	34 (100.0)	25 y, 11 m

Source: LAC, National Personnel Records Centre, Ottawa, Confidential Personnel Files of Canadian Expeditionary Force Personnel.

St Mary's Cathedral Parish, Calgary, has two data sets, one from the parish list and one from the men listed in the military demobilization papers for southern Alberta and sent to Calgary.

resent a good cross-section of Catholic men, both regular participants in parish life and those who were not. While it cannot be stated definitively that practising Catholics, as discovered in the honour rolls of parishes, were less likely to violate the sixth commandment than Catholic soldiers with no apparent parish affiliation, the padres might have been able to conclude from interviewing and hear the confessions of their "boys" that "careless" Catholics and fornication were comfortable bedfellows.

There appears to be little difference between rates of VD among different groups of Catholics, although there may have been some regional variations. Units and regions sampled in which Irish Catholics were the dominant group had VD levels as high as Catholics of French Canadian or Scottish origin. At times these units, such as the 240th Battalion, had VD levels that exceeded the national average for the CEF. The 240th, raised in the upper Ottawa Valley, was a forestry battalion filled with lumbermen and imbued with a culture of masculinity that drove many of the resident padres to distraction. Maritime-based battalions such as the 105th from Prince Edward Island and the 26th from the Saint John, New Brunswick, area, had low rates of VD, which seems to confirm the reports from chaplains about the "good character" of the men from these parts of Canada. There seems to have been little difference between reported rates of VD in battalions where Irish Catholics and their Acadian, Scottish, Ojibwa, and French Canadian co-religionists were mingled, and the rate of VD in the CEF as a whole. Perhaps of greater interest is that there appeared to be no appreciable difference between VD rates in battalions where a priest was present – this would include the 22nd, 163rd, 199th, 132nd, and 25th – and battalions without a priest. Thus the arguments made to the CCS by O'Gorman and others that providing more priests would enhance Catholicity in the ranks appear to have been naive, at least with respect to preventing sin. If anything, the presence of the priest may have offered the assurance that if sins of the flesh (drinking, carousing, fornication, and self-stimulation) were committed, confession and absolution were possible before the battle. Thus Catholics, the Irish included, influenced by the ethos of the military life in wartime, and dominated in the ranks by single men, tended to behave sexually much like soldiers all around them, regardless of religious background. The single caveat is that Irish Catholic soldiers with a demonstrable link to a specific parish community were less likely than the "unchurched" to succumb to temptation.

The one thing that appears clear is that defining the religious culture of Catholics in the CEF is a complex and frustrating undertaking. The anomaly pointed out by Doyle – sacramentality, yet immorality – is at the heart of understanding Catholicity in the CEF. The same Catholic men who, for the most part, attended the sacraments – and some of whom earned good conduct badges – seemed unable to translate this personal religiosity into moral scrupulosity, particularly regarding sex. The chaplain at Etchinghill noted the devotion of the many Catholic patients and their zeal for the sacraments. There is no easy accounting for this apparent contradiction. But perhaps the same uncertainty and fear that propelled many Catholic men, particularly the "unchurched," into the care of the chaplains had also prompted them to take risks that they might not normally have taken. Not to be ruled out is the peer pressure inherent in a male military culture characterized by the cohesiveness of units and regiments, "group narcissism," ostentatious masculinity, and an "almost universal preoccupation with sex."[169] Thus, the pressures of a culture that urged one to test one's sexual prowess, and the psychological stress of witnessing human carnage, prompted many men to partake of passions of the flesh proscribed by the Catechism.[170] Most of the Catholic men infected with VD were young, unmarried, away from home for the first time, and – for many of the French-Canadians described by Major Filiatrault – separated from the security and strict moral boundaries of their parish life and curé. In such a context, their moral indiscretion is understandable. If they lived to their next Confession, absolution awaited them. Their sin would be forgiven.

Such reasons might not have been so easily understood by a priest as new to his vocation as Father Doyle. Others, however, remarked on the need for compassion when dealing with the men infected with VD. For Father James Patrick Fallon, brother to the bishop, and fellow padre Father Antoine Lamarre, a soldier who had committed a sexual indiscretion was not necessarily a lost soul. The hospital at Etchinghill became Father Fallon's opportunity to extend compassion and love to the Catholics and non-Catholics in his care, men to whom even the Red Cross would not send packages, nor would the CEF pay when they were undergoing treatment. There, the churched and previously unchurched recreated the devotional and symbolic universes inherent to ultramontane Catholicism – dutiful attendance at Mass, frequent confession, and the practice of individual acts of piety.[171] The Etchinghill experience underscored the stark contrasts of Catholic religious culture in the CEF: the missionary zeal of priests, the men's participation in the sacramental and devotional life of the Church, and the fragility of the human condition when it came to upholding Catholic morality.

When assessing the religious life of the Irish Catholics and their non-Irish co-religionists in the CEF, however, Church officials recognized a problem that they may have been reluctant to acknowledge in civilian life. Given the numbers of the "unchurched" to whom they ministered in the CEF, it was clear to chaplains and bishops alike that the domestic Church was failing in its efforts to secure the fidelity and regular religious practice of young Catholic men. The difficulties of the chaplains in labour, railway and forestry battalions, the sacramental indifference of many recruits from the West, and significant levels of disciplinary infractions and VD among those soldiers sampled from lists not generated by parishes, is perhaps a statement about popular male Catholic religious culture in Canada itself, rather than being germane only to life in the CEF. Fathers Doyle and Fallon, among others, suggested that the crisis they faced was rooted in the domestic Church. A frustrated Fallon wrote, "The majority of them never had much of the fervour of the early Christians ... some time ago I spoke of the number of soldiers in units attended by me, who were Catholics only on paper."[172] It is no coincidence that the tough observations of chaplains came at a time when Bishop Emile Légal of St-Albert had complained of negligence and indifference among many Catholics in his diocese, and the newly appointed archbishop of Winnipeg, Alfred A. Sinnott, begged his friend Archbishop McCarthy for just one priest to help save his troubled territory. "The indifference to religion in this part of many," observed Sinnott, "cannot be described as anything but astounding."[173] While the appearance of the "unchurched" in the CEF, according to Bishop Fallon, offered the opportunity for "missionary work" that yielded "very favourable results," the harvest of the red vineyard had been sown elsewhere.[174] What appeared in the early years of the war to be a battle by the chaplains and bishops in defence of the faith against Steacy and Hughes, was in fact a war within the Church itself between the pulpit and the pew. Although Irish Catholics did not appear prominent in this internal struggle, except where language was concerned, they still formed part of the problem of religious practice, or carelessness thereof. After the war, the padres and bishops who sent them would have to tend to the state of a church "militant and triumphant" at home.

5

Between Resistance and Rebellion

Father John J. O'Gorman was seething. It was June 1917, and he was a patient at the Ottawa General Hospital on Water Street (now Bruyère), recovering from the serious shrapnel wounds he received in France. On the feast of Corpus Christi, the hospital, run by the Grey Sisters of Ottawa (Soeurs de Charité d'Ottawa), was decked out in flags – the Papal flag, the tricolour of France, the French-Canadian fleurs-de-lis, and the Union Jack – for the annual procession and exposition of the Eucharist that was expected to wind around the streets of Lower Town near the Basilica of Notre Dame. Observing that an Irish presence was missing, O'Gorman had two Irish harp flags hung outside his window. His unauthorized decorations were spotted by a French Canadian nurse who, according to the indignant O'Gorman, took swift and arbitrary action: "[I]n spite of my protests, the Rev Sister and treasurer of the hospital, entered and rudely tore down the Irish flags from the window, adding that she was obeying an order of the Sister Superior."[1] Spitting mad, O'Gorman told the local press that there was more to this insult than met the eye: "Ireland, the most Catholic nation in the world, cannot be excommunicated from a Corpus Christi procession by the decree of an excited French-Canadian nun." For O'Gorman, this was an insult not just to one Irish-Canadian priest, but to all Irish Canadians working in the hospital and to Irish Catholics in Ottawa who, through "the civic and provincial grant," supported the institution, which "proclaims itself to be a general hospital, not a racial one." For him, the incident was typical of the activities of a "clique of fanatical Nationalists" who were entirely unlike the French Canadians he had worked with at the front. He demanded but did not receive an apology, and resolved to buy an Irish flag and a Canadian flag for his room, to remain as long as he was in it.[2]

Perhaps knowing full well how formidable the Ottawa priest could be as an enemy, the hospital sidestepped O'Gorman's criticisms and claimed that, for safety reasons, nothing should be suspended from the upper windows of the hospital. O'Gorman retorted that, if this was the case, how did it come to pass that an orderly had retrieved the old Irish flags from a cupboard and hung them up for him? And why was it that when the Irish flags were removed the others – including the French tricolour – remained dangling from the fourth-floor windows?[3] The *Ottawa Citizen* subsequently reported that the nun in question had been egged on to remove the flags by an "anti-British" physician.[4] Although the controversy passed – and six months later O'Gorman confessed to Archbishop Gauthier that he should have "accepted the humiliation in silence"[5] – the "flag incident" not only reopened the old wounds between O'Gorman and his French Canadian detractors in Ottawa, but also exposed the fragile position of Irish Catholics within their own Church and the Canadian war effort. Time after time, Anglo-Protestant reporters, politicians, and civic leaders would question Irish Catholic loyalty on the basis of the behaviour of Catholics elsewhere in Canada and in Ireland. Catholic loyalty was under scrutiny throughout the war because of the alleged pro-German sympathies of Pope Benedict XV, the alleged disloyalty of the Ukrainian Catholic Eparch, the allegedly pro-Austrian sympathies of many of the most recent Catholic migrants to Canada from eastern Europe, and – after April 1916 – because of Irish disloyalty to the Crown, as evidenced by the Irish Republican Brotherhood's failed insurrection on Easter Monday in Dublin. Closer to home, Irish Catholics found it increasingly difficult to distinguish themselves in the public mind from their French Canadian co-religionists, who had been reluctant to enlist in large numbers and in 1917 vigorously opposed the Borden government's move to legislate the conscription of able-bodied men into the battered CEF.

From mid-1916 to the end of 1917, Irish Catholics found themselves constantly defending their loyalty to Canada, the Empire, and the war effort largely because of other Catholics beyond their sphere and events beyond their control. While bishops and the Catholic press easily dismissed the anti-papal and anti-immigrant rhetoric offered by certain Protestant journalists, politicians, and members of the Orange Order, their ability to distance themselves from the French Canadian hierarchy and outspoken pundits such as Henri Bourassa proved to be more difficult. With respect to French-Canadian attitudes toward the war, Irish Catholic leaders had to be careful not to damage, whether in reality or in the public perception, the solidarity of all "races" in the Faith, while making careful distinctions between French Canadian statements of a Catholic nature, and those that came from a purely nationalist or cultural position. Given the way in which language, culture, and religion were intricately intertwined as the living fibres of French Canadian identity, Irish Catholics were constantly frustrated in their attempts to sort out the Faith from other factors. Certainly, Irish-French relations in the Church had been soured before the war by Irish Catholic support for the abolition of bilingual schools in Ontario; by Irish and French competition for the support of new Catholic Canadian immigrants; and by episcopal struggles over the succession of bishops, English-speaking or French-speaking, to the vacant or newly created bishoprics in Canada. In many ways, the Catholic Church in Canada was deeply divided in 1914, a circumstance that only worsened within the context of the war. By 1918, and through the articulation of O'Gorman, Irish Canadian Catholics offered themselves as an example of double duty: working for Home Rule in Ireland by constitutional means; and winning the war, which was being fought so that small nations might be free. At home, Church leaders such as Toronto archbishop Neil McNeil were forging an entente between Irish and French Catholics, while asserting an unflinching loyalty to Canada and the Empire and a determination to win the war.

Historically, the papacy has often been the target of fierce criticism of the Church by non-Catholics. Seen at best as a centralized, hierarchical administrative structure, and at worst as an authoritarian and tyrannical entity that dictated the belief of the faithful, the role of the Holy See (more commonly called the Vatican) has always been the subject of intense debate in Christian circles.[6] Popes could be loved as living saints or reviled as autocrats perpetuating an alleged paganism foreign to Bible-based Christianity. In this way, one of the longest serving popes, Pius IX (1846–1878), could be regarded before the Roman Revolution of 1848 as a moderate, liberal, and charismatic pope of the modern world, only to be denounced as the anti-Semitic and anti-democratic author of the *Syllabus of Errors* and the enemy of modernity.[7] His successor, Leo XIII, was an elderly and affable man who was elected by the College of Cardinals upon Pius IX's death in the certain knowledge that, given his age, he would be in the office only for a short time, would do little, and would give the electors more time to think about the type of Bishop of Rome they might have for a longer term. Leo XIII fooled them all and reigned until 1903, while issuing some of the most important encyclical letters of the century, including a comprehensive teaching on the relations between labour and capital in the modern world. In 1903 the new pope, Pius X, encouraged daily Eucharist among all Catholics and spent a good deal of his pontificate trying to silence progressive theologians and biblical scholars, who were labelled as heretical "Modernists." Pius died in 1914, lamenting that he could not manage to reconcile the great powers and avert a general war in Europe.

Benedict XV succeeded to the papal throne on 3 September 1914, a little over a month after the great alliances of Europe had declared war on one another. Born in Genoa on 21 November 1854, Giacomo Paolo della Chiesa had been a papal diplomat and was so bird-like and frail in appearance that the residents of his former Diocese of Bologna nicknamed him *il piccoletto*.[8] With his skill as a diplomat, and as a student of the consummate Vatican secretary of state and politician, Cardinal Mariano Rampolla, Benedict knew how to creatively remain neutral, despite the fact that the Pope had essentially been a prisoner in the Vatican palace ever since the forces of a reunited Italy invaded Rome and made it the national capital in 1870.[9] He also knew that the Cardinals who had elected him came from both sides of the conflict. Even when the Kingdom of Italy became a combatant on the side of Britain and France and their allies, Benedict retained his neutrality, promoting peaceful solutions to the war as frequently as he was able. There were millions of Catholics on both sides of the war; hence, Benedict felt obligated to try to broker peace between the Entente and the Central Powers. In November 1914 he issued his first encyclical, *Ad beatissimi Apostolorum*, imploring the world "for the sake of human society and the sake of the Church" to lay down its arms and negotiate a just peace.[10] He could please neither side with his entreaties.

A year after his election, in 1915, Benedict made a second plea for peace even more graphically than the first:

> In the holy name of God … We conjure you whom Divine Providence has called to govern the fighting nations to put an end once and for all to this awful carnage which has for a whole year dis-

> honoured Europe. It is the blood of brothers which is being poured out on sea and land! The most beautiful regions of Europe, the garden of the world, is sewn with corpses and ruins … [L]isten to our prayer.[11]

His overture for peace met the same cold reception as had the earlier encyclical.[12]

Benedict made himself available to delegations from both sides. In October 1917, Canon Frederick George Scott, the larger-than-life Anglican chaplain of Canada's First Division, took forty-six soldiers on two weeks' leave to Rome. Scott noted the flow of cardinals from both sides into Rome, trying to carry on the business of the Church as normally as possible[13] while the war raged on. In 1917, the Pope proposed concrete terms for peace, including a preliminary exchange of wounded prisoners of war,[14] but the powers rejected his plan: given the sacrifice of so many lives, only total victory would suffice. There would be no compromises. The problem was that neither the Allies nor the Central Powers believed that Benedict was sufficiently neutral, and suspected that he secretly harboured support for one side over the other. The editors of the *Sentinel,* the official organ of the Loyal Orange Lodges in British North America, declared they would have "No Pope's Peace." The Pope, they maintained, was an "Ally of the Kaiser," and his plan was "Made in Germany."[15]

The accusations of partisanship made against Pope Benedict XV during the war became a headache for the Irish Catholic leadership in the Canadian Church. The press in Canada recognized that, despite his best efforts to effect peace, Benedict had been pilloried by both the Allies and the Central powers. French papers called him the *Boche* Pope, while the Germans referred to him as Maledict XV, among other names.[16] In Canada, the Methodist *Christian Guardian* suggested he might be pro-Austrian,[17] while the *Sentinel* was relentless in its repeated accusations that the Pope and the Kaiser were in league with one another. The Toronto *Telegram* constantly fed its Orange readership with what the *Catholic Register* described as an "unspeakably vile campaign against the Vicar of Christ."[18] Every faulty and unfounded hypothesis imaginable about the Pope's purportedly sinister aims was used by Orange editors to explain to their readerships why Quebec, Ireland, Australia, and Catholics in America were either disloyal to the Empire or, in the case of the Americans, entertained its demise.[19]

Non-Catholics who believed the Pope was on the "other" side might understandably conclude that his minions in the rest of the world supported him. Writing in October 1916, Norman Murray, publisher of the *Sentinel*, took aim squarely at Catholic disloyalty:

> Another great surprise in store [during this war] was the indifference and apathy of the Roman Catholic part of the population of the British Empire. The situation in the Catholic portion of Ireland and in Quebec is almost identical, with a little to the good in favour of Catholic Ireland in the matter of recruiting to the British Army ... While the Canadian hierarchy is said to have advised its people to do their part like their fellow countrymen by enlisting in the imperial army this advice seems to have no effect whatever ... It has been suggested that the Church is playing a double game and that, while it openly proclaims its loyalty, it is secretly working the other way through the confessional and otherwise.[20]

Murray continued by presenting the recruitment of Irish Catholics in Montreal as an abject failure. His paper made repeated attacks on the allegedly pro-German papacy, disloyal Irish nationalists, French-Canadian shirkers, and the "pro-Austrian" Ukrainian Catholic Eparch of Canada.[21] Attacks on Catholicism and the Papacy by the Orange Order were neither new nor surprising, but when similar arguments began to appear in the secular daily press and came from the mouths of politicians such as former Mayor Horatio Hocken of Toronto,[22] or Liberal politician Newton Wesley Rowell,[23] or from Protestant ministers such as E.I. Hart, English-speaking Catholic leaders knew their denomination would not be credited with the loyalty they had professed or the blood spilled by young Catholic soldiers and nurses.

The uncomplimentary writing in the Toronto *Telegram*, when combined with tirades from the *Sentinel* and the Toronto *Globe*'s suggestion that the Pope could not be neutral, prompted Archbishop McNeil to swing into action. In February 1918 he published a pamphlet, *The Pope and the War*, which was widely distributed and sold out of its first print run. McNeil carefully analysed the Pope's position in the conflict, explored the historical interests of the Catholics among the combatants, and concluded that neutrality was the Pope's only reasonable option under the circumstances.

> The Pope is necessarily neutral in this way. He is in justice obliged to be impartial ... Catholics are patriotic in their respective countries. The war has made this clear. Whether right or wrong in judgement, they are convinced of the justice of their respective countries' cause, whether French or German. If the Pope condemned either group of belligerents at the outbreak of the war, or at any stage in it, he would thereby place millions of Catholics in the agonizing necessity of choosing between their Church and their country, and he would favour one section of the Church at the expense of another. The war would go on in any case.[24]

The pamphlet won praise from within and outside of the Catholic community and was even significant in switching the position formerly taken by the *Globe*.[25] The *Sentinel* and its readers were unmoved, and the paper's attacks continued, but this time they were answered.[26] The Knights of Columbus at Ottawa's oldest and largest Council no. 485 pledged full support for McNeil's pamphlet and launched a counter-campaign against what it considered an anti-Catholic press.[27]

Dealing with criticism of the Pope was neither new nor unexpected for Irish Catholic leaders in Canada. In fact, since the Pope was remote from the Canadian scene and perhaps more of a phantom than a direct menace to Canadian Protestants, their criticism of him paled in comparison with what some Canadian Protestants were pointing to as potentially greater dangers at home. In the two decades leading up to the war, Canada had received nearly a million immigrants. Although the majority were from the British Isles and the United States, hundreds of thousands came from Europe, and the majority of these were Roman or Byzantine-Greek Catholics. Notable Canadians such as J.S. Woodsworth, a Methodist minister and author of *Strangers Within Our Gates*, and the popular novelist Ralph Connor, pen name for Presbyterian minister C.W. Gordon, warned Anglo-Protestant Canada in his novels about the consequences of any failure to assimilate these "papists." Although the "sturdy peasants in sheepskin coats" provided much needed labour in Canada's cities, capital works projects, railways, lumber yards, and uncultivated prairie agricultural lands, they also provided linguistic, cultural, and religious challenges to the British Canadian way of life.[28] As a result, over a decade before the war, various Protestant denominations and the Catholic Church battled one another for the souls and loyalty of these new Canadians. Presbyterians attempted to proselytize the Ukrainians and Hungarians, Methodists the Italians, and Anglicans any groups along their chain of railway missions. Meanwhile, French and English-speaking Catholics, often known to prairie francophone bishops as "*les maudits Irlandais*" vied for the allegiance of newly arrived Catholics who spoke neither official language.[29]

When the war erupted, a new challenge was presented both to the government and to Anglo-Canadian citizens: What was to be done with "enemy aliens" who had recently arrived as settlers, particularly in the Canadian West? Many eastern European Catholics now discovered they were targets, not just because of their religion or culture, but because their countries of origin were now at war with the British Empire. Prior to the war, Monsignor Alfred E. Burke, then president of the Catholic Church Extension Society, estimated that there might be as many as 150,000 Ruthenians (Ukrainians of the Eastern Rite) in Canada whose homeland was part of the Austro-Hungarian Empire.[30] There were also thousands of immigrants who were branded as naturalized members of enemy powers: Hungarians from Austro-Hungary, Poles from German- and Austrian-occupied Poland, and Maronite Catholics from the Ottoman Empire. German Catholic immigrants were implicated in the same way, as were German Canadians who had been living in Canada for generations. Irish Catholic leaders were caught between having to defend the Catholic immigrants whom they had spent a decade trying to incorporate into their branch of the Church, or playing the disloyalty card, as so many Anglo-Protestant Canadians were prepared to do. The Catholic press and bishops drove a careful path down the middle: they defended the Catholic immigrants as having a new loyalty to Canada, while dismissing any of the old-world claims upon the allegiance of these new loyal members of the Church.

Such lofty sentiments were fine in print, but specific incidents confirmed some Canadians in their belief that foreigners from an enemy nation could not be trusted. Nykyta Budka, the first Ukrainian Catholic Eparch (bishop) of Canada, presented the Canadian Catholic Church with the first major public relations disaster on the enemy alien question. Budka had come to Canada in 1912 to administer a diocese of Ukrainian Catholics of the Eastern Rite that encompassed the entire country. Irish Catholics in eastern Canada, particularly those affiliated with Burke's Catholic Church Extension Society, had done much to prod the Holy See to appoint an Eparch and had financed his travel, provided funds for his churches and a newspaper, and secured him additional clergy.[31] With close ties to the Austrian court, and having served in the Austro-Hungarian Army as a chaplain, Budka had a loyalty to Emperor Franz-Josef. In the wake of the assassination of Archduke Franz Ferdinand, Franz-Josef's heir, and the declaration of war between Austria and Serbia, the Eparch delivered a pastoral letter to his flock in early August 1914, urging them as former citizens of the Austro-Hungarian Empire to return home and defend their Emperor from his Russian and Serbian enemies.[32] The appeal to Ukrainian immigrants was poorly timed: within a week, Great Britain and Canada were at war with Germany and her ally, Austria-Hungary – and now Budka, although he had withdrawn his comments, looked like a Catholic traitor.[33] Anti-clerical Ukrainians used the opportunity to distance themselves and attack Budka, while some Anglo-Canadians pounced on Budka as a traitor and eventually pressed for legal action to restrain the bishop.[34] The English-speaking Catholic bishops and their Catholic Church Extension Society, which had supported Budka and the Ukrainian home missions, appeared guilty by association. Despite the fact that, by the end of the war, Budka had been acquitted of all fourteen counts of sedition, the possibility of disloyalty among new Canadians hung like a stench across the Canadian Church.

The English-language Catholic press swung into action, taking every opportunity to blot out this stain of disloyalty. In Antigonish, the *Casket* broke the story shortly after the Budka indiscretion was noted, and the editor warned that the matter of Budka making his statement eight days before the British declaration of war would be conveniently overlooked by "anti-Catholic writers and preachers for years."[35] His prognostications were correct, and the *Casket* and other Catholic papers accordingly continued their defence. The *Casket* vouched for the loyalty of Ukrainian Canadians to the Empire by pointing out that Ukrainians themselves had been victims of Prussianism when their bishop in Lemberg (now Lviv, Ukraine) was silenced and placed under house arrest.[36] Editors at the *Canadian Freeman* in Kingston, the *Northwest Review* in Winnipeg, and the *Catholic Register* in Toronto all gave unreserved endorsements of Budka's loyalty and that of his flock.[37] But the defense went beyond newspapers. The Ancient Order of Hibernians in Winnipeg not only affirmed Ukrainians' loyalty but also insisted that their language and that of

Poles be respected in Manitoba's schools. "The British Empire," argued the AOH, "is battling today for the principle that small peoples have the right to live without being oppressed by their greater neighbours, and carrying out this principle, Canada, as a loyal member of the Empire, should grant the various peoples within her borders the greatest freedom and liberty to cherish and perpetuate their mother tongue."[38] The Catholic Church Extension Society under Burke continued their vigorous appeal for the support of Ukrainian churches, all the while defending their loyalty to the Empire.[39] Finally, in British Columbia, where many Austro-Hungarian nationals and "aliens" were interned during the war, the Archdiocese of Vancouver, through its Children's Aid Society, was engaged in taking care of Ukrainian children whose parents had been interned in a camp at Vernon.[40]

When they were not deflecting criticisms about the potential Prussianism of their Pope or rebutting accusations against enemy aliens housed in Canada's Catholic Church, Irish Catholics had to keep an eye on the volatile situation in Ireland. The outbreak of war had brought a degree of calm to recent troubles in Ireland, which in events leading up to August 1914 appeared to be on the brink of civil war. When John Redmond's Parliamentary Party agreed to delay the enacting of the provisions of the Home Rule Act (Government of Ireland Act 1914) until after the successful completion of the war, it appeared that peace had returned to Ireland. Most of the Ulster Volunteer Force, northern-based and Protestant, formed the corpus of the 36th (Ulster) Division, and over two thirds of the overwhelmingly Roman Catholic Irish Volunteers found themselves enlisting in the 10th (Irish) Division, the 16th (Irish) Division, or other units in the British Expeditionary Force.[41] Redmond's brother William, a sitting member of the Irish Parliamentary Party, enlisted. In fact, by August 1916 over 100,000 Irish had been recruited into the British Army and had been fighting at Gallipoli, Ypres, and the Somme.[42] Canada's Irish Catholics were aware of these actions in the "homeland," as Catholic newspapers boasted of the high levels of Irish recruitment, and the interest of the Irish in winning the war and then securing Home Rule.[43] In 1916, for instance, the *New Freeman* of Saint John, once again responding to attacks by the *Sentinel*, refuted claims of Irish "slacking" with statistics: "The facts are that Ireland is doing its duty nobly and will continue to do it.[44] This Canadian Catholic enthusiasm for Ireland's engagement in the war effort was crystallized by, of all papers, the Toronto *Globe*, a paper that had supported Home Rule and that could have been summing up Irish Canadian hopes when it wrote: "No longer is Ireland divided into hostile camps; no longer are Irishmen separated by racial and religious difference. Orange or Green, Protestant or Catholic; they are now Irishmen all."[45]

Canada's Irish Catholics and many politicians, particularly those affiliated with the Liberal Party, had a strong a connection with and appreciation for the work of John Redmond, leader of the Irish Parliamentary Party. As a constitutional nationalist, Redmond had sought non-violent ways to win Home Rule concessions at Westminster through his party. The fact that Redmond looked at Canada as a model for self-government within the context of the Empire resonated powerfully with Irish Catholic Canadians and many non-Irish.[46] He had visited Canada to secure support and money for Irish self-government prior to the Home Rule Bills in the 1890s and in 1912 and maintained a healthy correspondence with circles of friends in Ontario and Quebec, including former prime minister Wilfrid Laurier. His own planning documents for negotiations with the British Government included a detailed plan to replicate Canadian-style autonomy for Ireland.[47] For their part, Catholic newspapers continued to pay attention during the war to the work Redmond was doing to support the war effort and secure Irish autonomy. In a special message to Canada, penned for St Patrick's Day in 1915, Redmond wrote: "Canada will rejoice to learn that although the war cloud today ever shadows Ireland as it does so much the rest of Europe, yet the outlook for the old country was never brighter. Irishmen never had more reason to look forward with hope and confidence in the future." Redmond would add that victory for the cause of "civilization and freedom ... and the cause of Christian civilization" would lead to a united and federated Empire.[48]

One might say that the Great War brought eased tensions that might otherwise have ignited civil war in Ireland in 1914. It provided the burden of proof for Irish loyalty that Canadian Catholics could use in the face of opinions to the contrary coming from the usual suspects. This was not a "made-in-Toronto" conception of Irish Catholic pundits, but rather, in the first two years of the war, a view of Ireland shared across the diverse Irish Catholic communities of Canada. In Nova Scotia, the *Casket* outlined in great detail how the former English attitude of suppressing its Celtic neighbours had now been overtaken by a new principled spirit of co-operation and higher statesmanship. The paper credited the example of Canada and Australia for their influences and, in particular, the legacies of Charles Gavan Duffy in Australia and John A. Macdonald and Thomas D'Arcy McGee in Canada: prominent Celtic advocates of autonomous dominions within a larger Empire.[49] London's *Catholic Record* was quick to applaud the co-operative efforts of both Redmond and Edward Carson to support the fragile Liberal government of Herbert Asquith and win the war.[50] In Winnipeg, editors of the *Northwest Review* commented that in recent meetings the local Ancient Order of Hibernians (the largest Irish Catholic fraternal association) had chastised American Irish nationalists for being out of touch. According to the editor, "The Ireland of today is far removed from the oppressed isle of our forefathers." In a backhanded swipe against Irish Americans who did not fully appreciate how far Ireland had come under Redmond, the paper continued, "It is to be feared that the Irish Parliamentary Party is to be judged by a standard which is not recognized across the water."[51] The war helped to bring a perceived new Ireland into sharper focus for Irish Catholic Canadians, prepared them better for attacks against Irish disloyalty, and satisfied them that their Irish cousins would soon share what they as Canadians had already won and shared by peaceful means: Home Rule and responsible government.

Few Irish in the homeland or in the diaspora expected anything more than to celebrate the feast of the Resurrection of Jesus Christ on the Easter weekend of 1916. The liturgical celebrations and family gatherings on Easter Sunday, April 23, gave way to a shocking revolt in Dublin on Easter Monday. The Rising, as it would come to be known, was poorly planned and ineptly executed by the Irish Republican Brotherhood (IRB) and members of the radical labour Irish Citizen's Army. Most of the IRB-dominated Irish Volunteers were denied participation in the Rising, when ordered to stand pat by their General Eoinn MacNeil, and the British captured rebel Sir Roger Casement on the coast of Kerry at Banna Strand, during a failed *rendez vous* attempt to secure German arms and ammunition near Cahersiveen.[52] However, when Patrick Pearse, one of the IRB's leaders, emerged from the General Post Office on O'Connell Street (then Sackville Street) and read the proclamation of the Irish republic, a chain of events was initiated that would forever alter Ireland's relationship with Great

Britain. Using remnants of the Irish Volunteers who had refused to join the British Expeditionary Force, Pearse and his cohort of intellectuals, republicans, socialists, and dreamers seized positions within the inner city of Dublin, few of which had any strategic value. Over the course of the following week, the rebels, numbering about 250 and armed with Mauser rifles supplied by Germany, withstood the increasing pressure of the British Army, which employed heavy artillery to blow the IRB out of its hiding spots. By the time of the IRB surrender on April 29, 450 people had been killed (including 64 rebels, 132 British soldiers, 254 civilians), 2,600 civilians had been wounded or injured, and much of downtown Dublin north of the River Liffy was in ruins. General Sir John Maxwell assumed command of Ireland and imposed martial law.[53]

At the time, a shocked population saw the IRB actions as cowardly, betraying the British Empire when it was in a death grip with imperial Germany. As rebels were marched to jail through the devastation of downtown Dublin, bystanders jeered, spat on them, and threw vegetables at them in derision.[54] Both the *Irish Independent* and the *Irish Times* condemned the rebellion outright. Ulster Unionists who had feared the worst from their southern neighbours before the war were very much convinced that their initial fears about the Irish Nationalists had been justified. Not so General Botha of the South African forces fighting alongside the BEF, who sent John Redmond his sympathies. Redmond himself was fit to be tied. He condemned the rebellion outright, but the irony of the situation was that while his supporters in the Volunteers were fighting and dying for the imperial cause and Home Rule, in France, Belgium, and Turkey his more radical detractors and their Volunteer support stayed home and plotted what would eventually become Redmond's own demise as an effective Irish leader.[55]

If the English-language Catholic newspapers in Canada are to be considered a rough sounding of Catholic opinion, Canadian Irish Catholics condemned the Easter Rebellion and its leaders unequivocally. The *Catholic Register* and its new editor, James Wall, described the rising as "an unspeakable outrage and colossal folly" perpetrated by a "small and unrepresentative element."[56] The *Register*'s provincial rival, the London *Catholic Record*, was equally strident, although like many Canadians they would mistakenly blame the Sinn Fein movement rather than the IRB:

> The criminal folly of the abortive Sinn Fein rising has caused such profound sorrow to all sane Irishmen and all true friends of Ireland everywhere. The Sinn Feiners are not Irish nationalists, but the bitterest opponent of the Irish national movements. Often John Redmond and his followers protest against the puerile pleadings and insane ebullitions of this handful of mischief makers.[57]

Other papers across the country joined in the chorus, once again denouncing Sinn Fein instead of the IRB. The *New Freeman* branded the Sinn Fein rebels as "anarchists," while the *Casket* described the rising as an act of "folly" and "stupidity."[58] Patrick Henry, the Irish nationalist editor of the *Northwest Review*, condemned the rising and the attempt to undermine Redmond, while the *Canadian Freeman* creatively compared the rebel leadership to the nationalist voices from Quebec: "[Sir Roger Casement] is no more the mouthpiece of Ireland than Armand Lavergne is the mouthpiece of Canada."[59] Even rank and file Catholics weighed in. Maxine Meagher, a student at Loretto High School in Guelph, defended the British Parliament and called out Sinn Fein as "intellectuals, who have failed to keep pace with modern conditions."[60] In France, in the thick of the action, Canadian artillery officer William O'Brien wrote in his diary that he had "[h]eard about disgraceful Sinn Fein riot in Dublin on the 24th." Word of the rebellion must have travelled quickly: O'Brien knew about it a day before the IRB's surrender.[61]

Although Irish Catholic opinion in Canada appeared solidly against the leaders of the Rising, albeit misrepresented as the Sinn Fein, their summary execution caused considerable consternation throughout the Irish diaspora. Under martial law, General Maxwell had rounded up the rebel fighters, jailed them, and added about three thousand potential political prisoners to the Mountjoy and Kilmainham jails. Within a span of ten days in May, after brief court martial proceedings, Maxwell oversaw the execution of fifteen IRB leaders, including Casement, Pearse, and John Connolly, the head of the Irish Citizen's Army.[62] Eamon de Valera was spared execution, not necessarily because of his American citizenship, but due to the fact that by the time of his trial a civilian leadership had replaced the temporary rule of Maxwell and the army. The executions essentially redirected the outrage of the Irish people toward the ruthlessness and haste of Maxwell's actions. Bishop Edward O'Dwyer of Limerick, Bishop Joseph

Hoare of Ardagh and Clonmacnoise, and Bishop Michael Fogarty of Killaloe all condemned the executions and brought the weight of the Church to bear on the ongoing debate. "There is hardly a second opinion in Ireland as to the savagery with which the Government has been acting," O'Dwyer wrote. "But it will do good. The country was being hypnotised by the politicians, but it was being revived these days."[63] Revived it was: Maxwell had now created martyrs, and Redmond gave the appearance of colluding with the British. His opponents in Sinn Fein could now step into the breach, and despite their passivity during the rising could now mount an effective public alternative to Redmond and the Irish Parliamentary Party.

In Canada, the Catholic papers and most Irish Catholic leaders retained their denunciation of the Rising but became equally shocked and disgusted by the so-called British "fair play" or justice meted out by General Maxwell. Several lines of argument began to emerge in the Catholic press and from some leaders of Catholic voluntary associations regarding the relationships between Canada, Ireland, and the Empire. Most Irish Catholic leaders in Canada remained convinced that John Redmond's constitutional means of achieving Home Rule was still the best policy and that he was the politician worth supporting. There was a sense of frustration, however, that the misguided leaders were summarily executed, particularly given the knowledge that, in 1913 and 1914, Unionist leader Sir Edward Carson and his Ulster Volunteers were prepared to engage the Crown supplied by German arms and were left untouched by authorities. According to the *New Freeman*, "there would not be an armed man today in Ireland, excepting soldiers and the constabulary, but for Carson's rebellious policy."[64] The inconsistency of British policy was clearly problematic for Irish Catholic editors, who now walked a fine line between promoting the war effort so that small nations might be free and supporting an Empire that was willing to take such harsh measures against a small, predominantly Catholic nation that was the land of their ancestors. Angered by the executions, the *Northwest Review* reminded readers that the German militarism that spells "the destruction of the natural rights of nations" must be defeated everywhere and that "we ought not to forget what we are fighting for."[65]

The *Casket*, however, saw the hands of Germany behind the Dublin fiasco and supported carrying out the death sentence for Casement for his part in the "hideous spectre of insurrection."[66] Alternatively, the

Catholic Register acknowledged that the actions of Ulster Unionists were partly to blame for the continued tensions in Ireland, but reprinted the opinion of the Dublin *Irish Catholic*, which condemned the IRB leaders for treason.[67] The *Catholic Record* judged its rival's position as too strident and potentially divisive for Canadians. Instead, the *Record* expressed a nuanced understanding of the motives of the rebels as sincere, while judging their actions as "folly." The paper regretted the executions, but it still labelled Pearse's actions as criminal because he and his followers failed "to present a united front under the guidance of [Ireland's] elected leader, John Redmond, who is supported by almost the entire hierarchy of the land."[68] The *New Freeman* agreed, as did the *Northwest Review*.[69] While slightly different in their analysis after the executions, all of Canada's largest English-language Catholic weeklies remained firmly supportive of John Redmond's loyalty to the Crown and to winning the war, and particularly his dedication to bringing forth Home Rule by constitutional means.

The *Canadian Freeman*, which was undergoing a transition from private ownership to ownership by the archdiocesan priests, carried perhaps the sharpest words on Irish affairs after the executions. The editors had condemned the Rising unequivocally, but their condemnation of the executions was equally passionate:

> The executions in Dublin are worse than a crime – they are a blunder, and a blunder that seems calculated to revive old hatreds and old misgivings. The Sinn Fein outbreak afforded England the golden opportunity to make atonement for her wicked past. She has chosen deliberately to ignore it. As a result of her criminal blundering, old wounds have reopened. By her stupid policy of repression she has glorified a riot into a revolution. If her intention was to make martyrs out of a handful of fanatical dreamers she has succeeded admirably.[70]

The *Canadian Freeman*, however took support of Redmond to the next level by drawing a parallel between Ireland's aspirations and Canada's experience. Editors advised the British to commission Redmond to repair the damage and make new laws for Ireland. The key was to understand that only through self-government could Ireland be loyal, just as Canada's loyalty had been maintained and nourished by the achievement of its own self-government. "Were there not mutterings of rebellion in Canada before self-government was conceded?" the *Freeman* argued. "Canada did not receive self-government because she was loyal; she is loyal because she enjoys self-government."[71] In the days and weeks after the Dublin fiasco the *Freeman*'s call for the implementation of Irish Home Rule, sooner than later, would be a commonly held position by Catholic editors across Canada.[72]

Apart from the voices of the English-language Catholic newspapers on the subject of the Easter Rising, only fragmentary evidence points to the thoughts of ordinary Irish Canadian Catholics on the matter. Priests were generally silent on the subject, and there were no official pronouncements of any kind from anglophone bishops. Interestingly, when commenting on the events in Dublin almost a year later, artillery officer William O'Brien, who was still alive and well at the front, took a position very similar to that of the moderate Catholic newspapers back home. As for Sinn Fein, O'Brien described them as "young misguided dreamers." He feared, however, that the British treatment of the rebels had "spread the organization."[73] Elsewhere at the front, Father Miles Tompkins, serving as chaplain with the 60th Battalion, lamented that "Ireland is in a sad state" and that this state of affairs was dampening recruiting efforts there.[74] Among the Ancient Order of Hibernians (AOH) there was a growing rift between radical members in the United States and members in Canada who, while holding on to their sentimental attachment to Ireland were loyal to Crown and Empire. Earlier in the war, Canadian AOH branches had threatened to succeed from the American AOH because of the latter's pro-German and anti-British stances. In fact, the Canadian AOH demanded that the official organ of the Order, the *American Hibernian*, be seized at the border as seditious literature. John H. Barry, an AOH executive from Fredericton, New Brunswick, where the Order was particularly strong, was adamant that "the order in Canada is worth saving though not at the tremendous cost of treason to our country."[75] The crisis passed, but the Easter Rising only increased the tension between the Canadian and American branches of the AOH.

Two months after the executions, the AOH sympathies in Canada became clear. In July 1916, the North American branches held their convention in Boston, where a New Brunswick priest, Father C.J. McLaughlin, drew a line in the sand with the Americans on the issue of Canadian Irish Catholic loyalty. In a stirring address to the convention he instructed the Americans as follows:

> Patriotism ever burns in the heart of the Hibernian. I would remind you Mr. President and brothers that this organization is composed of members owing allegiance to different flags and, sir, may I inform you that the fires of patriotism burn not the less bright within the bosoms of the Canadian Hibernians for the British flag than it does within the breast of the American citizens for the Star Spangled Banner ... Hibernian that I am, I am also a British subject. Britain's flag is our Talisman. The Roman citizen of old gloried in the title of Roman citizenship. Let me, sir, assure you today that the Canadian delegates here assembled glory in the proud title of Canadian-British citizenship, and, sirs, I would indeed be unworthy of the race and the land from which I came if I were to sit here this morning and offer no protest to some of the remarks that I have heard made here ... If the Dublin people followed John E Redmond and his Nationalists we would not today be mourning the loss of life in that unfortunate affair ... Let me answer it here by telling you that the hearts of the Canadian Irish beat true and that Canadians of all classes, Irish included, are prepared to stand by Britain in this crisis to the last man and the last dollar.[76]

The *New Freeman* reported that this speech was received warmly by "hundreds" of delegates and that some of the resolutions on foreign affairs against which he protested were subsequently modified.[77] Unafraid to test this message at home, McLaughlin delivered a similar address in August to the AOH in Moncton and was answered with repeated cheering.[78] McLaughlin's speech was reprinted with favourable commentary in other parts of Canada and came roughly at the same time as several bishops, including Archbishop McNeil of Toronto and Bishop James T. McNally of Calgary, issued strong public reassurances of Catholic patriotism and loyalty to the Empire's cause.[79]

The Irish question remained in the news for the duration of the war. Irish Catholic Canadians watched carefully as the Asquith government fell in 1916 and as David Lloyd George, a radical Liberal with little sympathy for Ireland, became prime minister. Canadian support for Redmond continued throughout 1916 and 1917 as he attempted to restore Asquith's assurances that Home Rule would be honoured at the end of the war – whenever that might come. The survivors of the Rising, such as Eamon de Valera, were breathing new life into Sinn Fein, which was fast becoming the principal rival of Redmond's Irish Parliamentary Party. Sinn Fein vilified Redmond for being too well ensconced with the British. In 1917, several by-elections were won by Sinn Fein candidates, including de Valera in East Clare and another in South Longford, the seat formerly held by Redmond's brother Willie, who had been killed while serving with the BEF. Although they did not abandon Redmond in his constitutional negotiations, several Canadian Catholic newspapers and the AOH continued to make resolutions demanding that the government of Lloyd George enact Home Rule for all of Ireland immediately, in order to secure Irish loyalty to the war effort. According to the *Canadian Freeman*, which was becoming increasingly vocal on the issue, the reasons for urgency on Home Rule were clear from a Canadian perspective. Irish Canadians are loyal, remarked the editor, because "they enjoy the priceless boon of liberty [and] ... they believe that Canadian liberty is worth defending."[80] Coinciding with St Patrick's Day 1917, prominent Irish Catholic Canadians joined with rank and file Catholics to demand that the Borden government apply pressure on Lloyd George to effect Home Rule in Ireland immediately. From across Canada, petitions and words of support came from the AOH, the Irish Catholic Benevolent Association, Archbishop Spratt of Kingston, Bishop Fallon of London, Member of Parliament Charles Murphy, J.J. Leddy, the Catholic Conservative scion of Saskatoon, and former mayor of Montreal, Patrick Keane, among many others. The plea was for constitutional change and to honour the principles for which Canada was fighting in Europe.[81] None of the leading subscribers to these resolutions would be considered cool to the war effort; in fact, support came from Charles J. Doherty, Borden's minister of justice and an Irish Catholic MP for St Anne's riding in Montreal. Privately, Doherty thought the Rising and the stalling on Home Rule might have hurt Irish Catholic recruitment in Canada.[82] For editors at the *Canadian Freeman*, such demonstrations "dispelled forever the suspicion that [Irish Canadians] were apathetic about the Home Rule issue."[83]

Once again, Church leaders were notable in their efforts to mobilize Irish Catholic politicians. In March, Fallon wrote to Doherty, Murphy, and Ontario Tory MPP and provincial treasurer, T.W. McGarry, to meet with him in Ottawa to discuss a Canadian strategy to move the Home Rule agenda forward by applying Dominion pressure on Lloyd George. In his outrage over the British prime minister's foot-dragging and equivocation on Home Rule, Fallon had turned to this multi-partisan trio because he considered them the leading Irish Catholic politicians "in federal and provincial affairs."[84] All recipients responded with varying levels of support for Fallon's invitation. Doherty was perhaps the most careful and diplomatic. He had been in correspondence with several observers and participants in the Irish constitutional nationalist cause and was well aware of Redmond's weakness both politically and with respect to his public popularity in the wake of the Rising.[85] Doherty replied to Fallon that Canadian and Irish politics should be considered as distinct and that any actions in Canada should "be such as to leave clearly defined the dividing line between them."[86] He did, however, leave an opening for a meeting of more representative Irish Canadians than just politicians, to propose "prompt and effective" action for "kin" in the "Old Land who are in need and grave danger."[87] Earlier, Doherty had sent a personal telegram to Borden, who was in England, strongly urging him to pressure Lloyd George to enact Home Rule immediately, lest the Irish question "help the Germans to prolong the war."[88] In the months that followed, Canadian Irish Catholics and politicians from coast to coast did meet to express their concern, sometimes heatedly, that Ireland deserved what other dominions enjoyed. It should not be forgotten, however, that behind the scenes Catholic prelates were often the guiding hands prodding the laity.

One of the more notable of these Fallon-inspired meetings took place in Ottawa on 24 April 1917. Chaired by Charles Murphy and attended by many Irish Catholic politicians and community leaders, such as Justice Frank Anglin, Chief Justice Charles Fitzpatrick, and lawyer Edward J. Daly, the meeting resulted in a resolution to be sent to Borden so that pressure might be applied on Lloyd George to enact Home Rule immediately. Although Doherty was in New Jersey on business and could not attend, he sent his endorsement of the resolution and a lengthy personal note indicating that being engaged in the fight "for the protection of the rights of outside small nations entitles Canadians to at least raise our voices on behalf of the small nation that is at the household of the empire."[89] The resolution itself, which was supported in person by Wilfrid Laurier, demonstrated clearly that the issues of winning the war and effecting Home Rule in Ireland were intimately linked:

> That with a view to strengthening the hands of the Allies in achieving equal rights for small nations, and the principle of nationality against the opposite German principle of military domination and government, without consent of the governed, it is in the position of this meeting of Canadian citizens assembled in the capital of the Dominion, essential without further delay, confer upon Ireland the free institutions long promised her.[90]

In as concise a fashion as possible the resolution struck the main chords of what was coming to be a consensus among most Irish Catholic Canadian leaders, clerical and lay: a stress upon winning the war; the assertion that the "small nations" principle for which the war was being fought be applied by the Allies themselves in Ireland; and an assurance that the promoters of such a notion were proud and loyal Canadians.

In the larger view, the resolution exemplified Doherty's strong advice to Fallon that any public actions on the Home Rule issue had to be measured and viewed within the context of several other burning domestic issues of the time. In 1917, Canada's Irish Catholics appeared unwilling to take a radical position on the Irish question, lest it be mistaken for any sympathy for Irish rebellion while the Empire was deadlocked in the war with the Central Powers. In the context of the unresolved Ukrainian question and continued sniping from the Orange Order, Mayor Horatio Hocken of Toronto,[91] and some Protestant clergy on the alleged collusion between the Pope and the Kaiser, the Catholic Church did not need the Irish question to make an already combustible domestic situation more incendiary for the Irish Catholic rank and file. The approach was a constitutional one, and one resting on sound precedents set by Britain's evolving relationship with its dominions. The *New Freeman* was clear to readers in Saint John that Irish affairs should not stir anger at the Crown; King George had nothing to do with the Dublin affair, and he was favourable to Home Rule.[92] An abiding hope was expressed by figures as different as Bishop Fallon and the controversial A.E. Burke that a peaceful, negotiated settlement could be had, and that the war aims would be honoured in the case of Ireland.[93] The *Catholic Register* even held out hope that American intercession on the issue, recognizing its pronounced support of Home Rule, would hasten a peaceful and constitutional resolution to the Irish troubles.[94] In Winnipeg, AOH branch no. 1 passed a balanced resolution that defended the Empire's war and the principle of freedom of small nations, and then pointed out that the "blunder" in Dublin needed to be remedied by Home Rule for the sake of the Empire.[95] D.A. Casey, who had become the editor of the *Canadian Freeman*, wrote to Archbishop William J. Walsh of Dublin to ascertain whether the IRB had committed atrocities during the rising. (They had.) He wanted to make certain of his facts regarding alleged "Sinn Fein" excesses.[96] In Ottawa, when Father Matthew J. Whelan addressed his St Patrick's Parish for its patron saint's feast day in 1917, he referred to Padraig Pearse's "fatuous Proclamation" during the "Rising" but offered grudging respect for those who wanted independence, and prayed that Britain not fall into a trap "worse than German 'kulture'" regarding Ireland.[97] More openly in support of Sinn Fein throughout the aftermath of the Rising was Katherine Hughes, a journalist and, ironically, the niece of the late imperialist Archbishop of Halifax, Cornelius O'Brien.[98] She claimed, and with some justification, that Sinn Fein had been misrepresented, and she became a tireless lobbyist for radical change in Ireland.[99]

By mid-1917, Canada's Irish Catholic leadership was facing heated questions about Catholic loyalty arising from circumstances beyond their control both domestically and in Europe. Such diversions came as editors, priests, bishops, and Catholic politicians continued to praise the Irish Catholic war effort and encourage greater enlistment to bring the war to an end. As had been the case so many times since the war began, it was O'Gorman who came to the fore to eloquently address the complexity of the Irish Catholic position in Canada. While he was convalescing in Ottawa, he developed the idea of "double duty" as best characterizing the position of the Irish Catholics of Canada. In an interview with the *Ottawa Citizen* – which was later reprinted in Catholic weeklies across the country – O'Gorman laid out what he considered to be the best course of action for Canada's Irish Catholics:

> To answer the question [no recruiting unless there is Home Rule in Ireland] we should consider the double duty of the Irish Canadian – the duty he owes to Ireland, and the duty he owes to Canada. For there certainly exists this double duty. There are some who claim that we of Irish descent are Canadians pure and simple; that

> Ireland was indeed the land of our ancestors, but it is not our land, and that consequently we have nothing whatever to do with it. This claim we Irish Canadians cannot admit. Ireland has bequeathed to us, in addition to the Catholic faith of St Patrick, an intellectual, moral, emotional and artistic inheritance which is of the highest spiritual value. It is our right as it is our duty to know Ireland's history, her great saints, her mighty men and women, to impregnate ourselves with the ideals which they realized, that we their descendants, may be imbued with their high spirituality.
>
> ... Canada is indeed our native land, but Ireland is our fatherland, all the dearer and nearer and we will be second to none in 1917.[100]

O'Gorman clearly outlined that Irish Catholic Canadians still had an obligation to the spiritual and cultural heritage passed to them from Ireland, whether they recognized it or not. But having once identified that the loyalty of his people was bifocal, it was an identity based on a debt to one nation and a present obligation to their current home.

O'Gorman claimed quite clearly that refusing to support the Canadian and imperial war effort hurt both Canada and Ireland. He eschewed the anti-conscription movement in Australia and the anti-English lobby in the United States, and regretted what appeared to be a negative impact on recruitment of the 199th Battalion in Montreal. O'Gorman admitted that there was anger in the Irish Canadian community after the executions in Dublin, but nevertheless for him the reasoning in any "anti-recruiting" movement was flawed because "[i]t directly aids the enemy and weakens our allies."[101] Moreover, he claimed that such a policy is one of "sulk[ing]" and advocates a "policy of self-sacrifice." Instead he reasoned in favour of the Irish Catholic double duty:

> [T]he duty we owe to Ireland, coincides with the duty we owe to Canada ... The interests of Canada, as a nation, as a part of the British Empire, and as a member of the world's family of nations, demanded that we enter this war against the Turco-Teutons, and that having entered it, we should prosecute it till we finish it or it finishes us. The few voices that are raised here and there, asking that we should halt till Ireland gets Home Rule, have rightly been disregarded by the vast majority of Irish Canadians. We do not intend to do wrong that good may come

> ... No matter how unjust be the policy of England towards Ireland, we shall not change. For our patriotism is the result, not of the changing conduct of individuals or institutions, but of principles as unchanging as our Catholic faith.[102]

O'Gorman did not mince words about the failure of the British government to handle the Rising and its aftermath effectively, but he did not see this as sufficient to divert Irish Canadian attention away from winning the war. For O'Gorman, Canada had to be a voice at the table for small nations, and he recognized in Prime Minister Borden, an equal partner with the British, as a strong voice for Canadian interests. As had been the case with every challenge he faced during the war, O'Gorman's position was well thought out, articulate, and able to balance the question of Irish Catholic loyalty with concern for the Irish situation. His position won praise, even from the *Canadian Freeman*, a Catholic weekly often noted for more extreme pronouncements on the Irish question. For its editors, this was about Christianity prevailing over *Kultur*, a struggle that could not be lost.[103]

Throughout early 1917, Irish Canadian Catholics, in groups both small and large, continued to meet in parish halls, public theatres, and private clubs to hear speeches and voice their support of Irish Home Rule. In Toronto, Father James Dollard, an Irish-born priest and poet, and also part-time chaplain in the local military hospital, hosted a large meeting that included a speech from Irish journalist and radical Robert Lindsay Crawford and a resolution demanding Home Rule for the sake of "the unity and safety of the Empire."[104] In Victoria, a public meeting hosted by MPP John Hart reinforced the point that Home Rule was precisely the cause for which the Empire was fighting. The AOH in Nova Scotia and New Brunswick passed similar resolutions.[105] In Ottawa, 1500 attended a meeting in which former prime minister Sir Wilfrid Laurier spoke eloquently in favour of extending to Ireland what Canada already had.[106] In neighbouring eastern Ontario towns other meetings added more voices to the Home Rule chorus. One discordant note came from W.E. Cavanaugh in Almonte, who provided one of the few critiques of O'Gorman's approach, claiming "his youthful zeal has led him into rash conclusions."[107]

Throughout 1917 the Catholic press kept a careful eye on the Irish situation, knowing full well that negative developments in Ireland might call into question the loyalty of Irish Catholic Canadians in the eyes of their non-Catholic neighbours. As the influence of Sinn Fein began to grow, reactions in the Catholic press covered the spectrum from fear to grudging support. The *Catholic Register*, long known for its conservative positions under editors Alfred Burke and J.A. Wall, appeared alarmed at Sinn Fein's growth and once questioned "Is Ireland Republican?"[108] The *New Freeman* chose to place the force of its criticism on Prime Minister Lloyd George's proposal to implement Home Rule but with several of the northern counties of Ulster excluded. The editors chose to criticize ideas of partition, shifting their support to John Redmond and his Nationalists, who had no choice but to leave "the house in disgust; red-blooded men could stand no more."[109] In their support of the Irish Nationalists, the *New Freeman* editors gave full treatment of a speech by Redmond's deputy, John Dillon, to the House of Commons in which he told parliamentarians that delay on Home Rule was simply driving Irish support into the arms of Sinn Fein, thereby destroying decades of constitutional approaches to the Home Rule question.[110] The *New Freeman* made clear its support for the constitutional processes by which Canada had benefitted greatly. What is most curious about papers like the *New Freeman*, however, is that they appeared to embody O'Gorman's idea of double duty on their front pages. It was not unusual to see a headline like "Home Rule Must Be Granted" right beside an article of equal prominence titled "They Died for King and Country."[111] Both issues were of importance to readers: the sacrifice being made by the men and women of Canada under the Union Jack, and the fight for Irish Home Rule – which was clearly, in their minds, an application of the principles for which they were fighting in Flanders and France. In this light, editors at the *Catholic Record* could write: "Self-government as we have it in Canada would be such a solution and the only one which would remove the far reaching effects ... of centuries of oppression and misgovernment."[112]

While the press statements and public meetings attest to the importance of the Irish question to Irish Catholic Canadians, one should resist the temptation to regard this as the only issue relevant to "descendants" in Canada or even the most important issue. One must remember that throughout 1916 and 1917 tens of thousands of Irish Catholic Canadians were fighting overseas or were waiting to join the struggle in Europe. Families were coping without sons and fathers, while young men were being called increasingly into non-traditional industrial jobs to keep the war machine supplied and the family economy buoyant. Meanwhile, the sniping from the Protestant and secular press on issues of Papal treachery, the dangerous enemy alien, and questions of Catholic loyalty continued. But perhaps the most divisive issue for Irish Catholics was their growing drift away from the policies and politics of their French-Canadian co-religionists. Although the war itself did not cause the rift within the Canadian Catholic Church, opposing positions taken by Irish and French Catholics on recruitment, the Union Government, and eventually conscription polarized the Church into seemingly intractable sides based on language and culture. Meanwhile French Canadian attitudes to the war, deemed "disloyal" by many Anglo-Protestant leaders, became a burdensome label all Canadian Catholics would have to bear. The ongoing crisis of Quebec and the nationalism of francophone Catholics would be one more leaden ball Irish Catholic leaders would have to juggle in the complex politics of religion, language, and loyalty during the Great War.

As discussed in the opening chapter, the seeds of disunion within Canada's Catholic Church had been sewn decades before the war. French Canadian and Irish Catholics had already been at each other's throats competing for the loyalty of new Catholic Canadian immigrants and the episcopal sees that would manage them in the Prairie West and British Columbia. In the east, the struggle for episcopal sees had been just as evident in the west, and the question of language in Ontario schools was a festering canker sore in the Church in Ontario. These pre-war issues were relived during the war, when many of the Irish Catholic leaders in the battle with their francophone coreligionists emerged as leaders of Catholic Canada's Great War initiatives. French Canadian Catholics, both leaders and the rank and file, could not help but be reluctant in their enthusiasm for the war, when a trio of their pre-war "enemies" – Fallon, Burke, and O'Gorman – all seemed to be well ensconced and supportive of the Anglo-Canadian and imperialist military establishment.[113]

It has been noted that when war was declared in 1914 all of Canada's Catholic bishops, regardless of language, were supportive of the imperial war effort. Despite the differences between the major linguistic groups within the Church, there was a great show of solidarity in the early months of the war.[114] At that point, even the outspoken French Canadian nationalist Henri Bourassa received fair reporting from Catholic English-language weeklies on his support for a Canadian contribution to the European struggle."[115] But it has also been demonstrated that the patience of Irish Catholic leaders and editors with Bourassa and his French Canadian allies began to wear thin, particularly when Bourassa's oppositional voice became sharper on issues such as recruitment. Nevertheless, as much as they were annoyed, and despite the risk of being seen in the public eye as disloyal to the Empire because of their shared religion with French Canadians, Irish Catholic clerics and politicians had to carefully nuance their criticisms of French Canadian nationalism, lest the Church appear divided at a time of national crisis. Bishops and editors had to make sure that their responses to the critique of Catholic Quebec "shirking its duties" carefully extricated the bishops and clergy from the rhetoric and actions of the Nationalists, while carefully identifying the problems stemming from Quebec as not emergent from anything Catholic, but as by-products of excited expressions rooted in language and culture – or, as described at the time, "race."

As has been examined earlier in this study, for the first eighteen months of the war Irish Catholic prelates, clergy, politicians, and the editors of the English-language Catholic weeklies worked carefully to maintain the fragile alliance within the Canadian Church. As recruitment began to fall off in mid-1916, and as pressure from many anglophone politicians for compulsory military service increased, the entente within the Church began to fracture. Finally, Irish and French Catholic leaders' hopes for peace among Canadian Catholics were crushed in a corner of southern Ontario in August 1917. After the death of an anti-Regulation 17 priest at francophone Our Lady of the Lake Parish in Ford City, Diocese of London, Bishop Fallon sent a more obedient French-Canadian priest, who was immediately rebuffed by the parishioners. Demanding a pastor who was "French-Canadian at heart and of the same aspirations and ideals as the great majority of the congregation," the crowd tossed Father Francis-Xavier Laurendau's baggage onto the front lawn of the parish property and barred his re-entry to the rectory. After a heated exchange of letters between Fallon and the protestors, the new parish priest was escorted by local constables to the rectory, only to be met by a mob of three thousand protesters. What ensued on 8 September 1917 was a full-blown riot involving hand-to-hand combat between police and protestors, many of whom were women wielding brooms and clubs. By the time the melee ended, the police had captured the church and rectory, nine protestors had been arrested, and several civilians, including a seventy-two-year-old woman, had been injured.[116]

The Ford City Riot made headlines across the country and further solidified the lines drawn between francophone and anglophone Catholics. The *Casket*, for instance, admitted that it had always been sympathetic to French Canadians, but it could not abide disobedience to episcopal authority as evidenced at Our Lady of the Lake Parish.[117] This Nova Scotia Catholic weekly then engaged in a verbal war with the nationalist *Le Droit* of Ottawa and its position that parishioners had a canonical right to resist the bishop's appointment.[118] D.A. Casey, editor of the *Canadian Freeman*, denounced the rioters as disgraceful and their actions as "utterly unchristian and un-catholic."[119] Casey, who had earlier expressed his exasperation with trying to balance the interests of Church and French Canada, saw the Ford City case as a potential tipping point in internal cultural relations within the Church: "We have never penned a line inimical to the French-Canadians. But if our French brethren want to alienate the sympathy of every Catholic worthy of the name they have but to uphold such conduct as that of the ill-advised enthusiasts of Ford, Ont."[120] Although Fallon was backed by anglophone supporters, who defended his authority as bishop, officials in Rome were not pleased. Cardinal De Lai, the Vatican's secretary of state, sent Fallon a note condemning the Ford City rioters and rebuking Fallon for his "anti-French Canadian" activities. "I read the letter with some pain and more astonishment," Fallon wrote in his diary. "If the policy of Card. De Lai is carried out in Canada, then there are bad days ahead for the Church in that Country. But God will decide."[121] Fallon was correct; the year 1917 would be remembered as an *annus horribilus* for the Canadian Catholic Church.

As police battled French Canadian parishioners, and relations between anglophone and francophone Catholics in Ontario and in the West soured to a point of no return, the federal government proposed conscription of manpower as a means of alleviating the shortage of troops in France and Belgium. French Catholics had long been suspicious that Borden's Conservatives were slowly moving in this direction as the war dragged on and voluntary enlistment figures dropped off after mid-1916. Although Borden was not prepared to move toward conscription as voluntary recruitment waned, there was pressure from within his Cabinet, principally from anglophone ministers, to draft able-bodied men to fill the ranks of the four fighting divisions. It was not until February 1917 that the 5th Division, based in England as a reserve division, was effectively broken up to fill the gaps in the four front-line divisions.

The government's first initiative to secure additional manpower for the war effort was the National Service program. In late 1916, Borden moved to implement a national registration of all human resources in Canada, to ascertain who was engaged in essential war industries and agriculture and who might be approached for voluntary military service. In private correspondence, Borden approached the two most powerful Catholic prelates in Quebec, Archbishop Paul Bruchési of Montreal and Cardinal Louis-Nazaire Bégin of Quebec City, to endorse the registration, promising them that it was not a prelude to conscription. Both agreed and were joined by Bishop Joseph-Guillaume Forbes of Joliette in the preparation of pastoral letters endorsing the registration and instructing parish priests to encourage their parishioners to register.[122] Bruchési assured his people that the registration was not conscription but a means of properly assessing human resources so that Canada might win the war. He added that participation served as an active expression of patriotism "and conformed with the teaching and tradition of the Catholic Church demonstrating deference towards civil authority."[123] Forbes was perhaps more poetic in expressing his appreciation to Bruchési, likening his colleague's pastoral as "rendering unto Caesar," akin to when Mary and Joseph went to Bethlehem to enrol in the census, so that "God's prophecy became realized." Accordingly, as a suffragan to Bruchési, Forbes issued his own pastoral letter endorsing registration.[124] Perhaps the most positive response offered to Borden was by Joseph-Simon-Herman Bruneault, bishop of Nicolet, who reaffirmed the historical relationship between the Quebec Church and the state, evident from the time of Bishop Olivier Briand after the Conquest of 1760: "[J]e ne fait que suivre l'exemple des Evêques de ce pays," wrote Bruneault, "qui, depuis la Conquête se sont toujours montrée le plus fidèle sujets de la Courronne Britannique, et j'ai voulu rappeler á tous le respect qui est dû á l'autorité civile lorsque'elle intervient pour le bien commun de la nation."[125] All had confidence in Borden when he said the National Service was not a prelude to conscription.

Irish Catholic bishops and the Catholic press were more willing to endorse the program and did so knowing that the compliance of the

Quebec Church might provide further proof that Catholics as a whole were loyal citizens of Canada and the Empire and were dedicated to winning the war. In Calgary, Bishop McNally issued his own circular directing his priests to make certain that the National Service cards were completed by all men between the ages of sixteen and sixty-five in their parishes. "It is not for us to question this," directed McNally, "As loyal citizens and as dutiful Catholics, we recognize the right of the government to call upon all of us in the hour of our country's need."[126] McNally made it clear that a Catholic's patriotic duty was inseparable from one's obligation to the Faith. In Toronto, Archbishop McNeil, upon the request of R.B. Bennett, Director of the National Service program, also issued a circular making clear the registry's purpose and the duty of Catholic men to complete it as directed.[127] The Catholic press was also quick to fall in line with the *Catholic Record*, which reminded its readers: "There should be a cheerful and ready response to the Government's request for this information ... to organize this country's resources for the supreme effort in the great struggle in which we were now engaged."[128] The *Catholic Register* was less cheerful, warning its readers not to be swayed by organized labour, which opposed registration: "[N]o labour organization can stand between them and their duty as citizens, upon their religion [Catholic] lays stress."[129] Regardless of tone, the National Registration brought francophone and anglophone leaders together, singing from the same hymnbook, perhaps for the first time since 1914.

Catholics returned thousands of registration cards through the early months of 1917, and the military apparatus now had a better idea of where potential recruits were to be found. In Toronto alone, the Christian Brothers reported that they had 100 per cent participation among the young men in Toronto's separate schools.[130] The good will extended toward registration, however, was not to be rewarded. In May 1917, after a visit to Europe, where he met the battered and wounded of the CEF and came to understand the crisis the allies faced in the third year of the war, Borden returned home convinced that conscription was needed. His announcement in the House of Commons of the coming introduction of a conscription bill sent shock waves through the Catholic community and placed extreme stress on the linguistic entente that had already proven itself to be fragile, if not ready to fall to pieces, in the context of the "race" and education questions in 1917. Given the bully pulpit that Bourassa, Lavergne, and others had built for themselves in Quebec, the government knew they had almost no support in French Canada; accordingly, intra-governmental memos identified the Catholic Church as an opponent of conscription.[131] Once again, another sector of Protestant Canada – in this case, elements in the overwhelmingly Anglo-Protestant federal Cabinet – associated French Canadian dissent regarding the war effort as stemming directly from the Catholic Church. Regardless of how many times Irish Catholic priests, bishops, lay leaders, and the press made the case for Catholic loyalty and sacrifice during the war, they had been made guilty by association because their francophone and immigrant co-religionists were considered inherently "disloyal."

The Military Service Act was introduced in the House of Commons in June 1917 and debated during the summer until it was passed. Sensing his fragility at the polls in the inevitable election that was to come before the end of the year, Borden invited former prime minister and opposition Liberal leader Sir Wilfrid Laurier to join him in a coalition government so that the country would not be split along linguistic lines as a result of conscription. Laurier declined. He disliked the idea of compelling men into military service and knew full well his French Canadian supporters would abandon him to Henri Bourassa's nationalists in Quebec if he united with Borden. In the autumn, Borden enticed many prominent English-speaking Liberals from Laurier's caucus and from the provincial Liberal parties to join him in a Union government, which would make the Military Service Act the chief electoral issue when Canadians went to the polls in December 1917. Canada was now bitterly divided, with French Canadians, organized labour, and anti-conscriptionists in one camp, and a noisy Anglo-Canadian "win-the-war" movement on the other. Farmers had been temporarily neutralized by promises of exemptions for agricultural workers.[132] English-speaking Catholics were now facing a perfect storm on the conscription issue, which had the potential to irreparably damage their relationship with their French Catholic brothers and sisters. At the same time, if they wanted to win the war, English-speaking Catholics could find themselves in an alliance with their Orange Lodge and Conservative partisan detractors. Added to this was the basic philosophical question of whether or not compulsion was an appropriate way to win the war; until now, voluntary enlistment had been viewed as the high ground in a democratic society.

It did not help relations in the Church that the politician front-and-centre in the conscription debate was the Irish Catholic member of parliament from Ste Anne (Montreal), Charles J. Doherty, the Minister of Justice and the cabinet minister with the principal hand in writing the Military Service Act. On 5 July 1917, Doherty stood in the House and offered a lengthy speech in which he refuted the objections of Opposition members, many of whom were fellow Quebec MPs, and demonstrated that the Act would amount to a far more careful deployment of Canada's human resources, assuring that men in essential industries and agriculture would remain in Canada while others who were of age would fight. "How many a father has left this country, "argued Doherty, "and gone over, to give his life in this great struggle, or to return crippled and unable to support that family; while men with no dependents, men of leisure, men with money, men who did not need to devote themselves to production, men without ties, men with no one dependent upon them, sat at home."[133] When David A. Lafortune, the honourable member from Montcalm, insinuated that Irish Catholics rejected conscription, Doherty deftly put him in his place by asking how this French Canadian could presume to speak for the Irish. Doherty mused that the Irish were "anxious to do their duty. I do not doubt there will be differences of opinion among them … But they will not as the member for Montcalm says they will, [act] in one body themselves as absolutely on one side of the question."[134] After a lengthy defence of the Act, Doherty concluded with great rhetorical flourish, imploring members to stand on their "honour," do their "duty" to the men who had already died, put aside partisan differences and regional differences, and remember "that there is come to us the great privilege, carrying with it the heavy burden of responsibility, of determining for Canada tonight the most important question that any Canadian Parliament has been called upon to determine … and upon the proper action following that decision depends the honour of our country, Canada."[135]

To Doherty's regret, there was no support for the Act from the Quebec bishops, who now felt betrayed by the Borden government after the promises made in exchange for their support for the National Service Registration just five months before. In a flurry of letters to the prime minister, Archbishop Paul Bruchési begged Borden not to enact conscription, fearing that it would hurt Canadian unity.[136] Bruchési knew that Bourassa and the Nationalists would now have the upper hand and that the Quebec episcopate would lose face because of its steadfast trust in the federal government. For the leader of Canada's largest Catholic diocese, there was no need for conscription now that the United States had entered the war, and in view of the fact that so many skilled workers were needed for the war industries at home and for the harvests that would be required to feed the nation. Bruchési simply feared the worst in terms of violence and protest in his home province.[137] In his carefully worded reply, Borden thanked the archbishop for his concerns and professed his undiminished respect. He reiterated that he had not intended conscription in 1916, but circumstances had changed. Not moving effectively to bring more troops to the front, Borden argued, "would involve the abandonment and betrayal of the men in the trenches who by the hundred thousand have freely offered themselves for the supreme duty of citizenship in order that Canada may live and that our liberties, institutions, and heritage be preserved."[138] Borden had cast the die and had lost the good will of Quebec's bishops in the process.

Doherty was correct that there was by no means unanimity among Irish Catholic leaders or the rank and file on the issue of conscription. The divisions crossed lines of political partisanship, region, and lay or clerical vocation. In the first camp, bishops, clergy, and some Catholic newspapers openly supported conscription as a means to win the war. A second group, primarily based among the editors and writers of some Catholic newspapers, accepted conscription but indicated it would not have been their desired approach to solving the question of manpower on the front, because it threatened to split the country along linguistic and cultural lines. A third group refused to engage in the debate, protesting its tone and the manipulation of arguments by extremists on both sides. Included in this non-committed camp were Catholic organizations that generally eschewed political involvement, but elected to make general professions of loyalty to winning the war without uttering the divisive "C" word. Finally, a fourth group, essentially composed of two newspapers and a handful of clergy and laymen who made their voices known in the public square, opposed conscription on principle: it was contrary to democracy and would destroy national unity. Each camp, though providing variations on a single theme of winning the war, were conscious that the situation in Quebec was still having a negative effect on the perception of Catholic loyalty, and that even benign arguments introduced by the Quebec bishops about exemptions could bring out the worst in the Anglo-Protestant supporters of conscription, the Orange Order, and the daily secular press.

The English-speaking Catholic bishops of both Irish and Scottish lineage led the Roman Catholic endorsement of conscription. Archbishop McNeil of Toronto, Bishop Fallon of London, Archbishop Casey of Vancouver, Bishop MacDonald of Victoria, Bishop McNally of Calgary, Archbishop Sinnott of Winnipeg, and Bishop Morrison of Antigonish all made public statements in favour of the government policies and conscription.[139] Like so many of his episcopal colleagues, Casey, a native of New Brunswick, implored his flock to accept conscription: "Our very life as a nation, our homes and our firesides, nay even the vital principles of humanity and civilization as we understand them, are at stake and at issue in this gigantic contest. We are, therefore to place our all, blood and treasure, at the disposal of the authorities of our nation, so that our duty to our country may be fulfilled to its uttermost degree."[140] In Winnipeg, Sinnott, a Prince Edward Islander by birth, indicated that if the government deemed conscription necessary, Catholics must not let anything interfere with their "manifest duty of loyalty to the state."[141] The Canadian bishops stood in contrast with their Australian colleagues, who opposed conscription in that country's second plebiscite on the issue in December 1917. In Australia, seminarians and teaching brothers would not be given an exemption under the conscription bill, whereas in Canada the issue of tonsure (see chapter 6) would keep most seminarians out of the draft.[142]

Canada's anglophone bishops were complemented in their support publicly by Doherty, the only Irish Catholic in Borden's Cabinet, the vociferous Father Lancelot Minehan of Toronto, Father A.B. O'Neill, Rector of St Joseph's University in New Brunswick, and A. Claude Macdonell, the Catholic Conservative MP for South Toronto.[143] Even the much maligned Nykyta Budka, Ukrainian eparch of Canada, wrote to Prime Minister Borden explaining that his Ukrainian Catholic flock would comply with conscription just as they had in the old country and wanted to demonstrate pride in their Canadian citizenship. Budka also suggested that Ukrainian conscripts not be sent to France, Romania, or Serbia, where they might have to fight against their fathers and brothers.[144] Borden said he would to try to accommodate Budka's wishes and would refer the matter to Doherty, who was administering the Military Service Act, but this response did not reveal the government's true position. Throughout 1917 the government was keeping a close eye on Ukrainian nationalists, their publications, and their alleged failure to participate in the National Service registration.[145]

The *Catholic Register* expressed unequivocal support for conscription. Since the paper served both as the official organ of the Catholic Church Extension Society and as the mouthpiece of the Archdiocese of Toronto, under the watchful eye of former journalist Archbishop McNeil, the *Register*'s opinions held considerable sway among subscribers. J.A. Wall, McNeil's hand-picked editor after Burke's resignation in 1915, was clear that the situation at the front –particularly the collapse of Russia on the Eastern Front – warranted urgent action. "It has become a question of whether the Allies can withstand the destruction of their shipping until they can beat back the huge armies of Germany."[146] Wall continued:

> We justify the Government's decision ... on the stern grounds of absolute necessity to the life of the Empire and the continued freedom of our own Dominion ... the safety of civilization requires that we still do more; and we must nerve ourselves to do it. It is as truly for the defence of Canada as if German shells were now crashing into Halifax or Quebec or Toronto.[147]

Columnist Henry Somerville, also hand-picked by McNeil to write on labour issues, expressed his regret of the racial divide the issue had created, but praised the support offered by many English-speaking Catholics who came out prominently in favour of conscription. While conceding the democratic right of people to dissent, except in the case of narrow sectional interests, he was harshly critical of those who said nothing on the issue, accusing them of a dereliction of "duty."[148] For Somerville, winning the war was a moral duty that encompassed "legal duties imposed on us by the state." In the end, wrote Somerville, "[p]atriotism is a Catholic virtue and national service is a Catholic duty."[149] The columnists at the *Register* remained committed to conscription throughout the war, even though at least one reader accused Wall of turning the paper into a "Conservative sheet" and being excessive in his criticism of Bourassa.[150]

Both the *Catholic Record* and the *New Freeman* offered support for conscription, but not without expressing reservations about the domestic trouble it might cause and questioning whether voluntary enlistment had in fact been exhausted. The *Record*, which had been sympathetic to the Liberal Party and to Laurier, did not want to appear to rebuke the latter's opposition to Borden's bill. Nevertheless, the editors accepted that conscription would be a way of "enabling Canada to do her full duty in the war," with the caution that national unity and peace could be maintained only if the Quebec clergy supported the measure.[151] Knowing how volatile the bill would be with respect to domestic politics, national unity, and the existing problems between the chief linguistic groups in the Catholic Church, the *Record* provided a highly nuanced legalistic argument in favour of the Military Service Act. Earlier in the year, the editors had expressed hope that conscription would not be necessary, or perhaps at worst could be implemented in a modified form, but once it was certain that the Military Service Bill would become law the paper accepted the authority of the state to enact such legislation: "Canada is at war, and her Parliament has the right to exact and enforce military service from every Canadian. And obedience is a duty binding in conscience."[152] The paper might dispute the wisdom or expediency of the Act, but the state had the right to legislate in these matters and citizens had the duty to obey. The *Record* would have preferred, however, a more democratic approach to the conscription issue, entrusting the people with the decision, instead of the government moving in a less consultative way amid the cries of the militarists.[153]

Editors at the *New Freeman*, also concerned about the damage that might be done to both national and ecclesial unity, took a similar legalistic and cautious approach. The paper lamented how the debate on conscription had descended into partisanship and "political kite-flying" on both sides and demanded a shift "away from party politics in such a time as this."[154] Editors questioned whether the voluntary method of enlistment really had failed, but were prepared to err on the side of the prime minister, who saw no recourse but conscription to win the war. Trying to nuance this acceptance, the paper suggested that "[c]onscription of men should be accompanied by conscription of resources," which was an open shot at speculators and Canadian businessmen who had made a tidy profit on the war thus far.[155] Not necessarily questioning the need for more troops, the *New Freeman* cited the *Montreal Star* and its call for calm and conciliation: "What we want is more soldiers to fight the Germans ... We will not get them if we must stir up trouble in Canada … No country can stand divided."[156] By September, and the beginning of the implementation of the Act through the registration and medical examination of draftees, and the formation of tribunals where men could seek exemptions, the *Freeman*'s editors pointed out that the relative calm in Quebec and the high levels of participation in Montreal were a strong rebuke of Quebec's detractors and an acknowledgement that not all Quebecois were of the ilk of the Nationalists.[157] While the *New Freeman* may not have been overjoyed at the passage of the Military Service Act, it provided no opposition to it, but rather criticism of the rhetoric that excited passions on both sides of the debate and tore at the fabric of national unity.

The *Casket* took a different stance, disavowing any endorsement or rejection of the Act. Traditionally, it had sidestepped partisan politics, and this case was no exception. "The *Casket*," explained editor Michael Donovan, "is taking no part in the Conscription controversy … Whatever may be the merits of Conscription, it is clear that there is a good deal of opposition to it apart from Quebec, and the effort to make it a French-English issue is entirely political and fraudulent."[158] The paper questioned the heightened rhetoric of the debate and even questioned whether the government would send the conscripts to the Western Front where they were needed. The dismemberment of units such as the 199th Battalion, Irish Canadian Rangers, ought raise concern that the Government might renege on original plans and promises to new recruits.[159] Donovan's policy throughout the crisis was to allow for discussion of the issue, criticize extremists on both sides of the debate, refute anti-French rhetoric, and eschew bullying, particularly by supporters of the Act and by groups of veterans who were breaking up public meetings organized by opponents of conscription.[160] As had been the case since the beginning of the recruitment crisis, any unanswered criticism of the Church in Quebec would wear poorly on the entire Catholic Church in Canada.[161]

A variant of the neutrality school were Catholics in groups that might not mention the conscription issue per se, but took the opportunity during the crisis to proclaim their patriotism. Just as Catholic newspapers might be free to take no particular side while exercising the liberty to criticize specific positions on conscription, Catholic organizations remained politically neutral while expressing a desire to win the war. The *Cathedral Magazine*, published in the Diocese of

Hamilton, did not directly address conscription, but in November 1917 it outlined the duty of Catholics during the war:

> Patriotism, or readiness to defend our flag and all it stands for, is the foremost virtue of the hour. A true and sincere Catholic is necessarily a true patriot, for Mother Church clearly inculcates the virtue of patriotism. She teaches it is an obligation for every Catholic to love, reverence and obey those who wield civil power, for 'All power comes from God.' On every battlefield in the glorious past Catholics have proved the truth of this statement, and the multitude of our boys who sprang to arms at the Empire's call shows that the same spirit lives to-day. The call has now gone forth again, and our war-weary brothers over the seas are anxiously awaiting the answer. Shall we not support them? … No man who is fit and free should seek exemption. The issue is too sacred, for while victory means freedom, defeat would spell slavery for ourselves and for posterity.[162]

The magazine indicated that in Bishop Thomas Joseph Dowling's diocese, young Catholic men were expected to act in accordance with the law. Similarly, in that same city, evading direct engagement with the conscription issue, the Knights of Columbus State Council (Ontario) convened its annual meeting and deemed that the national anthem would be sung at the meetings of each local Knights' council across the province. "A splendid spirit of true Canadian Catholic patriotism prevailed," one reporter stated.[163] Similarly, the Knight's State Council of Saskatchewan and Manitoba voted to "use every legitimate means" to secure victory.[164] Once again, the issue of conscription was not addressed directly, but Canada's fastest growing Catholic fraternal association wanted to make clear where its loyalties stood. Charles J. Foy of Perth, Ontario, an outspoken Irish nationalist and president of the AOH, was less cautious and openly announced his support for the Union Government and all that such an endorsement implied.[165]

Support for conscription also came from one of the war's most prominent Irish Catholic Canadian combatants, surgeon Robert James Manion. He was born in 1881 in Pembroke, in the Ottawa Valley, to parents of southern Irish descent, as he described them: Manions and O'Briens from Cork and Tipperary.[166] Manion's father moved the family to Fort William (Thunder Bay, Ontario) when Robert was a child.

Manion was educated locally and eventually pursued science and medicine for a year at Queen's University and, later, Trinity College, the site of the University of Toronto's medical school. After postgraduate work in Edinburgh and France, Manion returned to Fort William to practise general medicine and surgery, while making frequent trips to the Mayo Clinic in Rochester, Minnesota. When war broke out Manion resisted formal enlistment so he could serve the Entente on his own terms. In 1915 he travelled to Europe at his own cost with the aim of working as a surgeon in either Britain or France. After a brief sojourn as chief surgeon at a French hospital housed at the Château de Rimberlieu, near the front, Manion realized he was underused and returned to Canada to formally join the CEF. Serving at aid stations on the front lines with the 21st Battalion, which included performing surgical duties during the attack on Vimy Ridge in 1917, Manion would record his war experiences in *A Surgeon in Arms*. Because the memoir was published after he was demobilized home in 1917, in need of surgery for his back, Manion made no controversial statement in the book, nor did he offer the names of officers, enlisted men, or units, which are colourfully identified as a "blank." Modestly, he says nothing about having been awarded the Military Cross for bravery.[167]

Manion's actions in 1917 and subsequent autobiography, *Life is an Adventure*, demonstrate the lengths to which he would publicly support the Union Government of Robert Borden. Reflecting on his public support of conscription, Manion explained:

> I was one of those who came to the conclusion that if the war were to be carried on successfully, indeed if the war were to be carried on justly and fairly to our nation, conscription of man power was the only satisfactory method. While no one more devoutly desires, or is a more sincere advocate of, world peace, I am convinced that the only fair and just way of raising men is by conscription.[168]

In 1917 Manion, a Liberal like his father, was nominated to carry the party's standard in Fort William in the upcoming federal election. His Liberal ties were deep; Wilfrid Laurier was a friend, and his wife Zoé had been present at Manion's wedding.[169] Manion did not let personal ties compromise his principles, however. With the tabling of the Military Service Act, Manion was among the Liberals who abandoned

Laurier and joined the Union coalition. He stood as a Union candidate in 1917 and won the election and every subsequent election in the riding of Fort William until 1935. After the war he switched to the Conservatives and served in the Cabinets of Arthur Meighen and R.B. Bennett. From 1938 to 1940 he was the Conservative Party leader. King's Liberals handily defeated Manion and the Tories in 1940, within the context of the Second World War.

As to how typical Manion was of Irish Catholic servicemen is hard to determine. While he took great pride in his mother's pioneering Irish family in the Ottawa Valley, and admitted to having followed the constitutional nationalist cause of John Redmond, William O'Brien, and T.P. O'Connor as a young man – to such an extent that he laid "the blame for the unhappy condition [of Ireland] at England's door" – his views changed as he grew older. Manion admitted, "I came to the conclusion that Canada has quite enough problems to absorb the attention of all young Canadians, although they need not fail to keep a corner of their heart for the land whence their forefathers came."[170] Before leaving for duties in Europe, Manion left a sealed letter for his three sons containing paternal advice. Along with warnings about drinking alcohol and remarks on religious toleration, Manion tells his sons to be proud of both their Irish heritage and the French-Canadian culture inherited from their mother. One should not be held above the other, he advised.[171] Manion wrote about himself as a Catholic of Irish descent, and in both of his books made a point of distinguishing himself from the Irish who had been born in Ireland. They were not the same as Canadian Irishmen like himself; they were different. In his war memoir he dedicates an entire chapter to his batman, Private James Kelly, trying to amuse the reader (and likely himself) by having Kelly speak in his native brogue in witty lines,like some stereotypical leprechaun-like imp offering comic relief through the gore of battle and the tedium behind the lines. Even as Kelly lies dying from a shell wound, Manion cannot resist filtering his dying wishes through a heavily accented English: "Will ye tell them [Manion's children] sometimes of Kelly? An' tell thim that wid all me faults Oi lived their daddy and troied to sarve him well; an' that if Oi was sure me death would cause ye to be taken safely back to thim, Oi'd doie happy an' content."[172] As for Manion, despite his Irish roots he often referred to himself as "Anglo-Saxon," standing apart from Irishmen from Ireland and regarding them as great comrades, quaint in their ways but enmeshed in their own politics.[173]

There were other Irish Catholic Canadians who, unlike Manion, were vocal in their opposition to conscription. The reasons for their opposition ranged from a principled stand against the notion of compulsory military service, to a rejection of the government's right to enact such legislation because it had not gone to the people with question, to concerns about national unity, and just plain partisan politics. One suspects that some opponents held fragments of each of these views in addition to their own. There were three Catholic MPs who, unlike Manion, refused to leave Laurier's side when he rejected membership in Borden's proposed coalition of Union Government: Charles Devlin (Hull); Charles Murphy (Russell); and Charles Power (Quebec South). "Chubby" Power had been a captain in the 14th Battalion and was demobilized back to Canada after having been wounded. He believed fervently that conscription imperilled national unity and that a well-organized voluntary system would be an effective alternative.[174] He did not let his ideas alienate him from his Irish Catholic opponents, however; despite their political differences, Power and Manion remained lifelong friends.[175] Charles Murphy, however, was a zealous and noisy opponent of the Union Government, including two of its most anti-Catholic figures, former Toronto mayor Horatio Hocken and former Ontario Liberal leader Newton Wesley Rowell.[176] Murphy became a magnet for loyal Catholic Liberals.[177] Two priests joined the politicians in their opposition: Edmonton Jesuit Lewis Drummond, a Laurier supporter, and vociferous Ottawa pastor Matthew Whelan.[178] The latter had been an outspoken opponent of bilingual schools and an ardent supporter of the very successful recruitment of young men from his congregation at St Patrick's Church in Ottawa. Whelan attested to the loyalty of Catholics, and tangible proof of the sacrifice symbolized in the wreath commemorating the dead of his parish, but he deplored conscription as the "ugly forerunner of continental militarism." Nevertheless, Whelan admitted that now that the bill had become law, all citizens were compelled to live with it.[179]

The *Canadian Freeman* could hardly disguise its unhappiness with conscription and printed articles that tended to expose the defects of compulsory military service. By giving free reign to veteran Catholic journalist and former *Register* editor Patrick Cronin, the Kingston weekly exposed the editorial sympathies hiding behind feigned neutrality. Cronin lambasted the Military Service Act as an assault on the poor and yet another means to bully Quebec.[180] As the Act approached its passage in Parliament, editor D.A. Casey made a comparison between Canada and Ireland, questioning why the British Parliament might allow an Ulster minority to dictate the Ireland policy, while a Canadian Parliament would shut down a French Canadian minority trying to impose its will on the entire country. The *Freeman*'s analysis pointed to the Orange interests prevailing in whatever position – majority or minority – they may be found. "Wise counsels are none the less needed in Canada," Casey proclaimed, "but we have little hope that they will prevail. Orangeism and the 'big interests' must be placated."[181] For Casey, his paper's sympathies were clear: fair play was needed in Ireland and in Canada, particularly in French Canada, where his paper had subscribers.

The Irish-born editor of the *Northwest Review* was far less nuanced. His paper demanded that the issue of conscription be placed before the people of Canada in a referendum. "Conscription without a referendum implies a mistrust of the Canadian people or a fear of their decision. It is an admission," continued Henry, "that the war propaganda of the last few years has been a failure."[182] But Henry took his Winnipeg paper where none of the other Catholic weeklies would go. He simply declared that the growing nation of Canada needed men to work at home more than serve at the front. "Our urgent need is manpower, but our government thinks the allies need this manpower more than we do … Some of us think that the Empire's needs come first, others Canada's. We cannot serve two masters … Our future lies in Canada."[183] His remarks were conveniently in the special issue of the paper commemorating fifty years of Confederation, complete with the Canadian Ensign across the banner. The message coming clearly from right under Archbishop Sinnott's nose was that Canada had to assert the principles, particularly those concerning minority rights, upon which her foundations rested. The current conscription crisis underscored how fragile these rights might be. The *Northwest Review* dared to dream of a united Canada with "a distinctly Canadian sentiment appealing to native born Canadians as well as to hundreds of thousands of immigrants."[184] Conscription appeared to undermine such unity, but the paper did concede, once the Act received Royal Assent in August 1917, that the law would have to be obeyed.[185]

As Doherty had predicted in the House, there was no unanimity among Irish Catholics on conscription, but it appeared that – despite their diversity of outlook – all parties came to agree that the Military

Service Act was the law and would have to be observed. The best must be made of a divisive situation. Two issues remained that forced Irish Catholic leaders to be further vigilant: first, the manner in which the Military Service Act apparatus would be put in place with Catholic representation; and how to keep all elements of the Church united as Canada approached the election of December 1917. On the first point, much attention was paid to those who would be given exemptions from military service and how those exemptions would be adjudicated. One of the complicated issues for the bishops was the nature of the clerical exemption. This was a standard exemption for all clergy, but it was unclear whether seminarians would be included. Since within the Catholic tradition the seminarian was "tonsured" as clergy before ordination, Catholic seminarians would technically be exempt from the draft. This became a theological sticking-point between Catholics and Protestants, since divinity students and seminarians in the Anglican, Presbyterian, Methodist, and Baptist traditions were not technically clergy until ordination and so would not be exempt. Thus there was little understanding among Protestants about why Catholic seminarians could not be drafted but their own students could. Theological subtleties were buried in optics that screamed to some Protestants that Catholics were being favoured and were, once again, shirking their duties.

Once again, the French Canadian hierarchy came under fire and the English-speaking prelates and pundits were forced to tread carefully. When Cardinal Bégin made queries about whether clergymen were exempt, the *Sentinel* and several secular dailies took the opportunity to pounce once more on the Catholic Church, regarding the Cardinal's comments as further evidence of French Canadian Catholic disloyalty.[186] Caught in the anti-Catholic crossfire, English-speaking Catholic weeklies rose to the defence of the French Canadian hierarchy by demonstrating the ongoing loyalty of the Church while repeating that French Canadian bishops did not speak for the entire Church. In yet another of his fiery missives to the press, outspoken Toronto priest, Lancelot Minehan shot back at critics: "Bégin is not the Catholic Church … Now everyone not blinded by ignorance and prejudice knows that the opposition to recruiting and conscription in these countries [Ireland, Australia, Canada] is due to racial and political antipathies and that Catholicity as such has nothing whatever to do therewith."[187] The *Casket* simply pointed out the hypocrisy of the situation, whereby Protestant critics would attack Bégin or any Catholic bishop for appealing to a senator or a member of parliament for clarity on the implementation of conscription, while Protestant churches and the Orange Lodge routinely lobbied elected officials to secure their advantage. Demonstrating that not all Catholics are of like mind on the conscription issue, the *Casket* pointed out that Senator Lawrence Geoffrey Power, a Liberal representing Nova Scotia, thought that divinity students ought not to be exempt from conscription, claiming that "a year at the front would not hurt some of the clergy, and would do them good."[188]

Knowing that the anti-Catholic attitudes still had traction in the public square, Irish Catholic bishops became concerned about such bigotry translating into the unfair implementation of the Military Service Act. To ensure that Catholic men were not disproportionately refused exemption when it was required, the bishops lobbied the federal government and local Military Service Act officials to make certain that there was adequate Catholic representation on local tribunals. Catholic leaders were fortunate that Doherty was the minister responsible for the administration of the Act. Bishop Fallon made it clear to Doherty that "[i]t is of prime importance that one member of each local tribunal should be a Catholic. There are immediate rights at stake and future interests to protect, which make the presence of a Catholic on each local tribunal well-nigh imperative."[189] Clergy, bishops, and journalists across the country kept a careful eye on the activities of the tribunals, criticized publicly the unfairness of decisions or selection of officers when evident, or, in the case of certain bishops, interceded with Doherty and Borden when necessary to secure a just decision. Reports of there being no Catholic representation in parts of Ontario and New Brunswick brought swift reaction from the press and confirmed in some Irish Catholic minds that perceptions by some Canadian Anglo-Protestants of Catholic "disloyalty" would be difficult to combat.[190]

The election of December 1917 would be divisive both nationally and within the Catholic Church. Because Laurier had refused his offer to join a proposed coalition government, he had lost many of his English-speaking allies to the new Union coalition. The *Catholic Register* lamented such disunity on the eve of Canada's fiftieth birthday and hoped that the politicians would place partisanship aside and work out the military needs of the country: "If we fail to win the war, there will be no Canada to conserve."[191] The paper imagined the worst and got it. Catholics split along several lines, and most of the clergy were silent. In fact, Bishop McNally of Calgary publicly muzzled his priests from speaking on the election.[192] French Canadian Catholics voted for the Laurier Liberals, who promised an alternative to conscription to win the war. Irish Catholic MPs remained loyal to their parties, and Catholic papers were guarded in their sympathies. Candidate Charles Murphy professed that only Wilfrid Laurier could restore national unity, and Chubby Power advocated a conscription of "wealth not men."[193] Editors continued to carefully distinguish between issues that would naturally rouse a "Catholic" response, versus those to which reaction would be considered "cultural" or "racial," a word that contained a broader spectrum of definitions in 1917 than it does in our own time. Each paper took pains to promote national unity and refute what editors considered bigotry directed at Quebec; instead, English-language Catholic papers unpacked reasons why Quebec might oppose conscription – such as the province's rootedness in Canada, and its perception that Canada was not directly endangered – and validated Quebec's democratic right to dissent.[194] Most forceful, however, were the *Casket*, *Canadian Freeman*, *Catholic Register*, and *Northwest Review* when they took issue with the Wartime Elections Act, which effectively disenfranchised immigrants, many of whom were Catholic, who were former citizens of Germany and the Austro-Hungarian Empire. The Kingston paper urged "patriotic Canadians" to denounce the stripping of the right to vote from new Canadian citizens.[195] Although the *Record* sometimes offered detailed reports on Laurier, reprinted from other Liberal newspapers, only the *New Freeman* of Saint John appeared to be taking sides, although it later disavowed partisanship when it wrote of the Union Government that "All in all, the new platform is a strong one. The personnel of the cabinet has been considerably strengthened and the administration awaits the verdict of the people."[196]

Within the short time of the fall campaign all of the ugliness of the previous eighteen months was thrown in the faces of Catholics: disloyalty in Quebec; disloyalty in Ireland; disloyalty of the "alien" immigrants; the Prussian-ness of the Pope. Protestant ministers, some Union Party firebrands, and the Orange Order repeatedly stood on the soapbox of Catholic disloyalty.[197] In one of two dramatic moves by the Catholic hierarchy in the campaign, Archbishop McNeil spoke out harshly in response to the most recent anti-Catholic shrapnel coming from the mouth of the Montreal Protestant minister E.I. Hart. McNeil refuted each of Hart's public accusations against the Church, as only an effective former professor could: the Catholic Church was not pitted against the Empire; the attitudes of Quebec and a minority in Ireland were not representative of the Catholic Church; the protest by Quebec was "not religious, but racial; and the Catholic Church was a moderating influence in both Quebec and Ireland. Reaching the heart of his frustration, Toronto's archbishop proclaimed:

> Today the loyalty of the Catholic soldier and of the Catholic population is absolutely essential to the continued existence of the British Empire, and people are so confident that this loyalty can be depended on that they play with side issues which seem superficially to indicate that there is a difference between Catholics and Protestants in this war. There is no difference. We are all involved in the same issue.[198]

McNeil's points were clear and were heard. The *Canadian Annual Review* remarked that his was among the strongest episcopal voices during the election. McNeil had placed emphasis on the separation of religious from racial issues, and some journalists felt this might relieve some of the attacks made on the Church.[199]

In the last week of the election campaign the second episcopal bomb was dropped. Bishop Fallon issued a public letter urging Catholics to support the Union Government at the polls. On December 6 he wrote: "In the approaching election, the issue which dwarfs all others is Canada's effective continued participation in the war. This is the issue that compels us to disregard all others, however important they might be at another time."[200] Fallon had taken the next step in McNeil's separation of religion from race. In the context of the election and winning the war, Fallon reasoned that the right course of action was to place faith ahead of race and vote for the best available solution for Canada and the Empire's victory. Unionist papers hailed him as one of the most "respected and trusted" prelates of the Church.[201] An Anglican minister from Hamilton wrote to Fallon personally, thanking him and observing that Fallon deserved the "thanks of all loyal Canadians."[202] French Canadian Catholics saw this as yet another manifestation of Fallon's insensitivity to them. The sharpest critique of conscription on the Catholic side, the *Northwest Review*, without endangering its Catholic credentials and readership by insulting Fallon, simply dismissed the letter: "With Bishop Fallon's private political preferences we are not concerned. They are his own."[203] Fallon's own *Catholic Record*, despite its own historic Liberal leanings, was nuanced in its approach. Acknowledging that Fallon's letter was the most quoted letter across Canada and had won much acclaim even from Catholic Liberals, the *Record* claimed the epistle had the desired effect of cutting the legs out from under the "mountebank pulpiteers" with their anti-Catholic "stink pots" and it would reassure the Americans of Canada's commitment to win the war. "Once again," wrote editor James T. Foley, "let us hope finally and decisively, Bishop Fallon has demonstrated to the Canadian people, Catholic and Protestant alike, that the politics of Quebec are not the dogmas of the Catholic Church." For Foley, Fallon's letter took "moral courage."[204] Fallon might agree. Writing in his diary several months later while touring the Western Front, his expenses courtesy of the Borden Government, he reflected that the warm welcome he received from all he met stemmed from "my stand on public affairs since the war and my letter on the issue at the election."[205]

It is hard to determine exactly how much influence McNeil and Fallon had on Irish Catholic voters going to the polls on 17 December 1917, or how the Irish Catholic vote split between Liberals, Unionists, and Labour. In the heavily Irish, Scottish, and Acadian Catholic ridings of Antigonish–Guysborough, Inverness, North Cape Breton–Victoria, and South Cape Breton–Richmond, the Laurier Liberal candidates won handily.[206] In South Toronto, with a heavy Irish Catholic population, Claude Macdonell's Conservative seat was retained by the Unionists; the Irish Catholic candidate, D.A. Carey, who had a son wounded in France, stood for Labour in the riding and finished a distant third.[207] In Renfrew County, the Irish Catholic vote split, with the local Irish Catholic Unionist candidate, L.T. Martin, falling to the Liberals. Charles Doherty, the incumbent Unionist in St Anne's–Montreal won by over 2,000 votes, before the military votes were counted. Fort William elected newly minted Unionist Robert Manion. "Chubby" Power retained Quebec South for the Liberals by over 100 votes, while Charles Murphy captured Russell by a handsome margin.[208] The Liberals won no seats west of Ontario, and the Unionists took only three in Quebec.[209] Although a finely grained electoral analysis has not been done on a poll-by-poll basis, what remains clear is that the Irish

Catholic vote went in many directions in 1917, reflecting the great diversity of opinion within the community from party to party, region to region, and city to city across Canada.

The election brought to an end a frustrating year for Irish Catholics in Canada and their leaders. At a time when prelates like McNeil would have preferred Catholics to focus on winning the war and celebrating Canada's Golden Jubilee,[210] the Catholic Church faced criticism from its Protestant neighbours and was itself rife with division. Scholars who focus narrowly on Irish Catholic nationalism in this period do so at their own peril. Irish Catholics in Canada were challenged by complex and interwoven domestic and international issues, of which the war was central, and that were further complicated by ethnic, social, and political circumstances. The events of 1916 and 1917 testify that Irish Catholics behaved differently when faced with adversity and challenges depending on where they lived, which bishops were in control, and their proximity to other large groups of non-Irish Catholics. Questions about the Pope's neutrality, Catholic aliens, Irish revolutionaries, and French Canadian resistors put Irish Catholic leaders constantly on the defensive. Within their Church the unhealed wounds of French language schools and episcopal control festered until the community was completely fractured after the federal election. If Irish Catholics had wanted their French Canadian co-religionists to join them in common cause to win the war, their emerging leaders such as Burke, O'Gorman, and Fallon sent the wrong messages. It was understandable, in the end, why a French Catholic nurse tore O'Gorman's Irish flag off the hospital wall.

6

Winning the War, Saving the Peace

Marcus Doherty came from privilege in Montreal. His grandfather, also named Marcus, had been born in Ireland and emigrated to Montreal long before the Great Famine. The elder Marcus Doherty became a respected lawyer and a defender of Catholic rights, and rubbed shoulders with the leading politicians of his day, including the soon to become iconic Thomas D'Arcy McGee. He became a judge of the Superior Court of Quebec and married Elizabeth O'Halloran, the sister of yet another Irish Catholic justice (James O'Halloran) in that province.[1] Their son Charles Joseph – father of Marcus junior –, was educated in the best schools that Montreal could provide: the Christian Brothers elementary school, the Jesuit-run Collège Ste-Marie, and McGill University, where he won the Torrence Gold Medal for the Study of Law. Subsequently he earned legal degrees at St Francis Xavier University and the pontifical University of Ottawa. A successful lawyer and leader in countless Irish Catholic associations and causes in Montreal, Charles Doherty was named King's Council in 1887 and was appointed as a judge of the Quebec Superior Court in 1891.[2] During his busy legal career he had found time to serve as a captain in the 65th Regiment, which saw action during the Northwest Rebellion of 1885. The Dohertys were prominent in the Liberal-Conservative Party and, within a year of having helped suppress Riel's rebellion, Charles Doherty was elected as the Conservative member of Parliament for the Montreal Riding of St Anne's.[3] A confidant of Robert Borden, Doherty became justice minister in the new prime minister's Cabinet and served in that position throughout the Great War. As a family, the Dohertys were powerful, successful, and respected in Montreal and across Canada. Young Marcus had much to live up to.

By 1918, however, young Marcus, the only son of Charles, had not quite lived the life of his father. As Charles had done during the Northwest Rebellion, young Marcus had rushed to the aid of his country when it asked for his service during the Great War, but the medical examiners rejected him. Marcus was sickly; he had high blood pressure, poor kidneys, a weak physique, and had suffered from scarlet fever and diphtheria as a youth.[4] Unable to join the army, Marcus left Montreal and entered the novitiate for the Society of Jesus, with the intention of studying for the priesthood and service with the Jesuits. On the night of 7 June 1918, having just finished his evening prayers and readying himself for bed, the St Stanislaus Novitiate, located on a farm just north of Guelph, was surrounded by a local detachment of military police officers, who forcibly entered the residence to demand the arrest of alleged shirkers who were taking refuge there to avoid their duty under the Military Service Act.[5] Although news of this incident was suppressed by the military censors for about a week, for fear of a racial and religious backlash across Canada, the Guelph Novitiate Raid became one more wartime controversy that pitted Catholics against Protestants and heaped further indignity on the fractious linguistic divisions created by the war and subsequent government policies. The controversy was made more prominent by the fact that Marcus Doherty was allowed one phone call. Naturally, he called his father, the minister of justice.[6]

The Guelph Raid is somewhat microcosmic of the situation in which Irish Catholics in Canada found themselves enmeshed in 1918. Although the election of December 1917 had bitterly divided the country along linguistic, cultural and, in some cases, religious lines, Irish Catholic leaders, both clerical and lay, had used it as an opportunity to reassert that they had consistently supported the war and had assisted the government in matters of recruitment and registration, and that rank and file Irish Catholics, men and women, had joined the "colours" in robust numbers. Ironically, as far as the Guelph situation was concerned, the Jesuits had been very active in recruitment across Canada, in their schools, parishes, and in First Nations' mission stations. On the night of the raid, a demobilized and decorated soldier, J.P. O'Leary, was in the residence pursuing what he thought might be a career as a Jesuit priest. Also in residence was a Montreal Jesuit, Major William H. Hingston, who had served as chaplain to the 199th Montreal Irish Rangers Battalion. Even Marcus

Doherty could have been considered a young man who would have loved to don khaki, had only his body not let him down. Nevertheless, it appeared that old sectarian prejudices in Canada died hard. The slightest hint that a Catholic might not be doing his duty once more became, in the popular Protestant mind, further evidence that the disloyalty of Quebec, rebellion in Ireland, Prussian partisanship of the Pope, and perfidy of enemy aliens could be laid squarely at the feet of the Catholic Church. In 1918, during the closing months of the war, Irish Catholics would reassert their loyalties and work actively and ecumenically to support "the boys at the front." But certain quarters of Anglo-Protestant Canada would not be convinced. Politicians in Charles Doherty's own Union caucus, members of the Loyal Orange Order, and selected Protestant clergy would keep alive the idea that Catholics in Canada could not be trusted.

In the final eleven months of the war, Irish Catholics generally maintained their resolve to win the war, and during the Hundred Days Offensive that began in August 1918 and would eventually end the war, a second task became clear: to save the Church in peacetime. Peace came in two forms. First, given the split within the Church along linguistic lines, as exacerbated by the Ontario bilingual schools question and conscription, English-speaking and French-speaking Catholic leaders intensified their efforts to heal the cultural wounds that divided Canada's Catholics. Archbishop Neil McNeil of Toronto was instrumental in reaching out to French Canada in print and through the English- and French-speaking intellectuals engaged in the Bonne Entente movement, an informal round table to bring Canadians together, while fraternal associations such as the Knights of Columbus/Chevaliers de Colomb tried to unify all Catholics, regardless of language or culture, in a common effort to win the war. Church leaders also came to the defence of the Ukrainian Eparch, Nykyta Budka, as he faced serious charges in the courts regarding his alleged disloyalty. Secondly, the Knights and the seemingly ubiquitous John J. O'Gorman developed a national campaign to establish recreational centres for the troops. The Army Huts program was a herculean effort to help win the war by raising morale while bringing together Catholics and Protestants in common cause. In one sense, the Huts campaign provided two objectives: to support the troops and to bind the divided country. By war's end, however, neither objective – winning the war or saving the peace – met with unqualified success. The war had been won, but pockets of Protestant Canadians still believed this was in spite of the Pope and his minions. Riots in Quebec over conscription, French Canadian resistance to the Union Government, and the ongoing violent fallout from the Easter Rising in Dublin were three powerful pieces of circumstantial evidence to feed Protestant skepticism. As for reunifying the Church, efforts by clergy and laity moved slowly, and the peace that was forged between linguistic groups was fragile at best.

Aside from continuing their advocacy for enlistment, the purchase of Victory Bonds, and contributions to various war-related funds, English-speaking Catholic leaders used the Catholic Army Hut campaign to demonstrate an ongoing national commitment to the war effort. The project would be led by none other than chaplain, Major O'Gorman, who had recovered from his wounds and, as an active member of the Knights of Columbus, was prepared for this new challenge. The Knights were a fraternal benevolent Catholic men's association with councils in every province of Canada. Founded in New Haven, Connecticut, in 1882 by Father Michael McGivney, the Knights were intended as a working-class men's association that offered generous life insurance to its members and the promise of financial security to Catholic families.[7] The Knights would also dedicate themselves to the defense of the Faith and vowed to combat "the enemies of the Church by an intelligent defense of its teachings."[8] The order spread quickly across the United States and entered Canada in 1897 with the founding of Council 284 in Montreal, appropriately named "The Canada Council." Its membership was largely Irish Catholic; there were only six francophone members.[9]

Not all Catholics were excited by the emergence of the Knights. Some French-Canadian clergy and some Irish Catholic bishops, such as Denis O'Connor of Toronto, had been skeptical of the Knights, suspecting they might be a secret "masonic-type" society, and thereby had blocked its establishment in some parishes and dioceses.[10] Some Canadian Protestants were equally alarmed that as they grew in numbers the Knights might become a threat to their Faith and the political and cultural way of life within the Dominion. Some detractors of the Knights alleged that members swore a secret oath to the Pope that required them always to subordinate loyalty to the state to loyalty to the Supreme Pontiff. These allegations provoked such controversy in the United States that Canadian Protestants became alarmed that the growth of the order would be a blight on Canada. In Renfrew, Ontario, concern for the Knights and their oath was so great that the parish priest at St Francis Xavier Church, Francis French (soon to enlist as a chaplain) recruited four prominent Protestant citizens to investigate the claims made against this Catholic fraternal organization. In 1915, the investigators published their findings: they were satisfied that "the whole thing was manifestly overdrawn" and that the oath was a fake, the product of "political manipulators" in the United States.[11]

The charitable work of the Knights became proof of their value as a new social institution within parishes and civic communities. Following the American model, Canadian Knights supported the local Church, motivated by the guiding principles of fraternity, unity, and charity, and the espoused principles of patriotism by the Knights of the Fourth Degree (established in 1899); successes within American parishes and further timely interventions by several American bishops eventually convinced Catholic leaders in Canada that there was a greater benefit in having the Knights than in shunning them. Cardinal James Gibbons, the highly respected Archbishop of Baltimore, intervened with the Canadian hierarchy and assured them of the Knights' purely Catholic credentials and intentions.[12] After 1899, Catholic men founded councils in Quebec City, Montreal, Sherbrooke, Ottawa, Charlottetown, Kingston, Renfrew, Pembroke,[13] Saint John, Cornwall, and Sydney. In 1910, the Canadian Knights borrowed the American administrative structure and created two "State" sections, one for Quebec and one for Ontario and the Maritimes, to facilitate the oversight of sixty councils.[14] By the time of the Great War the Knights and their francophone counterpart, "Les Chevaliers de Colomb," had become the leading Catholic fraternal association in Canada and had "State" conventions in Ontario, Quebec, the Maritimes, and the three Prairie provinces. Numerous clergy joined the order, including O'Gorman and Bishop Michael Francis Fallon, who served as the State Chaplain for Ontario. In his correspondence with Archbishop Paul Bruchési of Montreal during the war, Archbishop McNeil envisioned the Knights as key players in healing the differences between francophone and anglophone Catholics. With support from the two key archdioceses in central Canada, the state deputies, Georges-Henri Boivin (state deputy of Quebec and a Liberal member of Parliament for the riding of Granby-Shefford), and J.L. Murray of Renfrew, State Deputy for Ontario (and brother of Ned, whom we met in chapter 3), began discussions for a grand project that would unite Catholics across Canada.[15]

Not to be lost in its influence was the Knights' reputation for patriotism. This principle or precept was cultivated by the Knights in the United States to demonstrate unwavering Roman Catholic loyalty to the Republic. It translated easily to a Canadian context, when councils substituted allegiance to Crown and the Empire for reverence for the Stars and Stripes and the American Constitution. In 1912, Charles Doherty, by then the new minister of justice, recognized the Knights as a valuable asset to Canada and as confirmation of Catholic loyalty. In an address to over five hundred Knights in Toronto, he said:

> You have within your ranks ... men of all races, and there is no distinction. You are all brothers, laboring for the promotion of the common Faith, and in doing your best for the furtherance of these things which have been a blessing upon this country's welfare. I am sure that every one of you here feels as I do, that Canada has a most glorious future. We are all happy to be citizens of a great, free and prosperous country. If you could only realize, as I have done, on the occasion of my recent visit to the Motherland, how large Canada looms in the eyes of the world, you would feel more proud than ever to be Canadians. It is a good thing for our country to be made up of different racial elements. We need the genius, the aggressiveness and the industry which has been coming here in recent years from many lands, which are being fused in the melting-pot of Canada ... in order to bring forth from the crucible of a nation which will be heir to all that is best and most progressive in European civilization.[16]

While the Knights to whom he spoke in Toronto would have been primarily Irish in background and clerical, professional, and skilled tradesmen in terms of occupation,[17] they were but the advanced guard of a larger male Catholic association that had the potential to bind Catholics, regardless of background, from sea to sea. As they grew in membership and influence, the Knights of Columbus would become one of the most prominent Catholic witnesses to dedicated citizenship and patriotic activity in Canada.

It was the intrepid Father O'Gorman who proved to be the catalyst for the launch of the Army Huts campaign. In April 1917 he was still in the Ottawa General Hospital convalescing from the wounds he had received in Europe while serving as a front-line chaplain. A member of the Ottawa Council of the Knights of Columbus, Council 485, O'Gorman would have been aware of the American Knights and their provision of recreational and spiritual centres for American troops serving under General John "Black Jack" Pershing along the Mexican border in 1916. With America's entry into the Great War, on the side of the Allies on 6 April 1917, cross-border communications seemed to indicate that the Knights would spring into action with the European war as their new focus. From his hospital bed in Ottawa, O'Gorman contacted Ontario State Deputy of the Knights, J.L. Murray of Renfrew's Council[18], and hatched a plan for the Canadian Knights to begin an Army Hut program. Murray agreed, first convincing the State Convention held in in Hamilton in May 1917, and then convincing the State Councils across Canada with the intent of raising one dollar per Knight in the fall of 1917.[19] For his part, O'Gorman wrote to each State Council and all of the bishops of Canada to solicit their support. By July the State Councils for Manitoba, Saskatchewan, Quebec, and Ontario had begun programs to levy the $1 per head. Meanwhile, the Supreme Council in New Haven, Connecticut, had mandated a $2 per head levy on every American Knight with the hope of raising one million dollars for a similar hut program.[20] The huts would combine the services of a hostel, cafeteria, recreation centre, reading room, and sacred space for soldiers of all religions.[21]

O'Gorman's letters to State deputies and the bishops were revealing about why the huts were needed and what the campaign would entail. First, he explained that the program was to be managed in the principal theatres of the war by Father Wolston Workman, now a Lieutenant-Colonel, the recently appointed assistant director of the Chaplain Service for Catholics. Workman and other chaplains knew that the YMCA had erected multipurpose recreational huts in the base camps in England and in reserve camps behind the lines on the Western Front. Here men could recreate and, on Sundays, attend religious services conducted by Catholic and Protestant padres who shared the facilities on a mutually agreed schedule. He identified Workman's most pressing need in his new role as ADCS as the erection of church huts or tents. "It will be readily understood," wrote O'Gorman, "how advantageous it is to the Catholic chaplains to have a Catholic tent. This can be used as a daily social centre, for Mass, confession, catechetical instruction, etc. The work that the YMCA has done in supplying the huts is well known, and like other chaplains I have frequently utilized their huts or tents for Mass on Sunday. It is evident, however, that a YMCA hut cannot be a Catholic centre, nor is there any reason that this interdenominational Protestant society should have all the glory of the work."[22]

O'Gorman also appealed to the American precedents, the Knights' vow of patriotism, and the presence of numerous Knights already serving in the CEF, which made the Knights' control of the campaign logical. Moreover, the men having experienced the huts, he argued, would bless the name of the Knights for providing a respite from the battle. The huts would be open to all, regardless of religion. Catholics in New Brunswick regarded the effort as confirming what they had already heard from some soldiers writing home: that there was a need for distinct places for Catholic soldiers to worship.[23] In addition, O'Gorman secured the support of the Knights, including an immediate $1,000 donation from the Alberta State Council,[24] and won enthusiastic public support from bishops McNally, Fallon, and McNeil, and editorial endorsements from the Catholic press.[25] For McNeil, the national campaign of the Knights was not just an example of Catholics exercising their patriotic duties, but also reflected his personal attempts with Archbishop Bruchési of Montreal to consider the Knights/Chevaliers as a means to bind the two solitudes of the Catholic Church in Canada together in common cause.[26]

O'Gorman and the Knights planned a national fundraising campaign for the autumn of 1917, with modest expectations. O'Gorman told the press that the goal for the campaign, scheduled from September 23 to 26, would be $15,000 and that all funds would go to the ADCS for the building of the huts, which would be open to all soldiers. There had been little indication that the first campaign, although national in scope, would be directed to anyone other than Knights and Catholic laypersons.[27] Coming during the conscription debate did not make for the best timing for the initial campaign, although the *Catholic Register* reported that the Knights had already collected $7,000 by late August[28] and expressed confidence that the bishops of Quebec would co-operate. The paper added that "Catholics whether lay or clerical, who flouted that appeal [from the bishops] deserve the strongest censure."[29] On the eve of the campaign, Knights of Columbus councils from every province except British Columbia (which did not hold a "state convention" to discuss the matter) pledged $20,000 to the campaign.[30] This amount attested to the commitment of the Knights to the war effort and indicated, given the dollar-per-head levy, that it was a large and increasingly significant player in the Canadian Catholic Church. Finally, Catholic women emerged as significant supporters of the campaign. In July, the Catholic Ladies Patriotic Society of Sydney, Nova Scotia, pledged $200 to the cause, and the Catholic Women's League of England became partners is the staffing and operations of huts overseas.[31]

In September 1917, the results of the national campaign surprised even the organizers. Although he had been impatient with what he considered a slow response to the campaign in August, O'Gorman made himself available for fundraising speeches in Ontario.[32] The campaign continued to be supported by the Catholic press and by local diocesan magazines, which trumpeted the needs of the chaplains to serve Catholic soldiers overseas. "Can there be any cause more worthy," suggested Hamilton's *Cathedral Magazine*, "than the spiritual needs of our Catholic soldier boys? The present is the first distinctively religious appeal to Catholics in connection with the war. What response are you going to make?"[33] Bishop Fallon sent a circular letter to every parish in the Diocese of London, urging their support.[34] At the end of the campaign, $80,000 had been raised, mostly in Ontario.[35]

This first drive gave impetus to O'Gorman and the Knights to create a more rigid infrastructure and plan for the next campaign. All of this came against the backdrop of the bitter election campaign of late 1917 and its aftermath in the New Year. In October 1917 the Catholic Army Huts (CAH) was formally incorporated, and nearly $100,000 was gathered into its coffers. In November, O'Gorman and the Knights established a Canadian office for the CAH in Ottawa, and the letters patent of incorporation were provided for a provisional board of directors to be named, including the representatives of each state council of the Knights. At that time, four overseas chaplains – Workman, French, Major Abbé Philippe Casgrain, and Captain Reverend John Knox – were added to the provisional board as overseas members. Money was already flowing from Ottawa to Workman in London. In January 1918, O'Gorman, Murray, and Boivin selected the permanent board.[36] J.J. Leddy, a Saskatoon businessman and prominent Knight, would also join the coordinating team comprising the Canadian board. Chaplains directed their requests for assistance to this board and an overseas board, headed by Workman, which managed the CAH operations in England and at the front.[37] In January, the CAH already had chapels and recreation facilities at Bramshott Camp, Witley Camp, Shorncliffe Camp, Purfleet, and Seaford, in England, and two projects were planned for London itself. Workman and O'Gorman, who now served as the secretary-treasurer overseas, also reported new huts at Le Treport and Étaples in France. This was a quick use of the CAH funds, although it should be clear that money from the Knights had begun flowing overseas in the summer of 1917. Workman and O'Gorman referred to the "work done" as merely a "satisfactory and prudent start."[38]

The next phase of the CAH campaign would be far more extensive and ecumenical and thus less Roman Catholic in its focus. O'Gorman wrote to McNeil to outline the game plan, which included securing the co-operation of Canada's bishops and McNeil himself liaising with Protestant leaders.[39] McNeil had garnered considerable respect among Canadian Protestants prior to the Huts intiative, and earned additional acclaim from Ontario Protestants for the first CAH campaign. One wrote personally to praise him for his excellent relations with non-Catholics, claiming there would be sectarian peace in Toronto as long as "such a man of God as Archbishop as yourself" is present.[40] With McNeil in this critical role, O'Gorman appeared to be broadening the mandate of the CAH campaign to include donors beyond the Knights and individual Catholics. If the huts were to be open to all, so should the fundraising. O'Gorman also noted that because of the implementation of conscription more Catholic chaplains would be needed. Ever vigilant, O'Gorman kept his eye on the broad political and social landscape within which the CAH campaign would be engaged, knowing full well that winning the war included a complicated interplay of issues beyond just the huts, including conscription, the reaction of Quebec, the inflamed situation in Ireland, and the action at the front.

The second CAH campaign was scheduled, depending on the region, for late September and early October 1918. The national campaign goal was an ambitious $500,000 (the equivalent of 7.2 million dollars in 2014)[41] for the provision of these recreational and spiritual spaces for all Canadian soldiers, whether serving at the Front, preparing or convalescing in the base camps in England, or in the training camps and military hospitals in Canada. The Catholic bishops of Canada openly endorsed the campaign, as did Pope Benedict XV.[42] Bishop Fallon went on a speaking tour to raise funds for the CAH across Ontario, and by his own estimation addressed "the largest gathering ever assembled" in Toronto's Massey Hall.[43] Although the bishop was known for his eloquent exuberance on such occasions, it was clear that the CAH effort was drawing significant attention. Even the sometimes contrary *Canadian Freeman* in Kingston raised the bar even higher when its editors announced: "This drive is the biggest thing the Catholic laity of Canada has ever attempted – and we must not fail … Stand behind the boys behind the guns."[44] Advertisements appeared in every major Catholic newspaper, including French-language weeklies in Quebec. The sizeable advertisements often included a Knight on horseback, holding a "K of C" banner in one hand and blowing a trumpet held in the other, with a caption above such as: "Le clarion appelle – AU SECOURS" [45] Other posters featured a Knight in full armour, bearing a shield with the crest of the Knights of Columbus and supporting a wounded soldier; a banner reads: "That HE may NOT need in vain" and "Won't you give as freely of YOUR MONEY as HE has of HIS BLOOD?"[46] Perhaps the most emotive was a scene of a mother weeping at a kitchen table, with an inset showing her son reading a letter from home in his dugout; here, the banner reads: "HE GAVE ALL – his Mother, his Home … WHAT WILL YOU GIVE TO KEEP HIM SMILING?" Advertisements such as these were published across the country as the campaign attempted to cut across religious lines with the message "Catholic Army Huts, All Are Welcome."[47]

The fact that the huts were to open to all soldiers (but reserved for Catholic services on Sundays) was a key theme in the second campaign.[48] Non-Catholic support for the K of C Army Huts was widespread and significant. Sir Robert Borden endorsed the campaign, as did Sir Arthur Currie, head of the Canadian Corps, and so did the Governor General, the Duke of Devonshire, who offered a personal donation of $100 ($1,430.68 in 2014 dollars).[49] In Manitoba, Premier T.C. Norris became an honorary patron of the campaign.[50] Even secular newspapers threw their support behind the campaign, as did many municipal councils and provincial governments.[51] Toronto's Orange scion and mayor, Thomas "Tommy" Church, pledged $15,000 of municipal funds (almost $215,000 in 2014 dollars).[52] The Conservative-leaning *Ottawa Journal* was particularly clear in its support of the ecumenical effort:

> [T]he part taken by the Knights of Columbus in the erection and maintenance of army huts is not sectarian … The Knights of Columbus army huts are for the convalescence and comfort of all the soldiers regardless of race or creed, and the call for funds to maintain them and provide more of them is to all the people … There have been many stories from the front of close cooperation in which chaplains of different faiths work.[53]

Similarly, Toronto's *Mail and Empire* commented in the wake of the campaign that "if Toronto had not responded to the call as it had done it would have been looked upon by the whole of Canada as a city of bigots."[54]

During the campaign there appeared to be no room for sectarian bitterness or the well-worn religious animosities that had dubbed some cities "the Belfast of Canada" or "the Derry of Canada." The Army Hut campaign had the appearance of religious co-operation from above and from the rank and file of Protestant and Catholic denominations. For their part, the state deputies of the Knights of Columbus had mandated every member to participate actively in the campaign, knowing full well that they would be working in co-operation with non-Catholics whose soldiers would be equally welcome in the Huts.[55] McNeil was blunt with his priests in the Archdiocese of Toronto that this was a joint effort between Catholics and Protestants – an effort in which, because of their numbers and organization, the latter "would do more" than the former.[56] Non-Catholics did not disappoint in this respect. The Great War Veterans Association (GWVA) wrote to J.L. Murray in his capacity as one of the campaign directors to indicate their endorsement of the CAH campaign and pledging their on-the-ground support.[57] Similarly, on the streets, the broadly "catholic" composition of the fundraising teams bore witness to the cooperation of non-Catholics in the soliciting of funds. The fundraising teams supplied by the Knights were joined by members of the YMCA and the Masonic Order. In Winnipeg, the Knights led teams of members and non-Catholic volunteers and businessmen, in carefully mapped-out canvassing areas across the city.[58] Reports from Saskatchewan indicated that the Knights were working co-operatively with the "Red Triangle" hut initiatives of the YMCA in Regina.[59] In Ontario, the non-Catholic cooperation was even more impressive as Knights joined with the YMCA, GWVA, Salvation Army, Masonic Order, Kiwanis

International, and Rotary clubs to collect funds door to door.[60] This unprecedented ecumenical fundraising campaign raised the anticipated $500,000 in Ontario alone and a whopping $1 million (the equivalent of $14.3 million in 2014 dollars) nation-wide.[61]

At the end of the campaign the Canadian Catholic bishops, notably McNeil and Fallon, acknowledged the enormous work of Protestant leaders and volunteers in helping the Knights surpass their target by 100 per cent. McNeil sent personal letters to the heads of major corporations, the YMCA, and other volunteers emphasizing that the campaign's success would not have been possible without them.[62] McNeil had every reason to be grateful: the Toronto campaign headed by Protestant Colonel W.S. Dinnick had raised nearly $200,000 ($2.8 million in 2014 dollars).[63] For his part, Dinnick was effusive in his praise of the ecumenical spirit displayed as teams went across the city of Toronto, just as they had in other Canadian centres. "I can say with all sincerity," wrote Dinnick to McNeil, "that I never worked in a campaign which I enjoyed so much and where such a fine Christian spirit was manifested." Dinnick confessed that much of the success of the co-operation was owed to McNeil's own "deep heartedness and broadmindedness," which Dinnick hoped would spread across Canada.[64] In Toronto, at a celebratory dinner attended by a who's who of Protestant and Catholic leaders, Fallon echoed Dinnick's enthusiasm, pronouncing that "the ghostly ghosts of bygone days have been laid and laid forever." Fallon commended Toronto for the "spirit" it had shown during the campaign, demonstrating to the rest of the country – perhaps for the first time – a religious cooperation that created "this blessed and beautiful occasion."[65] Fallon's speech was not idle rhetoric; he later warned Wolston Workman that in light of the ecumenical way in which CAH money was raised, "the most delicate care must be taken to avoid even the shadow of proselytism."[66] The huts were for *all*.

It would be naive to think that all Canadians, particularly non-Catholics, were enamoured with the CAH campaign. Although individual members of the Orange Order were notable in their co-operation with the campaign, the *Sentinel* never eased up on its accusations that Pope Benedict was aligned with the Central Powers, that Catholics shunned the Allies, and that the Catholic people were priest-ridden. As Protestants and Catholics took common cause in their door-to-door fundraising, the *Sentinel* continued to see the Vatican as the greatest obstacle to Allied victory, providing an interesting disconnect between the actions of ordinary Protestant citizens and the ultra-Protestant mouthpieces. Readers of the Sentinel could have mistakenly been given the impression that either the CAH campaign did not exist, or the campaign was a trifling diversion, distracting attention away from the salient issues of Papal perfidy and Catholic disloyalty.[67] The *Sentinel*'s duty, it appeared, was to remind those Protestants who might become soft on Catholicism that the Pope was pro-German and that the anti-Conscriptionist Australian Catholic bishop of Melbourne, Daniel Mannix, and the Irish Sinn Fein, were the true faces of Catholicism.[68] With respect to the outspoken anti-British Mannix, at least the *Halifax Herald* reported that "the loyal Catholics of Nova Scotia have nothing but contempt for the firebrand tactics and treacherous teachings of disloyal Catholic bishops in other parts of the Empire."[69]

Unflattering articles about the Knights in the *Sentinel* prompted the *Catholic Register* to point to the Orange Order as a major obstacle to the CAH campaign and to go so far as to accuse Toronto's Loyal Orange Lodges of trying to obstruct Mayor Church's pledge to the hut campaign.[70] Although there was some truth to Orange obstructionism during the CAH campaigns, the evidence is much stronger that the effort to fund and build these huts for all Canadian soldiers, regardless of creed, marked a bright spot in what was otherwise a year of bitter controversy between religious and linguistic groups over conscription, Irish affairs, the status of enemy aliens, and the near military disaster that befell allied troops in the face of a massive German advance on the Western Front in March 1918. Seen against the backdrop of Canadians at odds with one another in the last year of the war, the CAH campaign gives one pause, suggesting that Irish Catholic engagement with the war effort was far more complex than has been acknowledged by historians of the war and Irish nationalism. Even the most Irish nationalist of the Catholic weeklies, the *Canadian Freeman*, noted the local Protestant cooperation and praise for the CAH campaign in eastern Ontario. Some editors went further: "May it be the beginning of a more cordial relationship between the various creeds, and thus serve to promote that unity that is the desideratum of every lover of Canada."[71] The drive also garnered praise from Quebec's two leading Catholic prelates, Cardinal Louis-Nazaire Bégin, the archbishop of Quebec, and Archbishop Bruchési of Montreal, both of whom praised Murray for "salutary" and "grand "work" on behalf of the Knights and Chevaliers.[72]

The planning and execution of the CAH campaign transpired in the less happy context of the tortuous national implementation of the Military Service Act. For Irish Catholics, three issues were of primary importance during the crisis. First, Irish Catholic leaders, clerical and lay, would continue to pronounce publicly that Catholics, at least English-speaking ones, had done their duty in recruiting and would continue to do so under the rubrics of the new Act. Second, Catholic leaders argued that the clergy, and in particular tonsured seminarians, were exempt from conscription. Finally, although most Irish Catholics would not agree with the tactics undertaken by their French-Canadian co-religionists to resist the provisions of the Act, a careful public solidarity between the French and Irish would have to be maintained where matters of religion were concerned. Episcopal co-operation, however strained, would have to be maintained to ensure the success of the CAH program and the provision of adequate numbers of chaplains for the increased numbers of Catholic troops that would come with conscription.

As the "draft" boards under the terms of the Military Service Act came into operation in all of the Military Districts (MDs), Irish Catholics were vigilant that there was no discrimination in the manner in which men were selected for service. Men liable for service were to be between the ages of 20 and 45; this criterion was further refined by categories 1 through 6, the first being the most suitable for service and the sixth being the least desirable. Class 1 was composed of men aged 20 to 35 who were unmarried or widowers without children. Class 2 comprised men who were married or widowed with children. The remaining classifications included men who could be as old as 45, with priority given to unmarried men.[73] All men who fell under Class 1 were required to report for medical examination between October and November 1917, after which they would return home and await further notification about service. By the end of the year, approximately 404,395 men reported for the medical examination, of whom 308,510 sought inclusion under the special-exemption provisions of the Military Service Act.[74] The highest number of these requests came from the province of Quebec, although over 90 per cent of all men drafted nationwide requested exemption. In January, the first draft of 20,000 men, of whom 15 per cent were from Quebec, began their basic training.[75] By the end of the war, Canada sent over 24,000 conscripts to France and Siberia with the rest remaining in Canada.[76]

It appeared that the National Registration undertaken in early 1917 became the basis for the first set of lists of men eligible to be conscripted. Surviving lists from MD 3, with headquarters in Kingston and drawing on the counties of eastern Ontario, provide an interesting laboratory for assessing who appeared in the preliminary groups of prospective conscripts. It should be noted that use of the National Service of Canada *Recruiting Prospects Ledger* has several limitations, particularly for the purposes of the current study. First, the lists of Class 1 to Class 3 registrants capture the names only of those who were willing to complete cards during National Registration. It has already been established that the Catholic Church, in both its Celtic and French wings, strongly endorsed the Registration and demonstrated great pride in the extent to which Catholic men across the country participated. If Catholics were over-represented among the "drafted men," this could very well be an effect of their high participation in the National Registration. Secondly, the counties of eastern Ontario, particularly sections of Carleton, Peterborough, Renfrew, Lanark, Russell, Prescott, and Glengarry, had high proportions of Catholics in the general population.[77] Therefore, it is perhaps not surprising to find many Catholics on the list, although it has already been demonstrated in the case of Renfrew County, Ontario, and Pontiac County, Quebec, that high numbers of Catholic volunteers appear on the cenotaphs (see chapter 3).

The *Recruiting Prospects Ledger* for MD 3 focuses almost entirely on the city of Ottawa and a few towns in the region, including Pembroke, Peterborough, Perth, and Rockland, amounting to less than one per cent of the total (Class 1).[78] Approximately 780 men are listed on the ledger, along with their addresses and occupations; of these, 593 were Class 1 with an A level of fitness. There is no indication of the list as to self-identified ethnic origin or religion. The Class 1 men were mostly from the city of Ottawa; an overwhelming proportion were clerical, supervisory, and skilled workers. Moreover, judging from surnames, the French Canadian men on the list comprised about 15.4 per cent of the total, and were therefore under-represented relative to the proportion of French-speaking Catholics living in the city of Ottawa.

Although the Ottawa numbers indicate that Catholics (including the Irish), as identified on the basis of surname, were not unnecessarily discriminated against, accusations still flew from Catholic editors that bigotry on the Military Tribunals sometimes raised its ugly head. In February, the *Catholic Register* was convinced that, when dealing with eligible men from the Toronto Police Department, the Toronto Military Tribunal was biased against Irish Catholics. If this was not the case, argued the editors, why was it that six out of seven eligible Irish Catholics were drafted from the force, as opposed to only three out of twenty-five eligible Protestants? Moreover, seven out of ten eligible Catholic officers were drafted, against only eleven of sixty-nine Protestants.[79] As was to be argued by its competitor, the *Catholic Record*, the "calumny" that Catholics had not done their "bit" during the voluntary phases of recruitment was still popular currency among some Protestants. For its part, the *Record* presented data to proclaim that in, New Brunswick and Ontario, the Irish Catholic population was well represented in the voluntary phases of recruitment. Singling out Ottawa's St Patrick's Parish, the *Record* suggested that this parish's contribution to the ranks "ought to make the most impudent of 'loyal' and loud-mouthed slanderers slink in shame-faced silence away from the company of honest men."[80] The fact that bishops encouraged Catholics to participate in Registration as a sign of their patriotic duty suggests that Catholics would have been highly represented on the initial draft lists, and not necessarily because fewer had presented themselves as volunteers. What seems to be evident from the military's own admission is that the draft did not produce a surplus of Irish Catholics in the CEF, but a disproportionately large French Canadian Catholic contingent: so much so, that Workman appealed for at least eight new francophone chaplains.[81] Although the question still remains cloudy, and there may have been isolated instances of discrimination, there appeared to be no systematic effort to make certain that more Irish Catholics were drafted in order to compensate for a previous alleged lack of Irish Catholic volunteers. In fact, if there was a systemic bias in the conscription process, it appeared to be directed at French Canadian Catholics.

A major concern among Catholic bishops and clergy with the Military Service Act was the ambiguity surrounding the exemption of divinity students. The original legislation exempted members of the clergy but not students studying for the Protestant ministry or the Roman Catholic priesthood. Archbishop Bruchési would have preferred that all students in colleges be exempt, but Charles Doherty rejected the request, reserving divinity students only.[82] While this appeared to be a fairly clear-cut distinction on paper, in reality it was complicated by the nature of seminary preparation for young Catholics. Although Protestant divinity students did not become de facto clergy until formal ordination, Catholic seminarians became "clerical" upon their tonsure, which took place early during the course of their training. Therefore, many Catholic seminarians were technically clergy, and exempt, while all Protestant students were subject to the draft. Catholics bishops would have preferred a general exemption for all seminarians but would have to accept technicalities that would exempt only some seminarians.[83] In writing to an inquiring Cardinal Bégin, Senator Joseph Bolduc confirmed that Doherty had told him that "after having received tonsure they would be considered as clergy," even if they were given tonsure immediately upon arrival.[84] In the aftermath of the Quebec Conscription riots in 1918, Doherty confirmed this interpretation with Borden himself, stating clearly that "[y]oung men [who] aspired to enter the priesthood but who have not as yet reached that period of their studies where it has been customary to confer upon them the order of tonsure clearly do not come within the exemption made in favour of the clergy." Doherty added, however, that he was disturbed by the latitude applied to the "conferring of tonsure" on so many by the Cardinal Archbishop of Quebec.[85] The fine technicalities of holy orders did not wash in the court of Protestant public opinion when it appeared that Catholics, once again, were not doing their duty.

The conscription riots in Quebec City in March 1918 did little to ease the tensions between French and English Canadians, nor the fragile relations between French and Irish Catholics. On Easter weekend, between March 29 and April 1, troops that were enforcing the Military Service Act clashed with French Canadian protesters. At least four civilians were killed and five soldiers were wounded.[86] The popular violence against the conscription sent shock waves through the country, the Quebec Church, and Catholic parishes across Canada. In a circular letter issued to his priests during the riots in the heart of the old city, Bégin denounced the violence unequivocally: "La conscience chrétienne les réprouve et l'Église catholique les interdit."[87] Bégin ordered the priests to preach calm and moderation among their parishioners to prevent any further disturbances. The rioting continued for two more days. Shortly thereafter, on April 12, Bégin penned a lengthy letter to Prime Minister Borden describing the Church as "une école de louyauté," while urging that the government respect the education of seminarians and not remove them from their studies for military duty.[88] Suspicion, however, that the priests could have done more during Holy Week to prevent the rioting was not lost on other well-placed French Canadian leaders in Quebec. At least one former Conservative MP, Herménégild Boulay (Rimouski), who had been defeated in 1917, wrote to Borden urging that the government silence Henri Bourassa and shut down *Le Devoir*, which he blamed for the agitation that led to the riots. Although Boulay had voted against the Military Service Bill in mid-1917, he believed that the war must be won and that the bishops of Quebec had to rein in their priests, who were disseminating Bourassa's opinions "too freely."[89] Brigadier General J.P. Landry, Commander of MD 5, urgently requested Cardinal Bégin to meet with his priests and mandate their support of the Military Service Act. Landry pointed out that if by August 24 there was no cessation of the desertions in Quebec and the flouting of the provisions of the Act, no more amnesty would be granted and the strict letter of the law would be applied to those who disobeyed their summons to duty.[90] In Montreal, Bruchési had already warned his priests to cease criticizing the Military Service Act from their pulpits.[91] The *New Freeman* in Saint John appeared to sum up observations of the riots from the Irish Catholic anglophone perspective: "[T]he whole affair will always remain as a monumental piece of folly. What the originators hoped to gain from it is not clear; to think that anything could be gained by mob rule is absurd. Conceived in brutality, it ended in tragedy."[92] Although the editor pointed out abuses of local constabularies toward draft evaders, the paper's sympathies were with the military, particularly with French Canadian troops serving under Generals Landry and Lessard.

The wounds inflicted on one another by the two principal linguistic groups within the Church were still raw after the clashes over the elimination of bilingual schools in Ontario and the strong support given by several leading anglophone Catholics to Borden during the federal election in 1917. "Nos persécuteurs catholiques" were named and criticized *by Le Droit*'s editor, Albert Foisey, in mid-1916.[93] In an effort to ease the growing tensions within the Church and to at least make a plea for national peace in the wake of the incendiary election of December 1917, individual anglophone Catholics made overtures to French Canada.[94] The most notable came from Archibishop McNeil after the anti-conscription riots. The multilingual McNeil had long tried to maintain good relations with Quebec and by late 1917 was considered by some Quebeckers to be a respected cleric who might bridge the growing cultural divide in the Church.[95] In the wake of the riots, McNeil reached out privately to church leaders in Montreal: "Racial differences and antagonisms can become a real danger to the Catholic Church in Canada," he wrote. "I am simply trying to lessen that danger."[96] He was referring to a series of articles, written by him, that were solicited by and published in Montreal's *La Presse* and reprinted in the *Montreal Star*.[97] McNeil's public advocacy for moderation, reconciliation, and peace between the French and the English for the sake of Canada won considerable acclaim from both sides. J.A.H. Cameron, a Protestant from Montreal, wrote to McNeil, explaining to him that his article "has made a most profound impression and as nearly as I could learn has been received in the most kindly and affectionate manner by French Canadians."[98] A month later, Cameron repeated his praise, claiming the McNeil letter had helped change negative sentiment in Quebec, while a letter from a writer identified only as "A Pea Soup" thanked the archbishop for the "magnificent" letter, adding that the "Shamrock [and] Fleur-de-lis should grow in the same pot."[99] McNeil's efforts at rapprochement and his presence in the Bonne Entente movement helped to create an atmosphere in which the Catholic bishops from both sides of the Ottawa River, at least, could work together to see the war effort to its successful conclusion.

One area in which cooperation was critical among the bishops was in the management and appointment of new chaplains. As the conscription of Canadian men moved more rapidly in 1918, it was clear to clerical leaders that the increased numbers of Catholic conscripts would necessitate the selection of more chaplains, particularly French speakers, since it was thought that many of the new Catholics would be French Canadian. Although a new management structure was in place in the Canadian Chaplain Service overseas, with Lt. Colonel Rev. Workman serving as assistant director of the Catholic branch, formal supervision and oversight of the entire Catholic chaplaincy by the Canadian bishops was still not complete in 1918. Bishop Fallon had provided ad hoc oversight of the recruitment and selection of chaplains for Catholic troops, but his position was not official, nor was there much confidence among French Canadian bishops that Fallon, given his track record on bilingual schools, conscription, and the assertion of Irish Catholic power in the Church, was the best person to lead the chaplaincy initiative. Thus, in 1918 the Canadian bishops, with the approval of the apostolic delegate and the Holy See, made preparations for the appointment of an *episcopus castrensis* – a military bishop – formally appointed to be the supreme ecclesiastical authority over Canadian Catholic chaplains. The idea had been suggested as early as 1916, when French Canadian Chaplain Adolphe Sylvestre suggested that the Canadians adapt Italy's model of appointing a bishop to supervise chaplains.[100] First, however, Bishop Fallon's role had to be clarified, and once it was determined by his colleagues that his role had been completely at the discretion of the Ontario bishops, a new bishop who could incorporate the national and linguistic characteristics of the Church was to be considered.[101] After considerable discussion a compromise candidate was found in the bilingual and moderate Joseph-Medard Emard, bishop of Valleyfield, Quebec. A French Canadian born near Laprairie outside of Montreal, he would represent the majority francophone presence in the Church. Also, since he had previously earned considerable praise for his advocacy for enlistment in the CEF in his western Quebec diocese,[102] he satisfied the anglophone concern that someone with clearly loyal credentials hold the position.[103] Emard would serve as head of the Catholic chaplains from 1918 through the end of demobilization. In 1922 he was promoted to archbishop of Ottawa, where he became noted for his ability to navigate the Church around the linguistic and cultural tensions that historically troubled that diocese.[104]

In the time leading up to his eventual replacement by a formal *episcopus castrensis*, Fallon made a lengthy visit to England and the front at the invitation and expense of the Borden government. In February 1918, Major-General Sidney C. Mewburn, Hughes' replacement as the minister of militia and defence, confirmed with Fallon that the director of the Chaplain Service wanted the bishop to visit the Canadian troops and Mewburn added that his visit "would be greatly appreciated."[105] It appeared from the ensuing correspondence that Fallon's favourable position toward the Union government could be exploited; it would be to Borden's advantage to have the outspoken Catholic prelate visible at the front to promote winning the war and religious unity in the cause. Fallon did not disappoint. Having sought the approval of the apostolic delegate and the assistance of the federal government for transportation, he ventured to England in May and toured the front in June, before heading to Rome for consultations with the Vatican.[106] His diary of the trip reveals that he met with leading Canadian and British officials and generals, including Prime Minister Borden, Sir Edward Kemp, the minister of the Overseas Military Forces of Canada, and Kemp's superior, Sir George Halsey Perley, the Canadian high commissioner in London.[107] He was received cordially by politicians and quizzed for his wisdom on the "Irish Question" and an assortment of other political issues. At the front he met with Sir Arthur Currie and Catholic chaplains, fired a howitzer on the front lines, and – despite his reputation among the French Canadians – was cheered by the Royal 22nd Regiment, the famous "Van Doos."[108] In one of the most poignant moments of the tour, a visit to the cemeteries at Vimy Ridge, he wrote: "I walked through the long lines of Canadian graves and read many familiar names on the little crosses at the head of each grave. The thought ran through my mind as I knelt to say a *De Profundi*, was mainly the thousands of people at home who would have given so much for the consolation of looking on the last resting place of their loved ones out here in France."[109] It appeared his trip had firmly entrenched his own commitment to win the war, but it also served the interests of the government of Canada. Fallon provided the friendly face of the Irish Catholic hierarchy to the military establishment, and a symbolic commitment of those he nominally represented, that the war would be won with their unceasing support.

Fallon's European tour also included visits to forestry battalions in France, a sojourn in Italy, and eight days in Ireland. Perhaps the Vatican visit, according to his diary, gave Fallon the greatest degree of confidence that, in terms of the linguistic wars in the Canadian Church, he and the English-speaking hierarchy had strong support in Rome. Fallon could be caustic and mercilessly critical when he discussed leaders, clerical and otherwise, in his diary. Not so in this account of meeting and dining with the former apostolic delegates to Canada, Rafael Merry del Val, Donato Sbaretti, and Pellegrino Stagni, all of whom he praised for their grasp of the Canadian situation and their support of the strong role the Irish needed to play in the Canadian Church, in the face of "narrow" French Canadian nationalism.[110] Fallon came to learn that, since the Irish Catholics were the largest

Catholic group in the Empire, the British needed the support and stability offered by Irish Catholic prelates. In fact, British rapprochement with the Church during the war was, in fact, a continuation of enhanced diplomacy between the Vatican and Britain, dating back to secret meetings between representatives of both powers in the late eighteenth century.[111] Perhaps it was Fallon's forty-five minute audience with Pope Benedict XV, however, that gave him the greatest boost of confidence. He entered the private meeting prepared to defend himself against his role in the Ford City riots, particularly in regard to what he deemed a reprimand from Cardinal De Lai, encapsulated in a letter written to Fallon in early June. Instead, Benedict told him the letter was not a reprimand and that he understood the tension in the Canadian Church better than Fallon suspected. In a lengthy conversation on July 27, Benedict told Fallon twice that the French Canadians "do not recognize realities."[112] One of these realities, according to Fallon, was the necessity for the anglophone Church to have primacy outside of Quebec. Fallon was stunned when Benedict intimated that there had been an effort (presumably by agents of the French Canadian prelates) to oust Fallon from London and transfer him back to the United States, on grounds that he never should have been selected to be bishop of London (in 1909) while he was a resident priest in Buffalo, NY. When the rumours (of which Fallon claimed he had been unaware) of his transfer spread from the Vatican to England, Robert Borden met immediately with British authorities and, with them, petitioned the Vatican to leave Fallon in his see. Evidently, Fallon's work was far too valuable to be disrupted. When Fallon returned to England, ADCS Wolston Workman assured him that the alleged plot was real, but the French Canadian efforts to remove him from Canada had failed.[113] Fallon was now convinced of his own righteous cause and his support in the highest corridors of power in both the Catholic Church and the British Empire.

It was ironic that while Fallon was cementing positive ecumenical relations at the front between the Catholic Church and the Canadian and British military establishment, the opposite was taking place just outside of his diocese, in the nearby town of Guelph, Ontario. As outlined earlier in the chapter, the (Protestant) Guelph Ministerial Association, in its zeal to ensure that every man was doing his duty under the terms of the Military Service Act, had isolated the Jesuit novitiate and farm, St Stanislaus, just outside the town, as a haven for young

Catholic shirkers. On June 7, without giving a thought to the fine canonical points of tonsure as a process of clericalizing seminarians, Captain A.C. Macaulay, the assistant deputy provost marshall from London, Ontario, led his team of Military Service Act enforcers to the Jesuit novitiate at dusk. Demanding that the rector assemble all the young men in the house, Macaulay intended to apprehend the draft-evaders present. The rector, Father Henri Bourque, Father William Power, the Jesuit Superior-General, who was by coincidence visiting the house, and Major William Hingston, who was in his military kit, began a heated discussion with Macaulay, despite the fact that the latter had orders to "proceed with tact and discretion."[114] After a protracted discussion, Macaulay was certain that at least a dozen of the novices were defaulters, but he arrested only three because he had no means to transport all of the men in question. Unfortunately for Macaulay, one of the designated three was Marcus Doherty, who became critical to the unravelling of the raid and, subsequently, Macaulay's career. After the young Doherty's phone call, and subsequent apologies from Ottawa, Charles Doherty and General Sidney Mewburn, Sam Hughes' successor as the minister of militia and defence, determined there was to be a media silence on the unfortunate events at Guelph.[115] Subsequent reports on the affair by Provost Marshal Colonel Godson-Godson (18 June 1918) and a Royal commission (the Chisholm–Middleton Commission) after the war criticized the military's activities on June 7, and Macaulay found himself transferred to Winnipeg.[116] The incident might likely have died under the cover of the censor had it not been for the Toronto *Star* leaking the story the day after Godson-Godson made his report.[117]

In the emotionally charged climate created by reactions to the Military Service Act, the responses to the "raid" were all too predictable. The *Sentinel* and Sir Sam Hughes, from the backbenches of the House of Commons, railed against the disloyalty of Catholics and their pope, and their wilful disobedience of the Military Service Act. The Reverend Kennedy Palmer, a Presbyterian minister from Guelph, embarked on a national tour in the summer to denounce the Jesuit activities, incite the Orange Lodge to action, and demand a national inquiry into the affair. Palmer had long believed that the Jesuit claims for exceptionality under the Act was just another case of Catholics demanding special privileges under Canadian law.[118] Palmer's cry for "equal rights for all, special privileges for none" harkened back to an era in Canadian politics, energized by the Jesuits Estates controversy, the Riel Rebellion, and the battle for separate schools, all of which were marred by sectarian bigotry and rhetorical excess.[119] For his part, Sam Hughes, likened to a dog with a bone, was still agitating against the Jesuits five months after the end of the war. In April 1919 he addressed the House, accusing the Jesuits at Guelph of harbouring slackers – including Marcus Doherty – and claiming that the Catholic priesthood considered itself to be above the law.[120] Hughes's interjections successfully secured the establishment of the Chisholm–Middleton Commission, whose subsequent report in October 1919 undercut much of Hughes' own arguments.[121] The Guelph debate raged throughout the summer in many Canadian newspapers, while in Guelph itself the controversy abated within a month as local leaders, selected ministers, and the press tried to calm the sectarian tension lest it appear that the town of Guelph was a cauldron of religious bigotry.[122]

The Catholic press, not to be outdone, saw a conspiracy of a different sort behind the raid. Just as some Protestants had pointed the finger at the old chestnut of Catholic perfidy, Catholics resorted to the familiar tune of a people falsely accused of disloyalty by a band of bigots. Within a week of the leaking of the story by the *Star*, almost all of Canada's English Catholic dailies had expressed their shock and anger over the military's action at the Guelph novitiate or, as the *Canadian Freeman* referred to the affair, "Romophobia in Guelph."[123] While acknowledging that most of the young men at the novitiate did not fall under the terms of the Military Service Act, because of either their age or health classification (including one student, who by merit of his American citizenship was exempt!), the *Casket* described the raid as simply "brought about by the urgings of bigots whose heads are full of 'Maria Monk' and all the favourite religious reading of enlightened Ontario."[124] The *New Freeman*, less tongue and cheek in its approach, accused extreme factions of Ontario Protestantism with "sordid bigotry … which may well make more responsible non-Catholics hang their heads in shame." The editors kept their sights carefully focused on the narrow band of extremists, without tarring all Protestants with the same brush when they continued that "[t]he Orange *Sentinel* that unlovely publication … and certain Protestant ministers today occupy that uncomfortable position of being caught in one of the most dastardly attempts to discredit a leading Catholic institution."[125] Like most Catholic papers, the *New Freeman* was almost gleeful when the military authorities in Ottawa apologized to the Jesuits, the minister of justice emerged as a champion of Catholic rights, and it was acknowledged that his son Marcus had never shirked his duty but was physically unable to serve.[126] Adding insult to injury for Macaulay and his armed cohort, the *Catholic Register* reprinted a list of the entire staff and student body of the novitiate, demonstrating empirically that most of the junior scholastics were underage (including Marcus Doherty, who had not reached his 20th birthday and therefore was not subject to Category 1 under the draft).[127] The *Register* also used the incident as a teaching moment to instruct detractors of the Jesuit novitiate of the various levels of progression within the Society of Jesus and the process of accepting tonsure and membership. For the *Register*, there was no excuse for Protestant ignorance on the question clerical exemptions. Protestant agitators claimed the *Register* ought to have been aware that the Jesuits and other religious orders were aware of the details of conscription: "Nothing but fanaticism can account for the assumption that our Orders of men are governed by fools."[128]

While Fallon and other Catholic leaders had made considerable advances in ecumenical co-operation, incidents like the raid at Guelph confirmed that old sectarian rivalries would be hard to exorcise from Canadian society. For Fallon, far removed from the context of Guelph, the unappreciated position of the Catholic Church in Canada was most perplexing. He confided in his diary: "I find that Quebec and Ireland are a very real difficulty for most of the people I have met. They are fair-minded and honest but they cannot understand the position taken up by the Irish [in Ireland] and French Canadians. The regrettable feature of the matter is the increase of prejudice against the Catholic Ch[urch]. Many a mind that has begun to feel the divine attraction of catholicity is thrown back by this consideration."[129] There was no easy trajectory or explanation to account for Irish Catholic participation in the Canadian war effort, or the recognition of such participation by non-Catholics. Even though recruitment statistics provided strong evidence of Catholic participation, the bishops became zealous supporters of the war effort, and ecumenical efforts such as the Catholic Army Hut program brought Catholics and Protestants together in what McNeil might call common cause, there were always mitigating factors at work. Old prejudices died hard on both sides. Old rhetorical flourishes could be revived when the sectarian lightening rod presented itself. During the war it might easily be concluded that Irish Catholics had come of age in presenting themselves as loyal defenders of Canada and the Empire within which it stood, but such an assessment was premature, given the fragility of the new bonds of unity that were being forged and the regional variations that engaged distinctive Irish Catholic communities with their neighbours. Moreover, Fallon was correct when he thought external factors often scuttled what might have been a greater Protestant appreciation of the Catholic partnership in Confederation.[130]

The events in Ireland continued to be among those mitigating external factors. In the wake of the Easter Rising of 1916 and General Maxwell's ill-advised hasty trial and execution of many of the leaders of the Irish Republican Brotherhood, the Irish situation spiralled out of control. Once again, Irish affairs were on the Canadian Catholic radar screen, particularly given the fact that if the CEF was fighting so that small nations might be free, what was happening in Ireland appeared to make the Empire look hypocritical. The new British prime minister, David Lloyd George, initiated negotiations with John Redmond's Nationalists, but the proposed segregation of the six most Protestant counties of Ulster became a wedge issue in the talks, particularly for Nationalists who envisioned an autonomous and united Ireland of thirty-two counties. Not so for the Ulster unionists, led by Edward Carson, who wanted nothing to do with Home Rule, which in their own minds was tantamount to Rome Rule. Complicating matters further was the continuing presence of republican elements, which were now coalescing with other radical nationalists under the banner of Sinn Fein and an increasing anti-imperial bitterness among the Irish people given what they viewed as the injustice of Maxwell's executions. Sinn Fein was slowly eating away support for Redmond's constitutional Irish Parliamentary Party (IPP), as it began to win by-election after by-election, including the one South Longford, which had been left vacant when Redmond's brother William was killed in action while serving in the British Expeditionary Force. Finally, in 1917 and 1918, the threat of the imposition of conscription on Ireland pushed Anglo-Irish relations almost to the breaking point, and the response to the proposed draft from many within the Roman Catholic hierarchy was openly hostile. With Redmond's death on 6 March

1918, the last prominent voice for Home Rule by constitutional means was gone, and Catholic Canadians of Irish descent took note of Ireland's increasingly precarious situation.[131]

In 1918, Canada's Irish Catholics continued to look upon the Irish Home Rule situation with considerable frustration. The Catholic press remained steadfast in their support for Irish Home Rule, regarded conscription in Ireland under the circumstances as a mistake, became increasingly critical of the Lloyd George government, and was openly critical of Sinn Fein, favouring the constitutional approach of John Redmond and his successor John Dillon. On Redmond's death, while the British government's efforts to resolve the Home Rule question teetered on the brink of failure, numerous Catholic editors in Canada rose in tribute to the fallen leader and his peaceful approach to Irish self-rule. The *Canadian Freeman* eulogized Redmond and saw his death as a great blow to solving the Irish question.[132] The *Northwest Review* agreed that in the wake of Redmond's death and the loosening hold of his party, "conditions in Ireland appear to be worse."[133] The paper cited the three-way race in an Armagh by-election as proof: the IPP and Sinn Fein candidates split the vote, thereby allowing the Orange candidate to win the seat. By July, when negotiations for a renewed Home Rule agreement seemed on the point of collapse, and Lloyd George's government, Dillon's surviving IPP, and Carson's Ulster unionists were in a deadlock, even the *Catholic Record*, which was usually measured in its assessments, referred to the Irish situation as "discouraging."[134]

With Redmond's sudden death and the growing popularity of Sinn Fein, there was little enthusiasm in Canada for a new political movement in Ireland that appeared to veer sharply from dominion status for Ireland, or indeed for any movement willing to use violent means to reach its objectives. Canadian commentators took seriously Cardinal Michael Logue's anti–Sinn Fein position and attempted to steer clear of the movement, now headed by Eamon de Valera.[135] While many in Sinn Fein publicly espoused republican principles and did not eschew violence to achieve them, the movement grew out of a dual-monarchy approach to Irish self-rule and in reality became a catch basin for a variety of Home Rulers, not all of whom were republicans.[136] While visiting the Front and talking to military brass, Fallon admitted that "few Irishmen – priests or laity – are sincere Sinn Feiners in the extreme sense."[137] In April 1918 the *Catholic Record* repeated to its readers that its initial assessment of Sinn Fein after the Rising had not changed: "Sinn Feinism is the outgrowth of narrow, unreasoning, sentimental nationalism which in Canada as in Ireland is a menace and a hindrance to peaceful national development."[138] For its part, the *Record* rejected a republic of Ireland and preferred to endorse John Dillon's constitutional means to secure dominion status for Ireland. Nevertheless, the whole Irish situation provided an unwelcome distraction from the ongoing the struggle to win the war:

> However much we explain, however sympathetic may be our understanding, the tragedy of the situation which sent John Redmond broken-hearted to the grave darkens and burdens every Irish heart. No matter who shoulders or shares this tragic responsibility, [there is] no reflecting Irish man or woman but feels the ten thousand pities that young Ireland is not freely fighting shoulder to shoulder, and heart to heart, sharing the victory or going down together in defeat with armies of liberty on Flanders fields.[139]

The *Casket* certainly agreed with respect to the linkage of the war with the Irish question, finding it difficult to swallow that Ireland was the only part of the British Empire to which self-government was refused – a fact that made Sinn Fein's growing popularity understandable. Disgusted with the current policy on Ireland at Westminster, and wary of Sinn Fein, the *Casket* among other Catholic papers and individual Catholic leaders – Fallon, Charles Doherty, and O'Gorman included – demanded self-rule in Ireland and promised a great voice in the affairs of the Empire after the war.[140] The crux of the Irish Catholic Canadian position was that Home Rule and winning the war were not an either–or proposition; in fact, they were compatible. One of the principles on which the war was fought was the self-determination of peoples such as the Belgians; it was only natural that the same status be accorded to Ireland as another dominion in the British Empire.

Canadian Catholic dissatisfaction with Lloyd George's government was more overt by the middle of 1918. Catholic journalists were particularly critical of the British prime minister's pandering to Carson and the Ulster Protestant minority who were opposing Home Rule.[141] Similarly, on the issue of imposing conscription in Ireland – which the British proposed as the war worsened on the Western Front in early 1918 – there was consensus in the Canadian Catholic press that this was not a good idea while the Home Rule issue remained unsolved. The *Canadian Freeman* rejected the idea outright, unless it was passed by an Irish Parliament.[142] Similarly, the *New Freeman* supported the notion of conscription only in the event of a separate Irish parliament bringing such a bill forward. Here the editors, like other commentators, took a careful tack, citing the opposition of Cardinal Michael Logue of Armagh to conscription: "To enforce conscription here without the consent of the people would be perfectly unwarrantable, and would soon and inevitably end in defeating its own purpose."[143] In this and other matters relating to the Irish question, the *New Freeman* was following a line of argument that would be adapted by many Canadian Catholic commentators for the next few years: they would watch two key elements in Ireland – the opinion of the Irish hierarchy on Home Rule and the expression of the popular will. Both the *Catholic Register* and *Catholic Record* targeted the misgovernment of Ireland by Westminster over the conscription question as a principal reason why support for the war in Ireland had lagged. The latter paper simply called for Lloyd George's government to reverse its policy entirely, away from the "humiliating proposal of compulsory service."[144] At the beginning of the war, continued the *Record*, "Irishmen freely, generously, enthusiastically sprang to the aid of Great Britain, gladly hailing the new era when justice and cooperation were to replace age-long oppression and hostility."[145] The implication made here was that since 1916 the Anglo-Irish relations had slid back to confrontation and violence. The outspoken Toronto priest, Lancelot Minehan, was one of the few clerics "delighted" to support conscription in Ireland in order to win the war, but only if it were achieved by the granting of Home Rule to a Dublin parliament.[146]

With the Irish question burning on both sides of the Atlantic, and while Fallon toured in Europe, the war took two dramatic turns in 1918: the German offensive in March, and its reversal by the Allied counter-offensive in August. During that time Irish Canadian Catholics, Fallon included, kept their eye on winning the war. At the same time, they were engaged in domestic questions, navigating the tricky relationship with French Canadian Catholics, and monitoring the deteriorating situation in Ireland. Irish Catholics were far from being a one-trick pony: they managed all of these issues, just as people in their everyday lives find time to balance, or juggle, family responsibilities, political affiliations, concern for world issues, work, and the occasional crisis that arises. It would be as unfair to characterize Irish Catholics as having a singular preoccupation with the "old country" as it would be to view them as obsessed with winning the war every waking hour of their lives, regardless of personal and regional concerns. The case of Fallon's visit to Europe amid the conscription crisis, the Irish Question, Germany's Spring Offensive, and CAH programs was a case in point. His primary mission from May to July was to engage with military and civilian leaders in England and France, visit the troops, and manage the religious needs of the Catholic chaplains. Amid all of his rambles, official dinners, spot visits to the trenches, and official meetings, a whole variety of issues were raised with him not the least of which was the Irish Question. In the course of his conversations he endorsed dominion rule for Ireland, expressed opposition to Melbourne's Archbishop Daniel Mannix and his anti-conscription crusade, and offered criticism of the Lloyd George administration; several times, military and civilian officials suggested to him that he venture to Ireland to be a mediator and even a recruiter for the BEF. [147]

On 10 June 1918, Fallon met with Colonel J.R. McLean at the Ministry of Information at the War Office. In a lengthy conversation with the Protestant officer he spelled out an Irish Catholic Canadian perspective that might have won support among his co-religionists at home. His response to McLean's inquiries on Home Rule in Ireland prompted the following articulation from the bishop of London:

> I then asked him to let me put my position before him. My interest in Ireland, I said, though real is but sentimental and secondary. But my interest in the political ideal of a Br[itish] Commonwealth is both real and practical and primary. I explained how I had reached my convictions on the Imperial Commonwealth among Germans in Holland and many tribes in Rome more than twenty years ago and it had been my experience of the past eighteen years in the U.S. and Canada. That political ideal is now in extreme jeopardy. The failure to make Ireland content constitutes the main element in the menace – for the Irish in Australia, Canada & U.S will not desert the land of their fathers. I pointed out the danger of throwing the Irish Americans and the German Americans into each other's arms and said that no political party in the U.S. could

> successfully oppose such and alliance and would not attempt it. If Paris is taken – which it now seems inevitable – the U.S will be forced out of the war by this alliance and the British Empire is at an end.[148]

Although one ought not to be presumptuous about drawing a group position from the ideas of one member of the group, particularly one who overestimated the success of the Spring Offensive, Fallon's words give us pause. He did not forget the problems faced by Ireland, the birthplace of his parents, but he framed them in a much larger context that engaged both the life he lived within Canada and the broader imperial and North American contexts. Given the writings of editors and the views of his fellow Catholic leaders, already presented, it is not hard to imagine that Fallon would have discovered a broad Irish Catholic consensus in Canada for his stand with McLean in 1918. The war mattered; Ireland mattered; the Empire mattered; but all would be lost without winning the war and honouring the principles for which it was being fought.

By August, Fallon had moved on to Rome to discuss matters relating to his diocese, not the least of which was the riot at Ford City. That same month the Canadian Corps was part of a massive allied offensive that broke through the German lines and transformed the war from a sedentary one in the trenches to a mobile overland war. Known to military historians as the "Hundred Days," this final push into Belgium and eastern France brought about the eventual retreat of the German army and the declaration of the Armistice on 11 November 1918. Within this final phase of the war, which was not anticipated as such at the time, Catholics and their neighbours undertook the CAH drive and Victory Loan drives,[149] and endured the ongoing painful process of assessing and drafting young men to fill the depleted ranks of the four Canadian divisions in the field. Bishop Budka, the Ukrainian Catholic Eparch, was placed on trial for sedition, which gave the Catholic press an opportunity to offer a public defense of his loyalty to the Empire and offer the bishop himself to speak publicly in his own defence. He did. "We Canadian Ruthenians," Budka exclaimed, "will stand loyally for our country's interest because Canada is for our children their native country. National means with us Canadian ... we stand under the British flag with everything we are and everything we have."[150] With his eventual acquittal it appeared that one of the external factors that had gnawed away at public perceptions of Catholic loyalty was gone.

In August 1918, while editors, prelates, priests, and politicians in Irish Catholic Canada agitated for immediate Home Rule, Bishop Fallon visited Ireland for eight days as part of the final fortnight of his European tour. While in Dublin he dined with Irish politicians, including Sir Horace Plunkett, and then travelled across the Irish countryside, where he was distressed by the strong presence of British troops.[151] It was his conclusion, he wrote in his diary, that "[t]he Nationalist Party is dead."[152] Expressing the mistrust of his fellow Irish Catholic Canadians back home, Fallon conceded that "for good or evil" Sinn Fein was to be a more permanent fixture on the Irish political scene. Outlining his thoughts in unusual detail in the diary, Fallon conceded that he admired Sinn Fein's love of the Irish language, literature, and culture. On the other hand, he considered the movement a "grave danger" and one that "bred a sort of insanity." Perhaps he reflected on his experiences of what he considered his hyper-nationalist French Canadian nemesis, when he considered what Sinn Fein's "exaggerated nationalism" might do should they take control of the island. Fallon also was clear that the movement needed "safe wise and prudent leadership," and he dreaded a confrontation between the Church and the revolutionaries.[153] Confirming the confidence that British authorities had in him, the British military invited him to help the recruiting drive in Ireland; he declined, citing the need to return to Canada after a four-month absence.[154] What remains striking about Fallon's account of his Irish experience is that he found that he had been made firmer in his willingness to be "an advocate of the British Commonwealth ... [a] family of self-governing nations wherein the individual nationality would be secondary."[155]

On the morning of 11 November 1918 the Canadian Expeditionary Force attacked Mons in a symbolic and perhaps wasteful move to hold the same section of Belgium held by the British Expeditionary Force in 1914. The assault ended at 11 a.m. when an armistice was declared. The war was effectively over. Canadians, Catholics included, celebrated and wept when word was received that the greatest slaughter in human history had come to an end. For Canadians the war had been marked by significant military moments, such as the defence against the first German gas attack at Ypres in 1915, and the capture of Vimy Ridge in 1917, and by controversy on the home front, not the least of which was the division caused by the implementation of conscription. Drawing from its population of over 7.5 million people, Canada had put over 620,000 men and women in uniform, most of them volunteers. Although many of the initial recruits had been born in the British and Irish islands, by war's end the scales had tipped in favour of Canadian-born men in khaki and women in nursing blues.[156] Catholics had comprised the second-largest share of the contingent, at 22.9 per cent, behind the Anglicans and slightly ahead of the Presbyterians.[157] Although the majority of the Catholic volunteers had been Irish or Scottish by birth or descent, the French Canadian share of the Catholic total assuredly rose during the period of conscription. The total cost of the war in human suffering was staggering. Approximately 425,000 members of the CEF served overseas, of whom 60,661 died. The war's toll included fourteen killed, seventy wounded and two missing in that last effort against Mons.[158] In total, 172,950 Canadian soldiers and nurses were wounded, as well as 1,130 Canadian pilots in the Royal Flying Corps.[159] This means that over half of the members of the CEF who served overseas were killed or wounded as a result of the war. At home, few Canadian towns or villages were untouched by this enormous butcher's bill.

Canadians, particularly those of Irish Catholic birth or descent, celebrated the war's end and mourned the horrific loss of life and the shattered lives of the wounded who returned. Catholic newspapers were replete with stories of the heroic fallen, and it was not long before lists from parishes, urban and rural, were published in the weekly papers – a practice that had begun during the war.[160] Editors waxed poetic on themes of sacrifice and nation-building, and some prognosticated on the kind of world that might be reconstructed on the ruins of Europe and the broken bodies of the war's fallen. For the *New Freeman* it was a "victory for Christianity … a victory for the right … a victory for civilization."[161] The paper added, though, a somber note, remembering the sacrifices of families, and expressing the hope that the fallen were in paradise chanting "*Te Deum Laudemus*," for which all Christendom, now in peace, is grateful. The *Casket* expressed exhaustion and a little hope: "Thank God it is over! Thank God we have won. Thank God such a war is not likely to occur again for many years. Yet wars will come unless the world gives God His peace."[162]

On the Prairies, the editors of the *Northwest Review* were more detailed in their reflection, although they admitted that the new crisis of the day – influenza – had already descended upon the people of the province. "For over four long bloody years," wrote P.J. Henry,

> the representatives of Force made a shambles of three continents in an effort to establish a principle which, had they been successful, would have turned the hands of progress backwards and placed mankind at the mercy of these savage methods from which Christianity had rescued it ... Unless the principle of self-determination as laid down by President Wilson be accepted and adopted – not grudgingly but unhesitatingly and willingly – much of the sacrifice shall have been in vain.[163]

Henry's reference to Ireland's situation, given his past comments, was scarcely veiled, as he linked the sacrifice of "Canada's victorious sons" with the principles of democracy and self-determination of peoples. Canada was clearly to be celebrated for this achievement over tyranny, but this was only a beginning. "We would be unworthy of them and guilty of treason to the great cause for which they stood, Henry wrote, "if we fail them now."[164]

In churches, priests and bishops urged their congregations to pray in thanksgiving for the end of the struggle and for the repose of the souls of the war's dead. On the Monday of the declaration, the bells of St Ninian's Cathedral in Antigonish peeled the end of the war. Bishop Morrison led a service of Thanksgiving, including a full recitation of the rosary accompanied by thirty priests and altar servers.[165] In Hamilton, Bishop Thomas Dowling ordered masses of thanksgiving and a solemn *Te Deum* to be sung on the first Sunday after armistice.[166] Alfred Sinnott, Archbishop of Winnipeg, urged the continued support of the Victory Loan campaign, proclaiming that 11 November 1918 was the "most glorious day in the history of the British Empire."[167] However, despite his joy that the war was over, Sinnott echoed the mixed thoughts of many Canadians in his circular to be read in all Churches: "It has caused rejoicings in those homes which have been most sorely affected, for, if peace cannot bring back the dead to life, it crowns their sacrifice with the consolation that their blood was not shed in vain."[168] In Calgary, the celebrations of victory were soon eclipsed by the perplexing job of receiving demobilized Catholic veterans, particularly conscripts stationed within Canada. Father Newman at St Mary's Cathedral was presented with lists of names of

Catholic men, many of whom he did not know, thus raising the suspicion that perhaps there were more unchurched Catholics hailing from the diocese than church authorities had realized.[169] Finally, amid his own prayers of thanksgiving, and in anticipation of the Versailles peace conference, Cardinal Bégin of Quebec petitioned his flock for prayers, in the hope that the world could be rebuilt and revolution avoided in the days and months following the conflict.[170]

As the demobilized men returned home in 1919, and families mourned those who did not, Catholic parishes, like their Protestant neighbours, began to compile lists of names that might be immortalized within the sacred spaces of their churches. In some Canadian dioceses, such as Pembroke, the bishops mandated the collection of names for honour rolls.[171] In Victoria, the list of the dead in St Andrew's Catholic Cathedral included dozens of local men and one woman, nurse Christina Campbell, a faithful parishioner who had drowned in the Atlantic when the *Llandovery Castle*, a hospital ship used for transporting the wounded, was torpedoed by a German U-boat near Ireland in June 1918.[172] The lists could be lengthy, including both the living and those "who paid the supreme sacrifice," like the parchment rolls at St John the Baptist Parish in Perth, Ontario, the framed list at St Columban's in Cornwall, and the bronze plates prominently placed in the foyer of St Joseph's Church in Ottawa. The parishioners thought so highly of the latter memorial that when the church was destroyed by fire in the 1930s volunteers recovered the tablets so they could be displayed in the new church – where they are today, on the campus of the University of Ottawa. Across town at St Patrick's, parishioners under the direction of anti-conscriptionist Father Matthew Whelan erected a massive painting of the "front" in the foyer of the church. It depicted a fatally wounded soldier dying at the feet of the crucified Christ, yet awaiting a choir of angels coming to take him to his just reward. Beneath are the calligraphed names of the fifty-nine men of the parish who would never grace its pews again.[173] The fallen Catholics of downtown Halifax were immortalized in a bronze wall monument at the doors of St Mary's cathedral, within sight of all who might enter. The message left by the commemorators was clear: "Sacred to the Memory of / Our Soldiers of St Mary's / The Noble Dead Whose Names are Here Inscribed / And the Honored Living / They Have Shown Us Manhood Knighted / Idealized, Transfigured, Capable of the Highest." Across the country Catholic parishes began to remember and memorialize, stating powerfully in paper, metal, and stone that this had been their war, too.[174]

The memorialization of the war dead in public sculptures appeared to bind together the country's ethnic, religious, and cultural communities. Whether the memorials included all who served, or recognized only those who had paid the supreme sacrifice, all names were equal when carved in stone. In Pembroke, a large plinth topped by an armed soldier ready to charge is the centrepiece of a memorial garden that commemorates local participants in all of Canada's wars since 1914. The names carved there appear alphabetically, regardless of class, religion, rank, place of birth, or ethnicity. The Irish Catholic Ned Murray, for example, memorialized as Edward Francis Murray, is flanked by two Presbyterians who survived their battles, bookkeeper Freeman Munro and labourer Campbell MacDonald. Not far away, are French Canadian Joseph Poitras, who volunteered in 1915, and Michael Stoqua, of the Golden Lake First Nation, who died at Vimy Ridge. Public monuments became the great leveller: whether or not those remembered were close to one another in life, in death they were all part of the same body. Along the Ottawa Valley, on either side of the river, are similar testaments to the Great War with similarly diverse honour rolls. In each monument, the most important badge of identity for those who served and died is the community that commemorated them. Much the same can be said for the monuments erected in socially, religiously, and culturally mixed communities across Canada.

The idea of the importance of this shared burden of the war between Protestants and Catholics was frequently memorialized by Catholics, who did not want the public to forget that this had been their war, as much as it had been of Canada's Protestants. In Eastern Nova Scotia, the patriotism and heroic virtue of Catholic troops was celebrated in *Catholics of the Diocese of Antigonish, Nova Scotia and The War, 1914–1918*, a commemorative volume published in 1919 through the joint efforts of faculty members at St Francis Xavier University and St Ninian's Council 1105 of the Knights of Columbus. The book offered complete nominal rolls of volunteers and conscripts from each parish in the diocese, along with photographs, biographies of the leading Catholics from the area engaged in the war effort, including Chief Matron Margaret MacDonald, vignettes on the chaplains, and edited texts of letters and speeches. The editors explained the purpose of the volume as follows: "Catholics … labored hand-in-hand with their non-Catholic fellow-citizens in non-denominational bodies, and no record was kept. This volume was proof of the Catholic 'staunch support of the allied cause.'"[175] The volume reveals the collective effort of Irish, Scots, Acadian, Mi'kmaq, and Italian Catholics in the exercise of their patriotic duty, lest it be forgotten or overlooked. Similarly, at St Michael's College in Toronto, faculty and students dedicated a huge section of its 1919 yearbook to list the fallen students, alumni, and staff from the college, and included their photographs and lists of decorations for valour.[176]

Also in Toronto – a city that bore a sometimes deserved reputation for sectarian tension – was the historic unveiling of a war memorial exclusively for Catholics. In June 1921, on the steps of St Paul's Church near Cabbagetown, Archbishop McNeil was joined by Mayor Tommy Church, an unrepentant member of the Orange Order, as hundreds of parishioners viewed the new memorial to the eighty-one members of the congregation who had died in the Great War. What made the monument so significant was that it was not reserved for the sacred space inside St Paul's, but dominated the Queen Street side of the church's entrance way, built into the base of the bell tower. Above a massive bronze plaque bearing the names of the fallen was a towering white marble angel holding the cross of the faith aloft with one hand and a wreath of laurels directed down toward the names of those who had won them.[177] The speeches made by Archbishop McNeil and local MPP, John O'Neill, praised the parish for its 762 men in uniform; the latter claimed he had never been "so proud as now" of his native parish. For his part, the Orange Mayor congratulated the Catholics of Toronto on their enormous efforts and sacrifices during the war and paid tribute to Dean John Laurence Hand, pastor of the parish, for his ongoing work for the poor. The tribute finished with three cheers for Archbishop McNeil and three for King George V. The St Paul's school choir then belted out three songs, reflective of their hybrid Canadian-Irish identity: "O Canada," "Men of the North," and the Irish fighting ballad "The Minstrel Boy."[178]

CONCLUSION

The Principles and Outcomes of War

On the morning of 11 November 2014, bishops from across Europe gathered at the site of the Verdun battlefield in France, where 700,000 men were killed or wounded during one entire year of fighting during the Great War.[1] Bishops from France, Germany, England, and other former combatant nations said prayers and lit votive lamps at the ossuary where the bones of 130,000 unknown soldiers have their final resting place. In their communiqué, the Commission of the Bishops' Conferences of the European Union commented on the "sheer folly of war" and the fact, as they understood it, that "World War One need not to have happened." In this light, the bishops appeared to exude some pride in the fact that European countries and cultures, a century later, had overcome their gravest differences and now "recall with gratitude the achievements of the European Project and the way the vision of the founding fathers of the European Union … have contributed to peace and understanding among nations." Amid their prayers, however, the collected bishops were ashamed of the fact that "even churchmen stoked the fires of conflict and fuelled nationalist passion; it is a recollection tinged with regret and shame. But we also remember how stoically and persistently Pope Benedict XV advocated cessation of arms and promoted peace."[2]

These prayerful reflections by the participating bishops, while genuine in their expression of regret and memorialization, offer little insight into why their episcopal forebears endorsed the war in the manner that they did. Perhaps the spirit of Bishop Edward Thomas O'Dwyer of Limerick might have smiled, knowing that he had been one of the lone episcopal voices in the United Kingdom that opposed the war from the outset and chastised those who differed from his position.[3] His Canadian colleagues of Irish birth or descent could not confess the same. They had been enthusiastic and zealous in their support of the war against Germany and her allies; they had personally assisted in recruitment, co-operated with the government in the registration of manpower and conservation of resources, and rarely missed an opportunity to convince their French Canadian colleagues to see the war through the lens of the Catholic duty of patriotism. Although unanimity was lacking among the anglophone Catholic bishops during the conscription crisis, their key spokesmen were firmly committed to the cause of winning the war, even if that meant young able-bodied men would be drafted into the ranks of the Canadian Expeditionary Force. Throughout the war, the bishops and their clergy helped to knit together, a little more tightly, the Irish Catholic communities across Canada that geography, time, social circumstances, and economic opportunity had kept at a distance for generations. The bishops, their supporting clergy, and Catholic editors regarded participation in the war as both a Christian duty and an imperial one. Many Irish Catholic Canadians, now two and three generations in North America, appeared to agree and enlisted in high numbers.

The position of the Catholic Church in Canada on the war had implications for Catholics in their engagement with the greater community and in their relations with other Catholics in Canada. Irish Catholic leaders used the Great War as a means of leveraging themselves as meaningful actors in the public square. Irish Canadian bishops and their clergy can to be seen as community leaders loyal to the Crown and attentive to public service, whether in recruiting, working on the Patriotic Fund, or marshalling Catholic support for a variety of government-sponsored initiatives.[4] Catholic editors crowed about the high levels of Catholic participation during the voluntary phases of enlistment and lent their support to the public campaign to register manpower in 1916. Catholic laymen and clergy alike navigated a careful course around controversies generated in Ireland, Quebec, the Vatican, and communities of "new Canadians" in order to keep the public perception alive that Irish Catholics and their Church were loyal to the Empire, to Canada, and to the cause of winning the war. In the process, Catholics and Protestants were often seen working co-operatively on the recruiting platform, when raising funds for Army Huts, or among the padres at the front; such co-operation in a time when ecumenism was not a word in fashion, particularly among Catholics, was noted and celebrated. The *Catholic Register* devoted plenty of ink to the praise that C.W. Gordon, a.k.a. the popular writer Ralph Connor, gave to the Catholic war effort after his return from the front. Given the unsympathetic portrayal of Catholics in his novels before the war, the *Register* boasted that "Ralph Connor's views of Catholicism are among the things that have changed by the terrible conflict."[5]

Although the Great War may have enhanced a long-sought respectability for Irish Catholics in Canada, it did not put to an end the tensions between Protestants and Catholics in many regions of the country. Mayor Tommy Church's kind and effusive words about Catholic service from St Paul's Parish, in the heart of Toronto, did not satisfy the skeptics among his Orange brothers and their ongoing belief that Catholics were inherently disloyal. Witnessing anti-conscription sentiment in Quebec and the rise of Sinn Fein in Ireland, Canadian Orangemen could still find ways to pillory their Catholic neighbours, whether in the pages of the *Sentinel* or in the corridors of power.[6] In 1926, Archbishop McNeil received an anonymous letter from a Catholic complaining about discrimination against Catholics even in the Liberal party, despite the fact, the author claimed, that the party had been "saved" by English-speaking Catholics from the likes of Newton Wesley Rowell and Clifford Sifton, who had defected to Borden's Union government.[7] Irish Catholic leaders during the war were not naive enough to think that all Protestants would embrace Catholics as brother in arms, although there was some hope that Catholic contributions to the war effort would be recognized and accorded respect by a majority of the non-Catholic populace. It would still be over forty years before a major Protestant organ might give a nod to the papacy; in 1961, the *United Church Observer* would comment that Pope John XXIII was "the best Pope Protestants ever had."[8] In 1919, Benedict XV would have never won such accolades from a leading Canadian Protestant weekly.

If the Great War had brought mixed results regarding Irish Catholic acceptance and respectability in the public square, it caused more serious difficulty between the major ethnic and religious groups within the Canadian Catholic Church. The period leading up to the war had been a time of serious tension between Irish Catholics and French Canadian Catholics over issues such as immigration, home missions, schools, and management of the Church outside of Quebec. The war simply worsened a bad situation. If, on the one hand, the war had acted as a centripetal force for Irish Catholics, binding their leadership closer together, employing national communications more effectively, and finding more common cause with Canadians who spoke English, the war had the opposite effect for Irish–French relations within the Church. In the latter case, the war acted as a centrifuge, throwing French Canadian Catholics away from their co-religionists on matters of national vision, the British Empire, and patriotism. The public perception of Catholic unity was shattered through the words, actions, and agency of such prominent Catholics as Michael Francis Fallon, John J. O'Gorman, Alfred E. Burke, and Henri Bourassa. Conscription became a powerful fault line between French Canadians and Irish Catholics, who had different visions regarding the war and how it could be won. All of the efforts of the Bonne Entente and the Knights of Columbus, and the personal efforts by archbishops McNeil, Bégin, and Bruchési could barely disguise the fact that the war had disfigured the Church. By 1919, the Catholic Church in Canada was in serious need of healing, both in terms of relations among its bishops and with regard to cultural understanding and tolerance between laypersons who shared a faith but differed in language and ethnicity.

Nor did the end of the Great War put to rest the Irish Catholic Canadian concern for the events unfolding in Ireland. While a comprehensive study of this issue could fill several books, what should be emphasized here is that Irish Catholic Canadian service in the war was linked to events in Ireland. The hope of Home Rule in 1912 and the promise made by the Asquith government of its implementation at the end of the war was crushed in the aftermath of the Easter Rising and the disintegration of Irish support, including episcopal support, for the constitutional approaches to Home Rule proposed by John Redmond and the Irish Parliamentary Party.[9] In Canada, bishops, Irish Catholic clergy, and most of the Catholic weeklies clung to their support of the dreams proffered by Redmond and his successors, confident that he and his party could bring to Ireland the autonomy within the Empire that Catholics in Canada enjoyed.[10] With the massive Sinn Fein electoral victory in late 1918, and the deployment of the brutal paramilitary "Black & Tans" to keep the peace in Ireland, Irish Catholic Canadians became louder in their demands that Ireland enjoy the constitutional rights that Canadians already possessed.[11] It is on this point that the editors at the *Catholic Record* were most eloquent: "Canada has a form of Home Rule which secures for her the utmost liberty of action in arranging her own affairs, developing her resources and framing her laws. Her people are happy ... The reason is because our ancestors fought for and obtained their rights, just as the people of Ireland are doing now."[12]

In this issue the Great War played a key role in Irish Catholic thinking: if Irish Catholics fought the Empire's war that small nations might be free, it only stood to reason that this principle be applied in Ireland. According to the *Canadian Freeman*, which had been among the most sympathetic supporters of Sinn Fein's approach to Home Rule after 1920,[13] the editors made a clear link between the Great War and Irish autonomy: "Irish people are rightly struggling to be free; Irish people must rightly choose their course according to the principles fought for by the allies; Canadian soldiers fought for this principle of self-determination; the British army of occupation [of Ireland] is a direct threat to 'Liberty and Democracy.' Irish towns are being sacked, homes burned, citizens murdered ... Canadians will not deny others the freedoms that they enjoy."[14]

In the minds of many Canadian Irish Catholics, there was no contradiction between taking pride in their participation in the Great War as an Imperial player and demanding that the Empire be a place where the principles for which the war was fought be honoured. It was logical that constitutional Irish self-determination be supported. The *Cathedral Magazine* in Hamilton acknowledged that even the Catholic hero of Belgium's struggle for independence, Cardinal Mercier, wrote publicly to Cardinal Michael Logue, Primate of Ireland, proclaiming his view that at the Paris Peace Conference the question of the self-determination of peoples in a post-war world should include Ireland.[15]

As a matter of justice, sentiment toward the birthplace of their ancestors, and outrage at the atrocities committed by the Black and Tans, a large number of Irish Catholic Canadians, from coast to coast – including newspaper editors, clergy, and the Ancient Order of Hibernians (AOH) –sent subscriptions to the Irish Relief Fund to assist the cause of Home Rule.[16] By 1920, there was also widespread Irish Catholic Canadian support for the Self-Determination League for Ireland, which pressed for Home Rule by holding "monster" meetings in several Canadian cities, including Vancouver, Winnipeg, Halifax, Montreal, and Ottawa. Notable at the Toronto meeting on July 5 were local Irish Catholics who had been prominent in their support for the war effort; these included Thomas O'Hagan, a poet, and C.J. Foy, who had supported Borden's Unionists in 1917.[17] Public meetings were not without controversy. In Winnipeg, Archbishop Sinnott prohibited the use of a church hall for a self-determination rally, preferring that politics be kept out of the Church. *Northwest Review* editor Patrick Henry retreated from his support of the use of the church hall, carefully stating that the archbishop's disapproval did not signal a lack of sympathy for the cause but merely reflected caution, since his "diocese includes so many races and languages [and he] must be neutral and fair to all."[18] In Montreal, French-Canadian nationalists joined more ardent Irish Home Rulers in the protest. This was not surprising, given the instincts of that city's Irish Catholic "double minority," who tended to wear their Irishness more vociferously than most other Irish Catholic communities in Canada and were seen as natural Catholic allies for Bourassa's nationalists.[19] The AOH was most vocal in its support for Sinn Fein, although some Irish Catholics in Quebec, including Charles Fitzpatrick, disapproved of such demonstrations, which appeared to be anti-England.[20] Nevertheless, it was a rare, albeit local, demonstration of Irish–French rapprochement.

As the Irish situation became uglier, however, Canadian Catholic voices became shriller. In 1920, when the mayor of Cork was murdered, the *Catholic Record* pounced on the story, claiming that if the murder "had occurred in Belgium during the German occupation [it] would have rung around the world as one more instance of the incredible brutality of Prussianism."[21] For its part, the *Record* stood by its support for constitutional Home Rule and demanded the British Government make right on its promise to Ireland and the principles for which the war was fought.[22] A small minority of Irish Catholics, the most notable of whom was journalist Katherine Hughes, favoured a republic for Ireland.[23] When civil war erupted in Ireland between republican dissidents, led by Eamon de Valera, and the supporters of the newly formed Irish Free State, led by Michael Collins, the battle lines among Irish descendants in the Canadian diaspora were clearer. The Irish Catholic press in Canada generally supported Collins, whose forces eventually prevailed.[24] Irish Catholic Canadians recognized that Ireland had won a constitutional status similar to that of Canada.[25]

In the immediate aftermath of the war, however, international issues were perhaps less pressing than the much anticipated opportunity for battle-scarred veterans to return home and resume their lives. For Irish Catholic soldiers and nurses it was a time to re-establish themselves in whatever a "normal" life might be once they returned home. Catholic priests and bishops were forced to redirect their attention to the pastoral questions of the day, and to healing the ethnic and linguistic wounds within the Church. Many Catholic families had to come to terms with life without a loved one who was soon to lie in a well-maintained plot, or with his or her name inscribed on a memorial headstone, provided without cost by the newly created Commonwealth War Graves Commission.[26] This may have brought some consolation, despite the fact that the deceased fathers, sons, brothers, sisters and daughters rested so far away from their native soil. Not all of the thousands of stories of the Irish Catholic "returned" can be told here, of course, but some vignettes might help to illustrate the transitions, sometimes difficult, made by those living in the aftermath of war.

For the Irish Catholic chaplains, the return to Canada meant a resumption of pastoral duties or, in the case of many men in religious orders, a resumption of their missionary and educational careers. Father Benedict Murdock returned to his parish in Chatham, New Brunswick, and began work on his war memoir *The Red Vineyard*. While not as well known nor as frequently reprinted as Canon Frederick Scott's *The Great War as I Saw It*, Murdoch's work provides one of the few reflections by a Canadian Catholic priest, in English, about the life of infantrymen at the front. Another chaplain, Father Ivor J.E. Daniel, teamed up with D.A Casey, editor of the *Canadian Freeman*, to write *For God and Country*, a tribute to the work of the Knights of Columbus and the Catholic Army Hut program. The inclusion of Father Casey as an author reinforces the connectedness between the Great War effort and the Irish question. Although Casey was adamant about Irish autonomy, and at the time of publication had supported Sinn Fein, he never lost the sense that Irish Catholic Canadian service in the CEF was an act of patriotism and citizenship worth celebrating.

Curiously, the Irish Catholic padres who returned to Canada – and indeed all the padres, regardless of background – never appeared to be celebrated by their own bishops.[27] Most padres simply returned to their pastoral duties in the domestic Church. Such was the case of Ambrose Madden, perhaps the mostly highly decorated Catholic Chaplain in the CEF. Madden returned to British Columbia and served in parishes in Kamloops and Chilliwack. He volunteered for duty during World War II and was appointed Command Captain for the Chaplain's Service in Vancouver. He died peacefully in his beloved province in 1968 at the age of 93.[28] The example of Madden, who was acknowledged as a war hero but slipped quietly back into pastoral life, appeared typical of Irish Catholic Canadian padres after the war. Despite their acts of bravery, selfless dedication to the men and women at the front and behind the lines, and their numerous decorations for valour, none was ever made a bishop after the war. Although a thorough study is needed to determine why this might have happened, a few conjectures might be raised for the time being. Had the padres been too ecumenical in spirit at the front, leaving some doubt as to their steadfast obedience to the canons of the Church in peacetime? Had they suffered from undiagnosed trauma that excluded them from selection? By contrast, several padres from the Second World War became bishops after the war was over.

Had he lived longer, perhaps the indefatigable Father O'Gorman might have been awarded the mitre – although one suspects not, if any French-Canadian prelate had a say in the matter. When the war ended, O'Gorman was awarded the Order of the British Empire for his exemplary service, particularly with the Canadian Chaplaincy Service.[29] He returned to Blessed Sacrament parish in the Glebe and continued the energetic life he had left behind in 1916: building schools, erecting a new church building, contributing to social service agencies, researching and writing about Ireland and its culture, planning (but never writing) a biography of Thomas D'Arcy McGee, writing on Catholic pedagogy, playing golf and tennis, and continuing his fight against the restoration of bilingual schools by local Franco-Ontarian educators.[30] His rekindled public skirmishes with the French-Canadians, particularly regarding his claims about their "imposition" of unqualified teachers on the board,[31] once again earned him a warning from Archbishop Gauthier not to publish articles in the secular press.[32] His pastoral successes, however, were beyond dispute, as Catholic families gravitated to O'Gorman's parish. Between 1914 and 1929 his flock nearly doubled in size, from 251 to 480 families.[33] On the morning of 24 April 1933, however, Ottawans would wake to the shocking news that O'Gorman had died from complications arising from a ruptured appendix. The *Ottawa Citizen* paid tribute to him as "one of Canada's most brilliant English-speaking priests."[34] The rival *Ottawa Journal* might have brought a smile to O'Gorman's face, capturing the priest's sense of patriotism, Irish ethnicity, and imperial citizenship: "Although deeply interested in the affairs of Ireland, Dr. O'Gorman was a staunch supporter of the British Commonwealth and above all he was one who upheld in every respect the traditions of the Dominion in which he was born."[35]

The war did not conclude the many labours of Montreal MP and minister of justice, Charles J. Doherty. He continued in this portfolio for prime ministers Sir Robert Borden and Arthur Meighen, until the Union Government was defeated in 1921.[36] Doherty was the Canadian delegate at the Versailles Peace Conference in 1919 and later served as Canada's delegate to the League of Nations from 1920 to 1922. His promotion to the imperial Privy Council in 1920 allowed him to use the title Right Honourable for the remainder of his life. Although a Montrealer at heart, Doherty and his family retained their residence in Ottawa while he engaged in his new international roles.[37] Publisher Hector Charlesworth's assessment of him in 1919 was rather flattering and demonstrated the extent to which some Irish Catholic politicians in Canada had attained a high degree of respectability: "The Minister of Justice is recognized by men of all shades of political opinion as an honourable man of exceptional ability and energy and is greatly esteemed by all classes for his splendid character, his capacity, his probity, worth and public spirit."[38] He died in 1931. Despite the high drama at St Stanislaus Novitiate in Guelph, his only son, Marcus Doherty, did become a Jesuit after the war. Marcus was a much beloved pastor and Church historian who loved to retell an embellished version of the night he was wrongfully arrested as a "shirker."[39]

Peterborough-born artillery Lieutenant William O'Brien survived the war and managed to record many of his experiences in a little notebook, which became a treasured heirloom among his children and grandchildren. Bill immediately resumed his legal studies at Osgoode Hall in Toronto, and was called to the Bar of Ontario on 20 May 1920.[40] In October of that same year, he married Mary Corrigan and settled in Toronto, where they had eight children. He dedicated much of his private time to family and Catholic organizations – the Newman Club, the Children's Aid Society, Catholic Charities, and the Knights of Columbus. For his tireless service to the Church he was awarded the "Pro Ecclesia et Pontifice" medal by Pope Pius XII, which he wore next to his military decorations. In 1933 he attended the reunion of CEF veterans in Toronto, which included a special dinner for "gunners" at the King Edward Hotel, where O'Brien was reunited with his favourite officer, General Archibald C. "Batty Mac" Macdonnel. O'Brien died in 1943 at the age of fifty-six.[41] His eldest son, William Jr, served in the artillery in the next war and after demobilization became a priest of the Congregation of St Basil and a teacher at St Michael's College School in Toronto. Another son, James R., known to his friends as "Jim" or "Reg," rediscovered his father's war diary in his father's ammunition box in the 1970s. The elder O'Brien had redacted it after the war, but the original notebook remained, as one Irish Catholic's testimony to war.

The Irish Catholic Canadian soldiers who returned home had stories as varied and idiosyncratic as the individuals themselves. Arthur Augustine McGrory was a law student who waited until 1916 to enlist in his native Prescott, Ontario. He spent his first two months of duty guarding the St Lawrence canals from potential saboteurs, but was later moved to Europe, where he was placed with the Princess Patricia's Canadian Light Infantry (PPCLI). He thrived with the unit, won a field promotion to Acting Sergeant (although he requested that he remain a private), was wounded in the head by bullets, and later was awarded the Military Medal for bravery.[42] He was demobilized in 1919, settled in Ottawa, had a large family, and was so enamoured by his old unit, the PPCLI, that he named one of his daughters Patricia. Perhaps more flamboyant and more in the public eye than McGrory's return, was the homecoming of the Bawlf brothers, all of whom were officers: Louis Drummond, David Leland, Clarence Nicholas, and Nicholas Jr. They were four of the eight children born to Catherine Madden and millionaire Nicholas Bawlf, a Manitoba grain merchant and businessman who died three months after the outbreak of the war.[43] The Bawlf boys came from privilege and each had chosen a different path to war service. Nicholas Jr played professional hockey in the National Hockey Association, but retired to Ottawa in 1905 in order to study.[44] Working as a civil servant in Ottawa, Nick joined the 154th Battalion in Cornwall, for whom he served in the non-combatant role of paymaster for the duration of the war.[45] His youngest brother Louis took a more focused and perhaps more glamorous, if regimented, trajectory to the CEF; after having served in the 90th Winnipeg Rifles and having graduated from St Thomas Military Academy in St Paul, Minnesota, Louis enlisted in the 144th Battalion. He eventually transferred to 203 Squadron, the Royal Flying Corps, where he joined his older brothers, "knights of the air" David Leland and Clarence Nicholas, nicknamed "Choney" during his distinguished athletic career.[46] David was killed in action in 1918 and buried near Pas-de-Calais, France.[47] Nick, Clarence, and Louis survived the war, but returned to Canada knowing that their dear Irish mother had died in 1918.[48] Nick was demobilized at Kingston and eventually coached lacrosse at Cornell University, while Louis and Clarence returned to the family in Winnipeg. Louis never lost interest in his military career and, when the time came, re-enlisted and served in the RCAF during World War II.[49]

Lance Corporal William McGowan, however, did not want to go home. McGowan was born in Kirkintilloch, Scotland, in 1896, the eldest son of the eleven children of Patrick McGowan and Mary Rodden. Like so many others of his generation in Northern Ireland in the late nineteenth century, Patrick's father, William Sr, had immigrated to the Glasgow area in search of gainful employment. With the same adventurous spirit of his grandfather, William Jr, of mixed Irish and Scottish heritage, had immigrated to Toronto just prior to the war. At the outbreak of hostilities he joined the 15th Battalion, formed out of 48th Highlanders of Toronto, and sailed with the first Canadian Contingent. William was fortunate that he never saw action with his unit at the deadly gas attack at Langemark (Gravenstafel Ridge) in April 1915, because he had been seconded to the signals corps; he was later re-attached to the 15th Battalion. With only a short leave in 1917 to return to his birthplace to be married, William spent the remainder of the war in France as a signaller and won the Military Medal with two bars – essentially, three decorations for bravery in the field. At war's end he re-enlisted and in 1919 served as a military policeman. By 1920 he was back in Toronto with his war bride, working as a riveter, and in close proximity to his younger brother George, who had just been demobilized from the Royal Flying Corps. Life was not easy for William, a man who probably lived with post-traumatic stress disorder (before its diagnosis was known) and was certainly tortured by the loss of so many comrades in the 15th. His marriage fell apart and he died, alone, in a rooming house on York Street, Toronto, in 1958.[50] The Last Post Society, a benevolent burial fund provided by the Department of Veterans Affairs, ensured that his body was laid to rest in Holy Cross Roman Catholic Cemetery, north of the city.[51]

Mona Whelan returned to Canada in 1917, having been invalided from the nursing service because of recurring respiratory ailments. It is not known whether she returned to the family farmland of Admaston Township; it is probable that she did so for a short time before returning to Ottawa. She was likely in the region when her mother, Johanna Whelan, passed away in 1919. Two years later, in 1921, Mona married Dr. Orland Kingsley Gibson, a man fifteen years her senior, and whom she had likely met while working as a nurse after the war. They resided at 9 Thornton Street, in Capital Ward, which included the more fashionable houses of the leafy Glebe neighbourhood. This was the same neighbourhood served by Father O'Gorman, who had returned to serve at Blessed Sacrament parish just a few blocks away. Mona probably did not connect with the former chaplain, since she elected to leave the Catholic Church and practise the Methodism of her husband. Her new role as wife of a respected doctor also changed the course of her vocation. Like many women of the time, Mona experienced the letdown of ordinary life, having had been a nurse caught in the drama and horror of war, assisting with the wounded in their convalescence, and offering comfort to the dying. In civilian life she became a housewife; her occupation was listed as "none" when she was enumerated in the census of 1921. For her part, Mona Gibson became a wife and eventually a mother in the Glebe, flanked by two servants in her new domestic theatre of operations.[52]

After the war, Catholic bishops spent much of their time either mending fences with their Catholic neighbours or asserting their rights when under fire from the Orange Order or zealously Protestant politicians. Bishop Fallon and Archbishop McNeil continued to serve their respective dioceses for nearly fifteen years. Fallon remained in London for the remainder of his career, and although he smoothed over the linguistic tensions in the diocese, he was still able to stir the pot over the issue of separate schools. Perhaps his finest hour for Catholic education came in 1922, when he spearheaded the movement to extend public funding to Catholic secondary schools. On 11 February 1922, sponsored by the Catholic Women's League, he gave a three-hour oration to a packed Massey Hall in Toronto, demanding "constitutional rights" not "sectarian privileges" for Catholic schools in Ontario. Arguing for more equitable funding, in his typical bombastic style, Fallon took "mudslinging" journalists to task for their misreading of the historical facts about Catholic schools. His passion helped to launch the legal challenge made by Tiny Township, in Simcoe County, for educational grants to be extended to Catholic high schools. Complications arising from diabetes took Fallon's life in 1931. McNeil, on the other hand, became known for his moderation and his concern for working-class Canadians and immigrants. He forged close ties with Toronto's Jewish community, pressured governments for equity in hiring practices when it came to religion, and promoted greater understanding between Catholics and Protestants in Toronto and the rural areas of his diocese. When he died in 1934, the usually Orange-sympathizing *Toronto Telegram* eulogized: "In the life of the community he was respected and admired as a patriot, who was always ready and anxious to cooperate in any movement for the public good."[53] After the war, both bishops demonstrated the leadership that had been typical of each during the war: Fallon, the strong public advocate of Catholic rights, and McNeil the calm peacemaker, using the power of his reasoned, measured, and humble personality to advance the Catholic cause.

Perhaps the oddest vignette of the Irish Catholic contribution to the war is fictional but plausible. It may have taken place in Halifax after the demobilization of troops in 1919. The story may have transpired like this: a stranger walking in St Patrick's Parish in North Halifax and wandered north on to Gottingen Street, overcome by his curiosity to examine the damage left by the Halifax Explosion. On route he encountered two demobilized soldiers within a space of a few minutes. By a twist of fate, the soldiers both bore the same name. The first, John Patrick Joseph Meagher, a local Irish Catholic, had lived on Charles Street in the North End of city and was a member of St Patrick's Parish. In striking up a conversation with the young Meagher, our stranger may have learned that at the age of eighteen, Meagher volunteered for the 40th Battalion, a Nova Scotia unit in which 211 recruits listed their home addresses as Halifax. Meagher stood a diminutive 5'3" and had a fair complexion, gray eyes, and light brown hair. He had worked as a labourer at the Nova Scotia Furnishing Company, and as an unmarried man had little to risk socially as he embarked on the greatest adventure of his life. He had served in France, was wounded in 1917, and was now engaged to sweetheart Catherine Stroud.[54] Within minutes our stranger bumped into a second John Patrick Meagher, who told him he was living at 26 West Street, and then told him he was eight years senior to the first Meagher whom our stranger had just encountered. As the conversation bounced around issues ranging from Irish Home Rule, to the war, and the reconstruction of Halifax's North End, the older Meagher admitted to the stranger that he had refused to enlist. Only slightly taller than his namesake, and equally as fair, the elder Meagher had continued his work as a labourer and had failed to respond to his conscription notice under the terms of the Military Service Act in November 1917. Arrested as a defaulter in August 1918, the elder Meagher was escorted to the Aldershot Camp, where he was placed in the 1st Nova Scotia Depot Battalion until war's end. These parallel meetings that morning in 1919 may well have left the stranger scratching his head, wondering which Meagher actually represented the Irish Catholic Canadian approach to the Great War that had just ended.

The different tales of two John Patrick Meaghers might raise serious questions for any casual observer of Canada's Irish Catholic history: one man boasted a record of service in compliance with the Empire's call, the other utter contempt and defiance for military service. Given the context of the deteriorating situation in Ireland, the evident linguistic tension lingering in Canada after the war, and the outpouring of grief at so many killed and wounded in four and half years of fighting it may be reasonable to ask where the Irish Catholics really stood during the war and at its finish. The answer to this puzzle is complicated, and certainly there is much evidence to suggest that both Meaghers embodied complexity of the Irish Catholic story. When all the evidence was examined and weighed, however, it was the younger Meagher who probably best represented the general norms of Irish Catholic male behaviour in Canada throughout the war. Ned Murray would have agreed.

Notes

ABBREVIATIONS

Religious Archives

AAD	Archives of the Archdiocese of Dublin
AAH	Archives of the Archdiocese of Halifax
AAK	Archives of the Archdiocese of Kingston
AAM	Archives of the Archdiocese of Montreal
AAO	Archives of the Archdiocese of Ottawa
AAQ	Archives of the Archdiocese of Quebec
AASB	Archives of the Archdiocese of Saint Boniface
AAV	Archives of the Archdiocese of Vancouver
AAW	Archives of the Archdiocese of Winnipeg
ACSSJ	Archives of the Congregation of the Sisters of St. Joseph (Toronto)
ADA	Archives of the Diocese of Antigonish
ADC	Archives of Diocese of Calgary
ADCh	Archives of the Diocese of Charlottetown
ADH	Archives of the Diocese of Hamilton
ADL	Archives of the Diocese of London
ADP	Archives of the Diocese of Peterborough
ADPb	Archives of the Diocese of Pembroke
ARCAT	Archives of the Roman Catholic Archdiocese of Toronto
ASJUCP	Archives of the Society of Jesus, Upper Canada Province
ASV-ADC	Archivio Segreto Vaticano, Apostolic Delegate, Canada

Public and University Archives

AO	Archives of Ontario
BIA	Beaton Institute Archives, Cape Breton University
CTA	City of Toronto Archives
CUA	Concordia University Archives
LAC	Library and Archives Canada
NLI	National Library of Ireland
NPRC	National Personnel Records Centre, LAC
NSA	Nova Scotia Archives
QUA	Queen's University Archives
TCDSBA	Toronto Catholic District School Board Archives
USMCA	University of St Michael's College Archives

INTRODUCTION

1 *Globe* (Toronto), 10 November 1899.
2 *Catholic Register* (Toronto), 20 July 1899. Criticism of Fitzpatrick came 10 November 1899.
3 Cecil Houston and William Smyth, *Irish Emigration and Canadian Settlement: Patterns, Links and Letters* (Toronto: University of Toronto Press, 1990), 337–40.
4 David M. Emmonds, *Beyond the American Pale: The Irish in the West* (Norman: University of Oklahoma Press, 2010), 20–1.
5 John Edward FitzGerald, "Michael Anthony Fleming and Ultramontanism in Irish-Newfoundland Roman Catholicism, 1829–1850," CCHA *Historical Studies* 64 (1998): 37–44.
6 John S. Moir, "The Problem of a Double Minority: Some Reflections on the Development of the English-speaking Catholic Church in Canada in the 19th Century," *Social History / Histoire sociale* 7 (April 1971): 53–67.
7 Mark Starowicz, producer, *Canada: A People's History*, Episode 8, *The Great Enterprise*, (Toronto: Canadian Broadcasting Corporation, 2000).
8 Simon Jolivet, *Le vert et le bleu : Identité québécoise et identité irlandaise au tournant de XX siècle* (Montréal: Les Presses de l'Université de Montréal, 2011).
9 William G Davis, "Thomas D'Arcy McGee: Irish Founder of the Canadian Nation," in *The Untold Story: The Irish in Canada*, ed. Robert O'Driscoll and Lorna Reynolds (Toronto: Celtic Arts of Canada, 1988), 453–63.
10 A good and diverse collection of essays on the subject of Irish nationalism in Canada is David Wilson, ed., *Irish Nationalism in Canada* (Montreal & Kingston: McGill-Queen's University Press, 2009). See also Brian Jenkins,

Irish Nationalism and the British State: From Repeal to Revolutionary Nationalism (Montreal & Kingston: McGill-Queen's University Press, 2006), 143–88.

11 This "exile" motif has been adopted in other histories of the Irish, including Emmonds, *Beyond the American Pale*, 8–9, and Kerby Miller, *Emigrants and Exiles: Ireland and the Irish Exodus to North America* (New York: Oxford University Press, 1985).

12 *Canadian Catholic Readers*, Fourth Book (Toronto: Copp Clark, 1899).

13 Michael Cottrell, "John Joseph Leddy and the Battle for the Soul of the Catholic Church in the West," Canadian Catholic Historical Association, *Historical Studies* 61 (1995): 41–51; Mark G. McGowan, *The Waning of the Green: Catholics, the Irish and Identity in Toronto, 1887–1922* (Montreal & Kingston: McGill-Queen's University Press, 1999), 215–6; R.J. Manion, *Life Is an Adventure* (Toronto: The Ryerson Press, 1936); Jolivet, *Le vert et le bleu*, 187.

14 Padraig O'Siadhail, *Katherine Hughes: A Life and a Journey* (Halifax: Penumbra Press, 2014), 30–2; Robert McLaughlin, *Irish Canadian Conflict and the Struggle for Independence* (Toronto: University of Toronto Press, 2013).

15 Allan Rowe, "Prairie Shamrock: Irish Settlement and Identity in Western Canada, 1870s–1930s" (PhD diss., University of Alberta, 2008); Sherry Olson and Patricia Thornton, *Peopling the North American City: Montreal, 1840–1900* (Montreal & Kingston: McGill-Queen's University Press, 2010); William Jenkins, *Between Raid and Rebellion: The Irish in Buffalo and Toronto, 1867–1916* (Montreal & Kingston: McGill-Queen's University Press, 2013); Patrick Mannion, "The Irish Diaspora in Comparative Perspective, St John's Newfoundland, Halifax, Nova Scotia, and Portland, Maine, 1880–1923" (PhD diss., University of Toronto, 2013).

16 Malcolm Campbell, *Ireland's New Worlds: Immigrants, Politics, and Society in the United States and Australia, 1815–1922* (Madison: The University of Wisconsin Press, 2008), 168–70.

17 J.L. Granatstein and J.M. Hitsman, *Broken Promises: A History of Conscription in Canada* (Toronto: Copp Clark Pitman, 1985); Simon Jolivet, "French-speaking Catholics in Quebec and the First World War," in *Canadian Churches and the First World War*, ed. Gordon L. Heath (Hamilton: McMaster Divinity College Press and Wipf and Stock, 2014), 75–101; J.L. Granatstein, "Conscription in the Great War," in *Canada and the First World War: Essays in Honour of Robert Craig Brown*, ed. David MacKenzie (Toronto: University of Toronto Press, 2005), 62–75; Carl Berger, ed., *Conscription 1917*, Canadian Historical Readings 8 (Toronto: University of Toronto Press, n.d.); Elizabeth Armstrong, *The Crisis of Quebec, 1914–1918* (Toronto: McClelland and Stewart, Carleton Library Series, 1974 [1937]); Robert Craig Brown and Donald

Loveridge, "Unrequited Faith: Recruiting the CEF, 1914–1918," *Revue international d'histoire militaire* 51 (1982): 53–79.

18 René Durocher, "Henri Bourassa, Les Evêques et la Guerre de 1914–1918," Canadian Historical Association, *Historical Papers* (1971): 248–75.

19 Robert Choquette, *Language and Religion: A History of English–French Conflict in Ontario* (Ottawa: University of Ottawa Press, 1975); Marilyn Barber, "The Ontario Schools Issue: Sources of Conflict," *Canadian Historical Review* 47 (September 1966): 227–48; Margaret Prang, "Clerics and Politicians, and the Bilingual Schools Issue in Ontario, 1910–1917," *Canadian Historical Review* 41 (December 1960): 281–307; John E. Zucchi, *The View from Rome: Archbishop Stagni's 1915 Reports on the Ontario Bilingual Schools Question* (Montreal & Kingston: McGill-Queen's University Press, 2002); Chad Gaffield, *Language, Schooling and Cultural Conflict: The Origins of the French-Language Issue in Ontario* (Montreal & Kingston: McGill-Queen's University Press, 1988).

20 Susan Mann Trofimenkoff, *The Dream of Nation: A Social and Intellectual History of Quebec* (Toronto: Gage, 1983), 203.

21 Richard S. Grayson, *Belfast Boys: How Unionists and Nationalists Fought and Died Together in the First World War* (London: Bloomsbury, 2009), xvi.

22 William D. Grant, ed., *Christendom Anno Domini MDCCCCI* (Toronto: William Briggs, 1902), 1:81.

23 Desmond Morton, *When Your Number's Up: The Canadian Soldier in the First World War* (Toronto: Random House, 1993), 278; Terry Copp, "The Military Effort, 1914–1918," in *Canada and the First World War*, ed. David MacKenzie, 37.

24 Jolivet, *Le vert et le bleu*, 213–49.

25 I.J.E Daniel and D.A. Casey, *For God and Country: A History of the Canadian Knights of Columbus Catholic Army Huts* (n.p: n.p., 1922).

26 Scott W. See, *Riots in New Brunswick: Orange Nativism and Social Violence in the 1840s* (Toronto: University of Toronto Press, 1993); Neil Gregor Smith, "Religious Tension in Pre-Confederation Politics," *Canadian Journal of Theology* 9 (October 1963): 248–62; A.J.B. Johnston, "Nativism in Nova Scotia: Anti-Irish Ideology in a Mid-Nineteenth-Century British Colony," in *The Irish in Atlantic Canada, 1780–1900*, ed. Thomas Power (Fredericton: New Ireland Press, 1991), 23–9; William J. Smyth, *Toronto, the Belfast of Canada: The Orange Order and the Shaping of a Municipal Culture* (Toronto: University of Toronto Press, 2015).

27 Peter Vronsky, *The American Fenian Invasion and the 1866 Battle That Made Canada* (Toronto: Penguin, 2011).

28 Brian P. Clarke, *Piety and Nationalism: Lay Voluntary Associations and the Cre-*

ation of an Irish Catholic Community in Toronto* (Montreal & Kingston: McGill-Queen's University Press, 1993).

29 J.R. Miller, *Equal Rights: The Jesuits' Estates Act Controversy* (Montreal & Kingston: McGill-Queen's University Press, 1979); Lovell C, Clark, *The Guibord Affair* (Toronto: Holt, Rinehart & Winston, 1971).

CHAPTER ONE

1 Anna Zurakowska, *A Concise Guide to Canadian Kashuby* (Barry's Bay, ON: Polish Heritage Institute Kaszuby, 2008); Joshua C. Blank, *Creating Kashubia: History, Memory, and Identity in Canada's First Polish Community* (Montreal and Kingston: McGill-Queen's University Press, 2016).

2 Whelan family monument, St Michael's Catholic Cemetery, Douglas, Renfrew County, Ontario.

3 *Fourth Census of Canada*, 1901, Admaston Township, Renfrew County, pp. 11–12. The 1901 census indicates that Stephen came to Canada in 1847 and lists his birth year as 1823. Carol Bennett, ed., *Founding Families of Admaston, Horton, and Renfrew Village* (Renfrew: Juniper Books, 1992), 79–80. Bennett lists Stephen Whelan as having been born in 1829. The family gravestone at St Michael's Cemetery in Douglas, Ontario, indicates that he died in 1906 at the age of 81, which would make the year of birth indicated in the census closer to the real date of birth than that given by Bennett. The family landed at Farrell's Landing (now Castleford) and lived in Horton Township briefly before settling in Lot 6, Concession 9, Admaston Township.

4 *Eganville Leader*, 9 March 1906; www.geni.com/people/Stephen-Whelan/6000000016796317557, accessed 4 January 2017; *Acts of Parliament of the Dominion of Canada*, vol. 1 (Ottawa: Brown Chamberlain, Queen's Printer, 1888), 51 Victoria, c. 65, *An Act to Incorporate the Ottawa and Parry Sound Railway Company*, 4 May 1888, 66–72.

5 *Fourth Census of Canada*, 1901, Ontario, Renfrew County South, Admaston Township, 11. The census lists her birthday as 19 March 1891, although her attestation paper claims 19 March 1889: LAC, RG9, Attestation Paper, Mona Whelan, 3 June 1915.

6 *Eganville Leader*, 27 August 1915.

7 *Toronto Star*, 3 November 1917.

8 Cecil Houston and William J. Smyth, *Irish Emigration and Canadian Settlement: Patterns, Links, and Letters* (Toronto: University of Toronto Press, 1990), 3–9, 338–9.

9 George Casey, "Irish Culture in Newfoundland," in *Talamh an Eisc: Canadian*

and Irish Essays, ed. Cyril Byrne and Margaret Harry (Halifax: Nimbus Publishing, 1986), 211.

10 John J. Mannion, "Old World Antecedents, New World Adaptations: Inistioge (Co. Kilkenny) Immigrants in Newfoundland," in *The Irish in Atlantic Canada – 1780–1900*, ed. Thomas P. Power (Fredericton: New Ireland Press, 1991), 32; Houston and Smyth, *Irish Emigration and Canadian Settlement*, 192. For more information on land use and the differences between Ireland and the New World, see John J. Mannion, *Irish Settlements in Eastern Canada: A Study of Cultural Transfer and Adaptation* (Toronto: University of Toronto Press, 1974), 74–5.

11 J.J. Mannion, "Old World Antecedents, New World Adaptations," 30–95.

12 Houston and Smyth, *Irish Emigration and Canadian Settlement*, 69 and 90; Terrence M. Punch, "Finding Our Irish," *Nova Scotia Historical Review* 6, no. 1 (1986): 47; Canadian Catholic Historical Association, *Historical Studies*, Occasional Paper 81 (2015). This is a special edition of the annual journal titled "Irish Catholics in Halifax from the Napoleonic Wars to the Great War," ed. Mark G. McGowan and Michael E. Vance. To date it is the most comprehensive anthology on the Irish Catholics in Halifax.

13 *Census of Canada, 1901*, vol. 1, table XIV, 422–3. A.A. MacKenzie, *The Irish in Cape Breton* (Antigonish: Formac Publishing, 1979), 23–4. See also Canadian Catholic Historical Association *Historical Studies* 81 (2015), ed. Mark G. McGowan and Michael Vance, "The Irish Catholics of Halifax, from the Napoleonic Wars to the Great War."

14 Peter Ludlow, "'Disturbed by the Irish Howl': Irish and Scottish Catholics in Nova Scotia, 1844–1860," CCHA *Historical Studies*, Occasional Paper 81 (2015): 32–55.

15 Peter Toner, "The Origins of the New Brunswick Irish, 1851," *Journal of Canadian Studies* 23, no. 1–2 (1988): 104–9; Peter Toner, "The Irish of New Brunswick at Mid-Century: The 1851 Census," in *New Ireland Remembered: Historical Essays on the Irish in New Brunswick*, ed. P.M. Toner (Fredericton: New Ireland Press, 1989).

16 Scott W. See, *Riots in New Brunswick: Orange Nativism and Social Violence in the 1840s* (Toronto: University of Toronto Press, 1993).

17 Robert Choquette, "English-French Relations in the Catholic Community," in *Creed and Culture: The Place of English-speaking Catholics in Canadian Society, 1750–1930*, ed. Terrence Murphy and Gerald Stortz (Montreal and Kingston: McGill-Queen's University Press, 1993), 7–9; Sheila Andrew, "Gender and Nationalism: Acadians, Quebecois, and Irish in New

Brunswick Nineteenth Century Colleges and Convent Schools, 1854–1888," CCHA *Historical Studies*, 68 (2002): 7–23.

18 Peter Toner, "The Irish of New Brunswick at Mid-Century: The 1851 Census," and T.W Acheson, "The Irish Community in Saint John, 1815–1850," in *New Ireland Remembered: Historical Essays on the Irish in New Brunswick*, ed. P.M. Toner (Fredericton: New Ireland Press, 1989): 106–132 and 27–54.

19 Brendan O'Grady, *Exiles and Islanders: The Irish Settlers of Prince Edward Island* (Montreal and Kingston: McGill-Queen's University Press, 2004).

20 Rusty Bitterman, "Agrarian Protest and Cultural Transfer: Irish Immigrants and the Escheat Movement on Prince Edward Island," in *The Irish in Atlantic Canada*, ed. Thomas P. Power, 96–106.

21 Robert Grace, "Irish Immigration and Settlement in a Catholic City: Quebec, 1842–1861," *Canadian Historical Review* 84, no. 2 (June 2003): 217–52.

22 Wendy Cameron, "Selecting Peter Robinson's Irish Immigrants," *Histoire sociale / Social History* 9, 17 (May/mai 1976): 29–46.

23 All figures are derived from LAC, *Colonial Office papers*, reel 1746.

24 Donald Harman Akenson, *The Irish in Ontario: A Study in Rural History* (Montreal & Kingston: McGill-Queen's University Press, 1999), 29–32.

25 Helen I. Cowan, *British Emigration to British North America* (Toronto: University of Toronto Press, 1961), 288.

26 LAC, *Colonial Office papers*, 384/82, 175. The precise figure for New Brunswick is 16,589. Other colonies received fewer: 2000 emigrants disembarked in Nova Scotia and Cape Breton; 993 in Newfoundland; and 536 in Prince Edward Island. See Mark G. McGowan, "A Tale of Two Famines: Famine Memory in Nova Scotia, Canada," in *Irish Hunger and Immigration: Myth, Memory, and Memorialization*, ed. Patrick Fitzgerald, Christine Kinealy and Gerard Moran (West Haven, CT: Quinnipiac University Press, 2015): 57–68.

27 Houston and Smyth, *Irish Emigration and Canadian Settlement*, 34.

28 William A. Spray, "'The Difficulties Came Upon Us Like a Thunderbolt": Immigrants and Fever in New Brunswick in 1847," *The Irish in Atlantic Canada – 1780–1900*, ed. Thomas P. Power (Fredericton: New Ireland Press, 1991), 124. The figure presented is lower, namely about 1,600 or more, in Wright, "Partridge Island," *The Irish in Atlantic Canada – 1780–1900*, ed. Thomas P. Power (Fredericton: New Ireland Press, 1991 136, although this is below the official account for reasons unknown.

29 Houston and Smyth, *Irish Emigration and Canadian Settlement*, 21.

30 Mark G. McGowan, *Death or Canada: The Irish Famine Migration to Toronto,*

1847 (Ottawa: Novalis, 2009), 97. See also Gilbert Tucker, "The Famine Immigration to Canada, 1847," *American Historical Review* 36 (April, 1933): 533–49.

31 Houston and Smyth, *Irish Emigration and Canadian Settlement*, 4–5, 21–2. Recent unpublished research by Kathleen McGowan on Admaston Township, Renfrew County, and by Derek Nile Tucker on Hibbert Township, Perth County, reveal that there was significant rural settlement by Famine migrants by 1851. Derek Nile Tucker, "Successful Pioneers: Irish Catholic Settlers in the Township of Hibbert, Ontario, 1845–1847," (MA thesis, McMaster University, 2001).

32 The most complete accounts of Irish migration to the Americas are found in Akenson, *The Irish in Ontario*, 3–47; Houston and Smyth, *Irish Emigration and Canadian Settlement*, 13–42, and Kerby Miller, *Emigrants and Exiles: Ireland and the Irish Exodus to North America* (New York: Oxford University Press, 1985), 103–30. See also Kevin Kenny, *The American Irish: A History* (Harlow, UK: Pearson Educational Ltd., 2000), 105.

33 Mark G. McGowan, "Between King, Kaiser, and Canada," in *Irish Nationalism in Canada*, ed. David Wilson (Montreal and Kingston: McGill-Queen's University Press, 2009), 97–120.

34 David Wilson, ed., *Irish Nationalism in Canada*. William Jenkins, *Between Raid and Rebellion: The Irish in Buffalo and Toronto, 1867–1916* (Montreal and Kingston: McGill-Queen's University Press, 2013); Brian P. Clarke, *Piety and Nationalism: Lay Voluntary Associations and the Creation of an Irish-Catholic Community in Toronto, 1850–1895* (Montreal and Kingston: McGill-Queen's University Press, 1993); Michael Cottrell, "Irish Catholic Political Leadership in Toronto 1855–1882: A Study in Ethnic Politics" (PhD diss., University of Saskatchewan, 1988); Robert McLaughlin, *Irish Canadian Conflict and the Struggle for Irish Independence, 1912–1925* (Toronto: University of Toronto Press, 2013); Padraig O'Siadhail, *Katherine Hughes: A Life and a Journey* (Ottawa: Penumbra Press, 2014); Brian Jenkins, *Irish Nationalism and the British State* (Montreal and Kingston: McGill-Queen's University Press, 2009), 143–88; Richard Davis, "Irish Nationalism in Manitoba, 1870–1922," in *The Untold Story: The Irish in Canada*, ed. Robert O'Driscoll and Lorna Reynolds (Toronto: Celtic Arts of Canada, 1988), vol. 1: 393–416; Patrick Mannion, "Halifax Catholics 'Patriotic Work': Responses to Irish Nationalism," in *Historical Studies*, Occasional Paper 81 (2015); Simon Jolivet, *Le vert et le bleu: Identité Québécoise et identité ilandaise au tournant du XXe siècle* (Montreal: Les Presses de Université de Montréal, 2011); Mark G. McGowan, *The Waning of the Green: Catholics, the Irish, and Identity in Toronto, 1887–1922* (Montreal

and Kingston: McGill-Queen's University Press, 1999); Mark G. McGowan, "Canadian Catholics, Loyalty, and the British Empire, 1763–1901," in *Loyalism and the Formation of the British World, 1775–1914*, ed. Frank O'Gorman and Allan Blackstock (Woodbridge, UK: The Boydell Press, 2014): 201–22.

35 David Wilson, "Introduction," in *Irish Nationalism in Canada*, 3–8.

36 *Catholic Record*, 13 July 1901.

37 *Catholic Register* (Toronto), 7 October 1897.

38 George Sheppard, "God Save the Green: Fenianism and Fellowship in Victorian Ontario," *Histoire sociale / Social History* 20, no. 39 (1987): 129–44; Brian P. Clarke, *Piety and nationalism: Lay Voluntary Associations and the Creation of an Irish Catholic Community in Toronto, 1850–1895* (Montreal and Kingston: McGill-Queen's University Press, 1993), 168–98. See also Peter Toner, "The Rise of Irish Nationalism in Canada, 1858–1884" (PhD diss., National University of Ireland, 1974), ii–iv, 107–8, 121–2.

39 For a complete and detailed analysis of the battle of Ridgeway, see Peter Vronsky, *Ridgeway: The American Fenian Invasion and the 1866 Battle that Made Canada* (Toronto: Allen Lane/Penguin, 2011).

40 ARCAT, John Joseph Lynch papers, Circular Letters, 9 March 1866.

41 *Ottawa Times*, 19 March 1866.

42 David M. Wilson, "Was Patrick James Whelan a Fenian and Did He Assassinate Thomas D'Arcy McGee?" in *Irish Nationalism in Canada*, 52–82.

43 Cited in David Wilson, *Thomas D'Arcy McGee*, vol. 2, *The Extreme Moderate, 1857–1868* (Montreal and Kingston: McGill-Queen's University Press, 2011), 100.

44 David A Wilson, *Thomas D'Arcy McGee*, vol. 1, *Passion, Reason and Politics, 1825–1857* (Montreal and Kingston: McGill-Queen's University Press, 2008), 354.

45 Stanley W. Horrall, "Canada and the Irish Question: A Study of the Canadian Response to Irish Home Rule, 1882–1893" (MA thesis, Carleton University, Ottawa, 1966).

46 Mark G. McGowan, *The Waning of the Green: Catholics, the Irish and Identity in Toronto, 1887–1922* (Montreal and Kingston: McGill-Queen's University Press, 1999), 195–7. John Redmond's correspondence archived in the National Library of Ireland Manuscripts Division contains a substantial correspondence with Canadian supporters and politicians. NLI, Redmond papers, MS 15, 235/2 1897–1915, Canada.

47 NLI, Redmond papers, MS 15, 235/2, Letter from D'Arcy Scott (Ottawa) to John Redmond, 4 February 1902, and MS 15, 265/2, "Memorandum: History of the Government of Canada," 1918, 9 pages.

48 *Catholic Register*, 27 March 1913.

49 *New Freeman*, 30 May 1914.

50 Jane G.V. McGaughey, *Ulster's Men: Protestant Unionist Masculinities and Militarization in Northern Ireland, 1912–1923* (Montreal and Kingston: McGill-Queen's University Press, 2012):41–62.

51 *Casket*, 26 March and 30 July 1914 and 12 August 1915.

52 *Globe*, 28 and 30 September 1912.

53 *New Freeman*, 26 September 1914.

54 *Catholic Register*, 19 March 1914.

55 *Globe*, 17 September 1914; *New Freeman*, 26 August 1914; *Catholic Register*, 20 November and 11 December 1913 and 30 July 1914; *Northwest Review*, 29 May 1915.

56 *New Freeman*, 3 April 1915.

57 *Catholic Register*, 14 February 1901.

58 *Irish Canadian*, 31 January 1901.

59 *Catholic Register*, 28 May 1914.

60 This analysis is based on a sampling of issues: 2, 9, 16 and 30 May 1914; 1, 8 and 15 August 1914. McLaughlin was reassigned to a parish in 1916. *New Freeman*, 25 March 1916.

61 *New Freeman*, 30 January 1915.

62 *Casket*, masthead, 1914.

63 *Canadian Freeman*, 1 April 1914.

64 Ibid., 8 December 1915 and 15 March 1916. There had been repeated calls for people to pay their subscriptions. The paper was still in trouble in 1925 when the newly appointed manager, Alexander Givens, reported to Spratt that he found "business chaos" at the paper upon his arrival and $7,053.90 in unpaid subscriptions. AAK, Michael Joseph Spratt papers, HI IC3, Alexander Givens to Spratt, 31 December 1925. Givens had been in control for a year and had raised subscriptions from under 4000 to 5094 by year's end.

65 *Catholic Record*, 21 March 1903.

66 Ibid., 8 August 1914.

67 *McKim's Directory of Canadian Publications* (Toronto: A. McKim, 1899 and 1909).

68 *McKim's Directory of Canadian Publications* (Toronto: A. McKim, 1909 and 1919).

69 LAC, Wilfrid Laurier papers, Microfilm Reel 779, Walter Boland to Laurier, 24 September 1900, p. 49447.

70 *Catholic Record*, 28 January 1915.

71 ARCAT, Archbishop John Walsh papers, Director's Report of the *Catholic Reg-*

ister Printing and Publishing Company, 31 December 1895. *Canadian Newspaper Directory* (1899), 107; 1905 (108).

72 McGowan, *The Waning of the Green*, 187–92.

73 *Northwest Review*, 12 September 1885. See additional details about the early years of the paper in the *50th Anniversary Special Edition*, 1935.

74 Ibid., 12 September 1885.

75 Ibid., 19 September 1885.

76 Ibid., 21 June 1919 and 17 February and 30 October 1920.

77 Ibid., 21 May 1921.

78 *Northwest Review*, 50th Anniversary Edition, 1935, 8.

79 Terrence Punch, "The Irish Catholic: Halifax's First Minority Group," *Nova Scotia Historical Quarterly* 10 (1980).

80 Catholic scholars defined the transformation of the bread and wine into the actual body and blood of Christ during the consecration ritual within the Mass as Transubstantiation. In the actions of the priest celebrating the Mass, the substance of bread and wine is replaced by the substance of Christ, while the accidents of bread and wine (their physical appearance) remains the same. The doctrine of Transubstantiation came to symbolize, in the minds of Protestants, the profound theological errors and doctrinal corruptions within Roman Catholicism.

81 Michael Cottrell, "St Patrick's Day Parades in Nineteenth-Century Toronto: A Study of Immigrant Adjustment and Elite Control," *Histoire sociale / Social History* 25, no. 49 (mai/ May 1992): 57–73; Scott See, "The Fortunes of the Orange Order in 19th Century New Brunswick," in *New Ireland Remembered: Historical Essays on the Irish in New Brunswick*, ed. Peter M. Toner (Fredericton: New Ireland Press, 1989); A.J.B. Johnston, "Nativism in Nova Scotia: Anti-Irish Ideology in a Mid-Nineteenth Century British Colony," in Power, *Irish in Atlantic Canada*, 23–9.

82 Martin J. Galvin, "The Jubilee Riots in Toronto," CCHA *Report* 26 (1959): 93–107; Gregory S. Kealey, "The Orange Order in Toronto: Religious Riot and the Working Class," in *Essays in Canadian Working Class History*, ed. Gregory S. Kealey and Peter Warrian (Toronto: McClelland and Stewart, 1976), 13–34.

83 Franklin Walker, *Catholic Education and Politics in Upper Canada* (Toronto: English Catholic Education Association of Ontario, 1955); Michael Power, *A Promise Fulfilled: Highlights in the Political History of Catholic Separate Schools in Ontario* (Toronto: Ontario Catholic Schools Trustees' Association, 2002), 1–72.

84 Paul Crunican, *Priests and Politicians: Manitoba Schools and the Election of*

1896 (Toronto: University of Toronto Press, 1974); Arthur Silver, *The French Canadian Idea of Confederation, 1864–1900* (Toronto: University of Toronto Press, 1982).

85 Manoly Lupul, *The Roman Catholic Church and the Northwest School Question: A Study in Church–State Relations in Western Canada* (Toronto: University of Toronto Press, 1974); James R. Miller, *Equal Rights: The Jesuits' Estates Act Controversy* (Montreal and Kingston: McGill-Queen's University Press, 1979); E.F. Henderson, et al., *Historical Sketch of the Separate Schools of Ontario and the Catholic Separate School Minority Report* (Toronto: The English Catholic Separate School Minority Report, 1950).

86 *Canadian Catholic Readers*, Fourth Book (Toronto: Copp Clark, 1899); McGowan, *Waning of the Green*, 135–7.

87 Roberto Perin, *Rome in Canada: The Vatican and Canadian Affairs in the Late Victorian Age* (Toronto: University of Toronto Press, 1990), 187–213; ASV-ADC 157.37, Cardinal Rampolla, Secretary of State to Falconio, 1 September 1900; Mark G. McGowan, "Rethinking Catholic-Protestant Relations in Canada: The Episcopal Reports of 1900–1901," CCHA *Historical Studies* 59 (1992): 11–32.

88 ASV-ADC, 157.37, Louis Nazaire Bégin, Archbishop of Quebec to Falconio, 29 November 1900; Paul Bruchési, Archbishop of Montreal to Falconio, 30 November 1900; Joseph-Thomas Duhamel, Archbishop of Ottawa to Falconio, 21 November 1900. Some of the suffragans reported minor problems in rural areas, but in all the reports Quebec was characterized as a Catholic fortress.

89 Recent works such as William Smyth, *Toronto, The Belfast of Canada: The Orange Order and the Shaping of Municipal Culture* (Toronto: University of Toronto Press, 2015) continue to emphasize the Orange character of cities such as Toronto in the early twentieth century; nevertheless, there are hard data to suggest that Irish Catholics could live full and abundant lives and advance socially even in the Belfast of Canada, which was a much milder sociopolitical milieu than its namesake.

90 ASV-ADC, 157.37, O'Brien to Falconio, 29 November 1900; Cameron to Falconio, 15 January 1901; James Charles MacDonald, Charlottetown to Falconio, 19 November 1900; Timothy Casey, Saint John, to Falconio, 26 November 1900; Thomas Barry, Coadjutor of Chatham, NB, to Falconio, 5 December 1900.

91 ASV-ADC, 157.37, Macdonnell to Falconio, 21 January 1901. See also Richard O'Connor to Falconio, n.d., and Gauthier to Falconio, 12 December 1900.

92 ASV-ADC, 157.37 Denis O'Connor to Falconio, 20 November 1900, McEvay

to Falconio, 19 November 1900, and Thomas Dowling to Falconio, 8 December 1900.

93 ASV-ADC, 157.37, Denis O'Connor to Falconio, 20 November 1900.

94 ASV-ADC, 157.37, Adelard Langevin, Archbishop of St Boniface to Falconio, 5 February 1901; Emile Legal, Bishop of St Albert to Falconio, 15 November 1900; Mark G. McGowan, "'A portion for the vanquished': Roman Catholics and the Ukrainian Catholic Church," in *Canada's Ukrainians: Negotiating an Identity*, ed. Lubomyr Luciuk and Stella Hryniuk (Toronto: University of Toronto Press, 1991), 218–37.

95 ASV-ADC, 157.37, Langevin to Falconio, 5 February 1901.

96 Mark George McGowan, "A Watchful Eye: The Catholic Church Extension Society and Ukrainian Catholic Immigrants, 1908–1930," in *Canadian Protestant and Roman Catholic Missions, 1820s–1960s: Historical Essays in Honour of John Webster Grant*, ed. John S. Moir and C.T. McIntire (New York: Peter Lang, 1988), 221–44.

97 LAC, MG 27 II C 1, Sir Charles Fitzpatrick papers, vol. 12, Copy of letter from Archbishop Fergus Patrick McEvay to Archbishop Louis-Nazaire Bégin, 27 September 1910, p. 5816.

98 Mark G. McGowan, "Toronto's English-speaking Catholics, Immigration and the Making of a Canadian Catholic Identity, 1900–30," in *Creed and Culture: The Place of English-speaking Catholics in Canadian Society, 1750–1930*, ed. Terrence Murphy and Gerald Stortz (Montreal and Kingston: McGill-Queen's University Press, 1993), 204–46.

99 AASB, Adelard Langevin papers, Copy of a letter from Langevin to Archbishop Louis-Nazaire Bégin, Quebec, 21 August 1908; Langevin to Bégin, 20 September 1909; Langevin to Father Thomas Dauson, OMI, 24 October 1912; and Langevin to the Extension Society, 13 January 1913.

100 *Catholic Register*, 24 June 1915. While eulogizing the late Adélard Langevin, Alfred Burke could not help but add: "Propinquity to the United States, the preponderance of Britain in the world, the commercial character of this age and of the age to come, will make for a common vehicle of intercourse and that will not be French but English ... The way of our statesmen and Churchmen is bestrewn with difficulty but it must be kept clear for the advance of British civilization and effective religion."

101 Raymond Huel, "The Irish-French Conflict in Catholic Episcopal Nominations: The Western Sees and the Struggle for Domination Within the Church," CCHA *Study Sessions* 42 (1975): 50–69. This article remains one of the best explorations of the struggle between anglophone and francophone factions for control of the Canadian Church.

102 Marilyn Barber, "The Ontario Schools Issue: Sources of Conflict," *Canadian Historical Review* 47 (September 1966): 227–48; Margaret Prang, "Clerics, Politicians, and the Bilingual Schools Issue in Ontario, 1910–1917," *Canadian Historical Review* 41 (December 1960): 281–307.
103 Robert Choquette, *Language and Religion: A History of English-French Conflict in Ontario* (Ottawa: University of Ottawa Press, 1975): 249–58.
104 AO, James Pliny Whitney papers, Fergus McEvay to Whitney, 15 February 1910 and copy, Whitney to McEvay, 9 March 1910.
105 ARCAT, AE. 0155, McNeil papers, Education, Copy of Letter from Michael Fallon to Charles Hugh Gauthier (Kingston), 18 August 1910; John Zucchi, *The View From Rome: Archbishop Stagni's 1915 Reports on the Ontario Bilingual Schools Question* (Montreal & Kingston: McGill-Queen's University Press, 2002), xvi–xix.
106 Robert Choquette, *La Foi Gardienne de la Lange en Ontario, 1900–1950* (Montreal : Bellarmin, 1987), 39–40 and 52–9.
107 Pasquale Fiorino, "The Nomination of Bishop Fallon as Bishop of London," CCHA *Historical Studies* 62 (1996): 33–46.
108 John S. Moir, "The Problem of a Double Minority: Some Reflections on the Development of the English-speaking Catholic Church in Canada in the Nineteenth Century," *Histoire sociale / Social History* 7 (April 1971): 53–67.
109 John S. Moir, "Canadian Protestant Reaction to the *Ne Temere* Decree," Canadian Catholic Historical Association, *Study Sessions* 48 (1981): 78–90.
110 *Catholic Register*, 7 March 1912.
111 Ibid., 1 February 1912.
112 *Globe*, 28 May and 18 June 1912
113 *Catholic Register*, 23 November 1911.
114 McGowan, *Waning of the Green*, 104–16; ASV-ADC, 89.4, John R. Teefy to Donatus Sbarretti, 10 June 1906 and 11 July 1906.
115 ARCAT, Marriage Registers, 1887–1920; Dispensation Stub Books, 1887–1920; McGowan, *Waning of the Green*, table 3.1, 110. See also *Catholic Register*, 5 December 1912.
116 AO, Provincial Secretary, Registrar General's Office, *Report Relating to Registration of Births, Marriages, and Deaths in the Province of Ontario*, no. 47 (1916).
117 ADP, Michael O'Brien papers, Letter from F.J. O'Sullivan to O'Brien, 28 November 1913.
118 ADC, Bishop Emile Légal papers, Circular Letter, 2 April 1908; Biship Olivier-Elzéar Mathieu, Circular to the Clergy, 1 October 1914. In *Lettres pastorals*

et Lettres circulaires de S.G. Monsignor O-E Mathieu, Eveque de Regina 1914–1923 (Regina: Chancery Office, 1912–32) vol. 2, 415–8.

119 J. Albert Foisy, *Le Catholicisme en Ontario* (Ottawa: Imprimerie *Le Droit*, 1918, 480 and 53.

120 Carman Miller, *Painting the Map Red: Canada and the South African War, 1899–1902* (Montreal and Kingston: Canadian War Museum & McGill Queen's University Press, 1993), xi.

121 Inscription found on the front plate of *The Ontario Reader*, Fourth Book (Toronto: T. Eaton Co, 1909). The readers were designed for grades seven and eight in public schools and were also used in Catholic separate schools.

122 Estimates are based on Fourth Census of Canada, 1901, vol. 1, "Population" (Ottawa: S.E. Dawson, Printer to the King's Most Excellent Majesty, 1902) tables I, IX, X, and XI, which indicate that there were 580,229 non-francophone Catholics in Canada. See also Perin, *Rome in Canada*, 11–38.

123 *Census of Canada, 1901*, based on the total Catholic population of 2,229,600 in Canada. To arrive at a rough estimate of the number of Irish Catholics, I have subtracted 1,649,371 French Canadians, 10,834 Italians, 2,994 Belgians, 7,500 Germans (in Waterloo, Ontario), 12,000 Austrians, 15,965 Scots (in Prince Edward Island), 5075 Scots (in Glengarry County, Ontario), and 44,742 Scots (in eastern Nova Scotia).

124 Mark G. McGowan, "Rethinking Catholic–Protestant Relations in Canada: The Episcopal Reports of 1900–1901," CCHA *Historical Studies* 59 (1992): 11–32.

125 Census of Canada, 1901, vol. 4, table XIX, Churches and Sunday Schools For Canada and the Provinces. Calculations are based on these figures of actual participation when compared with basic rates of profession in the same census. See also Mark McGowan, "Irish Catholics," in *Encyclopedia of Canada's Peoples* (Toronto: University of Toronto Press, 1999), 751.

126 Some sources for this include McGowan, *The Waning of the Green*, 184–217; David Shanahan, "The Irish Question in Canada: Ireland, the Irish and Canadian Politics, 1888–1922" (PhD diss., Carleton University, 1988); Daniel C. Lyne, "Irish-Canadian Financial Contributions to the Home Rule Movement in the 1890s," *Studia Hibernica* 7 (1967); Stanley W. Horrall, "Canada and the Irish Question: A Study of the Canadian Response to Irish Home Rule, 1882–1893" (MA thesis, Carleton University, 1966).

127 *Catholic Record*, 29 October 1898. Similarly see Fitzpatrick's speech in the *Record*, 25 March 1899; *Catholic Register*, 13 May 1897; Dean Richard Harris, "Our Own Land," Speech to the 'Old Boys' Meeting at Beamsville, Ontario,

3 September 1900. University of St Michael's College, Rare Book Room, 1867a H3D6.

128 *Walsh's Magazine*, vol. 2, (April 1896), 5.

129 McGowan, *Waning of the Green*, 63–6; LAC, Laurier papers, reel 815, Charles Fitzpatrick to Laurier, 7 September 1904, p. 89419.

130 Gerald J. Stortz, "Thomas Joseph Dowling: The First 'Canadian' Bishop of Hamilton, 1889–1924," CCHA *Historical Studies*, 54 (1987), 100–2.

131 Alfred E. Burke, "The Irishman's Place in the Empire," in J. Castell Hopkins, ed., *Empire Club Speeches, 1909–1910* (Toronto: Warwick Brothers & Rutter Ltd.), 230; Katherine Hughes, *Archbishop O'Brien: The Man and the Churchman* (Ottawa: The Rolla L. Crain Company, 1906), 169, 172, 210.

132 ADCh, Bishop James Charles MacDonald papers, box 5, MacDonald to Cornelius O'Brien, 19 July 1901; MacDonald to Diomede Falconio, 31 August 1901; Laurie C.C. Stanley, "James Rogers," in *Dictionary of Canadian Biography*, vol. 13 (Toronto: University of Toronto Press, 1994), 893.

133 *Le Soleil*, 13 novembre 1899. O'Brien was in the public eye numerous times in the autumn of 1899, including on the occasion of the highly successful celebrations surrounding the consecration of the new St Mary's Cathedral in Halifax. *Morning Chronicle* (Halifax), 20 October 1899.

134 Perin, *Rome in Canada*, 65; LAC, Sir Wilfrid Laurier papers, V, II, Pastoral, 20 June 1896, p. 4359; ASV-ADC, 13.0, "Antigonish." See also Raymond MacLean, *Bishop John Cameron, Piety and Politics* (Antigonish: Casket Publishing, 1991), 152.

135 Miller, *Painting the Map Red*, 155.

136 *Register*, 4 January 1900; "Circulaire de Mgr L'Archeveque de Montréal au Clergé de son Diocese," 14 fevrier 1900, *Mandements, lettres pastorales, circulaires et autres documents* (Montreal: Arbour et Dupont, 1908–1925), 276–80.

137 Miller, *Painting the Map Red*, 154–5; Robert Page, *The Boer War and Canadian Imperialism* (Ottawa: CHA, Historical Booklet, No. 44, 1987), 16–9.

138 *Debates of the House of Commons* (Hansard), 63–64 Victoria, February 20, 1900, 668–9.

139 *The Morning Guardian* (Charlottetown), 24 October 1899. See Sullivan's obvious Tory connections in "Hon. William Wilfred Sullivan," in *The Canadian Men and Women of the Time: A Hand-Book of Canadian Biography*, ed. Henry James Morgan (Toronto: William Briggs, 1898), 985.

140 *Halifax Herald*, 2 November 1899.

141 W.L. Scott, KC, "Sir Richard Scott, K.C," CCHA *Report*, 4 (1936–1937), 59; Brian P. Clarke, "Sir Richard Scott," in *Dictionary of Canadian Biography*, vol. 14 (Toronto: University of Toronto Press, 1998), 915.

142 Miller, *Painting the Map Red*, 24.
143 Ibid.
144 Carman Miller, "English-Canadian Opposition to the South African War as seen through the Press," *Canadian Historical Review*, 55 (December 1974), 435. AOH branches in Moncton and Saint John repudiated the action of the Montreal branch. *St John Globe*, 16 October 1899.
145 My thanks to Shane Lynn, a PhD candidate at the University of Toronto, for his very interesting unpublished paper "The Obscure in Pursuit of the Plausible? Fenians on the Pacific" (24 September 2016) and the accompanying documents: LAC, RG 24, vol. 2020, file HQC-695, vol. 17, Sinn Fein Party to Attack Canada, 1909–1933," and LAC, RG 6-A-1, vol. 94, file 145, Lieutenant Governor of British Columbia – Reports from Captain Fagen commanding at Esquimalt re: Knights of the Red Branch (a Fenian Society) to blow up Esquimalt dockyard and helping the Boers, 19–26 January 1900.
146 Miller, "English-Canadian Opposition," 435; LAC, Laurier papers, vol. 33., John F. Coffey to Laurier, 14 January 1897, pp. 11,015–16.
147 *Catholic Register*, 20 July 1899. Criticism of Fitzpatrick came 10 November 1899.
148 Ibid., 26 October 1899, 19 October 1899, and 28 December 1899.
149 Ibid., 26 October 1899.
150 LAC, Laurier papers, vol. 33, John Coffey to Laurier, 14 January 1897, pp. 11,015–6; Thomas Coffey to Laurier, reel 760, 5 October 1898; reel 781, Thomas Coffey to Laurier, 5 December 1900, pp. 51,451–3.
151 *Morning Guardian*, 28 August 1899 and 31 October 1899; *Casket*, 10 August 1899; *Catholic Register*, 14 December 1899.
152 *Catholic Record*, 25 November 1899.
153 Ibid., 9 April 1898.
154 *Casket*, 10 August 1899.
155 Ibid., 31 August 1899; 26 October 1899 "Sacerdos" [pen name of author]; 2 November 1899; 26 November 1899; 14 December 1899.
156 Ibid., 10 August 1899 and 14 September 1899.
157 Ibid., 19 and 26 October 1899 and 21 December 1899.
158 *Catholic Record*, 18 November 1899, 25 November 1899, 16 December 1899, 24 March 1900, 29 September 1900, and 9 February 1901.
159 *Catholic Register*, 21 December 1899.
160 Ibid., 21 December 1899.
161 *Casket*, 2 November 1899; 25 January 1900; 15 and 22 February 1900; 24 May 1900; 12 July 1900; 17 May 1901; 24 October 1901. See Ray A.

MacLean, *The Casket, 1852–1992: From Gutenberg to Internet, The Story of a Small-Town Weekly* (Antigonish: The Casket, 1995), 102.

162 *Freeman*, 6, 13, and 27 January, 3 February, and 2 June 1900.

163 Ibid., 17 March (Phillips), 10 March (Patrick McCreary), and 7 April 1900 (case of John McDermott).

164 Ibid., 20 January 1901.

165 *Catholic Register*, 14 December 1899. A very proud rendition of the return of the second contingent can be found in the *Catholic Register* on 3 January 1901. See also 3 October 1901. On O'Leary, see Duff Crerar, *Padres in No Man's Land: Canadian Chaplains and the Great War* (Montreal and Kingston: McGill-Queen's University Press, 1995), 20–1. O'Leary was highlighted in *Le Soleil* as early as 2 November 1899 and in the *Freeman* on 28 July 1900.

166 *Catholic Register*, 28 December 1899.

167 Ibid., 3 January 1901.

168 Carman Miller, "A Preliminary Analysis of the Socio-economic Composition of Canada's South African War Contingents," *Histoire sociale / Social History* 8 (November 1975): 219–37.

169 Derived from McGowan, "Rethinking Catholic–Protestant Relations in Canada," appendices; and the *Census of Canada, 1901*.

170 The names were selected from 13 reels of microfilm in the RG 38 series (reels T2069, 2079, 2080-4) found in LAC. In total, the files of 234 non-francophone Catholics were discovered among the 2,496 files scanned. To determine Irish origin, the sample was analyzed by surname, given name, religion, place of birth, address, and next of kin. Of the 234, 165 (70.5 per cent) were Irish; 49 (20.9 per cent) Scottish; 13 (5.6 per cent) English or Welsh; and 7 (3.0 per cent) other. Surnames were verified by use of the following resources: Patrick Hanks and Flavia Hodges, *A Dictionary of Surnames* (Oxford: Oxford University Press, 1991; Patrick Woulfe, *Irish Names and Surnames* (Dublin: M.H. Gill & Son., 1923); Donald Whyte, *A Dictionary of Scottish Immigrants to Canada before Confederation*, vol. 1 (Toronto: Ontario Genealogical Society, 1986); Ira A. Glazier, ed., *The Famine Immigrants: Lists of Irish Immigrants Arriving at the Port of New York, 1846–1851*, vols 1–4 (Baltimore: Genealogical Publishing, 1984); and Robert Matheson, *Special Report on Surnames in Ireland* (Dublin: Printed for His Majesty's Stationary Office, 1909).

171 The Scottish Catholics had an even higher rate, at 92.7 per cent, and 95.5 per cent of French Canadians were Canadian born. The general figure comes from Miller, "A Preliminary Analysis," 221.

172 Houston and Smyth, *Irish Emigration and Settlement*, 38–42; McGowan, *Waning of the Green*, passim; Akenson, *The Irish in Ontario*, 3–47.
173 A Gordon Darroch and Michael Ornstein, "Ethnicity and Occupational Structure in Canada in 1871: The Vertical Mosaic in Historical Perspective," *Canadian Historical Review* 61 (1980): 305–33.
174 Figures for the entire contingent are derived from Miller, "A Preliminary Analysis," 230–2.
175 Canada, Department of Labour, *Labour Gazette*, vol. 1, no 11 (May 1902): 636–7.
176 Crerar, *Padres in No Man's Land*, 116–22.
177 See J. M. Bumsted, "Scottish Catholicism in Canada, 1770–1845," in Murphy and Stortz, *Creed and Culture*, 78–99. In my sample, 51 per cent of Scottish Catholics had previous militia or military experience. Catholic military traditions could even be overlooked by Catholics themselves: see *Catholic Register*, 3 September 1914.
178 Katherine Crooks, "The Charitable Irish Society of Halifax," Canadian Catholic Historical Association, *Historical Studies, Occasional Paper*, 81 (2015): 167–94.
179 Holy Cross Cemetery Historical Trust, Halifax, Database of Burials at Holy Cross Cemetery, 1845–1900.
180 *Calgary Herald*, 15 February 1900.
181 Notable is the publication of the *Canadian Catholic Readers* (Toronto: Copp Clark, 1899), with their overtly Canadian and Imperial selections of poetry and prose in the "Fourth Book" and the adoption of public school readers and texts by many Ontario Catholic schools, a fact already played out for Catholic schoolchildren in the single publicly funded systems elsewhere in eastern English Canada. *Catholic Register*, 24 August 1899; *Record*, 2 September 1899. ARCAT, Fergus McEvay papers, copy of letter of Michael O'Brien to John Seath, Department of Education, 15 January 1909; O'Brien to McEvay, 8 March 1909.
182 *Catholic Register*, 21 August and 16 October 1902; 15, 22, 29 October, and 12 and 19 November 1903; 28 June 1917. LAC, Charles Murphy papers, vol. 10, Father James T. Foley to Murphy, 25 March 1913, pp. 4134–5; Foley to Murphy, 13 June 1913, pp. 4137–4; Foley to Murphy, pp. 4,145–9; and Foley to Murphy, 17 December 1913, pp. 4158–61.
183 NPRC, Attestation papers and Personnel Files. See also *Catholics of the Diocese of Antigonish, Nova Scotia, and the Great War, 1914–1918* (Antigonish: St Francis Xavier University, c. 1919), 51–3; *Record*, 13 January 1917.

184 LAC, RG 9 III C 15, Canadian Chaplaincy Service, Personnel Files, vol. 4637, C-O-4, Peter M. O'Leary. In 1914, O'Leary re-enlisted at age 64 and served with the 12th Battalion and the 1st Canadian General Hospital. There were rumours about his intemperance, but these were hotly denied and fellow padres took up a petition in his favour (21 November 1915). In January 1917, he was promoted to Lieutenant-Colonel, and several months later was demobilized on account of his age. His influence as a "faithful and gallant" padre in South Africa was noted by the ADCS-Catholic. His popular influence is confirmed in Duff Crerar, "In the Day of Battle: Canadian Catholic Chaplains in the Field, 1885–1945," CCHA *Historical Studies* 61 (1995), 56.

185 *Record*, 26 July 1902.

186 McGowan, *Waning of the Green*, ch. 4.

187 *Debates of the House of Commons* (Hansard), 1917, vol. 3, 29 June 1917, 2854; LAC, Charles Fitzpatrick papers, MG 27 II C1, vol. 81, "Canada and the Empire," 7-01-1901, pp. 45154–58.

188 *Catholic Register*, 16 October 1902.

CHAPTER TWO

1 *New Freeman*, 21 November 1914.

2 Ibid., 8 January 1916.

3 Ibid.

4 Margaret MacMillan, *The War That Ended Peace: The Road to 1914* (Toronto: Allan Lane, 2013).

5 Jonathan Vance, *Maple Leaf Empire* (Toronto: Oxford University Press, 2012), 44.

6 Ian Hugh MacLean Miller, *Our Glory & Our Grief: Torontonians and the Great War* (Toronto: University of Toronto Press, 2002), 19; Desmond Morton, *Canada and War* (Toronto: Butterworths, 1981), 54–5.

7 John Moir, ed., *Church and State in Canada, 1627–1867* (Toronto: McClelland and Stewart, Carleton Library Series, 1967), 72–110; André Vachon, "Jean-Olivier Briand," *Dictionary of Canadian Biography* , vol. 4 (1771–1800) (Toronto: University of Toronto Press, 1979): 94–103.

8 *Eganville Leader*, 16 October 1914.

9 *New Freeman*, 31 October 1914.

10 *Northwest Review*, 8 August 1914. See also Alfred E. Burke, "The Irishman's Place in the Empire," in *Empire Club Speeches, 1909–1910*, ed. J. Castell Hopkins (Toronto: Warwick and Bros & Rutter, 1910), 225–32.

11 *Eganville Leader*, 13 November 1914.

12 ARCAT, Archbishop Neil McNeil papers, Circulars 1914; *Catholic Register*, 20 August 1914.

13 AAH, Edward McCarthy papers, Statistics on the Church in Canada, 1916. Included in the four ecclesiastical provinces were Halifax, Antigonish, Charlottetown, Chatham, Saint John, Toronto, Kingston, Alexandria, Hamilton, London, Peterborough, Pembroke, Sault Ste Marie, Vancouver, Calgary and Victoria. Missing was Winnipeg. It should be clear that Irish Catholics were large minorities in the dioceses of Ottawa, Montreal, and St Boniface (out of which Winnipeg was carved).

14 Mark G. McGowan, "The Maritime Region and the Building of the Canadian Church: The Case of the Diocese of Antigonish after Confederation," CCHA *Historical Studies* 70 (2004): 48–70.

15 Ibid., 59.

16 *Calgary Daily Herald*, 12 September 1914.

17 *Casket*, 13 August 1914. See Peter Ludlow, *The Canny Scot: Archbishop James Morrison of Antigonish* (Montreal & Kingston: McGill-Queen's University Press, 2015), 76–7.

18 *Casket*, 12 November 1914 and 25 November 1914.

19 ADL, Michael Francis Fallon papers, Circulars, 28 August 1914.

20 *New Freeman*, 19 February 1916.

21 ADPb, Bishop Patrick T Ryan papers, Circulars, 4 August 1914 and ADP, Bishop Michael O'Brien papers, Circular, 31 December 1914.

22 *Northwest Review*, 25 December 1915.

23 *Casket*, 13 August 1914.

24 Ibid., 1 October 1914.

25 Ibid., 12 November 1914.

26 *McKim's Directory of Canadian Publications* (Toronto: A. McKim, 1919), 45.

27 *Catholic Register*, 10 September 1914.

28 Ibid., 5 and 19 August 1915.

29 Ibid., 20 October 1914.

30 Ibid., 24 September 1914.

31 *Record*, 21 March 1903.

32 Ibid., 28 January 1915.

33 *McKim's Directory of Canadian Publications* (Toronto: A. McKim, 1919), 45.

34 *Record*, 15 August 1914.

35 Ibid., 22 August 1914.

36 Ibid., 30 October 1915.

37 Ibid., 8 January 1916.
38 *Casket*, 7 January and 25 November 1915; 24 February 1916.
39 Ibid., 6 August 1914.
40 Ibid., 12 November 1914.
41 *New Freeman*, 21 November 1914.
42 Ibid.
43 Ibid., 26 December 1914.
44 *Catholic Register*, 29 October 1914 and 21 January 1915.
45 *Northwest Review*, 14 August 1915.
46 *New Freeman*, 9 January 1915.
47 Ibid., 2 October 1915.
48 Ibid.
49 *Walkerton Telescope*, 10 February 1916; *Canadian Freeman*, 13 July 1916.
50 AAO, John J. O'Gorman, Personnel File.
51 AAO, O'Gorman to Archbishop Alfred A Sinnott of Winnipeg, 25 November 1931.
52 AAO, O'Gorman papers, Gauthier to O'Gorman, 5 November 1913 and Gauthier to S Hudon (Rockland), 4 November 1913 and O'Gorman to Gauthier, 24 March 1914. *Le Droit*, 28 October 1915 and 10 March 1914. J.J. O'Gorman papers, file 1, O'Gorman to Charles Hugh Gauthier, 30 October 1915.
53 AAO, O'Gorman papers, O'Gorman to Gauthier, 30 October 1915; Henri Bourassa to Gauthier, 6 November 1914 and Gauthier's response mentioned in O'Gorman to Gauthier, 11 December 1914. The dispute continued in *Le Droit*, 10 March 1914 and 28 October 1915.
54 AAO, O'Gorman papers, O'Gorman to Gauthier, 4 January 1916.
55 AAO, O'Gorman papers, Gauthier to O'Gorman, 8 January 1916.
56 LAC, RG 9 III, vol. 4636, file C-0-3, O'Gorman, J.J.
57 John J. O'Gorman, *Canadians to Arms!* (Toronto: Extension Print, 1916), 1.
58 Ibid., 5.
59 Ibid., 11.
60 *Catholic Register*, 20 January 1916 and *Record*, 22 January 1922.
61 J. Castell Hopskins, ed., *The Canadian Annual Review of Public Affairs* 16 [1916] (Toronto: Canadian Annual Review Publishing Company Ltd, 1917), 434–5.
62 Robert Matthew Bray, "The Canadian Patriotic Response to the Great War," (PhD diss., York University, 1977), vii–viii.
63 *Casket*, 15 October 1914. The *Casket* argued that Canada's fate would be settled in Europe, just as Louisbourg's had been settled in Europe in the eighteenth century.

64 *Register*, 29 July 1915.
65 *Catholic Record*, 13 February 1915.
66 *Ottawa Evening Journal*, 19 August 1914.
67 ADL, Bishop Michael Francis Fallon papers, Circular, 31 December 1916; *Pickering News*, 14 October 1918; ARCAT, Neil McNeil papers, Circular, "The Duty of Patriotism," 20 August 1914; ADPb, Patrick T. Ryan papers, Circular to the Clergy, 28 December 1914, and 27 December 1915. *Casket*, 18 March 1915.
68 *Northwest Review*, 16 January 1915.
69 Ibid., 20 March 1915.
70 *Ontario Catholic Yearbook* (Toronto: OCYB, 1915), 134.
71 Marjorie Power, "Editorial," *St Joseph's Lilies* 3, no. 2 (September 1914), 70.
72 *Casket*, 25 February 1915.
73 *Canadian Freeman*, 19 August 1914.
74 *New Freeman*, 21 August 1915.
75 *Catholic Record*, 2 January 1916.
76 Ibid. Also 4 December 1915.
77 *Ottawa Evening Journal*, 14 September 1914.
78 *Globe*, 13 October 1914.
79 *Register*, 2 March 1916; *Canadian Freeman*, 13 April 1916.
80 LAC, RG 9 III C 15, vol. 4636, O'Gorman File, C-03, *Canadians to Arms!* 9.
81 *Canadian Freeman*, 19 August 1914.
82 Beauford Nally, "In Freedom's Cause," *Cathedral Magazine* 1, no. 5 (April 1917): 29.
83 ATCDSB, Textbook Collection, Sir Edward Parrott, *The Children's Story of the War* (Toronto: Thomas Nelson & Sons, 1914). These booklets began publication and circulation in the schools in 1914 and sold for eight cents a copy.
84 F.B. Fenton, "Religion and the War," *St Joseph's Lilies* 6, no. 1 (June 1917): 92–3.
85 F.B. Fenton, "Some Moral Aspects of the War," *St Joseph's Lilies* 5, no. 4 (March 1917): 48–9.
86 *Montreal Tribune*, 7 November 1912, identifies Brophy as the parish priest and "the Reverend Doctor" of St Agnes Parish, Montreal.
87 *New Freeman*, 2 September 1916.
88 Ibid.
89 *Catholic Register*, 10 September 1914 and 18 March 1915.
90 Ibid., 18 March 1915.
91 *Canadian Freeman*, 8 March 1916.
92 LAC, RG 9 III C 15, vol. 4636, O'Gorman File, C-03, *Canadians to Arms!*, 8.

93 *New Freeman*,12 August 1916.
94 *Casket*, 15 April 1915.
95 O'Gorman, *Canadians to Arms!*, 4–5.; *Register*, 16 November 1916.
96 *New Freeman*, 9 January 1915.
97 *Northwest Review*, 5 September 1914; *New Freeman*, 21 November 1914 and 8 May 1915 and 26 February 1916. LAC, RG 9 III C 15, vol. 4636, O'Gorman File, C-03, *Canadians to Arms!*, 11; J. Castell Hopkins, "The Churches and the War in 1916," *Canadian Annual Review of Public Affairs*, vol. 16 (1916) (Toronto: Annual Review Publishing Company Limited, 1917), 435–6. The latter cites Fallon on the martyrdom of Belgium.
98 *Casket*, 7 January 1915.
99 Ibid., 24 September 1914; ADP, Michael O'Brien papers, Circular Letter, 26 November 1914; *Record*, 20 February 1915; H. Duggan, "Why England is at War," *St Joseph's Lilies*, vol. 3, no. 4 (March 1915), 132.
100 *Northwest Review*, 14 November 1914 and 26 December 1914.
101 *Tablet*, 9 January 1915. The English Catholic magazine printed Mercier's suppressed pastoral calling for the liberation of his people.
102 *Catholic Record*, 10 July 1915. See also *Canadian Freeman*, 24 February 1915.
103 ADP, O'Brien papers, Archbishop Desire Mercier to O'Brien, 4 October 1915.
104 *Northwest Review*, 29 May 1915.
105 *Catholic Record*, 12 September 1914.
106 Jane G.V. McGaughey, *Ulster's Men: Protestant Unionist Masculinities and Militarization in the North of Ireland, 1912–1923* (Montreal and Kingston: McGill-Queen's University Press, 2012), 71.
107 *Northwest Review*, 12 June 1915.
108 *New Freeman*, 24 October 1914 and 20 March 1915 and 8 January 1916; *Catholic Record*, 16 October 1915; *Canadian Freeman*, 9 December 1914 and 24 March and 8 December 1915; *Northwest Review*, 29 August 1914.
109 ARCAT, war box, Patriotic Fund Campaign, Pledge Card, Neil McNeil, 1914; *Canadian Freeman*, 2 September 1914.
110 ARCAT, McNeil papers, PC01.02, Circular Letter, 25 August 1914.
111 *Globe*, 14 and 15 September 1914.
112 Ibid., 26 and 28 August 1914.
113 *Catholic Register*, 30 September 1915; *Ottawa Evening Journal*, 12 October 1914; *Canadian Freeman*, 23 September and 9 December 1914; ADL, Fallon papers, Letter from Herbert Ames, Honorary Secretary, Canadian Patriotic Fund, to Fallon, 3 March 1916; *Mandements, Letters Pastorales, Circulaires et Autres Documents*, Diocese de Sherbrooke, 1915–1912 (Sherbrooke: Messager

de St-Michel, 1920), 399–403; *Mandements, Lettres patorales et Circulaires*, Trois Rivieres, 1914–1923 (Trois-Rivieres: Le Bien Public, Ltée, 1923), 121–5; AAQ, 60, CN, Gouvernement du Canada, X: ii, Letter from Herbert Ames to Cardinal Bégin, 4 decembre 1915; *Mandements, Letters Pastorales et Circulaires*, Nicolet, 1914–1924 (Nicolet: n.p., 1924), 161.

114 *Whitby Gazette*, 27 May 1915.

115 www.bankofcanada.ca/rates/related/inflation-calculator (accessed 28 July 2015)

116 *Walkerton Telescope*, 3 September 1914.

117 *Catholic Register*, 14 October 1915 and 16 March 1916; *New Freeman*, 17 November 1917.

118 *New Freeman*, 12 August 1916.

119 ADPb, Bishop Patrick T. Ryan, Circular Letters, 1 December 1915; Maly Przewodnik, *A Concise Guide to the Canadian Kashuby* (Barry's Bay: Polish Heritage Institute Kaszuby, 2008), 13 and 19.

120 *Cathedral Magazine*, January 1918, 9.

121 *Catholic Register*, 16 March 1916.

122 ACSSJ, *Annals*, 1 January 1916, 500.

123 *Casket*, 24 January 1918.

124 ARCAT, Our Lady of Lourdes Parish Box, Report of Eleanor Moore, Secretary, Patriotic Association, 13 November 1917. *Catholic Register*, 7 December 1916.

125 *Catholic Register*, 20 July 1916.

126 *Pickering News*, 24 March 1916.

127 ADPb, Patrick Ryan papers, Circular, 21 November 1916.

128 *Record*, 14 November 1914.

129 *Northwest Review*, 15 May 1915; *New Freeman*, 24 June 1916; *Canadian Freeman*, 26 May 1915.

130 LAC, MG 30 D 258, volume 3, Ethel Chadwick Journal, Tuesday, 8 June 1915.

131 *Northwest Review*, 20 November 1915; *Catholic Record*, 8 April 1916; *Catholic Register* 19 November 1914; *New Freeman*, 16 January 1915; *Renfrew Mercury*, 27 November 1914.

132 *New Freeman*, 20 November 1915.

133 Desmond Morton, "Supporting Soldier's Families: Separation Allowance, Assigned pay, and the Unexpected," in *Canada and the First World War: Essays in Honour of Robert Craig Brown*, ed. David Mackenzie (Toronto: University of Toronto Press, 2005), 210; Barbara Wilson, ed., *Ontario and the First World War 1914–1918: A Collection of Documents* (Toronto: The Champlain Society and the University of Toronto Press, 1977), xx and xxv–xxvi.

134 *Record*, 16 October 1915.

135 *Casket*, 4 February 1915; *Canadian Freeman*, 21 October 1914.

136 LAC, RG 9 III C 15, vol. 4665, Reports of the Roman Catholic Chaplaincy, Captain Reverend Thomas L Cooney, to Lt Col Reverend A. Sylvestre, 20 December 1918. Cooney's letter suggests they may be French Canadian priests in Victoria, including Monsignor Leterme. Cooney to Sylvestre, 24 January 1919.

137 *Catholic Register*, 22 October 1914, Quebec Bishops' Pastoral letter.

138 *Casket*, 22 October 1914; *Catholic Register*, 26 August and 18 November 1915.

139 *Casket*, 15 October 1914; *Catholic Register*, 15 October 1914.

140 *Northwest Review*, 26 December 1914.

141 *Casket*, 24 December 1914.

142 ARCAT, McNeil papers, war box, WE 07.07, Draft of letter from McNeil to Henri Bourassa, September 1914.

143 AAO, O'Gorman papers, F1, O'Gorman to Gauthier, 11 December 1914. The initial letter from Bourassa is in AAO, O'Gorman papers, F1, Henri Bourassa to Archbishop Charles Hugh Gauthier, 6 November 1914.

144 *Catholic Register*, 26 August 1915. As early as December 24, 1914, A.E. Burke had already editorialized that Bourassa had become "in love with himself, and was simply an "irate tribune."

145 *Catholic Register*, 20 January 1916. They presented similar criticism as early as 18 November 1915.

146 *Casket*, 10 February 1916.

147 Ibid., 27 January 1916.

148 Ibid., 3 February 1916.

149 Ibid., 5 November 1914.

150 *Canadian Freeman*, 12 January 1916.

151 *New Freeman*, 15 January 1916, and *Canadians To Arms!*, 4–5.

152 *Northwest Review*, 22 March 1916, citing Major Charles Leigh at the Quebec Recruiting Office.

153 James Day, "Our French Canadian Neighbours," *St Joseph's Lilies* 3, no. 4 (March 1915), 100.

154 Ibid., 101.

155 AAQ, Archbishop Louis-Nazaire Bégin papers, 60 CN, Government Correspondence, X: 24, Sir Charles Fitzpatrick to Bégin, 9 July 1916 and 60 CN, IX: 150a, Bégin to Fitzpatrick, 31 July 1916.

156 AAQ, Circulaire au clergé, Collecte pour la Croix Rouge, 5 novembre 1917.

157 AAM, Archbishop Paul Bruchési papers, Toronto Correspondence, 225-104, 917-3, McNeil to Bruchési, 10 April 1917 and 915-2, 10 November 1915.
158 ARCAT, Education papers, "Circular," Ontario Bishops, 24 January 1917.
159 AAM, Bruchési papers, Toronto Correspondence, 225-104, 915-2, McNeil to Bruchési, 10 November 1915.
160 *Sentinel*, 26 October 1916.

CHAPTER THREE

1 Census of 1871, Ontario, Renfrew North, District 82, Sub-district Pembroke, microfilm C-10021, item 368796.
2 LAC, RG 150, 1992-93/166, box 6525, file 52, Edward Francis Murray, 811814, Attestation Paper; RG 38, South African War Personnel Files, reel T2079, Attestation Paper.
3 LAC, RG 150, 1992-93/166, box 6525, file 52, Edward Francis Murray, 811814.
4 *Renfrew Mercury* 30 August 1918; LAC, RG 150, 1992-93/166, box 6525, file 52, Edward Francis Murray, 811814, Medical History Sheet, 13 November 1917 and 6 February 1918.
5 Newspaper obituary, available at www.veterans.gc.ca/eng/remembrance/memorials/canadian-virtual-war-memorial/detail/314494?Edward Francis Murray
6 Robert Craig Brown and Donald Loveridge, "Unrequited Faith: Recruiting the CEF 1914–1918," *Révue Internationale d'Histoire Militaire* 51 (1982), 56–63.
7 LAC, RG 9 III, Militia and Defence Records, volume 4652, "Establishments no. 8," Voluntary Enlistments to June 1, 1917.
8 Brown and Loveridge, "Unrequited Faith," 57.
9 LAC, RG 24, volume 4301, file 34-1-59, volume 3, Recruiting Pamphlets, c. 1914.
10 Dominion of Canada, Department of Labour, *Labour Gazette* 14 (June 1914): 14–15.
11 Ibid., 15 (September 1914): 340–1.
12 Ibid., 14 (May 1914): 1265–6 and vol. 15 (August 1914): 171; Barbara Wilson, *Ontario and the First World War 1914–1918* Toronto: The Champlain Society and University of Toronto Press, 1977), xxi–xxiii.
13 *Labour Gazette* 17 (September 1916): 1540.
14 Ibid., 1541–2.
15 Ibid., 1534–6.
16 Ibid., 1533.

17 Ibid., 1531. There appeared to be a shortage of labour in the rural areas of Nova Scotia, and farmers were forced to advertise for help in the local papers, such as the Antigonish farmer who sought "a sober man to work on farm. One who understands gardening, dairying, and the proper care of livestock." *Casket*, 9 November 1916. See also ADA, Morrison papers, Morrison to W.B.A. Ritchie, Halifax, 18 August 1916, no. 3397. Bishop Morrison reports that the "farmers are experiencing the greatest difficulty in saving their crops, as it is next to impossible to find farm help."

18 *Catholic Record*, 24 November 1917.

19 LAC, RG 9 III, vol. 4636, C-0-3, Memorandum to the Archbishops and Bishops of Ontario, October 1917, pp. 10–11; see also RG 9 III, vol. 4673, "Religious Statistics," and RG 24 , vol. 1249, HQ-593-1-77, 22 August 1916. Similar figures can be found in Sessional Paper 143-B, 1917, as cited in Elizabeth Armstrong, *Crisis in Quebec* (Toronto: McClelland and Stewart, Carleton Library Series, 1974), 247.

20 LAC, RG 24-V-1249, Frank Beard, Record Officer for the Adjutant-General, to Military Secretary, Department of the Militia and Defence, 1 November 1915; also vol. 1249, "Returns Showing Approximate the Various Religious Denominations of Men Attested for Overseas Service, CEF, 22 August 1916; and vol. 1249, "Surgeon General, Deputy Minister to Senator Farrell, 11–12 July 1917. The final tally before the figure became conflated with men drafted under the *Military Service Act* is RG 9 III, vol. 4657, "Statement Showing the Religious Denominations of the Canadian Expeditionary Force, Overseas to December 31, 1917. The Roman Catholic figure remains at 14.8 per cent, behind the Anglicans at 41.3 per cent and the Presbyterians at 21.8 per cent, but ahead of the Methodists at 12.8 per cent. See also *Catholic Record*, 24 November 1917.

21 Duff Crerar, "Bellicose Priests: The Wars of the Canadian Catholic Chaplains," CCHA *Historical Studies* 58 (1991): 21–40

22 LAC, RG 9 III, vol. 4652, "Establishments no. 6" – Statement Showing Religious Denominations of Troops that Had Proceeded Overseas up to 31 December 1916. Taken from the Attestation papers on File in the Record Office, Ottawa.

23 *Northwest Review*, 12 February 1916.

24 *Walkerton Telescope*, 10 February 1916.

25 *Casket*, 23 March 1916.

26 ADA, James Morrison papers, Circular on Recruitment, 15 February 1016, no. 2937.

27 *Northwest Review*, 8 April 1916 and 13 January 1917.

28 ARCAT, FWGC01.103, Neil McNeil papers, war box, Handbill, n.d. See also *Catholic Register*, 20 and 27 August and 19 November 1914; 7 and 16 January 1915.
29 Charles G. Brewer, "The Diocese of Antigonish and World War I (MA thesis, University of New Brunswick–Fredericton, 1975), 11–12.
30 LAC, RG 9 II B3, volume 80, "160th Battalion, Nominal Roll of Officers, non-Commissioned Officers and Men, October 19, 1916. Allan Bartley, *Heroes in Waiting: The 160th Bruce Battalion in the Great War* (Port Elgin, ON: Brucedale Press, 1996); *Walkerton Herald Times*, 9 November 1988.
31 *Canadian* (organ of the Catholic Mutual Benefit Association), May and October, 1918.
32 ADC, War Correspondence.
33 *Northwest Review*, 13 January 1917.
34 Ibid., 3 March 1917.
35 *Canadian Freeman*, 20 April 1916. The published names were primarily Irish Catholic such as Clancy, Doolan, Flanagan, Aikens, Ryder, and Barry.
36 *New Freeman*, 15 December 1917.
37 *Northwest Review*, 19 January 1918.
38 *New Freeman*, 2 February 1918.
39 Fred McEvoy et al., *Enduring Faith: A History of Saint Patrick's Basilica Parish, Ottawa 1855–2005* (Ottawa: Saint Patrick's Basilica, 2005), 143.
40 *Northwest Review*, 19 January 1918. See also *New Freeman*, 6 November 1915.
41 *Casket*, 21 October 1915.
42 *Catholic Register*, 12 August 1920.
43 ARCAT, St Helen's Parish Box, photos file, St Helen's Church Honour Roll, 4 April 1917.
44 LAC, National Personnel Records Centre, Files of James Mitchell Cooney, 404303, Patrick Arthur Cooney, 681391, John Thomas Cooney, 405724, and Cornelius Vincent Cooney, 404724.
45 LAC, RG 150, box 6468-36, no. 47127, John Mulholland.
46 LAC, RG 150, box 6468-34, no. 2165, John Patrick Mulholland.
47 Email correspondence, Dr. Susan Marie Martin to the author, 7 September 2016. Martin is the great-granddaughter of John Mulholland and has his entire military record.
48 *Northwest Review*, 11 September 1915. The *Catholic Register* made a great clamour about how Catholic families in Toronto were doing their bit, citing the Smith family of 75 Lee Avenue, having offered four sons, one of whom, Captain Neil Smith, had won the Carnegie Medal for Bravery and

had been wounded at Vimy. The Dafoe Family of Sultan Street lost two of three sons who enlisted; see *Catholic Register*, 31 January 1918.

49 AAO, Charles Hugh Gauthier papers, Toronto Correspondence, Correspondence des civiles, 1901–1919, Berta Wadham to Gauthier, 8 October 1915.

50 *Catholics of the Diocese of Antigonish, Nova Scotia, And the War, 1914–1919* (Antigonish: St Francis Xavier University Press, c. 1919), 55–6.

51 *Casket*, 9 August 1915 and 17 January 1918; *New Freeman*, 2 March 1918.

52 *Northwest Review*, 4 March 1916.

53 CUA, President of Loyola fonds, 1147/7, box 430, Cadets 1919–1922, Rector of Loyola, Father William H. Hingston to W.F.C. Sullivan, QMG [Quarter Master General] of Military District 4, 5 September 1919. His letter requested an issue of 114 uniforms and great coats for the students at the College, indicating that the military traditions of Loyola continued after the war.

54 GABF, A-11 and A-13, St Michael's College letters, Father Henry Carr to Father Frank Forester, 11 June 1918.

55 St Michael's College, year book 1916, 47–50.

56 Ibid., 53.

57 St Michael's College, year book 1918, 55–9. This does not include the Catholics who were enrolled at the University of Toronto but not at St Michael's College. University of Toronto, *Roll of Service* (Toronto: University of Toronto Press, 1921), 10, 17, 26, 37, 44, 47, 57, 67, 85, and 122.

58 St Michael's College, year book 1917, 21.

59 Christopher J. Kaufmann, *Faith and Fraternalism: The History of the Knights of Columbus, 1882–1982* (New York: Harper and Row, 1982).

60 Mark G. McGowan, *The Waning of the Green: Catholics, the Irish and Identity in Toronto* (Montreal and Kingston: McGill-Queen's University Press, 1999), 174–6.

61 I.J.E. Daniel and D.A. Casey, *For God and Country: A History of the Canadian Knights of Columbus Catholic Army Huts* (Canada: n.p., 1922), 14.

62 *Catholic Register*, 8 October and 31 December 1914; 30 June, 7 July, 6 and 19 September 1917.

63 Daniel and Casey, *For God and Country*, Introduction.

64 ACSSJ, *Annals of the Sisters of St Joseph* (January 1916), 500. The annals mentions cadet drilling at St Mary's School. The *New Freeman*, 6 November 1915 and 8 July 1916, mentions Ancient Order of Hibernian Cadets drilling in Saint John; the *Catholic Register*, 26 April 1917 reports on the drill of 168 cadets at De LaSalle Collegiate in Toronto.

65 LAC, MG 27 III B8, Charles Murphy papers, vol. 49, Undated Speech to St

Theresa's Parish, p. 22178. His claims that seven hundred men from the parish had enlisted defies hard evidence.

66 *Northwest Review*, 3 March 1917.

67 *New Freeman*, 29 December 1917. The same claim had been made earlier by the paper in relation to the volunteers from St. Dunstan's Parish in Fredericton, *New Freeman*, 15 December 1917.

68 The March, May, June, and December 1918 issues of the *Canadian* (the official organ of the Catholic Mutual Benefit Association) make clear the association's initiatives during the war.

69 *Catholic Register*, 22 February 1917.

70 David Murphy, *Irish Regiments in the World Wars* (Oxford: Osprey Publishing, 2007), 3–23.

71 Ibid., 28.

72 Edward Atkinson, "Canada's Irish Regiments," *Archivist* (July–September 1991), 3.

73 Ibid., 22–3; Robin Burns, "The Montreal Irish and the Great War," CCHA *Historical Studies* 52 (1985): 67–81. The best account of the Irish tour thus far is Niabh Gallagher, "Irish Civil Society and the Great War, 1914–1918" (PhD diss, University of Cambridge, 2014), 175–99.

74 LAC, *Guide des sources pur les unites du Corps expéditionaire canadien* (Ottawa: LAC n.d.), 605; and LAC, RG 9 II B 3, vol. 80, "218th Battalion: Nominal Roll of Officers, Non-Commissioned Officers and Men, February 17, 1917."

75 Atkinson, 23; LAC, RG 9 III, volume 4703, folder 79, file 4, Historical Record 208th Battalion and RG 9 III, vol. 4946, folio 461, War Diary 208th Battalion.

76 Burns, 72–3.

77 *New Freeman*, 6 May 1916.

78 Simon Jolivet, *Le vert et le bleu: Identité Québécoise et identité irlandaise au tournant du XXe siècle* (Montreal: Les Presses de l'Université de Montréal, 2011), 190–3.

79 *The Irish Canadian*, Overseas Number (April 1917), 36.

80 *New Freeman*, 18 March 1916.

81 Elizabeth Smyth, "'Developing the powers of the youthful mind': The Evolution of Education for Women at St Joseph's Academy, Toronto, 1854–1911," CCHA *Historical Studies* 60 (1993–94), 125.

82 CTA, Irish Regiment of Canada fonds 70, series 340, subseries 6, file 50, The Irish Canadian: History of the 208th Overseas Battalion, 1917, privately bound, 21.

83 LAC, RG 24, volume 1249, HQ 593-1-77, "Occupations," Military District no. 2, 18th to 85th battalions, June 1916.

84 Atkinson, 23.

85 Burns, 72–3. Jolivet, *Le vert et le bleu*, 185–94.

86 Brown and Loveridge, "Unrequited Faith," 60; *Labour Gazette* (November 1915): 559; (December 1915): 688; (January 1916): 778–9, (March 1916): 986; (April 1916): 1084; (May 1916): 1184; and (June 1916): 1278.

87 Burns, 77.

88 LAC, RG 9 II B 3, vol. 80, "218th Battalion: Nominal Roll of Officers, Non-Commissioned Officers and Men, February 17, 1917." All calculations are my own.

89 ADA, Morrison papers, Frank MacEachern, Barrister, Halifax to Morrison, 26 October 1915. MacEachern reports that 20 per cent of the 26 Battalion and 22 per cent of the 25th Battalion are Catholic. He also indicates that 27 per cent of the 64th Battalion of Nova Scotia are Catholic.

90 *Catholic Register*, 31 January 1918.

91 LAC, RG 24, vol. 1581, file HQ 683-234-4, Colonel Commanding Military District no. 3 to Secretary of the Militia Council, Ottawa, 12 April 1916 and 24 March 1916.

92 Robert M. Clements, *Merry Hell: The Story of the 25th Battalion (Nova Scotia Regiment) Canadian Expeditionary Force 1914–1918*, edited by Brian Douglas Tennyson (Toronto: University of Toronto Press, 2013): 4–5.

93 Ibid., Clements, 15 LAC, RG 9 III-B-3, vol. 79, Canadian Expeditionary Force, 25th Battalion, Nominal Roll of Officers, Non-Commissioned Officers and Men, Embarkation, S.S. Saxonia, 20 May 1915.

94 Terry Copp, "The Military Effort, 1914–1918," in *Canada and the First World War: Essays in Honour of Robert Craig Brown*, ed. David Mackenzie (Toronto: University of Toronto Press, 2005), 37.

95 Census of Canada, 1901, vol. 1, table XIV, Birthplace of the People By Districts, pp. 422–3. Alan G. Green and David A. Green, "Balanced Growth and Geographical Distribution of European Immigrant Arrival to Canada, 1900–1912," *Explorations in Economic History*, 30 (1993), 38. In 1901 only 5.1 per cent of Haligonians (3,779 of 74,662) had been born in the United Kingdom, as compared with 7.4 per cent in Saint John, New Brunswick (pp. 416–17) and 7.3 per cent in Canada as a whole (pp. 420–1).

96 LAC, RG 9 III-B-3, vol. 79, Canadian Expeditionary Force, 40th Battalion, Nominal Roll of Officers, Non-Commissioned Officers and Men, 14 October 1915; June 15 1915; 9 October 1915.

97 LAC, *Guides des sources pour les unités du corps expéditionnaire du Canada : Bataillons d'infanterie* (Ottawa : Library and Archives Canada, n.d.,), 200.

98 Desmond Morton, *When Your Number's Up: The Canadian Soldier in the First World War* (Toronto: Random House, 1993), 279.

99 For the best appraisal of the phases of voluntary recruitment, see Robert Craig Brown and Donald Loveridge, "Unrequited Faith: Recruiting the CEF, 1914–1918," *Revue Internationale d'Histoire Militaire* 51 (1982): 56–63.

100 *Labour Gazette*, vol. 14, "Reports of Local Correspondents," Halifax (July 1914), 15.

101 *Labour Gazette*, vol. 14, "Report of Local Correspondents," Halifax (September 1914), 338.

102 *Labour Gazette*, vol. 15, "Report of Local Correspondents," Halifax (May 1915), 1258, and vol. 16 (February 1916), 870.

103 LAC, RG 24 volume 1249, District Officer, Military District 10, Fort Osborne Barracks, Winnipeg, to J.M. Rittal, Secretary to Militia Council, 21 August 1915; Commanding Officer, Military District no. 13, Calgary, Alberta, to Adjutant General, 21 August 1915; and Captain J.H, Gillespie, DAA, Vernon BC, to Adjutant General, 21 August 1915.

104 Allan Rowe "Irish Immigration, Settlement, and Identity in Western Canada, 1870–1930" (PhD diss., University of Alberta, 2008).

105 Raymond Huel, "The Irish–French Conflict in Episcopal Nominations: The Western Sees and the Domination Within the Church," CCHA *Study Sessions* 42 (1975): 51–70.

106 The first forty identifiable Irish surnames on the sailing list were selected, in the order in which they appeared, from officers to enlisted men.

107 LAC, RG 9 II-B-10, vol. 30, Nominal Roll, 138th Battalion, Edmonton, Alberta, 1916.

108 LAC, RG 24, vol. 4301, file 34-1-59, vol. 3, Recruitment Pamphlets, c. 1914.

109 *Casket*, 12 August 1915.

110 LAC, RG 24, vol. 1249, "By Military District by Nationality, of Members of 18th to 85th Battalions," n.d.

111 LAC, RG 150 1992-93/16 6, vol. 6525, Edward Francis Murray file, Service Record Card, Witley Camp, Acting Corporal, 138th Battalion, 4 September 1916. He reverted to private within a month when he was transferred 137th Battalion.

112 William J. O'Brien, *Send Out the Army and the Navy*, typescript, 4 May 1916. Courtesy of the O'Brien Family.

113 LAC, RG 150, 1992-93/166, box XX, William Leo Meagher, 622884, Copy of Report 13 October 1916, 10 Canadian Infantry Brigade, and Casualty Form, Active Service.

114 *New Freeman*, 10 June 1916.

115 *Ottawa Citizen*, 13 January 2005. His Stanley cup goal scoring record still stands.

116 Cynthia Toman, *Sister Solders of the Great War: The Nurses of the Canadian Army Medical Corps* (Vancouver: UBC Press, 2016), 38–9; C.A. Sharpe, "Canadian Enlistment in the Canadian Expeditionary Force: A Regional Analysis," *Journal of Canadian Studies* 18, no. 4 (Winter 1983–4), 17. The total number of nurses is disputed in Toman's count of 2,845, which was based on the number of attestation papers available, whereas Sharpe claims the number was 2,499. Matron MacDonald variously reported 2,951 and 3,141. The head of the CAMC, Sir Andrew Macphail, MD, claimed 2,428.

117 LAC, MG 30 E45, M.C. Macdonald papers, Unpublished Manuscript on the History of the Nursing service.

118 The best biography of Macdonald is Susan Mann, *Margaret Macdonald: Imperial Daughter* (Montreal & Kingston: McGill-Queen's University Press, 2005).

119 *Catholics of the Diocese of Antigonish, Nova Scotia, and the War, 1914–1919* (Antigonish: St Francis Xavier University Press, c. 1919), 53.

120 Mann, *Margaret Macdonald*, 42. She was a graduate of Mount St Vincent University, run by the Sisters of Charity, in Halifax.

121 RG 9 III, vol. 4650, "Force CEF Religion," c. 1918. The chart generated by the Department of Militia lists 2,854 nursing sisters, of whom 390 were Roman Catholic (13.7 per cent), 905 Anglican (31.7 per cent), 910 Presbyterian (31.9 per cent), and 346 Methodist (12.1 per cent).

122 The sample combined the graduate nurses of several Catholic hospitals and searches for Christian names and surnames.

123 Katherine Dewar, *Those Splendid Girls: The Heroic Service of Prince Edward Island Nurses in the Great War* (Charlottetown: UPEI, Island Studies Press, 2014), 205–20.

124 Ibid., 192.

125 LAC, RG 150, accession 1992-93/166, box 1007 – 17, Nora Gilbert file.

126 Robin Burns, "The Montreal Irish and the Great War," CCHA *Historical Studies* 52 (1985): 67–82.

127 *Saint Joseph Lilies* 4, no. 1 (June 1915): 87–8. *Catholic Register*, 29 April 1915.

128 LAC, RG 150, accession 1992-93/166, the files of Leila Brady, Irene Brady, Dorothy Smith, Florence Mary Kelly, Julietta Doherty Quinn, Catherine Regina Shea, and Katherine Byrnes.

129 LAC, Militia & Defence, RG 150 1992-93/166, Monica Marian Whelan Personnel File, 1915–1917.

130 Despite the excellent analysis of the work of military nursing sisters in Toman's book, she offers few vignettes of Catholic nurses.

131 Robert Rutherdale, *Hometown Horizons: Local Responses to the Great War* (Vancouver: UBC Press, 2004).

132 An examination of four local newspapers from 1914–1918 – *Eganville Leader*, *Renfrew Mercury*, *Pembroke Standard*, and *Equity* (Shawville) – demonstrate that war news was cheek by jowl with farm reports, local fairs, local and provincial politics, church news, and human interest stories.

133 *Eganville Leader*, 14 July 1916; *Pembroke Standard*, 12 November 1914 and 25 April 1917; *Equity*, 25 November 1915, and 25 February, 23 March and 10 May 1916.

134 *Equity*, 9 December 1915.

135 *Renfrew Mercury*, 6 December 1916.

136 Memorials include, in Quebec, Portage du Fort, Bristol, Fort Coulonge, Quyon, Bryson, Waltham, Shawville, Sheenboro, Otter Lake, and Chapeau. Ontario monuments include Arnprior, Renfrew, Douglas, Eganville, Barry's Bay, Mount St Patrick, Combermere/Wilno Cemeteries, and Pembroke.

137 Kathleen McGowan, "The Irish of Admaston Township, 1851," Senior undergraduate research paper, St Michael's College, 2013.

138 Carol Bennett McCuaig, *People of St Patrick's* (Renfrew: Juniper Books Limited, 1993), 56–7.

139 *The Renfrew Mercury*, 12 July 1918.

140 *Eganville Leader*, 12 April 1918.

141 *Renfrew Mercury*, 26 November 1915.

142 LAC, RG 24, vol. 4424, file 26-5-64-2, vol. 2, Lieutenant E.B. Manning, Assistant Senior Recruiting Officer, Military District no. 3, to Major C.G. Williams, Senior Recruiting Officer, Military District no. 3, 20 May 1916, p. 3. *Renfrew Mercury*, 10 December 1915, and 28 January and 31 March 1916.

143 *Pembroke Standard*, 17 June 1915; *The Equity*, 13 April 1916; *Eganville Leader*, 17 November 1916; *Renfrew Mercury*, 3 November 1916.

144 LAC, RG 150, 1992-93/166, box 6525, file 52, Edward Francis Murray, 811814, notification of burial.

145 Ibid.

CHAPTER FOUR

1 LAC, RG 9 III, vol. 4665, Reports of the Roman Catholic Chaplains, France, Ronald C. McGillivray to CCS, c. November 1917.

2 Duff Crerar, *Padres in No Man's Land: Canadian Chaplains and the Great War* (Montreal: McGill-Queen's University Press, 1995); Mark G. McGowan, ed., Frederick George Scott, *The Great War as I Saw It* (Montreal & Kingston: McGill-Queen's University Press, 2014).
3 Crerar, *Padres in No Man's Land*, 5–7, 10, 221.
4 Desmond Morton, *When Your Number's Up: The Canadian Soldier in the First World War* (Toronto: Random House of Canada, 1993), 279.
5 *Catholic Register*, 26 June 1919.
6 *Report of the Ministry, Overseas Forces of Canada, 1918* (London: Ministry of Overseas Military Forces of Canada, 1918), 409.
7 Crerar, *Padres*, 30.
8 Ibid., 33.
9 ADL, Bishop Michael Francis Fallon papers, Fallon to Apostolic Delegate Pellegrino Stagni, c. 25 November 1915.
10 Ibid., 20–1 and 31.
11 LAC, RG 9 III C 15, vol. 4623, James Patrick Fallon file, CF-4, Fallon to Wolston Workman, 19 April 1917 and 10 May 1917; vol. 4637, file C-O-4, Peter M. O'Leary File, "Petition," 21 November 1915 and Wolston Workman to Director Chaplain Service, 2 May 1917.
12 Crerar, *Padres*, 38–9.
13 Frederick George Scott, *The Great War as I Saw It* (Vancouver: The Clarke & Stewart Co., 1934), 34.
14 Duff Crerar, "Bellicose Priests: The Wars of the Canadian Catholic Chaplains, 1914–1919," CCHA *Historical Studies* 58 (1991), 23; *Casket*, 2 September 1915.
15 Alfred E. Burke, "Need of a Missionary College," in *The First American Catholic Missionary Congress*, ed. Francis C. Kelley (Chicago: J.S. Hyland and Co., 1909), 80.
16 Crerar, "Bellicose Priests," 21–39; the official number was 101. *The Official Catholic Directory* (New York: P.J. Kenedy, 1919), 151.
17 ADA, Bishop James Morrison papers, no. 2336, Morrison to Senator Lougheed, Acting Minister of the Militia, 13 August 1915. A full account of Morrison's battles to secure sufficient Catholic chaplains can be found in Peter Ludlow, *The Canny Scot: Archbishop James Morrison of Antigonish* (Montreal and Kingston: McGill-Queen's University Press, 2015), 78–86.
18 ADA, Morrison papers, no. 2477, Morrison to Frank MacEachern, Halifax, 28 September 1915.
19 ADA, Morrison papers, Copy of Report from the Ecclesiastical Province of Halifax, 20 October 1916.

20 ADA, Morrison papers, letter no. 2495, Morrison to Captain Joseph Hayes, MD, 85th Regiment, 8 October 1915. ASV-ADC, 130.1, file 2, Archbishop Pellegrino Stagni, Apostolic Delegate, to Archbishop Edward McCarthy, Halifax, 4 October 1916 and Bishop Michael Francis Fallon of London to Stagni, 30 September 1916.

21 ASV-ADC, 130.1 folio 1, Alfred A. Sinnott to Alfred E. Burke, 25 November 1916.

22 LAC, RG 9 III C, vol. 4641, C-S-28 John Joseph Sammon file, Bishop Ryan of Pembroke to Father Sylvestre, 18 November 1918.

23 ARCAT, Archbishop Neil McNeil papers, Charles Doherty, Minister of Justice, to McNeil, 27 October 1915; ASV-ADC, 130.1 file 1, no. 12841, Pellegrino Stagni to Fallon, 25 November 1915. AAK, Archbishop Michael J. Spratt papers, Meeting of the Bishops of Ontario, 12 October 1915. Spratt's papers indicate that Bishop Thomas Dowling of Hamilton and Bishop Hubert Dignan of Sault Ste Marie nominated Fallon.

24 ASV-ADC, 130.1 folio 2, Stagni to Archbishop Louis-Nazaire Bégin of Quebec, 3 March 1916.

25 ASV-ADC, 130.1 folio 1, Fallon to Stagni, 2 December 1915.

26 AAV, Archbishop Timothy Casey papers, box 6, folder 7, Ambrose Madden, OMI, to Casey 10 August 1915 and 30 September 1915.

27 LAC, RG 9 III C, vol. 4648, "England 1917–1918," Posting of Chaplains, 10 August 1917.

28 J.R. O'Gorman, "Canadian Catholic Chaplains in the Great War 1914–1918, Canadian Catholic Historical Association, *Reports* 7 (1939–1940), 72.

29 Crerar, "Bellicose Priests," 26–7.

30 ADA, Morrison papers, no. 2503, Sir Sam Hughes to James Morrison, 20 October 1915.

31 G.W.L. Nicolson, *The Canadian Expeditionary Forces, 1914–1918* (Ottawa: Queen's Printer, 1962), Appendix B, 545.

32 ADA, Morrison papers, no. 3261, Father Ronald MacDonald to Morrison, 31 May 1916. Also: Memorandum from 185th Battalion to Senior Chaplain, draft copy to Morrison, c.1917, indicates that a large number of Scottish Catholic recruits in Cape Breton were Gaelic speakers.

33 ADA, Morrison papers, no. 4331, Draft of Catholic Officers of the 185th Battalion to Senior Chaplain, c. April 1917; letter 2336, Morrison to Senator James Lougheed, Acting Minister of Militia, 13 August 1915; letter 2303, Father J.J. MacNeil (Dominion no. 4) to Morrison, 11 April 1915.

34 ADA, Morrison papers, no. 2508, Morrison to Hughes, 11 October 1915.

35 ADA, Morrison papers no. 3439, Morrison to J.J. O'Gorman, 10 September 1916.

36 ADA, Morrison papers, letter 3401, Father Wolston Workman to Morrison, 5 July 1916.

37 ADA, Morrison papers, no. 3612, Edward McCarthy Archbishop of Halifax to Morrison 4 November 1916. McCarthy's figures indicate that the 25th Battalion contained 315 Catholics.

38 ADA, Morrison papers, no. 3402, Father Wolston Workman, OFM, to Morrison, 26 July 1916. Workman includes the following figures: 1010 Catholics in the 22nd (99.4 per cent), 181 in the 24th (18.9 per cent), 259 in the 25th (26.7 per cent) and 342 in the 26th (33.8 per cent). Crerar, "Bellicose Priests," 24.

39 LAC, RG 9 III C 15, vol. 4618, file C-B-30, Canadian Chaplain Service Correspondence, Monsignor A.E. Burke to the DCS [Steacy], 26 November 1916.

40 ADA, Morrison papers, no. 2618, Donald Macpherson to Morrison, 16 September 1916 and no. 2364, Macpherson to Morrison, 1 August 1915.

41 ADA, Morrison papers, no. 3186, Morrison to Father D.M. MacAdam, 1 May 1916.

42 ADA, Morrison papers, no. 3051, Morrison to Sir Robert Borden, 23 March 1916.

43 *Catholic Register* 16 September 1915.

44 ADA, Morrison papers, no. 2963, McGillivray to Morrison, 5 January 1916.

45 ADA, Morrison papers, no. 2537, Morrison to Sam Hughes, 21 October 1915 and no. 2540, Morrison to Major General Rutherford, 21 October 1915.

46 ASV-ADC, 130.1 folio 2, Captain Rev. John J O'Gorman to Pellegrino Stagni, 21 July 1916. Enclosure from Father Rawlinson, General Headquarters, 2nd Echelon, 13 June 1916. Also J.J. O'Gorman to Steacy, 25 June 1916.

47 ADA, Morrison papers, no. 3402, Workman to Morrison, 26 July 1916.

48 ADA, Morrison papers, no. 3092, Morrison to J.J. McNeil, 1 April 1916. no. 3694, Father Wolston Workman, OFM to Morrison, 24 October 1916.

49 ASV-ADC, 130.1 folio 2, Major Alfred E. Burke to Pellegrino Stagni, 22 July 1916.

50 LAC, RG 9 III C 15, vol. 4636, O'Gorman File, O'Gorman to Workman, 30 July 1917 as cited in Crerar, "Bellicose Priests," 38.

51 *Canadian* (official organ of the CMBA), vol. 10 (December 1904), 5. Also see Art O'Shea, *A.E. Burke* (Charlottetown: Clarke Printing, 1993), 23–31.

52 Mark G. McGowan, "Alfred E. Burke," *Dictionary of Canadian Biography*, XV.

53 Francis Clement Kelley was born in Vernon River, PEI, 23 October 1870. He

died serving as the Bishop of Oklahoma City, 1 February 1948. He had served as founding president of the American Catholic Church Extension Society, in Chicago. André Chapeau, Louis-Philippe Normand and Lucienne Plante, eds., *Evêques Catholiques du Canada/Canadian R.C. Bishops, 1658–1979* (Ottawa: Université St-Paul, 1980), 111.

54 Francis Clement Kelley, *The Bishop Jots It Down: An Autobiographical Strain on Memories by Francis Clement Kelley* (New York: Harper, 1939), 149.

55 ADA, Morrison papers, MacGillivray to Morrison, 5 January 1916: ASV-ADC, 130.1, folio 1, Pellegrino Stagni to Cardinal Bourne of Westminster, letter 12640, 19 August 1915, and A.E. Burke to Pellegrino Stagni, 29 September 1915 (copy).

56 LAC, RG 9 II C 15, vol. 4618, file C-B-30, Alfred E. Burke to Director, CCS, 26 November 1915.

57 LAC, RG 9 II C 15, vol. 4618, file C-B-30, Alfred E. Burke to Canadian Bishops, 2 June 1916 (form letter); and Steacy to Burke, 1 June 1916. Steacy asks him to write to the Canadian Bishops.

58 *New Freeman*, 18 December 1915 and 13 May 1916.

59 LAC, RG 9 II C 15, volume 4618, file C-B-30, Alfred E. Burke to Sir Robert Borden, 17 April 1916.

60 ARCAT, CCES papers, James Morrison to Archbishop Neil McNeil, Toronto, 29 January 1913.

61 ASV-ADC, 130.1 folio 2, Copy of letter from J.J. O'Gorman to Burke, 22 June 1916.

62 Ibid.

63 ASV-ADC, 130.1 folio 1, Burke to Stagni, 9 November 1915.

64 ASV-ADC, 130.1 folio 2, P.H.D. Casgrain to Pellegrino Stagni, 10 February 1916 and 25 May 1916; this reaffirms 130.1 folio 1, Stagni to Casgrain, 22 November 1915.

65 LAC, RG 9 II C 15, vol. 4636, C-0-3, O'Gorman File, Memorandum from J.J. O'Gorman to Colonel R. Steacy, Director, Canadian Chaplain Service, 26 June 1916. In the same file is an earlier letter from O'Gorman, dated 15 June 1916; this was politely refuted by Steacy on 20 June 1916, prompting O'Gorman's more detailed response.

66 ADA, Morrison papers, Miles Tompkins to Morrison, 3 December 1916, no. 4208.

67 ASV-ADC, 130.1 folio 2, W.T. Workman to Stagni, 26 August 1916. ADA, Morrison papers, Workman to Morrison, 24 October 1916, no. 3694.

68 ASV-ADC, 130.1 folio 2, P.H. Casgrain to Sir Charles Fitzpatrick, 6 August 1916.

69 ASV-ADC, 130.1, folio 2, Workman to Casgrain, 2 August 1916.

70 ASV-ADC, 130.1, folio 2, Stagni to Burke, 16 July 1916, letter no. 13304.

71 ASV-ADC, 130.1 folio 2, Burke to Stagni, 16 August 1916 and 24 August 1916, "Confidential." In the former letter, his comments regarding the overzealous, busy-body clerics was a veiled attack on O'Gorman, as he indicated that such men had "grown up in the atmosphere of Ottawa."

72 ASV-ADC, 130.1 folio 2, Casgrain to Stagni, 6 August 1916.

73 LAC, RG 9 III C-0-3, Personnel File, J.J. O'Gorman, Original Medical History Form B 178 and Adjutant General to Department of Chaplain Services, 14 August 1916. The latter indicates that O'Gorman was appointed Honorary Captain on 4 February 1916 and promoted to Honorary Major 25 February 1916.

74 AAO, O'Gorman papers, O'Gorman to Gauthier, 6 October 1916 and Father Wolston Workman to Gauthier, 7 September 1916. Also see AAO, Charles Hugh Gauthier papers, Captain William B. Carleton, Chaplain, 4th Brigade to Gauthier, 1 October 1916. LAC, RG 9, Personnel File, J.J. O'Gorman, Medical History of an Invalid, 2 July 1919.

75 LAC, RG 9 III C15, vol. 4636, C-0-3, O'Gorman File, O'Gorman to Steacy, 26 June 1916; "Memorandum from Major John J. O'Gorman on the Position of the Catholic Chaplains in the Canadian Overseas Forces, 30 December 1916; O'Gorman to C.J. Doherty, 12 January 1917; O'Gorman to Wolston Workman, 28 February 1917; O'Gorman to the Minister of Militia, 25 July 1917; O'Gorman to Doherty, 31 August 1917; O'Gorman to Gauthier, 11 September 1917. Crerar, "Bellicose Priests," 32–5, and Crerar, *Padres in No Man's Land*, 53-55 and 61–2.

76 LAC, RG 9 III C 15, vol. 4636, C-0-3, O'Gorman File, O'Gorman to Wolston Workman, 28 February 1917; ARCAT, Memorandum from Father J.J. O'Gorman to the Archbishops and Bishops of Ontario, October 1917.

77 LAC, RG 9 III C 15, vol. 4636, C-0-3, O'Gorman File, O'Gorman to Minister of the Militia, 25 July 1917. There was a second ADCS for Protestants.

78 LAC, RG 9 III C 15, vol. 4618, A.E. Burke file, Steacy to Major-General J.W. Carson, 28 September 1916.

79 ASV-ADC, 130.1 folio 3, Memorandum, C.J. Doherty to Sir George Perley, 12 February 1917 (copy).

80 LAC, RG 9 III C 15, vol. 4636, C-0-3, O'Gorman File, O'Gorman to Minister of the Militia, 25 July 1917.

81 *Toronto Star*, 16 August 1917.

82 LAC, RG 9 III C 15, Assistant Director Chaplain Service RC, Neil McNeil to A Sylvestre, 19 August 1918; ASV-ADC, 130.1, folio 4, Msgr. Filippi, Apostolic

Delegation to Bishop Emard, no. 14849, 3 August 1918. LAC, RG 9 III C 15, vol. 4622, Bishop Emard File, GE-1, J.M. Almond, DCS, to General R.E.W. Turner, 13 August 1918. Emard would lead what became the Military Ordinariate, Workman would serve as assistant director of the Chaplain Service under Anglican J.M. Almond; Canon L.A. Sylvestre of Montreal would be Workman's assistant in Canada and F.L. French Workman's assistant in France. Almond recommended that Fallon still serve as a liaison with the government because he was well known. Minister of the Militia, A.E. Kemp, agreed. Ibid., Kemp to General Mewburn, 16 August 1918.

83 ASV-ADC, 130.1 folio 4, Canon A. Sylvestre to Stagni, 18 January 1916. At that time, Sylvestre recommended that Stagni make this kind of appointment based on the successful appointment of a similar position in Italy. Canon Sylvestre recommended a bilingual bishop.

84 ADA, Morrison papers, Sir Robert Borden to Morrison, 1 May 1016, Enclosure with comments from Father Ronald MacGillivray, no. 3399.

85 ASV-ADC, 130.1 folio 2, R.H. Steacy to Sir George Perley, 17 April 1916 (copy) and LAC, RG 9 III, vol. 4652, Steacy to Secretary, War Office, London, 19 August 1916. Steacy insisted that Catholic chaplains were overrepresented. There was one Church of England Chaplain for every 1,270 troops; one Presbyterian or Non-conformist minister for every 1,454 troops; and one Catholic priest for every 665 troops.

86 ADA, Morrison papers, Tompkins to Morrison, 11 June 1916, no. 3410.

87 ADA, Morrison papers, letter 2618, Donald MacPherson to Morrison, 16 September 1915; letter 3410, Miles Tompkins to Morrison, 11 June 1916. NA, RG 9 III, vol. 4620, C-8, Thomas L. Cooney File, Cooney to Canon Sylvestre, 19 December 1918; Murdoch, *Red Vineyard*, 36. Other ranks refer to non-commissioned officers and privates.

88 John Baynes, *Morale: A Study of Men and Courage, The Second Scottish Rifles at the Battle of Neuve Chapelle, 1915* (New York: Frederick A. Praeger, 1967), 205–8.

89 Duff Crerar, "In the day of Battle: Canadian Catholic Chaplains in the Field, 1885–1945," CCHA *Historical Studies* 61 (1995), 56.

90 LAC, RG 9 III, vol. 4621, CD-7, Maurice de la Taille File, de la Taille to W. Workman, 7 April 1918; ADL, Michael Francis Fallon papers, Circular Letter, 21 November 1917; J.J. O'Gorman, cited in John R. O'Gorman, *Soldiers of Christ: Canadian Catholic Chaplains, 1914–1919* (Toronto, 1936), 21–2; ASV-ADC, L.N. Bégin to Pellegrino Stagni, 7 March 1916. The sacerdotal importance of the priesthood is explicit in Bernard Ward, *The Priestly Vocation: A Series of Fourteen Conferences Addressed to the Secular Clergy* (New York: Long-

man's, Green and Co., 1918), 86–101, and Henry Edward Manning, *The Eternal Priesthood* (Baltimore: John Murphy & Co., 1883), 9–32.

91 ADA, Morrison papers, letter 4330, R.C. MacGillivray to Morrison, 21 April 1917. LAC, RG 9 III, vol. 4644, C-T-6, Miles Tompkins File, Workman to Bishop Morrison, 17 February 1919.

92 BIA, MG 10- 2-1a, James Tompkins papers, Miles Tompkins to James, from 60th Battalion, 13 June 1916.

93 LAC, RG 9 III C 15, vol. 4631, Ambrose Madden file, C-M-7, Colonel Richard Steacy, DCS, to Madden, 28 August 1916. Also Honour or Award Card, H.Q. 203-M-21. Entry for 2 October 1918.

94 AAO, O'Gorman papers, O'Gorman to Charles Hugh Gauthier, 4 January 1918. LAC, RG 9 III C 15, vol. 4656, Catholic Chaplains, Father Sylvestre to Father John E. Burke, CSP, Toronto Newman Club, 8 April 1919. Sylvestre reports that 101 priests volunteered during the Great War, of whom 89 served overseas. Two served in Siberia and 10 in Canada. One was killed in action and 12 received either the Military Cross or the DSO.

95 Michael McKernan, *Padre: Australian Chaplains in Gallipoli and France* (Sydney: Allen & Unwin, 1986), 35–6. Australian priest John Fahey joined his men during their assault on Galipoli. Cobourg, Ontario, native Francis P. Duffy earned the DSO, DSM, Legion of Honour, Croix de Guerre with Palm for his service at the front with the American 165th Battalion; Stephen L. Harris, *Duffy's War: Francis Duffy, Wild Bill Donovan and the Irish Fighting 69th in World War I* (Washington: Potomac Books, 2006). Ambrose Madden won the Military Cross for "conspicuous bravery under heavy fire" as he dug to free men buried alive in the trenches. LAC, RG 9 II C15, vol. 4649, "Ambrose Madden," and vol. 4665, Madden's diary, 1917. See also *From Easter Week to Flanders Field: The Diaries and Letters of John Delaney SJ, 1916–1919*, ed. Thomas J. Morrisey SJ, (Dublin: Messenger Publications, 2015); K.V. Turley, *Father Willie Doyle & World War I: A Chaplain's Story* (London: The Catholic Truth Society, 2014); Jeff Kildea, *Anzacs in Ireland* (Sydney: University of New South Wales Press, 2007), 97–102; Gary Browne and Darrin McGrath, *Soldier Priest in the Killing Fields of Europe: Padre Thomas Nangle, Chaplain to the Newfoundland Regiment WWI* (St John's: DRC Publishing, 2006).

96 LAC, RG 9 III C 15, vol. 4631, Lorenzo P. Lowry File, CL-3, Information sheet, wounded 30 October 1917.

97 LAC, RG 9 III C 15, vol. 4620, CC-21, Rosario Crochetière file, Wolston Workman to J.S.H. Brunault, Bishop of Nicolet, 19 April 1918.

98 A.J. Lapointe, *Souvenirs et impressions de ma vie de soldat (1916–1919)* (St-Ulric, Quebec: n.p., 1919), 81.

99 Murdoch, *Red Vineyard*, 174; ARCAT, FW GC 01.03, war box, Letter from Howard to his Mother, 19 July 1915; LAC, RG 9 III, vol. 4665, R.C. MacGillivray to Workman, c. September 1917.

100 ARCAT, war box, Doyle to Neil McNeil, 1 March 1918.

101 The term "red vineyard" was coined by Catholic chaplain Benedict J. Murdoch in his *The Red Vineyard* (Cedar Rapids: Torch Press, 1923.)

102 LAC, RG 9 III, vol. 4622, CD-16, Bernard Stephen Doyle File, Lt. Colonel Commanding 11th Railway Troops AAO to HQ, CRT, 8 May 1918. Requesting Doyle's removal, the commandant complains that "This Chaplain is a young man who just finished his college course shortly before enlisting. He seems to be entirely without experience in his duties as chaplain for a battalion of mixed denominations. He is, apparently, a conscientious priest and looks after some fifty odd [Roman Catholics] in the battalion but makes no effort to do anything for members of other denominations."

103 Robert Joseph Scollard, CSB, *They Honoured the Vestments of Holiness* (Toronto: Archdiocese of Toronto, 1990), 58.

104 ADA, letter 2361, Morrison papers, Duncan MacPherson to Morrison, 27 April 1915. MacPherson describes hearing confessions and saying Mass in the hold of a ship for the 25th and 22nd Battalions.

105 William J. O'Brien, Diary, "Call Out the Army and the Navy," Sunday, 10 December 1916. Used with the permission of the O'Brien Family, with many thanks. LAC, RG 9 III C15, vol. 4667, Chaplain's Reports, Michael Gillis, 4th Divisional Artillery, 19 May 1918.

106 LAC, RG 9 III C15, vol. 4321, Maurice de la Taille File, C-D-7, Invoice, R&T Washbourne, Publishers and Booksellers, 10 March 1916.

107 LAC, RG 9 III C15, vol. 4321, Maurice de la Taille file, Invoice of Mass Kit, 10 March 1916; vol. 4621, Ivor James Edward Daniel File, Daniel to Workman, 31 July 1917. ADA, Morrison papers, letter 5562, Donald MacPherson to Morrison, 4 September 1918. Murdoch, *The Red Vineyard*, 173.

108 LAC, RG 9 III, vol. 4622, GE-1, Bishop Emard file, Canon Sylvestre to Emard, 23 October 1918, indicates that Catholic soldiers had been dispensed from all fasting except on Good Friday. This dispensation included troops in Canada. ADP, Michael O'Brien papers, Neil McNeil to O'Brien, 25 February 1916.

109 A survey of 1073 personnel records of Catholic service persons indicates few men absent without leave (AWL) on Sundays, but rather high levels on other days, depending on the specific unit or region of origin. At least 22 per cent of the 104 men surveyed from Quebec's 22nd and 163rd battalions were indicted for being AWL. Among the 129 men surveyed from New

Brunswick's 26th and 132nd battalions, however, the cases of AWL amounted to only 14 per cent.

110 ADH, *The Cathedral Magazine* (July 1917), 27.

111 *Toronto Star*, 4 June 1917.

112 ADA, Morrison papers, Ronald MacGillivray to Morrison, 14 March 1916. NA, RG 9 III C 15, vol. 4618, C-B-30, A.E. Burke File, Burke to Colonel Steacy, c. 1916; vol. 4636, C-O-3, J.J. O'Gorman file, O'Gorman to Colonel Steacy, 26 June 1916. O'Gorman states that 95 per cent of Catholics are communicants; vol. 4665, Reports of the Chaplains, H.E. Letang, 23 June 1918; James Fallon, 28 April 1919; Roderick Macdonnell, 3 January 1918. *Catholics of the Diocese of Antigonish, Nova Scotia, and the War, 1914–1919* (Antigonish: St Francis Xavier University Press, c. 1919), 219.

113 ADL, Fallon diary, 30 June 1918. However, he added: "There is much carelessness among Cath[olic]s and no religion among the Protestants." The Chinese Catholics were praised by Father Francis Michael Lockary, LAC, RG 9 III, vol. 4665, Chaplain's Reports, F.M. Lockary, 2 December 1917.

114 Lapointe, *Souvenirs et impressions*, 16, 10, 13, 23, 36, 40 and 47–8.

115 One exception is chaplain Benedict Murdoch of New Brunswick, who while serving at Witley camp in England with the Fifth Canadian Division (Reserve) had a great mixture of Catholic Canadians at his Masses: "There were French Canadian lads from the Province of Quebec; Irish Canadian Rangers from Montreal; Scotch laddies with feathers in their caps from Ontario and Nova Scotia; Indian lads from Eastern and Western Canada." Murdoch, *Red Vineyard*, 52.

116 LAC, RG 9 III C 15, vol. 4623, James Patrick Fallon file, CF-4, Fallon to Wolston Workman, 17 May 1917.

117 Murdoch, *The Red Vineyard*, 95; LAC, RG 9 III, vol. 4620, CC-16, Frederick R. Costello file, Costello to Workman, no. 3 Canadian General Hospital, the Field, 24 May 1918.

118 O'Brien, Diary, 104. Great praise of the laity leading one another to the sacraments is given in ADA, Morrison papers, letter 2963, Ronald MacGillivray to Morrison, 5 January 1916. *Catholics of Diocese of Antigonish*, 219. A private from the 27th Battalion writes home saying that goes to Mass weekly even though he is at the front.

119 ASV-DAC, 130.1, Sylvestre to Apostolic Delegate to Canada, 15 November 1918.

120 ARCAT, McNeil papers, war box, FWGC 01.03, Howard to his Mother, 19 July 1915.

121 LAC, RG 9 III C 15, vol. 4665, Reports of the Roman Catholic Chaplains, France, week ending 7 April 1918.

122 Ibid., 15 July 1917.

123 Ibid., MacGillivray Report, Vimy Ridge, April 1917.

124 *Catholics of The Diocese of Antigonish*, p. 200.

125 St Peter's Seminary, London, Ontario, *Alumni Bulletin*, 1950, 12.

126 LAC, RG 9 III C 15, vol. 4665, Thomas McCarthy to Father French, Report on Vimy, letter began 7 April 1917. He reported news of the battle over the next five days.

127 Ibid., Madden to French, Report on Vimy, letter began 8 April 1917. This letter reported details of the battle over the next four days.

128 ADA, Morrison papers, Tompkins to Morrison, 14 May 1916, no. 3491.

129 LAC RG 9 III, vol. 4621, C-D-12, Doyon file, Doyon to Father Workman, 2 April 1918.

130 ADA, Morrison papers, letter 3491, Miles Tompkins to Morrison, 14 May 1916.

131 *Catholic Register*, 28 March 1918.

132 LAC, RG 9 III, vol. 4623, C-F-6, Michael Francis Fallon file, 5 September 1916; vol. 4618, A.E. Burke file, Burke to Colonel Steacy, 26 November 1916, indicates Doyon spoke English inadequately. vol. 4636, C-O-3, J.J. O'Gorman file, O'Gorman to Colonel Steacy, 15 June 1916. ADA, Morrison papers, letter 2963, Ronald MacGillivray to Morrison, 5 January 1916; letter 3360, MacGillivray to Morrison, 2 June 1916.

133 LAC, RG 9 III, vol. 4641, John Joseph Sammon file, Filiatrault to Workman, 30 January 1919.

134 AAO, John J O'Gorman papers, O'Gorman to Archbishop Charles Hugh Gauthier, 4 January 1918.

135 ADA, Morrison papers, letter 4331, draft of Catholic Officers to Senior R.C. Chaplain France, c. April 1917.

136 AAO, J.J. O'Gorman papers, O'Gorman to Archbishop Charles H. Gauthier, 4 January 1918. AAH, John T. McNally papers, Father A. Bernard MacDonald to McNally, Bishop of Calgary, 5 August 1918.

137 LAC, RG 9 III, vol. 4623, C-F-4, Patrick James Fallon papers, Fallon to Workman, 17 May 1917 and 11 July 1917. ADL, Fallon papers, Diary, 5 June 1918.

138 Murdoch, LAC RG 9 III, vol. 4667, Chaplain's Reports, Robert Moore, no. 3 Casualty Clearing Station, 28 May 1918 and Ewen MacDonald, 4th Brigade, 18 May 1918.

139 O'Brien, Diary, Sunday, 28 April, 1918; Sunday, 12 November 1916; Saturday, 10 August 1918; and Wednesday 14 August 1918.

140 *New Freeman*, 16 June 1917.

141 ASV-ADC, 130.1, Catholic Army Huts, Overseas Director's Report, W.T. Workman, OFM, 3 April 1919. LAC, RG 9 III C 15, vol. 4667, Chaplain's Reports, F.M. Lockary, 1st Brigade, 1 June 1918; *Catholic Register*, 10 October 1918.

142 LAC, RG 9 III C 15, vol. 4632, Robert John Moore File, Moorre to Workman, 7 May 1918; vol. 4637, John Robert O'Gorman file, O'Gorman to Workman, 7 June 1917.

143 ADA, Morrison papers, letter 2363, Duncan MacPherson to Morrison, 30 July 1915.

144 Ibid., and also NA, RG 9 III, vol. 4623, James Fallon file, Fallon to Workman, 2 November 1917 and 22 February 1918; vol. 4667, Chaplain's Reports, Miles Tompkins, 3rd Brigade CFA, 22 September 1918, and James Fallon, 1st Canadian CCS, 30 September and 31 October 1918. ADP, A.B. Coté to Bishop O'Brien, East Sandling Camp, 27 February 1917.

145 ADL, Fallon Diary, 24 May 1918, 31.

146 LAC RG 9 III C15, vol. 4665, Chaplain's Reports, J.P. Fallon, West Sandling, 7 October 1917.

147 Murdoch, *The Red Vineyard*, 29 and 150.

148 ADL, Bishop Fallon papers, War Diary, May 26, 1918, p. 45.

149 LAC, RG 9 III C 15, vol. 4665, Reports of the Roman Catholic Chaplains, A.B.W. Wood, Chaplain's Report, 3 February 1918.

150 ADP, Michael O'Brien papers, Father A.B. Côté to O'Brien, East Sandling Camp, 29 November 1916. Côté claims that 50 per cent of the Ontario Catholics there have not made their Easter duty "for periods of from five to twenty five years."

151 ADC, St Mary's Cathedral Records, D. Warner to Reverend A. Newman, 21 March 1919. Included were letters of introduction for forty-three men, dated 25 September 1918.

152 Murdoch, *Red Vineyard*, 29.

153 ADL, Bishop Fallon papers, War Diary, June 30, 1918, 131.

154 For thorough analysis of male military culture in the Great War: Denis Winter, *Death's Men: The Soldiers of the Great War* (Harmondsworth: Penguin, 1978) and Richard Holmes, *Firing Line* (London: Jonathan Cape, 1985).

155 Neil McNeil, Archbishop of Toronto, ed., *God's Armour is Prayer* (Toronto: Catholic Truth Society, n.d.), 33.

156 Several commuted death sentences (generally for desertion or disobedience) were noted in the confidential personnel files of 1073 Catholic recruits.

157 LAC, RG 9 III C15, vol. 4621, C-D-12, Constant Doyon file, Doyon to Work-

man, 28 March 1918. Jean-Pierre Gagnon, *Le 22e Bataillon* (Ste-Foy: Les presses de l'université Laval, 1986), 139–87 and 379–80; AAM, file group 732, Archbishop Paul Bruchési papers, doc. 225-915, Constant Doyon to Bruchesi, 27 Mars 1915.

158 LAC, RG 9 III, vol. 4621, Constant Doyon file, Doyon to Workman, 1 March 1918 and 7 March 1918; Workman to Doyon, 2 March 1918 and 26 March 1918.

159 LAC, RG 9 III, vol. 4621, C-D-6, Ivor Daniel File, Daniel to Workman, 7 March 1919.

160 LAC, NPRC, Selection of sixty files indicates ten Royal Red Crosses Awarded and four Médailles des Épidémies. Some nurses were taken from parish honour rolls in Nova Scotia, British Columbia and Ontario. Others were sampled from the Laval and St Francis Xavier Hospital Units. RG 9 III B2, vol. 3737, no. 6 Canadian Stationary Hospital, Nominal Roll, 1917.

161 LAC, RG 9 160th Battalion Sailing List; NPRC, Personnel Records of a sample of seventy-three Catholics of the 160th Bruce Battalion, Confidential; AJUCP, Cape Croker Diary, 1917–18.

162 ASV-ADC 130.1 [Instructions to French-speaking confessors of English Troops], Edmund Surmont, Vicar General, Westminster, 16 September 1915.

163 ADL, Fallon papers, John J. O'Gorman to Workman, [Report of the Meeting of Catholic Chaplains of the Canadian Corps with Bishop Michael Fallon], France, 24 May 1918.

164 Jay Cassel, *The Secret Plague: Venereal Disease in Canada, 1838–1939* (Toronto: University of Toronto Press, 1987), 122–3.

165 ADL, Fallon Diary, 6 June 1918. Father Gauvreau, OMI, blames the French women; 27 May 1918. Civil authorities in London and Paris are implicated. AAH, A. Bernard MacDonald to John T. McNally, Bishop of Calgary, 5 August 1918. The writer rejects the idea that England is a "Christian land."

166 Cassels, *The Secret Plague*, 122-44. LAC, RG 9 III C15, vol 4647, C-W-5, Wolston Workman file, Memorandum, 12 March 1918. Catholic chaplains protested the use of the prophylactic pack as merely encouraging the evil.

167 ADL, Fallon diary, 12 June 1918.

168 ADP, A. Coté to Bishop O'Brien, 27 February 1917. He reports that perhaps as many as 14 per cent of patients at Etchinghill are Catholic. Morton, *When Your Number's Up*, 200–1. Cassel, *The Secret Plague*, 130. My own sampling of patient lists for 1917 yields a figure of close to 20 per cent of patients as Roman Catholics. LAC, RG 9 III, B2, vol. 3718, 30-13-5 vol. 3, Canadian Special Hospital, Etchinghill, Nominal Roll of Patients over Two

Months, c. October 1917; vol. 3718, file 30-13-5, Etchinghill Hospital For Venereal Disease.

169 Holmes, *Firing Line*, 93–4 and 46–50.

170 *The Catechism of the Ecclesiastical Provinces of Quebec, Montreal and Ottawa* (1888), Question 432. ADP, A. Coté to Bishop O'Brien, 27 February 1917.

171 LAC, RG 9 III, 4623, CF-4, James Fallon to Workman, 27 November 1917; also vol. 4630, C-L-24, Antoine Ambrose Lamarre file, Lamarre to Colonel W. Beattie, 30 September 1919.

172 LAC, RG 9 III C 15, vol. 4623, James Patrick Fallon file, CF-4, Fallon to Workman, 1 November 1917.

173 NSA, Edward McCarthy papers, vol. II, no. 116, Sinnott to McCarthy, 1 March 1917. ASV-ADC, 130.1, A.E. Burke to Stagni, 24 August 1916, mentions "poor Sinnott alone in Winnipeg to face many problems"; ADC, Emile Legal papers, Legal to Stagni, 5 December 1911; LAC, RG 9 III, vol. 4620, C-8, Thomas Cooney to Ludger Sylvestre, 14/15 March 1918. Cooney says Catholicism in Victoria is "in a poor state."

174 ASV-ADC, 130.1/2, Fallon to Stagni, 7 October 1915.

CHAPTER FIVE

1 *Ottawa Evening Citizen*, 11 June 1917, 10.

2 Ibid.

3 AAO, John J O'Gorman papers, Clippings, *Ottawa Citizen*, June 1917.

4 *Ottawa Evening Citizen*, 12 June 1917.

5 AAO, J.J. O'Gorman papers, O'Gorman to Gauthier, 14 February 1918. O'Gorman was staying at the St Michael's Club, Grosvenor Square, in London at the time. He had returned to England 8 December 1918. O'Gorman to Gauthier, 4 January 1918.

6 John S. Moir, "Toronto's Protestants and Their Perceptions of Their Roman Catholic Neighbours," in *Catholics at the "Gathering Place": Historical Essays on the Archdiocese of Toronto, 1841–1991*, ed.Mark G. McGowan and Brian P. Clarke (Toronto: Canadian Catholic Historical Association and Dundurn Press, 1993): 313–28.

7 Marvin R. O'Connell, "Ultramontanism and Doupanloup: The Compromise of 1865," *Church History* 53 (June 1984): 200–17; Frank J. Coppa, "Cardinal Antonelli, the Papal States, and the Counter-Risorgimento," *Journal of Church and State* 16 (1974): 453–71. Paul Misner, *Social Catholicism in Nineteenth-Century Europe* (New York: Crossroad, 1991), 79–100. E.E.Y. Hales, *Pio Nono A Study in European Politics and Religion in the Nineteenth Century*

(New York: P.J. Kenedy & Sons, 1954); Frank J. Coppa, *Politics and Papacy in the Modern World* (Westport, CT: Greenwood Publishing, 2008).

8 Nicholas Cheetham, *Keeper of the Keys: A History of the Popes from St Peter to John Paul II* (New York: Scribners, 1983), 276.

9 David Bryan, "Benedict XV, Pope (1914–1922)," Michael Glazier and Monika Hellwig, eds., *The Modern Catholic Encyclopedia* (Collegeville: The Liturgical Press, 1994), 76.

10 *Ad Beatissimi Apostolorum*, 1 November 1914, paragraph 30.

11 *Catholic Record*, 25 September 1915.

12 *Catholic Register*, 9 September 1915; *New Freeman*, 11 September 1915.

13 Frederick George Scott, *The Great War as I Saw It* (Vancouver: The Clarke and Stewart Company Limited, 1934), 216–23.

14 *New Freeman*, 1 December 1917.

15 *Sentinel*, 16 August 1917 and 1 August 1918.

16 John F. Pollard, *The Unknown Pope and the Pursuit of Peace* (London: Burns & Oats, 2005), 87 and 89. J. Derek Holmes & Bernard W. Bickers, *A Short History of the Catholic Church* (Turnbridge Wells, UK: Burns & Oates, 1983), 257.

17 *Christian Guardian*, 1 January 1919.

18 *Catholic Register*, 10 January 1918.

19 *Sentinel*, 12 April, 19 July, and 4 October 1917 and 4 July 1918; 15 November and 11 October 1917.

20 *Sentinel*, 26 October 1916.

21 Ibid., 20 August 1914, 24 June 1915, 20 September 1917, and 4 and 25 July 1918.

22 ARCAT, war box, FWWE 07.20, James F. Coughlin to the Editor of the *Toronto Daily Star*, 22 March 1917.

23 *Canadian Freeman*, 28 March 1918.

24 Cited in *Globe*, 4 March 1918; ARCAT, McNeil papers, MN PO25.04, *The Pope and the War* (Toronto, February, 1918).

25 *Catholic Register*, 7 March 1918.

26 *Sentinel*, 1 March 1918.

27 ARCAT, Knights of Columbus box, M.J. Callaghan, Grand Knight, Council 485 to Grand Knight W.J. McCaffrey of Ottawa Council, 18 March 1918.

28 John Webster Grant, "The Reaction of WASP Churches to Non-WASP Immigrants," Canadian Society of Church History papers, (1968), 1–4.

29 AASB, Adelard Langevin papers, copy, Adelard Langevin to Archbishop Louis-Nazaire Begin, Quebec, 21 August 1908, and 20 September 1909; Langevin on the Extension Society, 13 January 1913; Langevin to Arthur Beliveau, 20 September 1909. ASV-ADC, 184.2, Langevin to Donatus Sbarretti,

10 June 1905. See also Raymond Huel, "The Irish-French Conflict in the Episcopal Nominations: The Westerns Sees and the Domination Within the Church," CCHA *Study Sessions* 42 (1975): 51–70.

30 Alfred E. Burke, "The Need of A Missionary College," in *The First American Catholic Missionary Congress*, ed. Francis C. Kelley (Chicago: J.S. Hyland and Company, 1909), 83.

31 Michael Power, *Singular Vision: The Founding of the Catholic Church Extension Society of Canada, 1908–1915* (Toronto: Novalis, 2013), 80–130; Mark George McGowan, "A Watchful Eye: The Catholic Church Extension Society and Ukrainian Catholic Immigrants, 1908–1930," in *Canadian Protestant and Catholic Missions, 1820s–1960s: Historical Essays in Honour of John Webster Grant*, ed. John S. Moir and C.T. McIntire (New York: Peter Lang, 1987): 221–44.

32 Stella Hryniuk, "Pioneer Bishop, Pioneer Times: Nykyta Budka in Canada," CCHA, *Historical Studies* 55 (1988), 34–5.

33 *Renfrew Mercury*, 11 September 1914.

34 *Sentinel*, 20 August 1914.

35 *Casket*, 3 September 1914.

36 Ibid., 25 March 1915.

37 *Canadian Freeman* 31 August 1916 and 29 August 1918, *Catholic Register*, 25 December 1919, and *Northwest Review*, 19 February 1916 and 18 March 1916.

38 *Northwest Review*, 19 February 1916.

39 *Canadian Freeman*, 21 March 1918.

40 ASV-ADC, vol. 130, Father J.S. Foran, Vancouver, to John Tomich, Vernon, 14 April 1919; Chairman of War Camp Committee to Father Foran, 3 May 1919; and Chairman of Camp Committee to Apostolic Delegate, 3 May 1919.

41 Jane G.V. McGaughey, *Ulster's Men: Protestant Unionist Masculinities and the Militarization of the North of Ireland, 1912–1923* (Montreal and Kingston: McGill-Queen's University Press, 2102), 83–7; David Murphy, *Irish Regiments in the World Wars* (Oxford: Osprey Publishing, 2007), 10–23; Timothy Bowman, *Irish Regiments in the Great War* (Manchester: Manchester University Press, 2003), 61–2; see also Tom Johnstone, *Orange, Green & Khaki: The Story of Irish Regiments in the Great War, 1914–1918* (Dublin: Gill and Macmillan, 1992); Niabh Gallagher, "Irish Civil Society and the Great War, 1914–1918," (PhD diss., University of Cambridge, 2014), 141–64.

42 Keith Jeffrey, *Ireland and the Great War* (Cambridge: Cambridge University Press, 2000), 7.

43 *Catholic Register*, 11 March and 25 March 1915; *Catholic Record*, 19 December 1914.
44 *New Freeman*, 26 February 1916.
45 *Globe*, 7 August 1914.
46 *Ottawa Journal*, 18 March 1915.
47 NLI, John Redmond papers, MS 15,235/2. 1897–1915, Canada. The file contains a sheaf of letters in which Redmond engages many Canadian supporters. MS 15 265/2 (1918) contains the draft of amended proposal for home rule with an overt Canadian flavour, "memorandum Working and History of Government of Canada," submitted by W.E. Ellis, Lord Dunraven, and Lord Middleton to the Irish Convention, 1918.
48 *New Freeman*, 25 March 1915.
49 *Casket*, 30 March 1916.
50 *Catholic Record*, 13 November 1915.
51 *Northwest Review*, 18 March 1916.
52 There are numerous accounts of the Easter Rising. One of the best and most even-handed is Charles Townshend, *Easter 1916: The Irish Rebellion* (London: Penguin, 2005).
53 David Fitzpatrick, "Militarism in Ireland, 1900–1922," in *A Military History of* Ireland, ed. Thomas Bartlett and Keith Jeffery (Cambridge: Cambridge University Press, 1996), 394.
54 Jeffery, *Ireland and the Great War*, 46–7.
55 Paul Bew, "The Strange Death of Liberal Ireland: William Flavelle Moneypenny's *The Two Irish Nations*," in John Horne and Edward Madigan, eds., *Towards Commemoration: Ireland in War and Revolution 1912–1923* (Dublin: Royal Irish Academy, 2013), 26–7.
56 *Catholic Register*, 4 May 1916.
57 *Catholic Record*, 6 May 1916. Editors continue their denunciations in the 13 and 20 May issues referring to Sinn Fein as anti-clerical, shirkers, and malcontents.
58 *New Freeman*, 6 May 1916, and *Casket*, 4 May 1916.
59 *New Freeman*, 6 May 1916, and *Casket*, 4 May 1916.
60 *The Rainbow*, Loretto College Toronto, vol. 25, no. 3 (July, 1918), 133.
61 *New Freeman*, 6 May 1916, and *Casket*, 4 May 1916.
62 Townshend, *Easter 1916*, 269–81; Jeffery, *Ireland and the Great War*, 53–4.
63 Jerome aan de Wiel, *The Catholic Church in Ireland, 1914–1918: War and* Politics (Dublin: Irish Academic Press, 2003), 107.
64 *New Freeman*, 13 May 1916.
65 *Northwest Review*, 13 May 1916.

66 *Casket*, 6 July 1916. *Northwest Review*, reprinting *Casket*, 27 May 1916.
67 *Catholic Register*, 18 May 1916, and *Catholic Record*, 3 June 1916.
68 *Catholic Record*, 27 May 1916. The *Northwest Review* argued that the *Record* was the most widely read Catholic newspaper in Ontario and "It may be safely taken as an index of Catholic thought and opinion in the sister province." *Northwest Review*, 28 July 1916. In comparison the *Canadian Freeman* was struggling and in September was taken over by the priests of the Archdiocese of Kingston. D.A. Casey remained at the helm of the paper and the new energy brought about 1,400 new subscriptions. Nevertheless, it was the smallest of the Ontario's Catholic newspapers, with a readership limited to Eastern Ontario, Montreal, and Western Quebec. *Canadian Freeman*, 15 June 1916 and 14 September 1916.
69 *New Freeman*, 20 May 1916; *Northwest Review*, 13 May 1916.
70 *Canadian Freeman*, 18 May 1916.
71 Ibid.
72 *New Freeman*, 17 June 1916.
73 O'Brien, *Send Out the Army and the Navy*, 30 April 1917.
74 ADA, Bishop Morrison papers, Miles Tompkins to Morrison, 3 December 1916, no. 4208.
75 AO, Charles J. Foy papers, box 3, file 14, J.H. Barry to Foy, 2 October 1915.
76 *New Freeman*, 29 July 1916.
77 Ibid.
78 *New Freeman*, 19 August 1916.
79 *Northwest Review*, 5 August and 12 August 1916.
80 *Canadian Freeman*, 8 February 1917.
81 Ibid., 22 March 1917; *Catholic Record*, 24 March 1917.
82 Cited in Simon Jolivet, *Le vert et le bleu: indentité Québécois et identité irlandaise au tournant de XXe siècle* (Montréal: Les Presses de l'Université de Montréal, 2011), 157.
83 *Canadian Freeman*, 22 March 1917
84 LAC, MG 27 II D6, Charles Doherty papers, vol.1, Michael Fallon to C.J. Doherty, Charles Murphy, and T.W. McGarry, 12 March 1917. Doherty's papers contain an undated clipping (likely after 17 March 1917) from the London Advertiser, reporting of Fallon's St Patrick's day speech in London in which he asserts: "Shall less be done for Ireland than has been claimed and successfully asserted on behalf of British democracy?"
85 LAC, Doherty papers, Shane Leslie to Doherty, 15 February, 20 and 22 April, 1917. His small collection of papers contains several files of correspondence

on the Home Rule issue and his personal support for Redmond's constitutional approaches to the question.

86 LAC, Doherty papers, Doherty to Fallon, 21 March 1917.

87 Ibid.

88 LAC, Doherty papers, Doherty to Fallon, 29 March 1917. The letter includes a copy of Doherty's cable to Borden dated March 8, 1917.

89 LAC, MG 27, Doherty papers, Draft of letter to Edward Daly, 22 April 1917.

90 Ibid.

91 *Northwest Review*, 21 October 1916.

92 *New Freeman*, 1 November 1916.

93 LAC, Robert Borden papers, vol. 204, "A.E. Burke to Robert Borden, 7 July 1916, pp. 113898–901. Archives of the Diocese of London, Fallon papers, "Diary of Visit to the Canadian Army in England and France, 19 and 23 May 1918 and 21 June 1918. Fallon quoted in *New Freeman*, 24 March 1917.

94 *Catholic Register*, 3 May 1917.

95 *New Freeman*, 6 January 1917.

96 AAD, Archbishop Walsh papers, D.A. Casey to Walsh, 2 November 1916.

97 LAC, MG 27 II D6, Doherty papers, vol. 1, copy, Matthew J. Whelan, "Thirty Minutes With the 'Irish Republic,'" 15 March 1917.

98 *Northwest Review*, 24 November 1917 and *Catholic Record*, 3 June 1916.

99 Padraig O'Saidhail, *Katherine Hughes: A Life and Journey* (Ottawa: Penumbra Press, 2014), 159–60 and 209–11.

100 *Ottawa Citizen*, 23 March 1917, *Canadian Freeman*, 29 March 1917, and *Catholic Register*, 29 March 1917. See also LAC, MG 30 D20, vol. 1, J.J. O'Gorman papers, file 2. The document is incorrectly dated 1925.

101 Ibid.

102 Ibid.

103 *Canadian Freeman*, 29 March 1917.

104 Ibid., 5 April 1917.

105 Ibid., 26 April 1917.

106 Ibid., 3 May 1917, and *New Freeman*, 28 April 1917.

107 *Canadian Freeman*, 5 April 1917.

108 *Catholic Register*, 17 May 1917, 10 May 1917, and 26 July 1917.

109 *New Freeman*, 17 March 1917.

110 Ibid., 5 May 1917 and 19 May 1917.

111 Ibid., 24 March 1917.

112 *Catholic Record*, 21 July 1917.

113 ADL, Michael Francis Fallon papers, HF 455, file 1, document 3, J.J. O'Gorman,

"A Personal Opinion on the Bilingual Propaganda," 19 July 1915. AAO, J.J. O'Gorman papers, F1, O'Gorman to Archbishop Charles Hugh Gauthier, 14 February 1918; O'Gorman to Gauthier, 30 October 1915. *Le Droit*, 10 March 1914 and 28 October 1915.

114 *Casket*, 22 October 1914; *Catholic Register*, 26 August and 18 November 1915.

115 *Casket*, 15 October and 24 December 1914.

116 Michael Power, *Bishop Fallon and The Riot at Ford City, 8 September 1917*, Occasional Paper No. 3 (Essex County: Essex County Historical Society, 1986), 20–3.

117 *Casket*, 30 August and 6 September 1917.

118 Ibid., 4 October 1917.

119 *Canadian Freeman*, 13 September 1917.

120 Ibid., 6 September 1917.

121 ADL, Bishop Fallon Diary, 29 June 1918.

122 LAC, Sir Robert Borden papers, vol. 16, microfilm reel C-4206, "Circular Letter of Archbishop L.N. Bégin, 4 January 1917 and C-4206, Copy of Circular letter of Archbishop Paul Bruchési, 3 January 1917, pp. 4029.

123 Ibid., Bruchési, p. 4029.

124 LAC, Borden papers, vol. 16, microfilm C-4206, Commentary on Bruchési Pastoral and Circular Letter of Guillaume Forbes, 3 January 1917, p. 4029.

125 LAC, Borden papers, vol. 16, d-4206, Bishop of Nicolet to Borden, 15 January 1917.

126 AAH, James T. McNally papers, Circular letter, 29 December 1916.

127 ARCAT, McNeil papers, PC 25, Circulars, January 1917. War box, R.B. Bennett to McNeil, 21 December 1916.

128 *Catholic Record*, 23 December 1916. *Casket*, 4 January 1917.

129 *Catholic Register*, 11 January 1917.

130 Ibid., 21 June 1917.

131 J.L. Granatstein and J.M. Hitsman, *Broken Promises: A History of Conscription in Canada* (Toronto: Copp Clark Pitman Ltd., 1985), 74.

132 J.L. Granatstein, "Conscription in the Great War," in *Canada and the First World War: Essays in Honour of Robert Craig Brown*, ed. David MacKenzie (Toronto: University of Toronto Press, 2005), 68–9.

133 LAC, MG 27 II 6, Doherty papers, vol. 2, file 52, "Duty is the Subject of my Story: Canada at War Speech by the Hon. Charles J. Doherty," House of Commons, 5 July 1917, 7. The speech was lifted from Hansard and published in a slender volume, double-columned, in 17 pages.

134 Ibid., 3.

135 Ibid., 17.
136 LAC, Borden papers, vol. 219, Bruchési to Borden, 27 May 1917, pp. 123403–6, and 2 June 1917, pp. 123412–3.
137 LAC, Borden papers, vol. 219, Bruchési to Borden, 22 May 1917, pp. 123339–402.
138 LAC, Borden papers, vol. 219, Borden to Bruchési 3 September 1917, pp. 123419–21.
139 J. Castell Hopkins, "Attitude of Canadian Churches in the War," *Canadian Annual Review of Public Affairs*, vol. 17 (Toronto: *Canadian Annual Review*, 1918 [for 1917]), 410–13. *Canadian Freeman*, 21 June 1917; *Northwest Review*, 9 June 1917. Charles G Brewer, "The Diocese of Antigonish and World War I (MA thesis, University of New Brunswick, Fredericton, 1975), 52–4.
140 Pastoral Letter, 25 November 1917, cited in *Canadian Annual Review* (1917), 412.
141 *Northwest Review*, 26 May 1917.
142 Jeff Kildea, "Australian Catholics and Conscription in the Great War," *Journal of Religious History* 26, no.3 (October 2002): 298–313.
143 House of Commons Debates, 7th Session of Parliament, 1917, vol. 3, 29 June 1917, pp. 2847–55; *Toronto Star*, 22 February 1916. *Canadian Annual Review* (1917), 413.
144 LAC, Borden papers, vol. 221, Nicetas Budka to Borden, 19 June 1917, pp. 124288–90.
145 Evidently, some Ukrainians thought the cards once signed was a mortgage on their property, so they refused to comply. LAC, Borden papers, vol. 219, H Mackie (lawyer) Edmonton to Borden, 2 January 1917, p. 123010; vol. 216, J.T. Ferguson, Calgary, to Borden, 5 January 1917, p. 122146; vol. 221, Borden to Budka, 23 June 1917, p. 124296.
146 *Catholic Register*, 24 May 1917.
147 Ibid., 24 May 1917.
148 Ibid., 28 June 1917.
149 Ibid., 23 August 1917.
150 ARCAT, *Catholic Register* fonds, Father Arthur O'Leary to Neil McNeil, 18 November 1917. *Catholic Register* 14, 21 and 28 June 1917; and 28 October and 18 November 1917.
151 *Catholic Record*, 26 May 1917.
152 Ibid., 7 July 1917. See also 10 February 1917.
153 Ibid., 4 August 1917.
154 *New Freeman*, 2 June 1917.
155 Ibid., 26 May 1917.

156 Ibid., 9 June 1917.
157 Ibid., 29 September 1917.
158 *Casket*, 19 July 1917.
159 Ibid.
160 *Casket*, 14 and 21 June; 9 and 16 August 1917.
161 Ibid., 9 August 1917.
162 *Cathedral Magazine* (November 1917), 19.
163 *Catholic Register*, 17 May 1917.
164 *Northwest Review*, 12 May 1917.
165 *Eganville Leader*, 6 September 1918.
166 R.J. Manion, *Life is an Adventure* (Toronto, Ryerson Press, 1936), 4, 34–5, and 37.
167 R.J. Manion, *A Surgeon in Arms* (Toronto: McClelland, Goodchild & Stewart, 1918), title page and photo.
168 Manion, *Life is an Adventure*, 224.
169 Ibid., 225.
170 Ibid., 69.
171 LAC, MG 27 III-B7, Robert J. Manion papers, vol. 1, file 1, Letter to Sons, 7 March 1915.
172 Manion, *Surgeon in Arms*, 49.
173 Ibid., 29, 32, 241 and 293; Manion, *Life is an Adventure*, 36–7, 169, 175–80, and 339–40.
174 QUA, C.G. Power papers, box 78 B, Federal Elections, "To the Electors of Quebec South," 11 December 1917.
175 LAC, MG 27 III B7, Manion papers, vol. 12, file 13, C.G. Power to Manion, 11 July 1938. The file folder contains evidence of a very warm and lasting friendship.
176 *Ottawa Journal*, 25 November 1935.
177 LAC, MG 27 III B8, Charles Murphy papers, vol. 16, file 18, Lt. A.M. Latchford to Murphy, 24 May 1917.
178 *Canadian Annual Review* (1917), 412.
179 *Catholic Record*, 12 January 1918.
180 *Canadian Freeman*, 31 May 1917 and 7 June 1917.
181 Ibid., 19 July 1917.
182 *Northwest Review*, 30 June 1917; 26 May 1917; 9 June 1916.
183 Ibid.
184 *Northwest Review*, 21 July 1917.
185 Ibid., 1 September 1917.
186 *Ottawa Journal*, 3 August 1917.

187 *Toronto Daily Star*, 18 August 1917.
188 *Casket*, 16 August 1917 and 23 August 1917
189 ARCAT, Neil McNeil papers, Education Files, Copy of letter from Michael Francis Fallon to C.J. Doherty, 14 June 1917.
190 LAC, Borden papers, vol. 16, Selection Board, J.D. Anglin, New Brunswick to Borden, 31 August 1917, reel C-4206, pp. 4007–8; ADA, Morrison papers, Senator E.L. Gimoir to Morrison, 19 September 1917; Associate private Secretary to Robert Borden, George Biskard to Morrison, 24 May 1918; General S.C. Mewburn, Minister of the Militia to Morrison, 23 May 1918; C.J. Doherty to Morrison, 31 May 1918; *Cathedral Magazine*, Hamilton (October 1917), 5. ARCAT, McNeil papers, war box, List of Toronto Police Under MSA, 1917; *New Freeman*, 29 September 1917; *Catholic Record*, 27 October 1917.
191 *Catholic Register*, 14 June 1917.
192 *Casket*, 3 January 1918.
193 LAC, MG 27 III B3, vol. 49, Charles Murphy papers, Speech notes, 1917, pp. 22178–85. QUA, Power papers, 2150, box 78, "To the Electors of Quebec South," 11 December 1917.
194 *Catholic Record*, 28 July 1917; *Northwest Review*, 27 October 1917; *Canadian Freeman*, 13 September 1917
195 *Canadian Freeman*, 13 September 1917; *Casket*, 14 June 1917; *Northwest Review*, 22 September 1917.
196 *New Freeman*, 27 October 1917; 15 December 1917.
197 Ibid., 1 and 8 December 1917; *Catholic Register*, 29 November 1917; 13 and 20 December 1917; anti-immigrant ideas were floating to the government, particularly from Conservative supporters in Saskatchewan and Manitoba. LAC, Borden papers, vol. 219, M. McKellar to Borden, 4 July 1917, reel C-4403, pp. 123112–14; J.A. MacDonald to R. Rogers (Minister of Public Works, copy, 29 June 1917, C-4403, pp. 123116–17; Saskatchewan Conservatives memorandum submitted to R. Rogers, copy, C-4403, pp. 123132–4; J.W Runions, Morden, Manitoba to Borden, 28 August 1917, C-4403, pp. 123261–8. Priests were implicated as presenting opposition to the government.
198 *Toronto Star*, 3 November 1917; *Catholic Register* 8 November 1917.
199 J. Castell Hopkins, *Canada at War: A Record of Heroism and Achievement, 1914–1918* (Toronto: Canadian Annual Review Ltd., 1919), 331; *Northwest Review*, 15 December 1917.
200 ADL, Fallon papers, Speeches, "Statement of Bishop Fallon in Favour of the Union Government," 6 December 1917; *Ottawa Journal*, 7 December 1917; *Catholic Record*, 15 December 1917.

201 *Ottawa Journal*, 7 and 10 December 1917.
202 ADL, Fallon papers, Correspondence, George Forneret to Fallon, 10 December 1917.
203 *Northwest Review*, 15 December 1912.
204 *Catholic Record*, 29 December 1917 and reprinted in the *New Freeman*, 5 January 1918.
205 ADL, Fallon papers, Diary, 30 May 1918, p. 59.
206 *Casket*, 20 December 1917.
207 *Canadian Freeman*, 27 December 1917.
208 LAC, Murphy papers, vol. 32, Election Returns, 1917, pp. 13295–7.
209 *Ottawa Journal*, 19 December 1917.
210 ARCAT, McNeil papers, Circular on Canada Jubilee, 21 June 1917, AR01.22

CHAPTER SIX

1 David Wilson, *Thomas D'Arcy McGee: The Extreme Moderate, 1857–1868*, vol. 2 (Montreal and Kingston: McGill-Queen's University Press, 2011), 197–8. See *Montreal Gazette*, 6 July 1903.
2 *Canadian Law Journal*, 27 (9 November 1891), 539.
3 Derived from Claude Belanger, "Charles Joseph Doherty," *Encyclopedia of Quebec*, 2005. Online version. Also: *Prominent People of the Province of Quebec*, 1923–24 (Montreal: Biographical Society of Canada, n.d.); LAC, MG 27 II D 6, Charles J. Doherty papers, vol. 2, Muster Roll, No. 7 Company, 65th Battalion, Fort Saskatchewan, May 1885.
4 *Ottawa Evening Journal*, 21 June 1918.
5 The best account of the raid is Brian F. Hogan, "The Guelph Novitiate Raid: Conscription, Censorship, and Bigotry during the Great War," Canadian Catholic Historical Association, *Study Sessions*, 45 (1978): 57–80.
6 LAC, MG 27 II D6, C.J. Doherty papers, vol. 2, file 26, Marcus Doherty to C.J. Doherty, 10 June 1918.
7 Christopher J. Kaufmann, *Faith and Fraternalism: The History of the Knights of Columbus, 1882–1982* (New York: Harper & Row, 1982).
8 David Murray, *A Columbian Souvenir* (Quebec: Commercial Printing, 1910), 2.
9 Kaufman, *Faith and Fraternalism*, 116–17.
10 Mark G. McGowan, *The Waning of the Green: Catholics, the Irish, and Identity in Toronto, 1887–1922* (Montreal and Kingston: McGill-Queen's University Press, 1999), 174.
11 *Renfrew Mercury*, 26 November 1915.

12 Kaufmann, *Faith and Fraternalism*, 116–7.

13 *Renfrew Mercury*, 28 May 1915. The Renfrew and Pembroke councils hosted a conference for eastern Ontario that month that attracted between four hundred and five hundred Knights.

14 Murray, *A Columbian Souvenir*, 6–7. *Kaufmann, Faith and Fraternalism*, 117.

15 AAM, 255.104, Toronto Correspondence, 917–3, Neil McNeil to Archbishop Paul Bruchési, 10 April 1917.

16 *Catholic Register*, 5 September 1912.

17 McGowan, *Waning*, 176.

18 *Renfrew Mercury*, 28 May 1915.

19 I.J. E. Daniel and D.A. Casey, *For God and Country: A History of the Canadian Knights of Columbus Catholic Army Huts* (n.p: [Knights of Columbus], 1922), 15–16.

20 *Canadian Freeman*, 12 July 1917.

21 *Ontario Catholic Year Book*, Toronto: Newman Centre, 1920), 26; *Catholic Register*, 3 October 1918. Daniel and Casey, *For God and Country*, 21–53. Detailed descriptions of Hut activities can also be found in *Canada and the Great War. Volume IV: Special Services Heroic Deeds* (Toronto: United Publishers, 1921), part 3.

22 ADA, Bishop James Morrison papers, J.J. O'Gorman to Dr. W.J.Mc Millan, Charlottetown, States Deputy, Maritime Provinces, copy, 17 April 1917. The copy was send by O'Gorman to Morrison, 24 April 1917.

23 *New Freeman*, 2 December 1916 and 7 July 1917.

24 ASV-ADC, vol. 130.113, Clipping of Army Huts Campaign, attached to letter from Delegate Pellegrino Stagni to J.J. O'Gorman, 19 April 1917. Bishop McNally received the $1000 from the Alberta Knights and passed it on to O'Gorman.

25 *Catholic Register*, 30 August and 6 September 1917. *New Freeman*, 7 and 14 July 1917.

26 AAM, 255.104, Toronto Correspondence, 917-3, Neil McNeil to Archbishop Paul Bruchési, 10 April 1917.

27 *Catholic Register*, 27 September and 4 October 1917.

28 Ibid., 23 August 1917.

29 Ibid., 2 August 1917.

30 *New Freeman*, 14 July 1917.

31 Ibid., 4 August 1917.

32 *Catholic Register*, 2 August and 20 September 1917.

33 *Cathedral Magazine* (Hamilton), vol. 1, no. 9 (October 1917), 1.

34 ADL, Michael Francis Fallon papers, Circular Letter, 26 August 1917.

35 Daniel and Casey, *For God and Country*, 16. About $10,117.31 was raised in the Toronto parishes alone. *Catholic Register*, 13 December 1917. See also ASV-ADC, 130.1, Catholic Army Huts Incorporated, copy, 8 November 1917, p. 3.

36 ASV-ADC, 130.1, Catholic Army Huts Incorporated, copy, 8 November 1917, p. 2.

37 *Catholic Register*, 22 November 1917 and ASV, ADC, 130.1, Overseas Director's Report, 3 January 1918.

38 ASV-ADC, 130.1, Overseas Director's Report, 3 January 1918.

39 ARCAT, Neil McNeil papers, war box, O'Gorman to McNeill, 6 November 1917.

40 ARCAT, McNeil papers, war box, J.S. Durham to McNeil, 2 October 1917.

41 For currency conversion adjusted for inflation, see www.bankofcanada.ca/rates/related/inflation-calculator/

42 *New Freeman*, 28 September 1918. ADPb, Bishop P.T. Ryan papers, Circular to the Clergy, 26 August 1918.

43 ADL, Fallon papers, Fallon to Workman, 19 October 1918.

44 *Canadian Freeman*, 12 September 1918.

45 *Action catholique*, 5 Septembre 1918.

46 *Catholic Register*, 12 September 1918.

47 *Action catholique*, 10 Septembre 1918; *Canadian Freeman*, 22 August and 5 September 1918; *New Freeman*, 24 August, 7 September and 14 September 1918; *Casket*, 8 August 1918; *Northwest Review*, 17 August and 7 September 1918.

48 *Catholic Register*, 3 October 1918.

49 Ibid., 19 September 1918. *Ottawa Evening Journal*, 14 and 23 September 1918; *Canadian Freeman*, 12 September 1918. For dollar conversion adjusted for inflation, see www.bankofcanada.ca/rates/related/inflation-calculator.

50 *Northwest Review*, 28 September 1918.

51 *Ottawa Evening Journal*, 17 September 1918. The editor also indicated that $30,000 was the target for Ottawa and the counties of Prescott, Russell, and Carleton, indicating the precision in which CAH organizers had divided the country with specific financial goals for each subdivision. The *New Freeman* reported that the Diocese of Saint John was asked to raise $20,000 and the Diocese of Chatham $23,000. *New Freeman*, 7 September 1918.

52 *Catholic Register*, 10 October 1918.

53 *Ottawa Evening Journal*, 19 September 1918. Editorial.

54 Cited in the *Catholic Register*, 10 October 1918. The Conservative *Mail and Empire* gave strong editorial support to the Catholic Huts Campaign and

was generous in providing updates of the activities of the collection teams and total funds raised from 2–4 October 2 1918. It was also clear that, given the daily half-page and three-quarter-page advertisements in the paper during the campaign week, the Hut's organizing committee valued the Toronto daily's large Tory readership. The advertisements were not overtly Catholic in any way, featuring drawings of the troops at the front with generic-looking "padres" and one poster containing a sketch of a rabbi (chaplain), who had constructed a makeshift cross of twigs, in order to comfort a dying Christian soldier at the front. The Campaign organizers were conscious in their emphasis of the interfaith character of the Huts and the need for religious solidarity among Canadians at the Allies' time of need. *Mail and Empire*, 30 September and 1–8 August 1918.

55 ADA, Bishop Morrison papers, Doc 5485, Letter from J.L Murray to Morrison, 20 August 1918, with enclosure of Knights Army Hut Appeal signed by J.J. Leddy (Saskatoon), J.L. Murray (Renfrew) and George Boivin (Granby), 21 August 1918.

56 ARCAT, McNeil papers, war box, Circular to the Clergy, 25 September 1918.

57 *Ottawa Evening Journal*, 19 September 1918.

58 *Northwest Review*, 28 September 1918.

59 *Regina Post*, cited in *Ottawa Evening Journal*, 16 September 1918.

60 *Ontario Catholic Year Book*, Toronto: Newman Centre, 1920) 25; ARCAT, Knights of Columbus papers, Colonel Dinnick's Speech for the Catholic Army Huts Campaign, 29 September 1918. The speech indicates that in the Toronto campaign three team captains included A.R. Auld, a Presbyterian, J.B. Hutchins, of the Masonic Committee, and Mr. Moneypenny of the YMCA. The teams were divided 50–50 Protestant–Catholic.

61 Ibid. Calculations of current value factoring inflation derived from www.bankofcanada.ca/rates/related/inflation-calculator. ARCAT, Knights of Columbus papers, J/L/ Murray to McNeil, 28 April 1919. Murray indicates that the final tally was $1,148,452.75. The preliminary estimate of one million dollars was confirmed by the *New Freeman*, 28 September 1918. The front page offered preliminary tallies by region amounting to $746,000. Quebec led with $275,000; Ontario $150,000; Nova Scotia $118,000; New Brunswick $75,000; Manitoba/Saskatchewan $65,000; Alberta $37,000; PEI $20,000; and BC $6,000. These provincial campaigns were undertaken at the end of September. Toronto's $200,000 placed Ontario first in the provincial rankings for giving and put the campaign near the one million dollar mark. The low tally from British Columbia was blamed by at least one Padre, Captain Thomas Cooney on low regard for Catholics in Victoria, where he

worked, some disloyal priests, and the pitiful state of the Knights in British Columbia. "I called upon the Knights twice – they are a dead crowd. They are not up and doing and have no officers to organize and promote movements." LAC, RG 9 III, Department of Militia and Defence, vol. 4620, C-8, Thomas Cooney, CSsR, Cooney to Rev. L.A. Sylvestre, 22 December 1918, 25 December 1918, and 20 December 1918.

62 ARCAT, McNeil papers, war box, McNeil to G.A Warburton, YMCA, 5 October 1918; McNeil to Ralph Connable, Woolworths Company, 10 October 1918.

63 *Catholic Register*, 10 October 1918. Calculations of current value factoring inflation derived from www.bankofcanada.ca/rates/related/inflation-calculator.

64 ARCAT, McNeil papers, war box, W.S. Dinnick to McNeil, 11 October 1918.

65 *Catholic Register*, 10 October 1918, citing the *Mail and Empire*, 2 October 1918.

66 LAC, RG 9 III, Department of Militia and Defence, volume 4623, file C-F-G, Michael Francis Fallon, Fallon to Workman, 19 October 1918.

67 *Sentinel*, 20 September 1917; 19 September 1918; 10 October 1918; and 24 October 1918.

68 Ibid., 30 August 1917.

69 *Halifax Herald*, 5 April 1918.

70 *Catholic Register*, 12 September 1918 and 28 August 1919. The *Register* reported on March 20, 1919, that the Board of Control had cancelled Mayor Church's pledge because city money could not be expended on sectarian projects. The editor chalked this up to "Toronto's intolerance and bigotry."

71 *Canadian Freeman*, 26 September 1918.

72 AAM, Archbishop Bruchési Correspondence, 732.256, (Copy) Cardinal L.-N. Bégin to J.L. Murray, 26 August 1918 and Bruchési to J.L. Murray, 31 August 1918.

73 J.L. Granatstein and J.M. Hitsman, *Broken Promises: A History of Conscription in Canada* (Toronto: Copp Clark Pitman Ltd., 1985), 84.

74 Ibid., 85. Also *The Canada Gazette*, Extra, Order in Council, Saturday, 20 April 1918.

75 J.L. Granatstein, "Conscription and the Great War," in *Canada and the First World War: Essays in Honour of Robert Craig Brown*, ed. David MacKenzie (Toronto: University of Toronto Press, 2005), 68.

76 Benjamin Isitt, *From Victoria to Vladivostok: Canada's Siberian Expedition, 1917–1919* (Vancouver: UBC Press, 2010), 72–3.

77 Mark G. McGowan, "Ecumenism," in *Planted By Flowing Water: The Diocese of Ottawa, 1847–1947*, ed. Pierre Hurtubise, Mark G. McGowan and Pierre Savard (Ottawa: Novalis, 1998), 226. In the 1911 census the proportion of

Catholics in counties contained in the Archdiocese of Ottawa were as follows: Carleton (32.5 per cent), North Lanark (18.7 per cent), Russell (65 per cent), Prescott (81.6 per cent), and City of Ottawa (50.1 per cent). When the entire territory contained within the archdiocesan boundaries is aggregated, 54.2 per cent of the people were Roman Catholic. All calculations were based on the Census of Canada, 1911.

78 RG 24, vol. 4404, file 26-5-64-2, vol. 1, *National Service of Canada – Recruiting Prospects*.

79 *Catholic Register*, 14 February 1918.

80 *Catholic Record*, 12 January 1918.

81 LAC, RG 9 III, vol. 4652, "Establishments 8," Lt. Col. Wolston Workman, ADCS (RC) to Director of Chaplain Service, 17 August 1918.

82 AAM, Archbishop Bruchési Correspondence, 723.254, Charles J. Doherty to Bruchési, 11 September 1917.

83 AAQ, 60 CN, Gouvernment du Canada, IX:171, Louis-Nazaire Bégin to C.J. Doherty, 30 July 1917 also IX: 190, Robert Borden to Cardinal Bégin, 25 October 1917.

84 AAQ, 60 CN, Gouvernment du Canada, IX:184, Joseph Bolduc to Archbishop Louis-Nazaire Bégin, 7 August 1917.

85 LAC, Robert Borden papers, vol. 222, C.J. Doherty to Borden, 19 April 1918, pp/ 124944 and 124950. See also AAQ, 60 CN, Gouvernmnet du Canada, X:103, Doherty to Bégin, 2 octobre 1918 in which Doherty questions Begin's liberal interpretation of the conferring of tonsure. Doherty asks for clarification earlier from Coadjutor bishop Roy, AAQ, 60 CN, Gouvernment de Canada, X:44, Doherty to Bishop Roy, 26 mars 1918.

86 Granatstein and Hitsman, *Broken promises*, 89. Elizabeth Armstrong, *The Crisis of Quebec, 1914–1918* (Toronto: McClelland and Stewart Limited, 1974 (orig. 1937), Carleton Library Series, No. 7), 227–30.

87 AAQ, 10 A, Mandements, vol. 17, typed draft signed by Bégin, 30 March 1918.

88 AAQ, 60 CN, Gouvernment du Canada, IX : 209, Bégin to Borden 12 avril 1918.

89 LAC, Borden papers, vol. 16, reel C-4106, H. Boulay to Borden, 7 April 1918, pp. 4078–81. Bourassa made his anti-Conscription position clear in *Le Devoir* 12 July 1917, which was a reprint of a statement he delivered in English to the *New York Evening Post*.

90 AAQ, 60 CN, Gouvernment de Canada, X : 93, General Landry to Bégin, 17 August 1918 (in French).

91 AAM, Bruchési Correspondence, 732.254, Louis Loranger, Military Service

Branch to Bruchési, 21 February 1918 and Bruchési to Loranger, 22 February 1918. See also 777.017, Bruchési to Doherty, 21 February 1918.

92 *New Freeman*, 6 April 1918.

93 *Le Droit*, 16 May 1916.

94 *Catholic Register*, 16 May 1918, praises work of Regina's Archbishop Mathieu for his work on changing the hearts of French Canadians. Poet-Professor Thomas O'Hagan publicly defended Quebec and her high moral standards, low crime rate, and historic loyalty. *Canadian Freeman*, 1 October 1918.

95 AAM, Bruchési papers, Toronto Correspondence, McNeil to Bruchési, 17 March 1917; ARCAT, McNeil papers, AS 13.05, A. Fitzpatrick, Montreal, to McNeil, 23 October 1917 (in French); and S, Lahy, Montreal, to McNeil, 28 February 1918.

96 AAM, Bruchési papers, Toronto Correspondence, 225–104, 918–1, McNeil to Chancellor Roy, 22 April 1918.

97 *La Presse*, 191 April 1918 and *Montreal Star*, 20 April 1918.

98 ARCAT, McNeil papers, AS 13.08, J.A.H. Cameron to McNeil, 25 April 1918.

99 ARCAT, McNeil papers AH 07.134, "A Pea Soup" to McNeil, 21 April 1918 and McNeil, war box, Cameron to McNeil, 29 May 1918. Added praise came from Oswald Mayrand, managing editor of *La Presse*, who gave McNeil an open invitation to publish in his paper. ARCAT, McNeil papers, AH 08.01, Oswald Mayrand to McNeil, 4 January 1919.

100 ASV-ADC, 130.1/4, Father A Sylvestre to Bishop Pellegrino Stagni, Apostolic Delegate to Canada, 18 January 1916.

101 ASV-ADC, 130.1/4, Archbishop Michael Spratt to Monsignor Filippi, 30 July 1918 and Cardinal Begin to Filippi, 29 July 1918.

102 *New Freeman*, 8 June 1918.

103 ASV-ADC, 130.1, Monsignor Filippi to Bishop J. M. Emard, Valleyfield, 3 August 1918, letter 14849. LAC, RG 9 III C 15, Assistant Director Chaplain Service (RC) fonds, file 1, Neil McNeil to A. Sylvestre, 19 August 1918.

104 Robert Choquette, "An Historical Overview," in Hurtubise et al., *Planted By Flowing Water*, 18.

105 ADL, Fallon papers, S.C. Mewburn to Fallon, 11 February 1918. See also copy Michael Francis Fallon to Mewburn, 23 February 1918. There is some evidence to suggest that Fallon himself planted the idea for his travel with Workman as early as November 1917, when he suggested to the ADCS (Catholic) that "It might bring some little consolation and encouragement to the noble brand of priests who are laboring so zealously for the spiritual welfare of our Canadian soldiers. If the military authorities invite me to do

so I shall endeavour to make arrangements to accept the invitation." ADL, Fallon papers, Fallon to Wolston Workman, 17 November 1917. Copy.

106 ADL, Fallon papers, Fallon to Archbishop P.F. Stagni, 13 February 1918; also Stagni to Fallon, 18 February 1918, Letter 14452; also Fallon papers, "Diary of Visit to Canadian Army in England and France at the Request of the Canadian Government," May–June, 1918. Transportation was arranged in Fallon papers, Mewburn to Fallon, 28 February 1918.

107 ADL, Fallon diary, 16 May 1918.

108 ADL, Fallon diary, 2 June 1918 (Currie); 23 May 1918 (chaplains); 25 May 1918 (howitzer); 30 May 1918 (Royal 22nd).

109 ADL, Fallon diary, 28 May 1918.

110 ADL, Fallon diary, 18 July, 24 July, and 25 July 1918.

111 S. Karly Kehoe and Darren Tierney, "'Like a Kind Mother': Imperial Concerns and Britain's Changing Perceptions of Rome, 1783–1815," CCHA *Historical Studies, Occasional Paper* 81 (2015): 11–31.

112 ADL, Fallon diary, 27 July 1918.

113 ADL, Fallon diary, 10 August 1918.

114 Hogan, "The Guelph Novitiate Raid," 65. Robert Rutherdale, *Hometown Horizons: Local Responses to the Great War* (Vancouver: UBC Press, 2004), 184.

115 Hogan, "The Guelph Novitiate Raid," 67.

116 Ibid., 68; *Commission to Inquire into certain charges by Rev. K.H. Palmer and Sir Sam Hughes relating to the administration of the Guelph Novitiate*, 1919. Chair: Joseph Andrew Chisholm. Debates of the House of Commons, Canada (*Hansard*) 1919 Session, vol. 2, 7 April 1919, p. 1220.

117 *Toronto Star*, 19 June 1918.

118 Rutherdale, *Hometown Horizons*, 186–7.

119 Note in particular J.R. Miller, *Equal Rights: The Jesuits Estates Act Controversy* (Montreal & Kingston: McGill-Queen's University Press, 1979).

120 Debates of the House of Commons, Canada (*Hansard*) 1919 Session, volume 2, 7 April 1919, pp 1219–59.

121 LAC, MG 27-II D6, Doherty papers, vol. 2, file 52, "Report of the Commissioners," 6 October 1919.

122 Rutherdale, *Hometown Horizons*, 189.

123 *Canadian Freeman*, 27 June 1918.

124 *Casket*, 27 June 1918.

125 *New Freeman*, 29 June 1918.

126 Ibid. also *Action Catholique*, 27 juin 1918; *Catholic Register*, 27 June 1918.

127 *Catholic Register*, 4 July 1918.

128 Ibid., 18 July 1918.

129 ADL, Fallon diary, 23 May 1918.

130 ADL, Fallon diary, 3 July 1918. LAC, Charles Murphy papers, vol. 23, Arthur O'Leary, Pastor St Joseph's Parish Toronto) to Murphy, 20 March 1918, p. 9915. Father O'Leary wonders why Catholics are still treated so poorly when "We all want to win the war and to help in the winning, but the graft of the past three years and the injustice of the last so-called election makes patience a virtue somewhat overstrained."

131 For a concise summary of events, see Michael Hopkinson, *The Irish War of Independence* (Montreal & Kingston: McGill-Queen's University Press, 2002), 3–21; Fearghal McGarry, "1916 and Irish Republicanism: Between Myth and History," in *Towards Commemoration: Ireland in War and Revolution 1912–1923*, ed. John Horne and Edward Madigan (Dublin: Royal Irish Academy, 2013), 46–53; David Fitzpatrick, ed., *Terror in Ireland, 1916–1923* (Dublin: Lilliput Press, Trinity History Workshop, 2012).

132 *Canadian Freeman*, 14 March 1918.

133 *Northwest Review*, 9 March 1918.

134 *Catholic Record*, 6 July 1918.

135 *New Freeman*, 25 May and 1 June 1918.

136 Fearghal McGarry, "1916 and Irish Republicanism: Between Myth and History," in *Towards Commemoration: Ireland in War and Revolution, 1912–1923*, ed. John Horne and Edward Madigan (Dublin: Royal Irish Academy, 2013): 46–53.

137 ADL, Fallon Diary, 19 May 1918.

138 *Catholic Record*, 20 April 1918. The *New Freeman*, 25 May 1918, strongly agreed.

139 Ibid.

140 *Casket*, 31 January, 15 March, and 25 April 1918; *Catholic Register*, 28 November 1918; *Catholic Record*, 7 September 1918.

141 *New Freeman*, 2 March 1918, and *Catholic Register*, 19 December 1918.

142 *Canadian Freeman*, 18 April 1918.

143 *New Freeman*, 13 May 1918 and 13 April 1918.

144 *Catholic Record*, 16 June 1918, and *Catholic Register*, 25 April 1918.

145 *Catholic Record*, 16 June 1918.

146 *Toronto Star*, 19 April 1918 and *Globe*, 22 April 1918. It was suggested by a correspondent to Neil McNeil that J.L. Murray, State Deputy of the Knights of Columbus in Ontario, also supported conscription in Ireland. ARCAT, McNeil papers, J.S. McGinnis to McNeil, 15 April 1918.

147 ADL, Fallon diary, 6, 7, 12, 14, and 21 June 1918; 3 July 1918.

148 Ibid., 10 June 1918.

149 *Casket*, 23 November 1917 and *Cathedral Magazine* (Hamilton), January 1918; *Catholic Register*, 8 November 1917 and 24 October 1918. ARCAT, McNeil papers, McNeil to J.C. O'Connor, 12 October 1918. McNeil indicates that Victory Loan signs will be placed in all churches.

150 *Canadian Freeman*, 29 August 1918. *Northwest Review*, 20 and 27 July 1918.

151 ADL, Fallon diary, 14 August 1918.

152 Ibid.

153 Ibid.

154 ADL, Fallon diary, 27 and 28 August 1918.

155 Ibid., 14 August 1918.

156 Desmond Morton, *When Your Number's Up: The Canadian Soldier in the First World War* (Toronto: Random House, 1993), 278.

157 Ibid., 279. Morton bases his figures on 619,636 attestation papers filed for the CEF.

158 Desmond Morton, *Canada and War* (Toronto: Butterworths, 1981), 81; Tim Cook, *Shock Troops: Canadians Fighting the Great War, 1917–1918*, vol. 2 (Toronto: Viking Canada, 2008), 578 and 612.

159 Cook, *Shock Troops*, 612.

160 *New Freeman*, 11 August 1917 and 24 May 1919.

161 Ibid., 16 November 1918.

162 *Casket*, 14 November 1918.

163 *Northwest Review*, 16 November 1918. The *New Freeman*, 23 November 1918 also made the link between the importance of the victory over Germany and Lloyd George following through with self-determination for Ireland.

164 Ibid.

165 *Casket*, 14 November 1918.

166 *Cathedral Magazine*, November 1918, 11.

167 *Northwest Review*, 16 November 1918.

168 AAW, Alfred Sinnott papers, Circular Letter, no. 9, 15 November 1918.

169 ADC, First World War File, Major D. Warner, Senior Chaplain to Father A. Newman, St Mary's, 23 July and 25 September 1918; 23 January and 21 March 1919.

170 AAQ, Circulars, No. 120, Circulaire au Clergé, 10 décembre 1918.

171 ADPb, Circular Letters, Bishop Patrick T. Ryan, Christmas 1917.

172 LAC, National Personnel Records Centre, Personnel File, Nursing Sister Christina Campbell. Katherine Dewar, *Those Splendid Girls: The Heroic Service of Prince Edward Island Nurses in the Great War* (Charlottetown: UPEI, Island Studies Press, 2014), 109–16. Dewar offers a very moving account of

the sinking of the *Llandovery Castle*, featuring nursing sister Rena MacLean, one of the six nurses who died.

173 Fred McEvoy, et. al., *Enduring Faith: A History of St Patrick's Basilica Parish, Ottawa, 1855–2005* (Ottawa: St Patrick's Basilica, 2006), 141–3.

174 Parish honour rolls from parishes in every province of Canada have been examined for this study. They vary in the materials used and sometimes were missing from parishes because of the physical renovations made to parishes after the Second Vatican Council in the early 1960s. In some cities, parishes passed hands from ethnic group to ethnic group, with subsequent groups remodelling the churches and disposing of some of the honour rolls, containing the names of Irish Catholics whose families had long since departed the parish. Such was the case at St Mary's in Toronto. In terms of mandated honour rolls see: ARCAT, McNeil papers, war box, Letter from Arthur O'Leary, St Joseph's Parish, 18 August 1918 and Father K.E. Morrow, St.Anthony's Parish to McNeil, 22 August 1918.

175 *Catholics of the Diocese of Antigonish, Nova Scotia and The War, 1914–1918* (Antigonish: St Francis Xavier University Press, c. 1919), foreword. ARCAT, Neil McNeil papers, Father J.R. MacDonald to McNeil, 22 December 1918. AP 05.18. MacDonald indicates that work on the book began and it was anticipated that 4,500 names would be collected. MacDonald was responsible for trying to secure funding for the project from the Catholic Army Huts funds, which evidently were not forthcoming as easily as promised. ADA, Morrison papers, N.R McArthur to Mr. O'Meara, Barrister & Solicitor, Ottawa, 11 January 1918, copy. Doc no. 8780.

176 USMCA, *St Michael's College Yearbook*, 1919, 5–11, 41, and 58–69.

177 Rev. Edward Kelly, ed., *The Story of St Paul's Parish, Toronto* (Toronto: n.p., 1922), 171–3.

178 Ibid., 173

CONCLUSION

1 *The Tablet*, 15 November 2014. Tim Cook, *At the Sharp End: Canadians Fighting the Great War, 1914–1918* (Toronto: Viking Canada, 2007), 321.

2 www.comece.org/site/en/press/pressreleases/mewsletter.content/1844.html ?SWS=25cef03cd9c8e21c382b1096f3b4ebf0, accessed 5 August 2015.

3 Jerome aan de Weil, *The Catholic Church in Ireland, 1914–1918: War and Politics* (Dublin: Irish Academic Press, 2003), 62–76.

4 For example, AAW, Alfred A. Sinnott papers, Circular Letter, 28 February 1918.

Sinnott mentions that support for the Government's food program is "a patriotic duty we cannot refuse."

5 *Catholic Register*, 1 February 1917.

6 Kevin Anderson, "Anti-Catholicism and English-Canadian Nationalism, 1905–1965" (PhD diss., McMaster University, 2013); John S. Moir, "Toronto's Protestants and Their Perceptions of Their Roman Catholic Neighbours," in *Catholics at the Gathering Place: Historical Essays on the Archdiocese of Toronto, 1841–1991*, ed. Mark G. McGowan and Brian P. Clarke (Toronto: Canadian Catholic Historical Association & Dundurn Press, 1993), 313–27. Raymond Huel, "The Anderson Amendments and Secularization of Saskatchewan Public Schools," 44 CCHA *Study Sessions* (1977): 61–76.

7 ARCAT, McNeil papers, AS12.85, "Adding Insult to Injury", c.1926.

8 *United Church Observer*, 15 November 1962.

9 Aan de Weil, *The Catholic Church in Ireland*. 79–125.

10 *New Freeman*, 2 February 1918. See Father Lancelot Minehan's comments on Sinn Fein in the *Toronto Star*, 22 January 1919.

11 *Catholic Register*, 9 January and 13 March 1919 and 4 November and 2 December 1920. *Canadian Freeman*, 12 December 1918.

12 *Catholic Record*, 25 September 1920. See also *Catholic Register*, 27 January 1921. Comparisons also appear in the *New Freeman*, 9 August 1919.

13 *Canadian Freeman*, 1 January, 3 June and 10 June 1920.

14 Ibid., 10 February 1921. The *Catholic Register* proposed the application of the war's "principles" as early as 2 December 1920. The *Northwest Review* commented on the war principles, 29 November 1919.

15 *Cathedral Magazine* (March, 1919), 37. See also *Catholic Register*, 20 March 1919 and 17 June 1920. The *Northwest Review* urged that the Irish issue be taken up at the Versailles conference, 5 July 1919.

16 *Canadian Freeman*, 27 January and 3 February 1921. In April 1921 about $953.75 was collected on the Prairies, although a large number of the donors bore Ukrainian, not Irish surnames, particularly in Regina and environs. *Northwest Review*, 16 April 1921.

17 *Catholic Register*, 1 July 1920. A similar meeting in Halifax also featured clergy and laymen who had been supportive of Canada's war effort. Patrick Mannion, "Halifax Catholics' Patriotic Work: Responses to Irish Nationalism, 1880–1923," in McGowan and Vance, eds., Canadian Catholic Historical Association, *Historical Studies* – Occasional Paper 81 (2015): 195–223. An Ireland rally was also held in Winnipeg. *Northwest Review*, 8 November 1919. In Vancouver the Irish National Association supported a loan appeal

to the Dail Eireann, the "parliament" held by Sinn Fein MPs, who were elected to Westminster but refused to take their seats. *Northwest Review*, 17 September 1920. Ottawa also hosted an SDIL meeting. *Northwest Review*, 30 October 1920.

18 *Northwest Review*, 16 April 1921. The Winnipeg situation is detailed, but without a national context, in Richard Davis, "Irish Nationalism in Manitoba, 1870–1922," *The Untold Story: The Irish in Canada*, vol. 1, ed. Robert O'Driscoll and Lorna Reynolds (Toronto: Celtic Arts of Canada, 1988), 393–416. Unfortunately, the article is the only scholarly source on Irish nationalism in Manitoba.

19 The best analysis of this local manifestation of more radical Irish nationalism is found in Simon Jolivet, *Le vert et le bleu: Identité Québécois et identité irlandaise au tournant de xxe siècle* (Montreal: Les Presses de l'Université de Montréal, 2011), 218–25 and 234–8.

20 Jolivet, *Le vert et le bleu*, 225.

21 *Catholic Record*, 3 April 1920.

22 Ibid., 10 April and 18 September 1920. The ideas and links to the principles fought for in the war are repeated in the *Catholic Register*, 3 March 1921.

23 Padraig O' Saidhail, *Katherine Hughes A Life and A Journey* (Ottawa: Penumbra Press, 2014), 217–49. The *Canadian Freeman* was perhaps the Catholic weekly most sympathetic to the republicans; see 10 February 1921.

24 *Catholic Record*, 17 and 24 and 31 December 1921 and 2 September 1922. *Catholic Register*, 8 and 29 June, 17 and 31 August, and 5 October 1922. *Northwest Review*, 10 December 1921. Frederick J. McEvoy, "Canadian Catholic Press Reaction to the Irish Crisis, 1916–1921," in *Irish Nationalism in Canada*, ed. David Wilson (Montreal and Kingston: McGill-Queen's University Press, 2009), 137. The *Canadian Freeman*, 5 January 1922, praised the Anglo-Irish Treaty as not perfect but it might have proven to be the road to something else. Although favouring Michael Collins and Arthur Griffith, it did acknowledge the right of de Valera to dissent.

25 LAC, MG 30, Austin Weir papers, CNR Radio, Addresses, No. 21, Grattan O'Leary, "The National Election in the Irish Free State," 21 February 1932.

26 David Crane, *Empires of the Dead: How One Man's Vision Led to the Creation of the Commonwealth War Graves Commission* (London: William Collins, 2014).

27 J.R. O'Gorman, *Soldiers of Christ: The Canadian Catholic Chaplain Service* (Timmins: n.p., 1936) and J.R. O'Gorman, "Canadian Catholic Chaplains and the Great War," CCHA *Reports* 7 (1939–40) are some of the only writings reflecting on the work of the Catholic chaplains who served in the CEF.

28 *Chilliwack Progress*, 13 June 1951; www.bytown.net/fanning.htm.

29 J.R. O'Gorman, *Soldiers of Christ*, 47, and J.R. O'Gorman, "Canadian Catholic Chaplains," 73.

30 *Ottawa Citizen*, 10 April 1922 (letter to the editor denouncing French Canadian conduct in the Ottawa Separate School Board) AAO, O'Gorman papers to A.A. Sinnott, 25 November 1931. He claims Archbishop Forbes has brought peace: "There are as yet a few professional French fanatics in this diocese (they are but few and their influence is waning in Ottawa) whose disordered imaginations are forever dreaming of Irish plots." *Ottawa Journal*, 24 April 1933. His publications included *Planning the Catechism Lesson: Suggestions Based on a Revised Munich Method* (Toronto: Extension Print, 1931); *The Catholic Church* (Toronto: Catholic Truth Society, 1924); *Catholic Women and Bible Reading* (Toronto: Catholic Truth Society, 1926); and *The Catholic Church and Liberal Education* (London: Catholic Unity League of Canada, 1923). His writings on McGee include LAC MG 30, D 20, John J. O'Gorman papers, "Thomas D'Arcy McGee, The Irishman – The Canadian – The Catholic," 1925.

31 AAO, O'Gorman papers, O'Gorman to English-speaking Secretary of the Ottawa Separate School Board, 19 August 1921,

32 AAO, O'Gorman papers, file 2, Father L.N. Campeau, Diocesan Administrator to O'Gorman, 10 April 1922.

33 AAO, Blessed Sacrament Parish Records, F56/5, Annual Reports, 1914, 1922, 1926 and 1929.

34 *Ottawa Citizen*, 25 April 1933.

35 *Ottawa Journal*, 24 April 1933.

36 www.parl.gc.ca/parlinfo/Files/Parliamentarian.aspx?Item=1d093884-066e-4154-90c4-5125c80965b9&Language=E&Section=ALL, accessed 10 August 2015.

37 Sixth Census of Canada, 1921, Ontario, District 110, Sub-district 38, Ottawa Centre Ward, page 8, line 40.

38 Hector W. Charlesworth, ed., *Cyclopaedia of Canadian Biography* (Toronto: Hunter-Rose, 1919), 156.

39 A.J. MacDougall et. al., eds., *Dictionary of Jesuit Biography: Ministry to English Canada, 1842–1987* (Toronto: Canadian Institute of Jesuit Studies, 1991), 87. Doherty received his early education at Loyola College in Montreal and returned to Montreal from 1921 to 1924 to study philosophy at Immaculate Conception College. He was ordained in 1930 and pursued his graduate degrees at the Gregorian University in Rome, from which he graduated in 1933. He taught Church history at the Jesuit Seminary in Toronto and by

the 1960s was engaged in pastoral work in Winnipeg, Thunder Bay, and Montreal. He died in 1970. Throughout his life he was tormented by illness and depression but was always noted to be a jovial, engaging, and dynamic personality, particularly in the classroom.

40 William Joseph O'Brien, *Send Out the Army and the Navy*, ed. by William H O'Brien, CSB, with appendices by James O'Brien (Private Family typescript), 240.

41 Ibid., 242–3.

42 LAC, RG 150, accession 1992–93/166, Box 6867–27, Personnel File Arthur A. McGrory, 639911.

43 Allan Levine, "Nicholas Bawlf," *Dictionary of Canadian Biography*, vol. XIV (1911–1920), www.biographi.ca/en/bio.php?id_nbr=7191; also see The Manitoba Historical Society, Memorable Manitobans, "Nicholas Bawlf," www.mhs.mb.ca/docs/people/bawlf_n.shtml. *Fourth Census of Canada, 1901*, Manitoba, Winnipeg City, Ward 2, page 8, line 45. Despite his unusual surname, Bawlf identifies himself as Irish.

44 Society for International Hockey Research, "Nick Bawlf," www.sihrhockey.org/login.cfm?accessdenied=%2Fmember_player_sheet.cfm%3Fplayer_id=8855

45 LAC, RG 150, accession 1992-93/166, box 516–21, Personnel File, Nicholas Bawlf, Captain.

46 Manitoba Historical Society, Memorable Manitobans, Clarence Nicholas Bawlf, www.mhs.mb.ca/docs/people/bawlf_cn.shtml; LAC, RG 150, accession 1992–93/166, box 516–19, Personnel File, Louis Drummond Bawlf, Lt.

47 LAC, RG 150, accession 1992–93/166, box 516–18, Personnel File, David Leland Bawlf, 1250090, transferred to RFC. Canada's Virtual War Memorial: www.veterans.gc.ca/eng/remembrance/memorials/canadian-virtual-war-memorial/detail/466750?David Leland Bawlf

48 *Manitoba Free Press*, 27 November 1918.

49 Canadian Great War Project, Louis Drummond Bawlf, http://canadiangreatwarproject.com/searches/soldierDetail.asp?ID=98000

50 Sixth Census of Canada, 1921, Province of Ontario, Parkdale, Sub-District 054, Toronto City, p. 8, line 37.

51 LAC, RG 150, Accession 1992-93/166, box 6852–18, Personnel File, William McGowan, 27242.

52 Sixth Census of Canada, 1921, Province of Ontario, District 110, Enumeration Sub-District 55, Capital Ward, Ottawa, p. 3, Lines, 19–22.

53 Cited in the *Catholic Register*, 31 May 1934.

54 Linda Gray-LeBlanc, *Halifax Heroes Remembered: The Story of Halifax Solders in World War I* (Halifax: by the author, 2012), 146–7. Even Gray-LeBlanc confuses the two, offering a very good description of the younger Meagher (415270) while offering the regimental number for the less-than-willing Meagher (40508343). LAC, RG 150, accession 1992–93/166, box 6086-40, John Patrick Joseph Meagher and John Patrick Meagher, box 6086–44.

Index

5th Brigade, 131, 163, 193; Chaplains, 171, 186–7; and language issues, 172–7, 187–8
5th Canadian Mounted Rifles (CMR), 64
5th Division, 120, 229
15th Battalion, 297
22nd Battalion (Van Doos), 127, 181; and 5th Brigade, 168, 171; and Bishop Fallon, 270; Catholics in, 193; and VD, 195, 197
25th Battalion, 127, 129, 131; and 5th Brigade, 168; occupations of, 133; recruitment of, 161; religion in, 172–3, 193
26th Battalion, 127, 131, 197; and 5th Brigade, 171
36th Ulster Division, 119, 210
40th Battalion, 129, 299; and chaplains, 168; in Halifax, 127, 131–3; occupations of, 133; recruitment of, 161
85th Battalion, 115, 168, 188
105th Battalion, 197
121st Battalion (Western Irish), 119, 122–4
130th Battalion (Lanark & Renfrew Highlanders), 127, 160
138th Battalion, 105, 137
154th Battalion, 127, 296
185th Battalion, 170
199th Battalion (Irish Rangers), 88, 117, 120, 123, 168; Catholicism in, 188; chaplain, 120, 197; disbanded, 120, 237; and J.J. O'Gorman, 223; recruitment of, 124; VD in, 194; and William Hingston, SJ, 250
208th Battalion (Irish Regiment of Canada), 120, 123; recruitment of, 122, 124; religion in, 121
218th Battalion (Edmonton Irish Guards), 120; ethnicity of, 126–7; recruitment of, 124
240th Battalion, 156, 197

Akenson, Donald H., 5, 6, 31
Alberta, 151; Catholics in, 76; and Edward Francis Murray, 68; and Knights of Columbus, 256; nurses from, 147–8; priests in, 191; recruitment in, 112–13, 134; and schools, 43

Almond, Colonel John M., 178
Ancient Order of Hibernians (AOH), 209–10, 212, 217, 291; and Boer War, 58, 61; and Boston Convention, 217–18; and Charles J. Foy, 238; and Home Rule, 35, 219, 222, 224; and Sinn Fein, 292
Anglicans (Church of England), 19, 46, 208, 243, 246; in 25th Battalion, 128, 131, 135–6; in 40th Battalion, 130, 132; and chaplaincy, 166, 170, 172, 178; and Frederick G. Scott, 167, 187, 205; nurses, 147; in Ottawa Valley, 152; and recruitment, 107–8, 110, 123, 134, 139, 282
Anglin, Frank (Judge), 51, 220
Anglin, Timothy Warren, 37
Asselin, Olivar, 9, 191

Bawlf, Nicolas, 296
B.C. Catholic, 37
Bégin, Louis-Nazaire (Archbishop of Quebec, 1898–25), 56, 103, 284, 290; and conscription, 243, 244, 266–7; and Knights of Columbus, 262; and National Registration, 299; and recruitment, 102; against riots (Quebec), 266
Belgian Relief Fund, 92–3, 95–6
Belgium, 10, 17, 22, 47, 72–3, 84, 150, 163; defence of, 77, 81, 91–2, 93, 109, 213, 228, 280; and Desiré Mercier, 89, 92, 291; and J.J. O'Gorman, 82; Jules Pirot from, 187; Mons, 281; self-determination of, 277, 292
Bennett, R.B., 230, 240
Black '47 (Great Irish Famine), 5, 29, 31
Black & Tans, 290–1
Bonne Entente, 16, 251, 268, 290
Borden, Sir Robert L., 79, 84, 175; and Bishop Fallon, 247, 269–71; and chaplains, 176, 178; and Charles Doherty, 249, 266, 295; and conscription, 202, 228–33, 244; and immigration, 161; and Irish Home Rule, 219–20, 224; and Knights of Columbus, 259; on Riots, 266–7; on Ukrainians, 234; Union government of, 238, 241, 289, 292
Bourassa, Henri, 9, 13, 15, 47, 99–101, 203, 226–7, 230, 290, 292; and Archbishop Bruchési, 101, 232; and Archbishop McNeil, 103; on Boer War, 56, 59; and Catholic press, 99–102, 235; against J.J. O'Gorman, 82–3, 100; and riots, 267; against Wilfrid Laurier, 231
British Columbia, 75, 120, 226; aliens in, 210; Ambrose Madden, OMI, in, 169–70, 293; and Boer War, 65; Catholics in, 169; and Knights of Columbus, 256; nurses from, 147–8; and VD, 194
British Empire, vi, 3, 10, 15, 20, 68, 84, 98; Alfred E. Burke on, 78–9; and Ancient Order of Hibernians, 210, 222; and Archbishop McNeil, 99–100, 203, 246; and Archbishop O'Brien, 64; and Bishop Budka, 209, 280; Bishop Fallon on, 87, 93, 246, 271; Bishop Sinnott and, 283; and Boer

War, 3, 12, 52, 57, 60–2, 67; *Canadian Freeman* on, 39, 86; *Casket* on, 60, 80, 99, 235, 277; *Catholic Record* on, 60, 80, 84–5; *Catholic Register* on, 62; Charles Fitzpatrick, 69, 81; and citizenship (Irish Catholic), 34, 26, 52–4, 113, 162, 202, 205, 217, 271, 275, 288, 290; and disloyalty, 227, 262; and Empire Club, 78; and immigration, 208–10; and imperial war, 72–8; and Ireland, 8–9, 19, 32–3, 35, 211–15, 217, 229; John Burke on, 71–2; J.J. O'Gorman on, 82–3; and Knights of Columbus, 87, 254, 279–80; *New Freeman* on, 39, 86; *Northwest Review* on, 41, 242; and Quebec bishops, 99, 230, 290; and schools, 69

Bruchési, Paul (Archbishop of Montreal, 1897–39), 56, 101, 103, 262, 290; and conscription, 229, 232–3, 265, 267; and Knights of Columbus, 253, 256

Budka, Nykyta (Ukrainian Eparch, 1912–28), 98, 208–9, 234, 251, 280

Burke, Alfred E. (Monsignor), xxv, 226, 248, 290; Canadian Chaplain Service, 174–80; Catholic Church Extension Society, 40, 46, 208, 210; and *Catholic Register*, 36, 78–9, 89, 225, 235; and Home Rule, 221

Burke, Edmund (Bishop of Nova Scotia), 25

Burke, John E., CSP, 71–3, 97

Burns, Patrick, 97

Calgary: Catholics in, 24, 46, 134; Diocese of, 47, 52, 75–6, 103, 218, 245, 234, 230; and demobilization, 283; and nurses, 148; and recruitment, 113, 144, 190; and St Mary's School, 68; VD, 195–6

Canadian birth, 161

Canadian Chaplain Service (CCS), 14, 16, 68, 83, 166, 170, 175, 186, 195; Catholic priests in, 167–70; and controversy, 176–9; and language issues, 171–4; structure, 110, 164, 269

Canadian Expeditionary Force (CEF), 13, 32, 79, 94, 105, 142, 189, 199, 281, 282; and francophones, 16, 99, 101, 117, 188; and Irish Catholics, 14, 23, 95–6, 107, 117, 126–30, 138, 161; and nurses, 146–50; and recruitment, 14, 67–8, 69, 89, 108, 109, 110, 111, 116, 288, 293; and religion, 164, 182, 184; and VD, 193–7

Canadian Freeman (Kingston), 37, 38, 39, 59, 101, 113, 209, 228, 273; on Catholic Army Huts, 259, 262, 293; and conscription, 241, 245; and declaration of war, 86–7; on Ireland, 214, 216, 219, 222, 224, 276, 278, 291; and Canadian Patriotic Fund, 94–5; on Cape Breton Island, 25, 38, 41, 47, 53, 77, 80, 112, 143, 163, 168, 247

Carr, Henry, CSB, 117

Carson, Sir Edward, 35, 93, 99, 212, 215, 275–6, 277

Casement, Sir Roger, 212, 214

Casey, D.A., 39, 222, 228, 242, 293

Casey, Timothy (Archbishop of Van-

couver 1912–31), 75, 76, 77, 86, 103, 169–70, 234
Casgrain, Philippe, 101, 176, 177, 257
Casket (Antigonish), 35, 37, 38, 99, 100, 101, 115, 209, 228, 273; on Boer War, 58, 60, 61; and Catholic Church Extension Society, 40, 46, 78, 175, 208–9, 210, 235; and Catholic Mutual Benefit Association, 53, 113, 119, 175; on conscription, 237, 243, 244, 245; and Great War, 78, 80, 86, 90, 282; and Ireland, 211, 214, 215, 277
Catholic Record (London, Ontario), 37, 38, 54, 92, 230; on Boer War, 58–9; and conscription, 235, 247, 265; on Great War, 79, 83, 84, 86; on Irish question, 32, 212, 213, 216, 225, 276, 278, 291–2
Catholic Register (Toronto), 3, 36, 37, 39–40, 51, 100, 127, 175, 205, 209, 256, 262, 274; and bilingual schools, 47–8, 49, 82, 103, 104, 169, 203 226, 241, 248, 251, 267, 269, 294; on Boer War, 58, 59, 69; and Catholic schools, 7, 9, 12, 15, 19, 32, 36, 42–6, 54, 68, 69, 82, 86, 88, 96, 102, 183, 214, 273, 286, 298–9; on conscription, 230, 235, 244, 245, 265; and Great War, 78, 79, 83, 172; and Irish question, 36, 213, 216, 221, 225, 278; and recruitment, 118, 156, 230
Catholic Women's League, 257, 298
cenotaphs, xv, xvii, xviii, 67, 111, 112, 114, 139, 153–4, 161, 206, 284, 285, 293. *See also* Memorials
Chadwick, Ethel, 96–7
Charitable Irish Society (Halifax), 67, 162
Chevaliers de Colomb, 251, 253, 256, 263. *See also* Knights of Columbus
Chisholm–Middleton Commission, 272, 273
Christian Brothers, 230, 249
Church, Thomas "Tommy" (Mayor), 259, 286, 289
Coffey, Thomas (Senator), 39, 59, 79
Collins, Michael, 292
Commonwealth War Graves Commission, xvi, 293
Congregation of St Basil, 296
Congregation of the Sisters of St Joseph, 95, 102
Connor, Ralph (C.W. Gordon), 186, 207, 289
conscription, 8, 15, 16, 110, 119, 228, 231, 232, 251, 256, 258–9, 262, 268, 269, 279, 282; and Guelph Raid, 250, 271–4, 295; in Ireland, 275–8; Irish neutrality on, 237; Irish opposition to, 114, 223, 232, 241–3, 284, 300; Irish support for, 232–7, 239, 243–4, 288; Military Service Act, 1917, 8, 15, 16, 106, 139, 154, 231–2, 235–6, 237, 239, 241, 243, 244, 250, 263, 264, 265–7, 271; Quebec, 9, 10, 202, 226, 229, 230–2, 265, 289, 290, 295; Quebec City Riots, 16, 252, 266–8. *See also* tonsure
Crochetiêre, Rosario, 181
Cronin, Patrick F., 3, 12, 36, 40, 59, 60, 241
Currie, Arthur (General), 188, 259, 270

Daniel, Ivor, OMI, 191, 192, 293
de Valera, Eamon, 214, 218, 219, 276, 292
devotions, 163–4, 166, 184, 188, 198, 199
Dillon, John 34, 225, 276–7
Dinnick, W.S. (Colonel), 261
Doherty, Charles J., 7, 81, 97, 177–8, 249, 254, 295; on conscription, 232, 233, 234, 242, 244, 247, 266; in Guelph Raid, 251, 272; on Irish question, 219–21, 277
Doherty, Marcus (Justice), 249
Doherty, Marcus, SJ, 249–50, 272, 273–4, 295
Donovan, Michael, 38, 60, 78, 80, 99, 237
Dowling, Thomas Joseph (Bishop of Hamilton 1889–24), 45, 76, 238, 283
Doyle, Bernard Stephen, 181–2, 190, 198, 199
Doyon, Constant Victor, 171, 172, 173, 187, 191

Easter duty, 172, 182, 185, 189
Easter Rising (Dublin 1916), xvi, 8, 15, 84, 106, 123, 149, 178, 202, 212–14, 217, 252, 275, 290
Election of 1917 (Canadian Federal), 15, 16, 18, 231, 239–40, 243, 244–8, 250, 257, 267
Emard, Joseph-Medard (Bishop of Valleyfield 1892–22), 178, 269

Falconio, Diomede, 44, 46, 47, 51
Fallon, James Patrick, 184, 198, 199
Fallon, Michael Francis (Bishop of London 1909–1931), 9, 48, 49, 75, 77, 79, 87, 93, 103, 189–90, 226, 269–71, 274, 275, 279, 290, 298–9; and Canadian Chaplain Service, 169, 177, 184, 190, 193, 199, 268–9; and Catholic Army Huts, 253, 256–7, 259, 261; and Ford City Riot, 227–8, 271; and Irish question, 219–21, 276–81
Fenians, 19, 33, 58, 70, 98; or Irish Republican Brotherhood (IRB), 8, 32, 33, 58, 98, 126, 156, 202, 212, 213, 214, 216, 222
First Canadian Contingent, 107, 143, 146, 166, 297
First Canadian Division, 166, 167, 205
First Nations, 46, 53, 165, 192, 250, 292
Fitzpatrick, Charles (MP and Chief Justice), 3, 112, 16, 51, 53, 56, 57, 59, 69, 81, 97, 100, 102, 120; on Irish question, 220, 292
Foisey, Albert, 267
Forbes, Joseph-Guillaume (Bishop of Joliette), 229
Ford City, Ontario, 227–8, 271, 280
Foy, Charles J., 238, 292
Foy, J.J. (Provincial Secretary, Ontario), 7
France, 17, 22, 146, 150, 162, 167, 173, 175, 178, 179, 182, 185, 189, 193, 201, 204, 213, 214, 225, 228, 234, 239, 247, 258, 264, 270, 279, 280, 287, 297, 299
French, Francis, 253, 257

Gauthier, Charles Hugh (Archbishop of Ottawa 1910–22), 55, 76, 82, 83, 100, 116, 202, 294

German Catholics, 21, 46, 53, 73, 86, 87, 11, 112, 134, 161, 208
German Spring Offensive, 1918, 262, 278, 279, 280
Gillis, Michael, 170
Glynn, Bernard, 183–4
Golden Jubilee (Canadian Confederation), 84, 242
Government of Ireland Act, 1912 (Home Rule), 34, 35, 36, 210. *See also* Home Rule
Grant, William, 12
Great Irish Famine (1845–51), 5, 7, 11, 19, 22, 23, 25, 26, 27, 28, 29–32, 70, 150, 156, 249. *See also* Black '47
Great War Veteran's Association, 260
Grosse Île, 22. *See also* Great Irish Famine
Guelph Novitiate Raid, 250, 271–4, 295. *See also* Chisholm–Middleton Commission

Halifax, 4, 7, 17, 19, 23, 24, 25, 29, 37, 42, 44, 50, 53, 76, 81, 149, 284, 299–300; and Boer War 56, 58, 61, 64–7, 70; and Irish question, 222, 262, 291; and recruitment, 6, 108, 109, 120, 127–8, 161–2; and VD, 193
Hamilton (Ontario), 29, 40, 45, 53, 55, 76, 88, 95, 127, 168, 183, 238, 246, 255, 257, 283, 291
Henry, Patrick (editor), 41, 214, 242, 283, 292
Hibernian Benevolent Society, 19, 33
Hingston, William H., SJ, (Major), 120, 188, 251, 272
Hocken, Horatio (Mayor), 99, 206, 221, 241
Holy Cross Cemetery (Halifax), 67, 134
Holy Cross Cemetery (Toronto), 297
Holy Name Society, 58, 119, 189
Holy See, 16, 25, 43, 47, 48, 50, 75, 203, 209, 269
Home Rule (Ireland), 6, 15, 35, 73, 217–18, 219, 220, 290–2; Canada and, 8, 9, 10, 20, 32–3, 40–1, 54, 84, 203, 210–12, 217, 219, 221, 222, 224, 225, 276–9, 281, 291–2; and John Redmond, xv, 34, 211, 290; legislation (Westminster), 19, 34, 38, 211, 213, 215–16
Houston, Cecil, 4, 5, 6, 23
Hughes, Katherine, 222, 292
Hughes, Sam (MP and Minister of Militia), 3, 79, 84, 273; and Canadian Chaplain Service, 166, 169, 170, 171, 173–4, 177–8, 199; in Militia and Defense, 79, 137, 269, 272

immigration, 17, 129, 134, 138, 161, 289; Irish, 4, 6, 11, 17, 23, 27–9, 31, 49, 70, 126, 160
Irish Canadian (Toronto), 33, 40, 121
Irish Parliamentary Party, 34, 178, 210, 212, 215, 219, 275–6, 290. *See also* John Redmond
Irish Republican Brotherhood (IRB). *See* Fenians
Irish Volunteers, xix, 35, 93, 210, 212, 213

Kaszub Poles, 21, 95, 152
Kelly, Florence, RN, 147–8
Kemp, Sir Edward, 270
Knights of Columbus, 17–18, 58, 83, 87, 96, 105, 113, 117–18, 207, 238, 251, 285, 290, 295; Catholic Army Huts, 252–63, 293. *See also* Chevaliers de Colomb
Kultur, 73, 87–8, 98, 222, 224

Labour Gazette, 109, 133
Landry, J.P. (General), 267
Langevin, Louis-Philippe Adélard, OMI (Archbishop of St. Boniface, 1895–15), 46, 47, 48, 137
Laurier, Wilfrid (Prime Minister), 34, 39, 43, 48, 55, 56, 57, 59, 60, 62, 79, 96, 101, 161, 211, 220, 239; and election of, 1917, 245, 247; on Irish question, 220, 224; and Union Government, 231, 236, 240, 241, 244
Laval University, 101, 117
Lavergne, Armand, 9, 101, 214, 230
LeBlanc, Edward Alfred (Bishop of Saint John 1912–35), 71, 80, 97
Leddy, John Joseph, 7, 219, 257
Le Devoir, 9, 82, 100, 267
Le Droit, 52, 82, 228, 267
Légal, Emile (Bishop of St Albert/ Edmonton 1902–20), 52, 112, 199
Llandovery Castle, 146, 284
Lloyd George, David (Prime Minister, UK), 218, 219, 220, 225, 275, 276, 277, 278, 279
Logue, Michael (Cardinal Archbishop of Armagh), 276, 278, 292
Loyal Orange Lodge (Orange Order), xvii, 7, 12, 13, 19, 37, 42, 43, 49, 79, 99, 104, 152, 166, 177–8, 202, 206, 211, 221, 231, 234, 242, 244, 245, 251, 261–2, 272, 286, 289, 298, 299; *Sentinel* 14, 18, 104, 205, 206, 261–2, 273
Lutyens, Sir Edwin, xv
Lynch, John Joseph (Archbishop of Toronto 1860–88), 33

Macaulay, A.C. (Captain), 272, 274. *See also* Guelph Novitiate Raid
MacDonald, Alexander "Sandy" (Bishop of Victoria 1908–23), 47, 75, 77, 98, 234
Macdonald, Sir John Alexander (Prime Minister), 33, 212
Macdonald, Margaret C., RN (Chief Matron), 68, 146–8, 192, 285
Macdonell, A. Claude (MP and Senator), 69, 234, 247
Macdonell, Alexander (Bishop of Upper Canada), 42, 45
Macdonell, Archibald C. "Batty Mac" (General), 189
Macdonell, Archibald Hayes (General), 61, 68
MacGillivray, Ronald, 163–4, 173, 179, 180, 182, 186
Macpherson, Donald, 172, 173
Madden, Ambrose, OMI, 169–70, 179, 180–1, 186, 293–4
Manion, Robert J., MD (MP), 7, 9, 238–9, 240; on conscription, 239–41, 247
Manitoba, 33, 53, 83, 97, 112, 296; and Boer War, 64–5; and Knights of Columbus, 96, 238, 255, 259; Manitoba Schools, 43, 210; migration to, 129, 143; and *North-*

west Review, 37; nurses from, 148; and recruitment, 134, 138, 137; and VD, 194
Mannix, Daniel (Archbishop of Melbourne), 262, 279
Mathieu, Olivier-Elzéar (Archbishop of Regina, 1911–29), 48, 52, 134
Maxwell, Sir John (General), 123, 213, 214, 215, 275
McCarthy, Edward (Archbishop of Halifax (1906–31), 76, 168, 169, 199
McCarthy, Thomas, 180, 186
McEvay, Fergus Patrick, 45, 46, 51, 55. *See also* Catholic Church Extension Society
McGarry, T.W (MPP, Renfrew, Ontario), 74, 219
McGee, Frank, "one-eyed," 97, 143
McGee, Thomas D'Arcy, 6, 33, 212, 249, 294
McGowan, George M., xix
McGowan, William, xix, 297
McGrory, Arthur, 296
McLaughlin, C.J., 38, 80, 217, 218
McNally, Hugh Francis de Sales, MD, xix
McNally, James T. (Bishop of Calgary, 1913–24), 75, 76, 103, 218; and conscription, 234, 235; and Knights of Columbus, 256; and National Registration, 230
McNeil, Neil (Archbishop of Toronto, 1912–34), 47, 51, 76, 90, 103, 235, 286, 289, 298–9; addresses nurses, 149; and conscription, 234, 235, 247–8; defends Pope, 206–7; descent, 23, 75; on French Canada, 99, 103, 203, 251, 253, 268, 290; and Great War, 75, 78, 82, 92, 94, 98, 99–100, 112, 245–6, 218; on National Registration, 230; supports Catholic Army Hut campaign, 256, 258, 260–1
Meighen, Arthur, 240, 295
Memorials, xv, xvii, 284, 285, 286, 293; in Ottawa Valley, 153–4, 161; at St Patrick's, Ottawa, 67, 114, 139, 285
Merry del Val, Rafael, 49, 270
Mewburn, Sidney (General), 269, 272
military districts (MDs), 110, 111, 113, 134, 267
Military Service Act, 1917. *See* conscription
military tribunal, 237, 244, 265
Miller, Carman, 52, 62, 66
Miller, Kerby, 6
Minehan, Lancelot, 234, 243, 278
Miramichi Valley, New Brunswick, 26, 27, 64
Moir, John S., 4, 50 120
Montreal, 4, 6, 8, 19, 21, 33, 38, 100, 109, 177, 249; and Ancient Order of Hibernians, 58; archdiocese of, xvi, 56, 82, 94, 103, 229, 253, 256, 262, 267; Irish in, 15, 17, 22, 23, 24, 50, 64, 219, 291–2; and Knights of Columbus, 118, 252–3, 256; and politics, 81, 219, 232, 247, 249; and recruitment, 88, 110, 111, 117, 120, 123, 126–7, 147, 153, 168, 171, 193, 206, 237, 246
Montreal Star, 236, 268
Morrison, James (Bishop of Antigonish, 1912–50), 75, 77, 78, 80, 92, 103, 187, 283; and Canadian

Chaplain Service, 167–8, 169, 170, 172–3, 176; and conscription, 234; support for recruitment, 234
Mount St Patrick, 21, 152, 156, 160
Mount St Vincent Academy, 148
Mulholland, John Joseph, 116
Murdoch, Benedict, 181, 190; his *The Red Vineyard*, 293
Murphy, Charles (MP, Russell), 118, 219; on conscription, 241, 245, 247; and Irish question, 220
Murray, Edward "Ned," 68, 105–6, 126, 137, 139, 143, 146, 153, 160, 162, 285, 300
Murray, J.L., 105, 162; and the Knights of Columbus, 253, 255, 257, 260, 263
Murray, Norman, 206. See *Sentinel*

National Registration, 106, 229–30, 235, 237, 250, 264–5, 288
nationalism: and the French Canadians, 15, 100, 102, 226–7, 270, 281; and the Irish, 4, 5, 6, 8, 32, 34, 40, 149, 248, 262, 277, 281
Ne Temere Decree (marriage), 50–1
New Brunswick, 25, 173; Ancient Order of Hibernians in, 217, 224; and the Boer War, 61, 64, 65; and the Canadian Chaplain Service, 169, 190, 293; and Fenians, 33, 98; the Irish in 26, 28, 53, 244; and Knights of Columbus, 96, 227, 131, 147, 168, 171, 197, 256, 265; newspapers in, 37–8, 59; nurses from, 148; and recruitment, 71, 77; schools in, 42, 43, 234; and VD, 193
Newfoundland, 4, 24, 25, 26, 27, 29, 39, 47, 67, 76, 90, 131
New Freeman (Saint John), 37–8, 80–1, 90, 101, 114, 273, 282; and the Ancient Order of Hibernians, 218; in Boer War, 74; on conscription, 235–7, 267, 274; on federal election (1917), 245; on Irish question, 34, 214, 215, 216, 221, 225, 278; on recruitment, 90–1, 119, 210
Northwest Rebellion (1885), 249, 250, 273
Northwest Review (Winnipeg), 37, 40–1, 99, 282; on Boer War, 74; and Catholic Church, 78; on conscription, 242, 245, 246; Great War support, 92, 101; and the Irish question, 212, 214, 215, 216, 276, 292; and Ukrainians, 211
Nova Scotia, 15, 25, 37, 38, 109, 228, 285; and Boer War, 57, 58, 64–5, 67; and Canadian Chaplain Service, 168, 169, 170–1, 176, 173, 172; and Catholic Church, 41, 75, 112; conscription in, 244, 262; Irish in, 25, 26, 27, 29, 30; Irish question, 224; nurses from, 68, 146–8; recruitment from, 80, 81, 91, 95, 112, 115, 127, 129, 131, 299–300; schools in, 42; and VD, 193
nurses (CAMC), 14, 17, 146–50, 165, 192, 201, 206, 248, 293; and casualties, 282, 284. *See also* Margaret C. Macdonald

O'Brien, Cornelius (Archbishop of Halifax, 1882–06), 44, 55, 61, 64, 222

O'Brien, Michael (Bishop of Peterborough, 1913–29), 51, 92, 93
O'Brien, William (RCA), 142, 183, 185, 188, 214, 217, 295–6
O'Connor, Denis, CSB (Archbishop of Toronto, 1899–1908), 45, 51, 55, 252
O'Dwyer, Edward (Bishop of Limerick, Ireland), 214, 215, 287
O'Gorman, John J., 8, 81–2, 294–5, 298; and Canadian Chaplain Service, 109, 111, 120, 171, 175, 176–80, 181, 188, 199; and Catholic Army Huts, 251–8; double duty talk, 18, 222–5; and French Canadian nationalism, 83, 100, 175, 226, 248, 290; on Irish question, 201–2, 224, 277; *kultur*, 87; on recruitment, 109–10; his *Render Unto Caesar*, 82–3, 89–90, 101
O'Leary, Henry J. (Bishop of Charlottetown, 1913–20), 95, 103
O'Leary, Peter, 61, 180; in Canadian Chaplain Service, 68, 166
Ontario, 7, 17, 53, 113; Boer War, 64–5; and Canadian Chaplain Service, 168–9, 178; Catholic Church in, 53, 55, 190; Catholic press in, 3, 37–8, 39–42, 79; Catholic–Protestant relations in, 45–6, 51; and conscription, 244, 247, 264–5, 271–4; election (1917) in, 267; First Nations recruits in, 112, 192; and French language, 9, 47, 103, 104, 203, 226–8; and Irish question, 211, 219–20, 224; Knights of Columbus in, 238, 253, 255, 257, 259–61; nurses from, 146–8; recruitment in, 102, 109, 111, 126, 127, 129, 134, 138, 151–60, 265; schools in, 7, 19, 42–3, 48–9, 68, 69, 88
Orange *Sentinel*. *See under* Loyal Orange Lodge
O'Reilly, John, 81, 91
Ottawa, 4, 12, 34; Catholic Church in, 48, 56, 73, 76, 85, 96, 114, 169, 284; Conscription and, 241, 264–5; and French Canadians, 49; Irish in, 50, 57, 201, 222, 224, 291; and Knights of Columbus, 207, 253, 255, 257; nurses from, 150; and politics, 39, 50–1, 58; recruitment in, 94, 109, 110, 111, 114, 118; schools in, 48; University of, 48, 82, 284
Ottawa "Silver Seven," 97, 143
Ottawa Valley, 4, 17, 21–4, 38, 69, 105, 111, 127, 182; and Canadian Chaplain Service, 197; Germans in, 73, 86; memorials in, 285; recruitment in, 151–61

Pearse, Padraig (Patrick), 126, 212, 213, 214, 216, 222
Perley, Sir George, 176, 178, 270
Polish Relief Fund, 95, 96
Pontiac County, Quebec. *See* Ottawa Valley
Pope Benedict XV, 14, 86, 103, 104, 175, 202, 245, 248, 251, 252, 259, 261–2, 271, 287, 289; criticism of, 204–7
Pope Leo XIII, 203, 204
Pope Pius IX, 42, 203
Pope Pius X, 85, 87, 204

Power, Charles "Chubby," 9, 241, 245, 247
Prince Edward Island (PEI), 95; Alfred Burke from, 46, 78–9, 175; Alfred A. Sinnott from, 46, 75; and Boer War, 53, 57, 65; Irish in 27, 29, 30, 44; James McNally from, 48, 76; nurses from, 147–8; recruitment in, 102, 138, 168, 197
Protestants, 4, 6, 24, 64, 129, 147, 284; and anti-Catholicism, 202, 206–8, 221, 226, 231, 246–7, 251; and Canadian Chaplain Service, 14, 166, 170, 175–6, 178, 180, 183, 187, 190; and Catholics, 5, 7, 11, 12, 13, 15, 18, 19, 25–6, 41, 43–7, 96, 104, 115, 274–5, 288–9, 299; and conscription, 234, 243–4, 255–6; in Irish battalions, 118–26; and Irish question, 35, 93, 210–1, 275, 277; and Knights of Columbus, 252–3; in marriages, 50–2; in Ottawa Valley, 22, 151–2, 160; and Papal aggression, 42; and schools, 42–3, 48–9. *See also* Anglicans; Catholic Army Huts; Guelph Novitiate Raid; Loyal Orange Lodge

Quebec, 19, 21, 28, 42, 195, 214; and Boer War, 56, 62, 64–5; and Canadian Chaplain Service, 174, 187–8, 269; Church in, 9, 13, 17, 25, 27, 44, 47, 70, 73, 82–3, 134, 154, 169, 232, 237–47; and conscription, 16, 227, 231–3, 236, 241, 245–8; Irish in, 3, 15, 22, 28–9, 33, 116, 241, 292; and Knights of Columbus, 253–5; nurses from, 146–8; opposition to war in, 99–101, 289; and recruitment, 104, 110–1, 116, 126, 138, 171, 193; and support for war, 94, 100–2; Valcartier, 14, 79, 107; and VD, 195. *See also* Catholic Army Huts; Nationalism, French Canadian; National Registration
Quebec Act (1774), 12, 41, 42

recruitment, 96, 97, 102, 107, 110, 118, 126–45; in Boer War, 54–61, 63–70; clerical involvement, 8–9, 10–11, 13, 71–80, 81, 88–90, 91, 95, 108, 109–10, 167–8, 172; by clubs, 118–9; in colleges, 116–7; by Irish Catholics, 13–14, 106–7, 111–15, 119–26; and Irish question, 222–34; and Quebec nationalists, 99–101; and nurses, 146–50. *See also* conscription; Ottawa Valley
Red Cross, 95, 97, 103, 115, 177, 198
Redmond, John (Leader, Irish Parliamentary Party), 34, 35, 93, 210–16, 217–18, 219–20, 225, 240, 275, 276, 290; death of, 276–7. *See* Easter Rising
Redmond, William, 210, 219
Regulation 17, 9, 49, 103, 227. *See* Catholic schools
Reynolds, William K. (*New Freeman*), 61
Rowell, Newton Wesley, 206, 241, 289
Royal Flying Corps, 140, 183, 282, 296, 297
Royal Red Cross, 150

Ryan, Patrick (Bishop of Pembroke, 1916–37), 76, 96, 152

sacraments, 17, 165, 167, 171, 176, 179, 180, 181, 182–91, 193, 198, 199; Blessed Sacrament Parish (Ottawa), 73, 82, 294, 298. *See also* confession
St Francis Xavier University, 76, 90, 114, 116, 249, 253, 285
St Joseph's Academy (Toronto), 86
St Joseph's Lilies, 86, 88, 102
St Joseph's Parish (Ottawa), 96, 143, 150, 284
St Joseph's University (New Brunswick), 234
St Michael's Cathedral (Toronto), 36, 59
St Michael's College (Toronto), 43, 117, 185, 286, 296
St Michael's Hospital (Toronto), 149
St Patrick's Parish (Halifax), 134, 299
St Patrick's Parish (Mount St Patrick), 156
St Patrick's Parish (Ottawa), 81, 85, 96, 114, 194, 222, 241, 265, 284
Saskatchewan, 43, 81, 148, 194; Germans in, 73, 86; and Knights of Columbus, 96, 238, 255, 260; recruiting in, 134, 138, 140
Sbaretti, Donato, 47, 270
Scott, Frederick George (Canon, Anglican Church), 167, 187, 205, 293
Scott, Sir Richard, 57–8
Scottish Catholics, 14, 23, 25, 27, 53, 91, 95, 165, 171–2; bishops, 25, 53, 56, 73, 75, 76; in Boer War, 62, 66; and Canadian Chaplain Service, 174, 182, 187; and conscription, 234, 247; and Gaelic, 188; and recruitment, 110, 112, 115, 117, 127, 282; nurse Christina Campbell, 146. *See also* Margaret C. Macdonald
Second Battle of Ypres (April 1915), 84, 116, 123, 137, 143, 149, 210, 281
Section 93, British North America Act, 12, 42
Self-Determination League for Ireland, 291
Sinnott, Alfred A. (Archbishop of Winnipeg, 1915–52), 46, 48, 75, 76, 78, 112, 168, 199, 234, 242, 283, 292
Sinn Fein ("We Ourselves"), 156, 213, 214–5, 216, 217, 219, 222, 225, 262, 275–7, 281, 289–90, 291, 292, 293. *See* Nationalism, Irish Catholic
Small, Teresa Korman, 122
Smith, Sir Frank (Senator), 33
Smyth, William, 4, 5, 6, 23
Society of Jesus (Jesuits), 19, 54, 85, 112, 120, 192, 241, 295; at Collège Ste-Marie (Montreal), 249; at Guelph, 250, 271, 274, 295; at Loyola College (Montreal), 117. *See* Guelph Novitiate Raid
Somerville, Henry, 235
Spratt, Michael Joseph (Archbishop of Kingston, 1911–38), 38, 76, 89–90, 219
Steacy, Richard H., 166–7, 170–4, 175, 176–9, 189
Sylvestre, Ludger Adolph, 185, 269

Teefy, John R., 43
Tompkins, Miles, 177, 179, 180, 186–7, 217
tonsure, 234, 243, 263, 266, 272, 274
Toronto, 4, 19, 42, 83, 230; and Boer War, 3–4, 54, 58–9, 60; and Canadian Chaplain Service, 168, 182–3; Catholic Church in, 23, 33, 45, 46, 51; Catholic press in, 36, 37, 39–40, 100; and conscription, 230, 234, 247, 265; *Globe*, 83, 99, 206, 207, 211; Irish in, 7, 8, 23, 29, 33, 50, 58, 120, 224; and Knights of Columbus, 96, 118, 252, 254, 259, 260–1; nurses from, 149; and recruitment, 108–9, 112, 116, 118, 120–1, 127; and St Augustine's Seminary, 76, 98; *Telegram*, 205, 206, 299. *See also* Loyal Orange Lodge; McNeil, Neil

Ukrainian Catholics, 46, 134, 208–10, 221, 234–5. *See* Nykyta Budka
Ulster Volunteer Force, 35, 93, 210, 215
Union Government, 226, 231, 238–9, 241, 245, 246, 252, 269, 289, 295
University of Ottawa, 48, 249, 284

venereal disease (VD), 193–6; at Etchinghill Hospital, 193, 198–9
Vimy, 143, 163, 186, 239, 270, 281, 285

Wall, James (*Catholic Register*), 213, 225, 235
Walsh, John (Archbishop of Toronto, 1889–98), 39
Walsh, William J. (Archbishop of Dublin), 222
Waning of the Green, 8
Welland Canal, 58, 98
Whelan, Matthew, 9, 85, 114, 222, 241, 284
Whelan, Monica (Mona), 22–3, 69, 150, 154, 297–8
Whelan, Stephen, 22, 28, 45
Whitney, James P. (Premier of Ontario), 43, 49
Winnipeg Catholic Club, 119p
Workman, Wolston, OFM, 173–4, 177, 178, 185, 265, 268, 271; and Catholic Army Huts, 255, 257–8, 261

YMCA (Young Men's Christian Association), 255–6, 260–1